25129

D1437298

LEEDS LIBRARY
DISCARDED

71 0140776 9   TELEPEN

The Weidenfeld and Nicolson Universal History

34: Europe 1919-45

Europe 1919-45

R. A. C. Parker

Fellow of The Queen's College, Oxford

Weidenfeld and Nicolson

5 Winsley Street London W1

JAMES GRAHAM COLLEGE
LIBRARYv
CLASS No:- 940·5
ACC. No :- 325123
2 2 JUL1970

710140776 -9

© 1967 by Fischer Bücherei GmbH,
Frankfurt am Main and Hamburg

English edition © 1969
by Dell Publishing Co., Inc., New York
and George Weidenfeld and Nicolson Ltd., London

First published in Great Britain in 1969

SBN 297 17602 1

Printed in Great Britain by
Morrison and Gibb Ltd, London and Edinburgh

Contents

LEEDS BECKETT UNIVERSITY
LIBRARY
DISCARDED

1   The Peace with Germany   1

2   The Peace with Austria, Hungary and Bulgaria   20

3   The Peace with Turkey   33

4   The Consolidation of Peace: Russia   41

5   The Consolidation of Peace: Great Britain, France and
    the German Problem   56

6   Europe between the Wars: Economic and Social Trends   94

7   Britain 1919–39   116

8   Italy 1919–40   137

9   France 1919–40   163

10 Spain 1919–45   190

11 Germany 1919–39   212

12 The End of the Peace: 1929–33   239

13 The Coming of War   258

14 The Second World War   337

    Notes   363

    Select Bibliography   383

    Index   387

List of Illustrations

(between pages 182 *and* 183*)*

1 President Wilson
2 Clemenceau in New York
3 Lloyd George at Versailles
4 Kemal Atatürk
5 Raymond Poincaré
6 Gustav Stresemann
7 Austen Chamberlain
8 Unemployment in Britain: a labour exchange
9 The General Strike: police clearing a street
10 J. H. Thomas, Stanley Baldwin and Neville Chamberlain
11 Fascist rally 1938
12 British Fascists 1939
13 New housing in Birmingham between the wars
14 Giovanni Giolitti
15 The March on Rome
16 Mussolini and his generals
17 King Victor Emmanuel III
18 Fascists saluting Mussolini
19 Italian fascist youth
20 Riots in Paris, February 1934
21 Léon Blum and his wife in England, July 1936
22 The Reynaud Cabinet, March 1940
23 Manuel Azaña and Luis Companys
24 Gil Robles
25 Nationalist forces during the advance on Madrid, 1936
26 General Franco in Burgos

27 The Spanish Civil War: nationalist troops, 1939
28 General von Seeckt
29 Alfred Hugenberg
30 Brüning and Curtius in London, July 1931
31 General von Schleicher
32 Franz von Papen
33 President von Hindenburg
34 Hitler and Hindenburg
35 Hitler's May Day speech, Berlin 1935
36 Joseph Pilsudski
37 Engelbert Dollfuss
38 Laval and Litvinov
39 Flandin in London, March 1936
40 Lord Halifax and Ribbentrop
41 Eduard Beneš
42 Chamberlain leaving for Godesberg, September 1938
43 Bonnet, Daladier and Gamelin after Godesberg
44 German troops in Prague, March 1939
45 Colonel Beck, April 1939
46 Belgian soldiers retreating, May 1940
47 The German occupation of Paris, June 1940
48 Dresden after the allied bombing

Acknowledgments

The publishers acknowledge with thanks the permission of the following to include plates in this book: the Keystone Press Agency, plates, 1, 2, 16, 25, 26, 34, 44 and 48; Paul Popper Ltd., plates 3, 5, 14, 15, 17, 23 and 24; the Radio Times Hulton Picture Library, plates 4, 6, 7, 8, 9, 10, 11, 12, 13, 18, 19, 20, 21, 22, 27, 28, 29, 30, 31, 32, 33, 35, 36, 37, 38, 39, 40, 41, 42, 43 and 45; the Imperial War Museum, plates 46 and 47.
The author wishes to thank Mrs Jennifer Loach for help in preparing this book.

Maps

European Frontiers 1919–37   31
Europe 1942   346

Author's Note

This book was first published in German translation, in October 1967. The German version forms part of a series making up the *Fischer Weltgeschichte*. Other volumes in that series deal with the world outside Europe and with Russia. This volume therefore concentrates on Western Europe. Limited space compelled a choice between relatively shallow treatment of a comprehensive range of topics or more detailed examination of some major themes in European history. I have chosen to follow the latter course and am fully conscious of the consequent omissions.

R.A.C.P.

1

The Peace with Germany

The citizens and the politicians of the major countries who fought the
First World War believed, except in Italy and in Japan, that they were
engaged in a defensive struggle. The Austro-Hungarian government
launched its attack in 1914 in order to save the monarchy from the
underhand machinations of Serbia; Russia believed herself to be compelled to resist the advance of Germanism towards domination in
south-eastern Europe and at the Straits; Germany sought to ward off,
before it was too late, the dangers of encirclement, to defend herself
against a Slavonic plot aimed at the destruction of her ally, a plot
hatched in St Petersburg with the encouragement of the French and the
connivance of the British Foreign Office; France stood firm against a
German attempt to break her defensive alliance with Russia, and found
herself invaded as a result; the British Foreign Office saw the European
balance of power threatened by Germany, and British public opinion
saw Belgium shamefully wronged. No doubt many of these powers took
up ambitious designs once the war had begun but none of them supposed
that their own country had entered the war for reasons other than self-
preservation. Even in Germany, where patriotic societies, publicists,
industrialists and so on were active before the war, in meditating or
preaching varied schemes for advancing the greatness of Germany, the
war when it came was one that was genuinely thought of as forced on
Germany by external events and those soldiers who deliberately
accepted war in 1914 urged the need for a preventive war against
dangerous enemies whose power was held to be growing; subsequent
military interest in conquest was a consequence of war, not its cause.
The United States, too, entered the war to defend something – international law and morality. Only Italy and Japan, among the great
powers, made war for the sake of territorial ambitions and both joined
in a war for whose outbreak they were certainly not responsible. In

1

short, the people and statesmen of all the great powers believed that someone else was to blame for the war.

On the allied side, the conviction was firmly established by the end of the war that Germany was to blame. German industrial power, and German military prowess kept the war going; to France, Britain, and America Germany had been the principal and most formidable enemy, and the conclusion was drawn that the contribution of Austria-Hungary to the outbreak of war must have been as small as her contribution to the fighting of it seemed to be to all the victorious powers, except, once again, to Italy.

Furthermore, the western powers assumed that this belief that Germany was responsible for the war was shared by the Germans themselves. Hence the writers of the 'war guilt' clause of the Treaty of Versailles thought they were making a simple statement of an obvious truth when they insisted that Germany was responsible for the consequences of a German war, and should make financial reparation for them. German resentment at this clause surprised the peace-makers at Paris and the formal protest of the German representatives there against this preamble to the reparations clauses was lightly dismissed.

The Allied and Associated Governments affirm and Germany accepts the responsibility of Germany and her allies for causing all the loss and damage to which the Allied and Associated Governments and their nationals have been subjected as a consequence of the war imposed upon them by the aggression of Germany and her allies.

To the drafters of the treaty it was self-evident that this was reasonable; to the Germans it involved a flagrant travesty of the truth. In May 1919, President Wilson commented on the German protest, 'Today they are still declaring that it was not they who caused the war. This attitude is unbelievable'.[1] This contrast explains how it came about that a peace which one side seriously thought to be the embodiment of justice seemed to the other to be iniquitous oppression. The opponents of Germany thought her guilty of a grave crime, the Germans thought themselves innocent. Thus justice for Germany implied different things to the Germans than it did to the allies. This was important since the promise was made to the German government before the armistice was signed in November 1918 that the peace would be just – this was the message of the President of the United States, Woodrow Wilson, in the speeches on the basis of which the armistice was made.

These notable utterances contained a majestic plan for a post-war settlement to ensure perpetual peace, a plan which aroused the applause of liberal-minded people and which gave moral justification to the allied fight against a Germany which had imposed on Russia at Brest Litovsk an old-fashioned peace of the most rigorous kind. Wilson's speeches laid down that peace could only be based on justice. International justice meant, above all, the exercise by all peoples of the right of self-determination, that is to say that frontiers should be drawn up according to the wishes of the population concerned. Then the peoples of the world would cease to wish to change frontiers and the major cause of war would go. Democratic forms of government would ensure that the contentment of the populations of states with their frontiers would be reflected in peaceful foreign policies. Democratic supervision of foreign policy would be made easy by open diplomacy. If genuine grievances arose the other nations of the world banded in a League of Nations would see that justice was done. If by mischance a state fell into the hands of old-fashioned diplomatists or irresponsible soldiers and became aggressive, the other states of the world would bring pressure to bear under the direction of the League of Nations. Economic or even moral pressure should be enough; if it failed, members of the League would be authorized to use armed force. As Wilson said in July 1918, 'What we seek is the reign of law, based upon the consent of the governed and sustained by the organised opinion of mankind'.

This impressive structure rested on impartial justice between nation and nation. Wilson declared in September 1918,

The impartial justice meted out must involve no discrimination between those to whom we wish to be just and those to whom we do not wish to be just. It must be justice that plays no favourites and knows no standards but the equal rights of the several peoples concerned.

In April 1918 justice was promised for Germany: 'To propose anything but justice, even-handed and dispassionate justice, to Germany at any time, whatever the outcome of the war, would be to renounce and dishonour our own cause.' But what was just for Germany? To the Germans anything short of equal treatment would be unjust, a betrayal of solemn pledges. To the peace-makers, however, justice for Germany did not mean equal treatment for Germany, for a criminal must be treated differently from his victims. Wilson believed this as strongly as did Lloyd George or Clemenceau as, indeed, careful reading of his speeches makes plain – thus in April 1918 Wilson declaimed,

Germany has once more said that force and force alone, shall decide whether justice and peace shall reign in the affairs of men, whether right as America conceives it, or dominion as she conceives it, shall determine the destinies of mankind,

3

and in September 1918, 'Germany will have to redeem her character not by what happens at the peace table but by what follows.' The nature of the most important part of the Peace of Paris, the Treaty of Versailles, cannot be understood unless it is accepted that all the peace-makers supposed Germany to have been aggressive and wicked.

The Peace of Paris was made up of four treaties, those with Germany, Austria-Hungary, Bulgaria and Turkey. The treaty with Germany, the Treaty of Versailles, was far and away the most important. The pre-war Habsburg monarchy had gone by 1918, Bulgaria's fate could have only local repercussions, the Ottoman Empire was already dismembered, but at the beginning of 1919 Germany remained intact and potentially, at least, easily the strongest power in Europe both economically and militarily. Indeed, Germany's relative potential strength seemed even greater in 1919 than in 1914, since Russia was convulsed by civil war. What to do about Germany was the major question in 1919 as it remained the major question in international affairs until 1945. If the wishes of whoever controlled Germany diverged from the wishes of the rulers of other European states Europe would be in danger of renewed war. There were broadly two ways of solving this problem: by making Germany powerless or by making enough Germans content with the new Europe to make it impossible for any German rulers to launch a war to change it. The treaty was a compromise between these two solutions and that is why it failed.

Most Frenchmen desired to weaken Germany, that is, to disarm her, deprive her of territory and even of unity, occupy her with troops, take away her money and surround her with powerful enemies. Most Frenchmen took the view, in 1919, that to attempt a reconciliation with Germany was to pursue an absurd chimera, and there was this truth in their view – that no conceivable settlement with Germany that would have been acceptable to the public opinion of Britain and the United States, let alone that of France and Poland, would have secured the assent of most Germans. No frontier, for instance, between Poland and Germany has ever been devised that simultaneously commends itself to Poles and Germans, and in 1919 it would have been impossible to curry favour with Germans by sacrificing Poles – although Lloyd George came near to trying to do so. In 1919, therefore, the French government aimed for a peace that would crush Germany. Divergences between Frenchmen, between President Poincaré and Marshal Foch on the one hand and Clemenceau, the Prime Minister, on the other, turned only on the question whether or not to risk the alienation of Britain and America in order to attempt to crush Germany.

4

Poincaré, Foch and the right in France thought Germany should be kept weak whether or not Britain and the USA acquiesced; Clemenceau and the left wished to maintain understanding with Britain and America and were ready to compromise in their German policies – this was a conflict in French thinking which continued throughout the next decade. Clemenceau was a moderate, and Germany between the wars owed much to his willingness to compromise and retreat. Clemenceau, as leader of the French delegation at the Peace Conference, worked brilliantly and triumphantly to avoid the loss of British and American support for France in Europe. France lost her allies later on because Wilson mismanaged the ratification of the treaty in the USA and because Poincaré alienated Britain.

The second solution was advocated by Lloyd George, the British Prime Minister, who was above all a politician, a man of compromise, of flexible principles and devious methods. Time and again it was he who produced the formula, the solution of intractable problems to which all could assent. He was responsive and sensitive to movements in public opinion and never ready to clash directly with it. Abstract principles of morality did not dominate his political action. This had an important consequence – it made him for practical purposes less hostile to Germany than was President Wilson. Wilson looked back on Germany's deeds and condemned them and was ready to discriminate against Germany; Lloyd George cared little for the wickednesses of the past, however recent, and sought only to mould the future. Lloyd George recognized, like the French, that the German question was decisive but, while the French sought to make Germany powerless, Lloyd George sought to induce Germany voluntarily to accept the postwar settlement. He had three reasons: to make Germany pacific, to make Germany and therefore Europe prosperous and to prevent Germany going Bolshevik. It was Lloyd George, not Wilson, who fought most strongly for German interests at Versailles – characteristically, it is true, with most clarity in areas which were of little interest to British public opinion, such as East Prussia and Silesia.

The picture of the Peace Conference, most brilliantly painted by Keynes in his famous book, *The Economic Consequences of the Peace*, of a clash between Wilsonian principles and European self-seeking in which Wilson was tricked and deceived by Lloyd George and Clemenceau into agreeing to the imposition on Germany of a harsh and unscrupulous peace is thoroughly misleading. To the French, the peace did not seem either harsh or unscrupulous and Clemenceau was, by some of them, accused of treachery; Wilson believed that he had secured justice for

5

Germany; Lloyd George was more dissatisfied with Versailles than Wilson was. It was, in fact, easier for Wilson and Clemenceau to agree than is usually argued – over the German treaty it was Lloyd George who made most difficulties for Clemenceau. Again, the major clashes among the leaders of the principal allied and associated powers (Britain, France, Italy, Japan and the USA) in their most intimate conferences came over the claims of Italy and over the partition of the Turkish Empire and not over Germany at all.

The treaty with Germany, the Treaty of Versailles, was the work of these three men, Clemenceau, Lloyd George and Wilson. Their final decisions were taken in discussions with each other, principally in the Council of Four, the fourth member of which was Orlando, of Italy, who took a minor part in the drafting of the treaty with Germany. German representations were considered only after a complete draft had been presented to German delegates summoned for that purpose. The work of the Council of Four was based on preliminary studies by commissions nominated by the four governments, after hearing representations made by the nations directly concerned. The Japanese delegates stood on an equal footing with the four European powers when Far Eastern and Pacific matters were discussed. The discussions of the Council of Four were, in principle, secret – open diplomacy thus proved to mean only that there should be no secret treaties, not that negotiation should be public. Less important issues were discussed by the foreign ministers of the great powers while the plenary sessions of the entire conference were purely formal affairs.

The great issues that the Treaty of Versailles attempted to settle were reparations, the frontiers of Germany, German disarmament and the fate of the German colonies. Over reparations the questions to solve were how much Germany should pay and how much Germany could pay. Wilson's fourteen points laid down that Belgium and the invaded portions of France should be 'restored'. On 5 November 1918, Lansing, the United States Secretary of State, wrote to the German government:

the Allied Governments feel that no doubt ought to be allowed to exist as to what this provision implies. By it they understand that compensation will be made by Germany for all damage done to the civilian population of the allies and their property by the aggression of Germany by land, by sea, and from the air.

The German government was thus forewarned before the armistice was signed of the extended interpretation to be given to the reparations clause of the fourteen points. By the treaty Germany was made to agree that she ought to pay far more than she could possibly pay, the actual figure to be worked out later; she was assured less clearly that she might perhaps, in the end, not be asked to pay more than she could pay, this figure too to be worked out later.

These clauses of the treaty aroused understandable dismay in Germany and an increasing volume of criticism from economists, led by Keynes. How had they come about? Lloyd George wished for three things: that life should be bearable in future for Germany, that Britain should have the largest possible share in German payments, and that British public opinion should suppose that Germany was being treated with the maximum harshness. The second and third objectives were secured at one stroke by the inclusion in the bill to be presented to Germany of pensions paid after the war by all the allies to widows etc. and to disabled soldiers together with separation allowances paid to dependants of fighting men during the war. A bearable future for Germany could only be secured by the postponement of any final statement of what Germany was to pay until public opinion had cooled down. Clemenceau wished the maximum payments for France. Wilson and his advisers wished to work out what Germany could reasonably be expected to pay and to demand that figure. Wilson, however, did not press his view with vigour, for his position was weakened by his own belief in German liability, and by the fact that even though the United States renounced financial reparation for itself, it refused to agree to any scaling down of allied indebtedness to the United States. Again, Wilson was constantly faced with the undoubted fact that Britain and France had suffered more from the war than had his own country – the casualty lists of France, Britain and Italy were repeatedly brought to his notice.

Lloyd George, on 2 June 1919, alarmed by the possibility that the Germans might refuse to sign the treaty, did suggest fixing a figure in advance, quoting the British delegation as criticising 'the indefinite and unlimited character of the debt imposed on Germany'. He soon changed his mind again and on 7 June we find him saying, 'the Americans insist on fixing a total figure at once; M. Loucheur [for France] thinks it is impossible; I agree with him,' and finally, on 9 June, 'Nothing would be more dangerous. Either the figure we would fix would terrify the Germans or on the other hand it would be impossible for M. Clemenceau as for myself to get it accepted by public opinion.'[2] The treaty postponed all decision: the amount of damage to which Germany was liable was to be determined by a Commission, with delegates from the great powers and from Belgium and Yugoslavia, which was to notify Germany of the figure by 1 May 1921 and draw up a schedule of payments discharging this obligation by 1951. The Commission could postpone payments after hearing German representations and considering German capacity to pay, but it could not cancel any part without specific authority from the governments represented on the Commission. Certain payments in kind were also demanded. They included notably the surrender of all German merchant ships above 1600 tons and a proportion of smaller ships, as well as deliveries of coal, livestock and chemicals. Thus dangerous and threatening uncertainty loomed over the German economy.

There was much dispute among the peace-makers over the fixing of German frontiers. One issue was decided without difficulty: Alsace-Lorraine should return to France. Wilson's eighth point laid down that 'the wrong done to France by Prussia in 1871 in the matter of Alsace-Lorraine, which has unsettled the peace of the world for nearly fifty years, should be righted in order that peace may once more be made secure in the interest of all.' French claims, however, went further, claims based precisely on the need to make peace secure. On 28 March 1919, for instance, Clemenceau told his colleagues, 'Do not believe that they [the Germans] will ever pardon us; they will only look for an occasion for revenge; nothing will destroy the anger of those who wished to establish their domination over the world and who thought themselves so near to success.' In reply Lloyd George declared, 'the English people are haunted by the fear of making new Alsace-Lorraines'.[3] French policy was based on the belief that justice to Germany would not create a pacific Germany; Lloyd George believed that injustice to Germany would make certain a future war; Wilson believed that injustice to anyone might bring war. The essential French demands, long premeditated (the acquiescence of the Imperial Russian government had been secured early in 1917) was that there should be an allied or French military occupation of indefinite duration of the left bank of the Rhine and of the main bridgeheads over the Rhine.

The arguments used, in documents and speeches by Marshal Foch, the French commander-in-chief of the allied armies, and in official and unofficial communications from the French government, were based on the conviction that even a republican Germany could not be trusted and might become as aggressive as Imperial Germany was supposed to have been. To frustrate these aggressive impulses whether directed to the east or the west, force might be needed. Russia must now be discounted, British and American help might come too late and on France must therefore fall, until in the remote and indefinite future the League of Nations could assume this burden, the prime duty of defending the world against the revival of German militarism. France, however, had fewer men and smaller industrial resources than Germany and so this disparity must be counterbalanced by securing to France that highly defensible barrier, the Rhine. In possession of the bridges, France could make difficult the rapid concentration of German armies in the west and could with ease deploy armies to strike a blow at the rear of any German forces menacing the new states in eastern Europe.[4] The French watch on the Rhine would be made easier if the Rhineland were separated from Germany. This, too, the French demanded, though rather more diffidently, and in the west of Germany a separatist movement was encouraged by the French general, Mangin.

Faced with determined resistance from both Wilson and Lloyd George, Clemenceau gave way – the indefinite occupation was given up; the French sponsors of a Rhineland Republic were ordered to cease their intrigues. This was the greatest concession Clemenceau made; it is a measure of his anxiety to preserve Anglo-American support. It earned for him a rebuke from President Poincaré, for which he cared nothing, the sulky hostility of Foch, which embarrassed him and it contributed to his defeat as candidate for the Presidency of the Republic, which certainly wounded him.

Of course, Clemenceau received major concessions, though only after receiving a document from Lloyd George of a kind deeply antipathetic to him, the Fontainebleau Memorandum of 25 March 1919 – *Some considerations for the Peace Conference before they finally draft their terms*. These were the considerations which dominated British foreign policy for the next twenty years – that peace could only be secured if it got the consent of the vanquished as well as of the victors. Germany must be prosperous – 'we cannot both cripple her and expect her to pay.' Germany must not be driven into communism – 'the greatest danger that I see in the present situation is that Germany may throw in her lot with Bolshevism.' Germany could not be left permanently weaker militarily than the other great powers – 'it is idle to endeavour to impose a permanent limitation of armaments upon Germany unless we are prepared similarly to impose a limitation upon ourselves.' 'In the end if she feels she has been unjustly treated in the peace of 1919 she will find means of exacting retribution from her conquerors' – the British notion of appeasing Germany took root even before the peace was made.[5] Lloyd George, though, wished peace to be made soon to bring back stability to Europe and to do that concessions had to be made to the French.

The most remarkable step was the promise by Lloyd George and

9

Wilson of a joint Anglo-American military guarantee of France in case she was attacked by Germany; this was a reversal of the foreign policies of both countries which proved too drastic for the United States Senate to accept. Again, both Wilson and Lloyd George expressed willingness to agree to a demilitarized zone and in the peace Germany was forbidden to send soldiers or maintain any military installations nearer to France than fifty kilometres east of the Rhine. At the same time, they agreed to an inter-allied occupation of the Rhineland, but only for a limited term of years, as a means of ensuring German fulfilment of the treaty and in particular of the reparations clauses. This gave an opening to Clemenceau to work for something equivalent to a permanent occupation and he made progress towards this end when he secured Wilson's agreement to a fifteen-year period of occupation, withdrawals to take place in three stages of five years. This agreement was made when Lloyd George was absent in England and when he returned he felt compelled to fall into line. Furthermore, Clemenceau secured agreement to the addition to article 429 of Versailles, on the occupation, of a paragraph stating that the occupation might last longer than fifteen years if at the end of that period guarantees against aggression on the part of Germany were not considered sufficient by the allied and associated governments. In addition, article 430 laid down that any German failure to fulfil the reparations clauses would mean immediate reoccupation.

In the closing stages of the discussion on the Treaty of Versailles, after the German government had commented on it, Lloyd George made another attempt to secure a reduction in the length of occupation. On 2 June, he included the occupation clauses among the parts of the treaty which should be modified, following German complaints, if Britain were to sign the treaty and join in compelling the Germans to sign. His suggestion that the occupation should be shortened met with determined resistance from Clemenceau and he was not supported by Wilson. What emerged – after discussion between the principal British and French delegates alone – was Clemenceau's agreement that the occupation could be brought to an end before the fifteen years were over if Germany fulfilled her obligations under the treaty.[6]

André Tardieu, who collaborated closely with Clemenceau in the peace negotiations, wrote on the Rhineland aspirations of France:

During the voyage from America to France, our ambassador to Washington, M. Jusserand, talked about them to President Wilson who seemed to recognise their weight and who, two months later, at the beginning of March had not, according to the testimony of his most intimate collaborators, opposed any objection to them. On the English side, on the contrary, a strong resistance emerged . . .

To him, there seemed only one point on which Clemenceau and Wilson came into sharp conflict – on the question of the Saar basin.[7] Here, the French demanded a tract of territory on historic grounds: that part of the Saar basin contained within the French frontier of 1814, as distinct from the frontier settled in 1815, together with the ownership of all the coal mines in this district on both sides of the proposed frontier. The claim to the mines was based on the systematic destruction by the Germans during the war of the French mines in the north-east. The claim to territory was based on the principle of self-determination; it was alleged that the populations were French, at least at heart, if not, perhaps, superficially, and the historic principle was deployed by showing that these territories had at some time in the past been linked with France. President Wilson detected, without difficulty, the feebleness of these arguments for annexation and offered firm resistance; for once, Lloyd George was less hostile to the French than Wilson and expressed readiness to agree that the French should have one or the other, territory or coal mines, but not both.[8]

Why was Wilson readier to defend the rights of Germans to self-determination in this part of Europe than in any other? Here it was a claim of France, not of Poland or Czechoslovakia, and it could hardly be argued that France could not exist without this territory; it was a dispute over the Franco-German frontier whose nature and history were far more widely familiar to Americans and Englishmen than were those of the frontier lands of Eastern Europe. This meant that 'experts' on the subject were in a much weaker position to get their views accepted than over Eastern Europe. Furthermore, the non-German expert on Polish or Czechoslovak questions was almost certain to be sympathetic to the national aspirations of those peoples while the far less esoteric knowledge required for Britons and Americans to understand the Saar issue did not tend to generate pro-German or pro-French feelings. Wilson's predisposition to sympathize with claims against Germany was thus in this instance balanced by the clarity with which this particular claim for sovereignty over territory could be seen to be a flat denial of self-determination. Why was Lloyd George's opposition to this claim against Germany weaker than his opposition elsewhere? The best answer is that he objected to what he supposed the Germans might object to and did not know what to object to until the Germans told him – he was concerned to make the peace as acceptable as possible to Germany and, as a result, his own objections to the peace became

11

clearest and most vigorous after the German objections to the draft had been heard – the Fontainebleau Memorandum of March, while stating the need to appease Germany, seldom escaped from generalities. The solution was a compromise suggested by Lloyd George – the creation of a small autonomous state of the Saar, within which the mines were to be ceded to France. As finally agreed, the state was to be administered by the League of Nations with a plebiscite to determine, after fifteen years, the eventual destiny of the territory, after which, if it were reunited with Germany, the German government could buy back the mines, a solution accepted by Wilson only with much repugnance.[9]

The frontier between Belgium and Germany was slightly changed – to include Eupen, Malmedy and Moresnet in Belgium; the frontiers between Denmark and Germany were altered, after a plebiscite, to include in Denmark the Danish parts of Schleswig-Holstein, a settlement which presented little difficulty since the Danish government made no attempt to go beyond the undiluted application of the principle of self-determination. On the eastern side of Germany, however, large numbers of Germans were included in Poland and Czechoslovakia. The Polish clauses of the treaty probably aroused more resentment in Germany than any other part of the treaty for though the fourteen points, which Germany had accepted, laid down, in point thirteen, that

an independent Polish state should be erected which should include the territories inhabited by indisputably Polish populations, which should be assured a free and secure access to the sea, and whose political and economic independence and territorial integrity should be guaranteed by international covenant,

it soon became evident that opinions sharply diverged on the meaning of the clause and in particular what was meant by 'indisputably Polish populations'.

The clash between Lloyd George and Clemenceau over the treatment of Germany showed itself at its clearest over the drafting of the Polish frontier with Germany. Here Lloyd George's anxiety to create a peace that Germany might accept – in the short run, by signing it, in the long run, by fitting into the new Europe – was not restrained by British parliamentary or public feeling and over this issue he spoke and acted as if he were an ingenious and rather unscrupulous delegate of the German government. Indeed, while the Treaty of Versailles was, in form, a dictated peace, it is untrue that German interests were neglected in the discussions that produced it, for the British Prime Minister represented Germany. Thus on 27 March 1919 we find Lloyd George telling his colleagues on the Council of Four, 'I think they [the Germans] will accept all the rest, including a very heavy indemnity; but what will hurt them most is the idea of abandoning millions of Germans to Polish domination'.[10] President Wilson tried to secure justice, a justice tinged with an anti-German feeling from which Lloyd George was exempt. To Wilson, justice for Poland meant the creation of a defensible, prosperous entity – a Poland that went beyond strict ethnological frontiers. 'It was therefore necessary to consider not only the economic but the strategic needs of this state, which would have to cope with Germany on both sides of it, the eastern fragment of Germany being one of a most aggressive character'.[11] Again, over Upper Silesia, Wilson remarked, 'I beg you not to forget that there are two sides to the question: as against the Germans, I admit that I am on the side of the Poles,' and when Lloyd George declared that British troops would not fight to give this area to the Poles without plebiscite, Wilson declared that American soldiers would support any people whatever against the Germans.[12] Wilson was influenced by the principal American expert on Polish affairs, Professor R. H. Lord, a keen advocate of Polish national aspirations. It must be remembered, too, that the cause of formerly oppressed nationalities was in 1919 a cause warmly espoused by those liberal, progressive people who supported most energetically the principles of Wilson's fourteen points. Thus Harold Nicolson, a member of the British delegation in Paris, who in general regarded the treaty with Germany as unduly harsh, wrote later, 'It was the thought of the new Serbia, the new Greece, the new Bohemia, the new Poland which made our hearts sing hymns at heaven's gate.'[13] Clemenceau's position was simple, Germany was the enemy, the stronger Poland was, the weaker Germany would be and the stronger the forces that might oppose Germany in the future would be. As for self-determination, Clemenceau said,

if one is obliged, in giving to these young peoples frontiers without which they cannot live, to transfer to their sovereignty the sons of the very Germans who have enslaved them, it is to be regretted and it must be done with moderation, but it cannot be avoided.[14]

The Commission on Polish affairs of the Peace Conference recommended that large areas of West Prussia, East Prussia, Pomerania, Posnania, and Upper Silesia should be ceded to Poland (territories including Danzig) and that a plebiscite should be held in the Allenstein region of East Prussia to determine its eventual fate, a plebiscite included at British insistence which led to this region remaining part of Germany.[15] Lloyd George immediately launched an attack on these recommendations and secured that there should be a plebiscite in the Marienwerder region (which meant leaving it to Germany) and that Danzig and the area around it should be made into a free city under the League of Nations. Already France's eastern European policy was beginning to clash with the need, felt by Clemenceau, to retain British friendship. After the German government had submitted its views on the draft treaty and stated violent objections to the loss of Upper Silesia, with its important industrial resources, Lloyd George reopened his campaign and secured a plebiscite here, too, which resulted in the end in the retention by Germany of about two-thirds of the territory in dispute. Over Danzig and Marienwerder, Lloyd George did not meet strong opposition; over Upper Silesia, he found it difficult to secure the consent of the Council of Four and the plebiscite for that area must be regarded as the British Prime Minister's greatest individual contribution to the peace with Germany.[16]

In spite of these changes, German opinion remained deeply shocked by the fact that over a million Germans were still to fall under Polish rule; to most Germans, this seemed unnatural, however reasonable it might be for Germans to rule over Poles, for, as the German observations on the draft treaty put it, 'as regards economic, social and cultural importance the German population is far superior to the Polish and Cassubian population.' That this social and cultural importance had been reinforced by German political domination was a point overlooked by the German government, but not by the allies who, in their reply, defended their work:

> It is true that there are certain areas, often far removed from the German frontier, such as Bromberg, in which there is a majority of Germans. It would be impossible to draw a frontier in such a way that these areas should be left to Germany while the surrounding purely Polish areas were included in Poland ... The Prussian Government ... has used all its immense resources to disposesss the original population and substitute for it one of German speech and German nationality ... To recognise that such actions should give a permanent title to the country would be to give an encouragement and premium to the grossest acts of injustice and oppression.[17]

It is to be noted that no one at Paris suggested the summary expulsion of populations of a particular nationality from disputed areas; that was a barbarism introduced into modern international practice in the Hitler-Stalin era.

The only really clear cut denials of the principle of self-determination are in the clauses of the treaty settling the new frontiers of Germany with former Austro-Hungarian territories. The solution adopted was attractively simple: to leave the frontiers unchanged. The result was to leave several million Germans in a Czechoslovak state of which many would have preferred not to form a part and to compel a still larger number of Germans to accept a separate existence from Germany in a new Austria. Of the delegations of the great powers only the French knew from the beginning, and with clarity, what it wanted – that is to say, to prevent these Germans becoming part of a greater Germany and to endow Czechoslovakia with the industrial resources and the defensible frontier of the German-inhabited areas of the borders. Once again, over Czechoslovakia, the relevant Commission reported in favour of a frontier based on strategic and economic considerations, though with certain modifications. The Council of Four decided the matter with casual rapidity. Colonel House, President Wilson's chief adviser, though he held no official position, deputized for Wilson in his absences from the Council, Lansing, the Secretary of State, being passed over. House and Clemenceau quickly agreed to make the old frontier between Germany and Austria-Hungary the new frontier between Czechoslovakia and Germany: 'It was so much simpler and less full of possibilities for trouble. We had but little difficulty in persuading both George and Orlando to accept our conclusion, George seeming to know but little about it.' In fact, Orlando said nothing, and Lloyd George accepted at once Clemenceau's skilful remark that it really had nothing to do with the German treaty at all but should be considered with the Austrian treaty.[18]

Lloyd George's lack of interest is odd, since at the end of the month before he had referred to the question of the Bohemian frontiers as something which might give Germany a grievance – probably this remark in the Fontainebleau Memorandum was included by a better-informed adviser. Lloyd George's own lack of interest can be explained by the lack of interest shown by the German government itself; Lloyd George was naturally not interested in securing concessions for Germany that the Germans themselves did not want and, in spite of an Austrian request, the German government did no more than urge self-determination for the Germans in Austria and Bohemia, without emphasis and without demanding that any part of Bohemia should be attached to Germany. It has been suggested that the Berlin government was anxious to avoid Czech intervention in case Germany refused to sign the peace; in fact, Germany cared, in any case, far more about the fate of those Germans who were to enter Poland than of the Germans of Czechoslovakia.[19] The Austrian government was much more concerned, but by the time its representations were submitted, the Treaty of Versailles was in its final form. Lloyd George was unlikely to trouble

15

himself greatly about the views of Austria, an altogether less important factor in Europe than Germany. As for Wilson, there is no sign that he ever gave any thought to this question; Lansing did – but Lansing's contact with the President was minimal.

A complete break with the principle of self-determination was contained in the provision of the treaty that the new Austria should be independent whether willingly or not. Almost certainly, a majority of German Austrians wished, in 1919, to become a part of the German *Reich*; the treaty laid down that they could not do so, except with the consent of the Council of the League of Nations, which required unanimity and on which, therefore, France had a veto. Thus the treaty prescribed that Austria could not unite with Germany without French permission, a provision that completely met French desires to prevent any strengthening of Germany. It was a decision whose full implications may not have been clear to Wilson. For Wilson insisted on upholding the right of all Austrians to decide their own fate, and when the subject came before the Council of Four, he opposed the French suggestion that Austrian independence should be 'inalienable' and himself suggested that the League of Nations might be required to permit Austro-German union, a proposal Clemenceau, of course, readily accepted. Lloyd George took little part in the discussion, probably because he shared the widespread British belief that German-speaking Austrians were something wholly different from Germans and therefore supposed that the Austrian desire for immediate unification was a passing whim, dictated by hunger and by the confusion of the defeat and dissolution of the monarchy; writing in 1938, he treated a prediction of 1919 that the *Anschluss* would eventually come as a sign of remarkable prescience.[20]

The frontier settlements, especially between Poland and Germany, and the reparations clauses – these were the parts of the Treaty of Versailles most disliked in Germany, which made certain between them that the peace of 1919 would never be accepted by German opinion without great revision; both these sections of the treaty were based on the assumption that Germany had been wantonly aggressive in 1914 and might be wantonly aggressive in the future, assumptions which were simply incomprehensible to most Germans. The military and naval clauses were resented by a smaller, though highly influential, section of public opinion, by German nationalists and conservatives, by those who believed that the army and the training it provided were the best schools for German citizens; the complete loss of German colonies mattered emotionally and practically least of all.

The disarmament of Germany and the prohibiting of German re-armament aroused little dissension among the peace-makers. On 12 February 1919, Wilson told the heads of delegations that 'he felt that until we knew what the German government was going to be, and how the German people were going to behave, the world had a moral right to disarm Germany, and to subject her to a generation of thoughtful-ness.'[21] The only disagreement in Paris was whether to insist on a German army composed of short-service conscripts or one of long-term volunteers. Allied generals asked for the former, Lloyd George and Clemenceau agreed on the latter; the generals were afraid that the small long-service army could provide highly skilled cadres for rapid expansion, the politicians that short-service conscripts would furnish dangerously large trained reserves. The politicians had the last word so that the German army was limited in the treaty to 100,000 men to serve not less than twelve years, a small army which, as Foch and his colleagues had predicted, provided highly competent leaders for a rapidly expanded army in the 1930s. There was to be no great general staff and the weapons allowed to the German army were carefully restricted – it was forbidden to have tanks, for instance. The German navy was equally drastically curtailed, and an upper limit of 10,000 tons displacement was put on newly built ships. Germany was forbidden to have an air force. The whole selection was made to harmonize with the fourteen points by prefacing the disarmament clauses of the treaty with the statement that German disarmament would 'render possible the initiation of a general limitation of the armaments of all nations.'

Article 119 of the Treaty of Versailles reads, 'Germany renounces in favour of the principal allied and associated powers all her rights and titles over her overseas possessions.' This presented no difficulty to the peace-makers, for it occurred to no one at Paris that Germany might be allowed to keep her colonies. Thus Wilson said to the Council of Ten in January 1919 'that he thought all were agreed to oppose the restor-ation of the German Colonies'; he took for granted that the German colonial record was too bad to permit any other interpretation of his own point five: 'A free, open-minded, and absolutely impartial adjust-ment of all colonial claims . . . the interests of the populations con-cerned must have equal weight with the equitable claims of the govern-ment whose title is to be determined.'[22] Difficulties arose rather over the redistribution of German territories and of her rights in China and over the tenure by which German colonies were to be held in future. The problem of tenure was solved by the introduction of the mandate system, which committed the recipients of the mandates to prepare the relevant territories for self-government in a more or less remote future, under the international supervision of the League of Nations. The German observations on the draft treaty complained that the taking away of Germany's colonies was contrary to Wilson's point five and that Germany needed colonies as markets and as areas for settlement of surplus population and claimed that Germany 'had looked after the interests of her natives'. In reply, the allies were able to point to past denunciations of German colonial rule in the Reichstag, especially by Erzberger and Noske. It could also have been pointed out that Germans had never shown any eagerness to settle in the German colonies and that German trade with her colonies had been insignificant.[23] Even so, the colonial clauses of the treaty, like the disarmament section, were resented in Germany as an example of unequal treatment.

Such was the German treaty; it left Germany potentially strong and immediately resentful – if Germany were not held down, and made to adhere to the letter of the treaty or if, on the other hand, Germany were not ultimately reconciled by concessions to the new European order, a new German war was almost certain. This is not an assertion based on hindsight alone: there were those who made this prediction as soon as the treaty was made, or earlier. Foch and Poincaré made it clear that they did not believe Germany could be held down indefinitely after the occupation of German territory had ended; on the other side General Smuts, the South African statesman who acquired during the First World War the habit which he never subsequently lost, of issuing wise pronouncements on all branches of the affairs of the world, published a statement immediately after the Treaty of Versailles was signed, explaining in the cloudy language of his assertively high-minded style that the peace treaty would not bring a 'fairer, better world,'[24] two members of the American delegation resigned and, above all, J. M. Keynes began to write his brilliant book *The Economic Consequences of the Peace* which showed conclusively, what the peace-makers knew all along, that the reparations clauses of the treaty were absurd, a condemnation which Keynes' readers extended to the treaty as a whole. Thus there began to grow up in France that bewildered feeling of having been somehow cheated of the security that victory should have brought and in Britain a feeling of guilt that Germany had been dealt with unjustly. British feelings of guilt strengthened the belief, expressed in private so frequently already by Lloyd George, that only through the reconciliation of Germany could European prosperity and peace be assured.

Part One of the treaty with Germany dealt with a more general theme; it was entitled 'The Covenant of the League of Nations'. Here

← L o/ N

was the great innovation: a world organization which would 'promote international co-operation' and 'achieve international peace'. On this document the hopes of liberal and progressive mankind rested and to the working out of this document President Wilson devoted his keenest attention in Paris, to the neglect, it must be suspected, of more parochial issues such as the borders of Bohemia. The Council was the chief organ of the League and was to consist of representatives of the great powers, the principal allied and associated powers, together with representatives of four other powers, while an Assembly of all the members was provided for. Articles 10 and 16 embodied the central provisions of the Covenant: members undertook to respect and to defend the territorial integrity and political independence of all members and in case of aggression the Council was to advise members on what they should do to carry out this pledge. Members would, without action by the Council, sever all economic intercourse with an aggressor and would receive recommendations from the Council on military action against the aggressor. Article 19 permitted the Assembly to 'advise the reconsideration by members of the League of treaties which have become inapplicable and the consideration of international conditions whose continuance might endanger the peace of the world'. Much of the whole structure was permissive and effective action depended on the voluntary co-operation of individual states, a state of affairs quite different from the situation the French had hoped to bring about in their abortive attempt to secure an international military force and an international general staff to enforce peace.

In fact, the League was likely to be effective only in mobilizing opinion, which President Wilson assumed would henceforth be the decisive factor in world affairs, but when the use of armed force was in question the League could rely only on friendly great powers.[25] In the 1930s, the international evil-doers were not of a sort to be restrained by moral disapproval nor were France and Britain, on whom, in practice, the duty of upholding international rights developed, very eager to take up the task. In consequence, the League had very little impact indeed. Its 'failure' is often ascribed to the abstention of the United States but it is far from evident that membership of the League would in itself have transformed American public opinion sufficiently to enable the United States to take a serious part in the defence of international order in the 1930s. Only if the League had been led and sustained by a continued coalition between Britain, America and France was it likely to be anything other than a failure, and divergent public opinions in these countries made such a thing impossible.

19

2

The Peace with Austria, Hungary and Bulgaria

The Peace of Paris was made up of the Treaties of Versailles with Germany, of St Germain with Austria, of Trianon with Hungary, of Neuilly with Bulgaria and Sèvres with Turkey – the Sèvres treaty proved too fragile and a new treaty of Lausanne was eventually signed with a new Turkey.

The most important fact of the Austro-Hungarian settlement was that Austria-Hungary ceased to exist. This was not a result of the work of the Peace Conference, for, by the time it met, the Habsburg monarchy had fallen apart and separate entities of Austria, Hungary, Czechoslovakia, and Yugoslavia had emerged. These states made claims, frequently mutually incompatible, to parts of the territories of the defunct Habsburg monarchy at the same time as claims were made by Poland, Italy and Rumania. By 1919, large armies would have been needed to reconquer the former Habsburg dominions if anything like the old Austria-Hungary was to be revived, and this line of action had understandably little appeal to the leaders of the great powers.

The Hapsburg monarchy had been held together by the same national antipathies that tore it apart. The monarchy had seemed useful, in varying degrees, to each of the nationalities within its borders as a means of curbing some other nationality. To Germans its existence prevented Czech dominance in Bohemia; to Czechs its absence might bring unrestricted German oppression (the Germans were proved right in 1919, the Czechs in 1939). To the Magyars of Hungary it provided the backing of a great power for the Hungarian kingdom and enabled them to oppress their Slavonic subjects; to the Croats it imposed some check on the Magyars inside the monarchy and on the Italians inside and outside. To the Poles it held back the Germans and Russians, and allowed them to dominate the Ruthenians. The monarchy provided little for Serbs, Slovenes, Rumanians and Ruthenes – but these were the

20

most backward and least self-conscious of the nationalities and even they could hope for something from Vienna, some anti-Magyar move, for instance, such as the Archduke Francis Ferdinand had allegedly been meditating before 1914. The power of the monarchy rested on the assent of the nationalities within its borders; that assent depended on fear of what other nationalities might do if the monarchy were removed; once it became clear, in 1918, that the power of the monarchy was anyway on the point of destruction, and that the new wielders of power in Europe, the allied and associated powers, were ready to deal direct with the nationalities, Austria-Hungary collapsed ignominiously and all the nationalities rushed to assert their separate existence in order to make the best for themselves of the new era of national self-determination. Now, the broker between the nationalities would no longer be the king and emperor but the Peace Conference and so the monarchy became irrelevant. That this should be so was the result of a decision of 1918, one of those revolutionary decisions, characteristic of great wars, taken without full recognition of its potential effects. This was the decision to endorse Czechoslovak and Yugoslav national aspirations.

During the war, the allies and the United States could adopt one of two alternative policies towards Austria-Hungary, the first to seek a separate peace with the Habsburg monarchy, the second to weaken and defeat it; the first meant acceptance of the Habsburg state, the second led to encouragement to the Slav populations of the monarchy to seek complete independence. Rumanian claims to Transylvania were less important in this context – without it Austria-Hungary could continue to exist, while without the territories claimed by Czechoslovakia and Yugoslavia it could not. The Poles could be fitted into either policy, for Austrian Poles felt little hostility to the Empire and might accept an autonomous Poland linked with it, while even if a completely independent Poland were erected the loss of Polish Galicia would not destroy Austria. Hence Wilson's Fourteen Points were much more clear on the Polish question than on the other national issues of Austria-Hungary: point thirteen laid down that 'an independent Polish state should be erected', while point ten was a masterpiece of ambiguity: 'The peoples of Austria-Hungary, whose place among the nations we wish to see safeguarded and assured, should be accorded the freest opportunity of autonomous development.' This was in January 1918: in April, negotiations with Austria-Hungary for a separate peace came to an abrupt halt; in June, President Wilson declared that 'all branches of the Slav race should be completely freed from German and Austrian rule', and in September, he recognized the Czechoslovak National

Council as a belligerent government.[26] It was the Czechs who destroyed the monarchy, above all Thomas Masaryk, who, almost throughout the war, had worked for an independent Czechoslovakia. His voice was decisive because of his own persuasiveness and because of the organization of Czech armed forces made up of deserters from the Austro-Hungarian armies and from prisoners taken by the Russian armies. The Yugoslav movement received less definite encouragment, partly because its spokesmen were not united, partly because of Italian suspicion that an independent Yugoslavia might block Italy's territorial ambitions. Even so, as President Wilson told the Austro-Hungarian government in what amounted to its death-warrant, the American government had also by October 'recognized in the fullest manner the justice of the nationalistic aspirations of the Yugoslavs for freedom'.[27] It is possible that Austria-Hungary, or some new form of Habsburg empire, might have survived, if Wilson and the allies had remained ready to negotiate with its government and had refused to deal directly with the nationalities; as it was, the destruction of the monarchy was assured before the Peace Conference assembled, as a by-product of the failure of peace negotiations with the Emperor and his ministers.

The peace-makers had to adjudicate, therefore, between the claims to former Austro-Hungarian territories, of new as well as of old states, those of Italy, Serbia, whose transformation into a part of the Serb-Croat-Slovene or Yugoslav state was recognized during the first months of 1919, Poland, Czechoslovakia, German Austria, Hungary, whose union with Austria ended on 1 November 1918 with the release by the King-Emperor of the Hungarian government from its oath of loyalty to him, and Rumania. Montenegro, which before the war had been an independent state bordering on the Hapsburg empire, was merged, amidst the protests of its exiled king, with Yugoslavia. Germany was excluded from joining in the partition of Austria-Hungary by the decisions that German Austria was not to be allowed to unite with Germany and that the old Bohemian frontier with Germany should be maintained. The dispute which caused most difficulty to the Peace Conference was that between Italy and Yugoslavia over their shares of former Austro-Hungarian territory around the Adriatic Sea, or, rather, the dispute over this question between Italy and President Wilson.

Italy had entered the war in return for specific promises of definite territorial gains. The Treaty of London of 1915 between France, Russia, Great Britain and Italy laid down that Italy should secure the Trentino and the south Tyrol (the Brenner frontier), Trieste, Istria, Gorizia and Gradisca, the islands of Cherso and Lussin and various smaller islands, the northern part of Dalmatia as far south as Cape Planka with adjacent islands, the Albanian port of Valona, with surrounding territory, full sovereignty over the Dodecanese Islands, the region of Adalia if Turkey in Asia were partitioned, and compensation in Africa if France and Britain increased their African colonies at the expense of Germany. Fiume was specifically not claimed by Italy – it was to be allotted to Croatia, which was apparently thought of as an autonomous state.[28] The agreement between France, Britain and Italy made at Saint Jean de Maurienne in 1917 which confirmed and extended Italian demands in Anatolian Turkey was subsequently condemned as invalid by Britain and France because the assent of Russia had not been secured.

With this programme, the Italian delegation led by Orlando and Sonnino came to Paris at the end of the war. The terms of the Treaty of London seemed to represent a discredited past which had disregarded international justice and national self-determination. The drafting of the Treaty of Versailles showed that the need to make states economically and militarily secure could sometimes override these high principles, but the unfortunate Italians were left in 1919 with no one to defend themselves against; the war had been, in a sense, too successful and Austria-Hungary, a great power against whom it might have been reasonable to seek strong defences, had gone. What is more, Italian claims could largely be met only at the expense of Yugoslavia, itself a product of the virtuous struggle of nationalities to be free from oppression. It could have been argued, for instance, that to detach Dalmatia from Austria-Hungary to give it to Italy was a 'liberation'; it was much more difficult to argue that detaching Slavonic Dalmatia from a Slav state had anything to do with liberation. Nor was it easy to see why harbours should be taken away from Yugoslavia and given to Italy in order to help Italy to defend herself against Yugoslavia or to give Italy equal access to the sea. However, for Italy to secure less than the Treaty of London had promised made the whole Italian war effort to that extent pointless. Furthermore, it was difficult for Italians to regard the new Serb-Croat-Slovene state of Yugoslavia as an allied power, as Italy was expected to do at the Peace Conference, for the Italians had, in addition to their historic memories of Croat oppression, recent experience of the determined fighting spirit of Croat troops serving in the Austro-Hungarian armies on the Italian front.

A clash between Wilson and Italy was certain and Britain and France would have been obliged to support Italy, in consequence of the Treaty of London, had not one Italian move saved them from a conflict with the United States which both Clemenceau and Lloyd George were concerned to avoid – this was the Italian demand for Fiume. This was in itself a not unreasonable demand, for the town of Fiume, as distinct from its suburb, Susak, was undeniably Italian. President Wilson, however, refused to allow the only major port available to Yugoslavia to be put under Italian sovereignty. For Britain and France the essential fact was that Fiume had not been promised to Italy by the Treaty of London, so that as successive Italian governments committed themselves more and more firmly to this demand, first backed and then frightened by a vociferous public outcry, Clemenceau and Lloyd George were able to put themselves in the position of mediators between Italy and Wilson and to decline to carry out their pledges to Italy. The demand for Fiume enabled them to argue that Italy was asking for more than the Treaty of London and that as a result they themselves were no longer bound by it. On 3 May, in the absence of the Italian delegation from Paris, Mr Balfour spoke thus to Lloyd George: 'The President of the United States thinks you are speculating on the impossibility, for the Italians, of simply abandoning Fiume. But if they did so, it must be recognised that the difficulty would become insoluble,' and Lloyd George answered, 'I agree, that is what I fear above all.'[29]

Wilson was exceptionally firm in his refusal to concede the Italian demands for Fiume – on this issue, his advisers had spoken with clarity at an early stage in the peace negotiations and the President seldom failed to follow any categorical advice from his own experts. His attitude on this point was in striking contrast to his conduct over the Brenner frontier which, in flat contradiction to the principle of self-determination, was given to Italy without any dispute arising. Here it seems that Wilson regarded the matter as settled in advance by one item of the set of comments on the Fourteen Points that Colonel House gave to the allies in October 1918, after Wilson had approved them, an item which interpreted the ninth of the Fourteen Points which called for 'a readjustment of the frontiers of Italy ... along clearly recognisable lines of nationality' as being compatible with giving the south Tyrol to Italy provided the cultural life of the Germans thus handed over was protected.[30] This frontier line was no doubt accepted because Austria was still thought of at the time as a great power, or more probably because it was thought that Austria might merge into Germany, against whom all agreed that defensible frontiers were essential. The Fiume question, on the other hand, proved beyond the powers of the Peace Conference to settle.

Eventually a direct arrangement was made between Italy and Yugoslavia and a treaty signed at Rapallo at the end of 1920. A free state of Fiume was to be set up, which was to include a special regime for Fiume proper, and Zara was to be Italian – these two provisions were considerable successes for Italy; in addition, the islands of Cherso, Lussin, Lagosta and Pelagosa were attributed to Italy. In 1924, Fiume became Italian. These terms were better than those Italy had been prepared to accept in 1919; it may be that the Yugoslavs were alarmed by the final defeat at the Presidential elections of 1920 of their hopes of continued protection from the United States.[31]

Elsewhere, Italian demands received little satisfaction: in Turkey they found themselves faced, first, with the preference of their allies for encouraging Greek ambitions and then, in common with the Greeks, with the fierce opposition of Turkish nationalists to foreign domination; from Albania the Italians eventually withdrew; in Africa, Britain and France showed little eagerness to compensate Italy for their own territorial gains and their arguments that they were only assuming burdens seemed not wholly convincing to Italian opinion. Even so, Italy secured substantial gains as a result of the war, but these gains, the Brenner frontier, Trieste and most of Istria, were overshadowed in Italian eyes by the Fiume question and its outcome. So intense had been the agitation in Italy over Fiume, that the neglect of Italian claims by her allies in 1915 and the direct opposition to them of Wilson, advertised by his manifesto of April 1919, dominated all else and gave to Italians the feeling that though technically victorious, they were being treated as a defeated power. After a war in which Italy's part had involved a painful loss of men and an exhausting economic effort and in which Italians believed that they had defeated Austria-Hungary single-handed, this feeling produced a dangerous disillusionment which readily generated a xenophobic nationalism which found its first overt expression in the activities of the poet Gabriele d'Annunzio. Only the socialists supported moderation in Italy's claims abroad. By the summer of 1919 there were rumours of a coup d'état planned by military men in association with Mussolini's organization of ex-soldiers to replace the allegedly weak and compromising politicians.[32]

On 12 September 1919, d'Annunzio seized Fiume with a contingent of volunteers, 'annexed' the town to Italy and proceeded to denounce America, the allies and the Italian government with energetic loquacity. It emerged that the Italian government was quite unable, despite its promises to the Peace Conference, to control d'Annunzio, that the armed forces could not be relied on to obey orders to act against

25

d'Annunzio and that Italian opinion, except among socialists, was sympathetic to him.[33] Indeed it was only the increasing unpopularity that the poet incurred in Fiume itself that made it possible for the Italian government to get him out of Fiume at the end of 1920. The conduct of Wilson, d'Annunzio's agitation, and the evasions of the allies made it unlikely that Italy could be counted on to support the final peace settlement and helped indirectly to foment anti-constitutional agitation in Italy, and a rancour not so much against Yugoslavia as against the whole victorious coalition.

Other parts of the Austrian and Hungarian treaties created new irritations or brought older rivalries and conflicts to the surface. Teschen, for instance, created ill-will between Poland and Czechoslovakia. Czechoslovakia had a strong historical and economic claim to the duchy of Teschen with its railways and coal fields; Poland a strong claim on ethnographical grounds. At first, it seemed that the two new states would arrange matters amicably by taking over the area inhabited by those who spoke the respective languages involved, and a provisional working agreement to do this was reached on 5 November 1918. Soon, however, the Czechs began to feel that they might successfully claim the whole territory and in order to reinforce their claim moved troops into the Polish occupied area, against Polish resistance, on 23 January 1919. The wound to Polish-Czech friendship opened on this day never healed. It was a clash of two reasonable claims: Polish claims were justified on ethnographical grounds, the Czechs, on the other hand, really did need the coal from the Teschen mine fields. This was an example of the sort of issue that European free trade would have resolved. The French backed Czechsolovak claims, through fear of driving Czechoslovakia into friendship with Germany, while they assumed that Poland was certain to be on bad terms with Germany, irrespective of Czech-Polish relations; few supposed, in 1919 or 1920, that the inclusion of the Sudeten Germans in the new Czech state would produce enmity towards Czechoslovakia on the part of Germany as distinct from Austria, and indeed these assumptions were invalidated only when an Austrian had secured control of German foreign policy.[34] The French representatives on the Supreme Council in Paris secured, in 1919, the rejection of a solution acceptable to Poland by playing the familiar card of a plebiscite; in 1920, at the Spa Conference, the Poles agreed, under the pressure of extreme anxiety to secure allied help against the Soviet Russian invasion, to submit the question, instead, to the arbitration of the allies who dictated a settlement giving complete satisfaction to Czechoslovakia. At Spa, Grabski, the Polish Prime

Minister, was bullied by Lloyd George and compelled to sign a document accepting the decision of the Supreme Allied Council on all Poland's unsettled frontiers.[35] The Poles never forgave the Czechs for taking advantage of their weakness.

The claims of Italy and the coming into existence of Czechoslovakia and Yugoslavia left the new Austrian republic a reduced fraction of the former Austrian part of Austria-Hungary. German-speaking populations were included in Italy and Czechoslovakia; with Yugoslavia, the new frontier followed ethnographic lines after a plebiscite had determined in favour of Austria the fate of the area around Klagenfurt. Independence, as we have seen, was imposed on this reduced Austria, which, unable to support itself economically, was thereby condemned to a hard struggle against unemployment and hunger.

The Hungary of the Treaty of Trianon of 1920 was similarly reduced to a remnant of the pre-war kingdom of Hungary. It contained what was left after most of the demands of Czechoslovakia, Rumania and Yugoslavia had been met (a relatively small, and largely German-speaking, area of Hungary was transferred to Austria). The old kingdom of Hungary had contained a central core inhabited by Magyars together with large territories in which politically and economically dominant Magyars were scattered among the populations of other nationalities. All these outlying territories were taken away from Hungary, together with some districts containing compact homogeneous Magyar populations. On the side of Slovakia, Magyar areas were detached on economic grounds – to give Czechoslovakia secure access to the Danube and because these areas were held to be economically linked with the territories further north rather than with lands south of the river. Ruthenia, an area largely inhabited by little Russians, which would certainly have been attached to Russia if that country had not been treated as non-existent in international affairs, was appended to Czechoslovakia; this was hardly a product of self-determination since the Ruthenes had scant national feeling, and in fact it is safe to say that the peacemakers had no idea what should be done with Ruthenia so that it went to Czechoslovakia simply because the Czechs asked for it. Czechoslovakia, therefore, took in from Hungary, nearly one million Magyars, about half a million Ruthenes, a quarter of a million Germans (Germans were to be found scattered throughout eastern and south-eastern Europe, especially in the towns) and rather under two million Slovaks. Transylvania was given to Rumania; here Magyar, Rumanian (and German) populations were inextricably intermingled, with areas of Magyar occupation to be found far to the east of the central Magyar core, and the territory ceded to Hungary contained nearly three million Rumanians as against one and a half million Magyars – once again some solid blocks of Magyars on the frontier were lost to Hungary, this time to include the only north-south railway in Transylvania inside the Rumanian frontier. The loss of the Banat, divided between Yugoslavia and Rumania, involved great difficulty in the division, where populations were inextricably mixed, but a relatively minor separation of Magyars from Hungary. Hungary lost large areas of Croatia and Slovenia to Yugoslavia – most of this loss was of incontestably non-Magyar lands which had had some measure of autonomy before the war – together with most of the territory lying between Szeged and Belgrade, in some of which homogeneous Magyar populations existed, an area given to Yugoslavia apparently in order to give Belgrade a larger bridgehead to the north of the Danube.[36]

The Magyars were thus split: two-thirds remained in Hungary; one-third found themselves in Czechoslovakia, Rumania and Yugoslavia. Most of the Magyars, perhaps two million or so of the three million lost to Hungary, were intermingled with other populations and it was thus a question of deciding who should govern whom. The Magyars insisted that their superior culture dictated that Magyars should do the ruling; the Czechoslovaks, Rumanians and Yugoslavs denied this superiority or attributed it to Magyar oppression. For the million or so Magyars in compact blocks near the frontiers the arguments used were economic or strategic – that Rumania and the new states were entitled to prosperity and safety. The Hungarians questioned the settlement by every means: firstly by force of arms under the ephemeral Bolshevik, Bela Kun, who attacked Czechoslovakia and Rumania and was overthrown by the Rumanian invasion that followed, and subsequently by incessant dialectic and propaganda.[37] Thus the Hungarian settlement, like the settlement of the German-Polish frontier, did not bring solutions to national problems, indeed 'solutions' could only be found by the methods introduced by the Turks and developed later by the Germans of compulsory resettlement of populations or mass murder, and, for all their faults, the peace-makers of 1919 would never have accepted even the milder of these barbarities. (Indeed, they insisted on the imposition on Czechoslovakia, Poland, Yugoslavia, and Rumania, of treaties which embodied pledges by these states to treat their minorities on equal terms with the dominant nationalities.[38]) The Hungarian treaty, like the German treaty, created resentment in the defeated country – stronger perhaps among educated Magyars than among Germans, since the peace-makers took Hungarian wishes far less into account than German wishes – Germany was much more powerful, actually and potentially, than Hungary. The new Hungary was a country that could never voluntarily accept the post-war settlement and which became a cause of fear and uncertainty among its neighbours.

Austria-Hungary could not have been resurrected politically in any form immediately after the war; but the fragmentation brought about by the new frontiers need not have brought about economic fragment-ation. One of three attitudes towards restrictions on international trade might have been taken by the peace conference: firstly to move towards a general reduction of tariffs, towards free trade; secondly to permit or to encourage restricted areas of partial or complete free trade, that is to say exchanges of preferences at one end, customs unions or 'common markets' at the other; thirdly to permit or encourage individual states to pursue isolated and selfish tariff policies. The territories of the old Austro-Hungarian monarchy had, in fact, made up a common market with free trade prevailing inside a rather high external common tariff; the test of commercial policy at Paris was the issue of what should become of this economic bloc. Wilson's third point sounded hopeful: 'The removal, so far as possible, of all economic barriers and the establishment of an equality of trade conditions among the nations consenting to the peace and associating themselves with its main-tenance,' but by the time Wilson went to Paris he had explained it away:

I . . . suggest no restriction upon the free determination of any nation of its own economic policy, but only that whatever tariff any nation might deem necessary for its own economic service . . . should apply equally to all foreign nations.

Discriminatory tariffs were to be employed only under the direction of the League to punish 'those who will not submit to a general programme of justice and equality'.[39] This meant that Wilson would support isolated tariff policies, provided that they were directed against the whole world outside and not against some parts of it rather than others. It followed that he would oppose customs unions, free trade areas and trading blocs. The French, sheltered behind high tariffs and fearful of a repetition of Prussia's advance to hegemony in Germany through a customs union, were unlikely to differ.

The result was that the peace treaties did nothing to curb the development of national policies of economic autarchy and the creation of more and more formidable barriers to trade. The treaties stipulated only that the ex-enemy states should not discriminate against the allied powers by granting more favourable tariffs towards anyone else's products. The Austrian government protested against this clause which meant the complete destruction of the pre-war tariff system of the Habsburg monarchy and would leave Austria 'in the position of the Palace of Versailles, deprived of its dominions'; it asked for preferential treatment to be allowed in Austria, Hungary and Czechoslovakia, that each of these countries should be able to reduce the tariffs they imposed on imports from the others. The Allied Economic Commission then contemplated making possible the revival of the old system by allowing mutual preferences in tariffs to the entire territory of the old monarchy – this was the scheme for an economic Danubian confederation. Since this would mean establishing internal customs barriers in Italy, Poland and Rumania, against which the Italian delegate protested, it was then proposed that preferential treatment could be given to each other by all states which had acquired territory from any part of the old Austro-Hungarian monarchy. Here was a grandiose vision which passed briefly before the conference only to be condemned, a scheme which, had it developed, could have changed the whole history of Europe and the world, and evolved into a scheme for a common market including Poland, Czechoslovakia, Rumania, Hungary, Austria, Yugoslavia and Italy. The Czech delegate to the Economic Commission protested that his country could not possibly face Italian competition on equal terms. At the Supreme Allied Council the project raised no comment except from Mr Balfour, of Britain, who was 'alarmed' by the 'proposal of establishing an entirely new customs system over half Europe'.[40] A much narrower solution was accepted – that Austria, Czechoslovakia and Hungary should be permitted, not compelled, to grant preferential customs treatment to each other, but for a five-year period only. Thus economic nationalism was reinforced by treaty; or, rather, the treaties laid down that economic understanding should be all or nothing, would include most of the world, or be impossible. Though it is arguable that the economic clauses of the treaties would permit a complete customs union between Czechoslovakia, Hungary and Austria, such a development was unlikely except as the final outcome of more tentative steps towards economic union and anything short of complete union was certainly ruled out by the prohibition of discriminatory tariffs after the five-year period had elapsed.

The Treaty of Neuilly with Bulgaria was less drastic than the other European treaties; it gave two small parts of eastern Bulgaria to Yugoslavia, on strategic grounds, in order to make the Bulgarian frontier more remote from the railway to Salonika, and it transferred western Thrace from Bulgaria to Greece, thus cutting off Bulgaria from the Aegean Sea. This latter provision was not based on ethnography

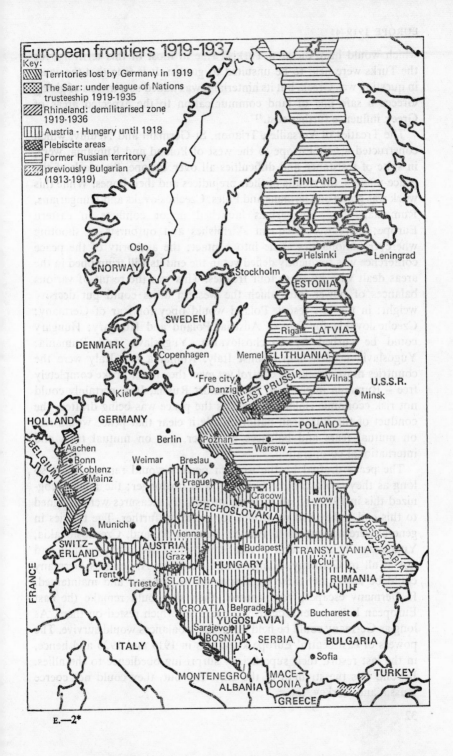

European frontiers 1919-1937

Key:
- ▨ Territories lost by Germany in 1919
- ▧ The Saar: under league of Nations trusteeship 1919-1935
- ▨ Rhineland: demilitarised zone 1919-1936
- ▥ Austria - Hungary until 1918
- ▨ Plebiscite areas
- ▤ Former Russian territory
- ▨ previously Bulgarian (1913-1919)

FINLAND

NORWAY

Oslo

Stockholm

SWEDEN

Helsinki

Leningrad

ESTONIA

Riga   LATVIA

DENMARK

Copenhagen

Memel   LITHUANIA

Vilna

Minsk

Kiel

Free city
Danzig

EAST PRUSSIA

U.S.S.R.

HOLLAND

GERMANY

Berlin

Poznan

POLAND

Warsaw

BELGIUM

Aachen
Bonn
Koblenz
Mainz

Weimar

Breslau

Prague

Cracow

Lwow

Munich

CZECHOSLOVAKIA

BESSARABIA

SWITZ-
ERLAND

Vienna

Graz

AUSTRIA

Budapest

TRANSYLVANIA

FRANCE

Trent

Trieste

SLOVENIA

HUNGARY

Cluj

RUMANIA

ITALY

CROATIA   Belgrade

YUGOSLAVIA

Bucharest

Sarajevo

BOSNIA   SERBIA

BULGARIA

Sofia

MONTENEGRO

ALBANIA

MACE-
DONIA

TURKEY

GREECE

which would have dictated Turkish rule in most of this territory, for the Turks were held to be unsuited to govern. It is true that the coast in question was Greek, but its hinterland was added as a means of giving Greece a safe line of land communication to the expected areas of Greek influence further east.[41]

The Treaties of Versailles, Trianon, St Germain and Neuilly, which constructed a new Europe to the west of Poland and Rumania, were, in spite of resistance and difficulties all over Europe, the work of the peace-makers, the results of their prejudices and their hopes. While this work was going on Germans and Poles, Czechoslovaks and Hungarians, Rumanians and Hungarians launched major conflicts in eastern Europe; there were frequent skirmishes and outbursts of shooting wherever nationalities came into contact; the authority of the peace conference was frequently defied yet in the end its will triumphed in the areas dealt with by these four treaties. This was the result of various balances of power into which the western allies could put decisive weight: in the last resort, Poland would obey for fear of Germany; Czechoslovakia for fear of Austria, Poland and Hungary; Hungary could be curbed by Czechoslovakia, Yugoslavia and Rumania; Yugoslavia needed help against Italy. Rumania and Italy were the countries most difficult to control yet even they never broke completely free – Rumania might need help against Russia, Italy certainly could not risk economic isolation. Even as the peace was being drafted, the conduct of the European nations made it clear that peace would rest on mutual fears and balances of power, not on mutual trust and international co-operation.

The peace drafted by the western powers would remain intact so long as they could control Germany and no longer; the allies recognized this in 1919 and all their major military measures were designed to this end – they had no troops for anything further. The treaties in general were acceptable to France, Belgium, Poland, Czechoslovakia, Yugoslavia, Rumania and Greece; much more doubtfully to Italy and not at all to Germany, Hungary and Bulgaria. As long as Germany could be kept quiet these treaties could be imposed and maintained. If Germany escaped from control, then she could remake the east European balances and destroy the treaties which rested on them. As long as Germany could be held down these balances would survive. The powers of east central Europe knew this in 1919 and 1920 and hence, in the last resort, their superficially surprising obedience to the allies. Beyond this the strength of the allies ran out, they could not coerce Russia and Turkey, too.

3
The Peace with Turkey

Neither the frontiers nor the degree of independence secured by Turkey in the inter-war years resulted from allied wishes. It is true that part of the Turkish settlement was imposed without difficulty, the detachment from Turkey of all Asiatic portions of the Ottoman Empire outside Anatolia. Here problems came from rivalries between France and Britain and from Arab ambitions and not from Turkish resistance. These problems, indeed, caused the worst quarrel between Britain and France of the entire period of the peace conference.

The situation at the end of the war was that soldiers of Britain and the overseas Empire had defeated the Turkish forces and were in occupation of the Arab areas of the Ottoman Empire. These forces had received some assistance, widely advertised, from Arab soldiers and irregulars led by the Emir Feisal and his British advisers, including T. E. Lawrence. Feisal and his father Hussein, the Sherif of Mecca, had, in exchange, received certain promises from the British government, the scope of which was capable of dispute, but which clearly promised the independence of the Arab lands subsequently conquered by the forces under the British commander Allenby, with reservations for the interests of France in part of those areas. In 1916, the Sykes-Picot agreement between Britain and France arranged that France and Britain should 'recognize and protect an independent Arab state or confederation of Arab states' and though the word 'protect' was subsequently replaced by 'uphold' (soutenir) it was clear that France and Britain, in fact, proposed to operate virtual protectorates in their respective spheres of influence – France in Syria; Britain in Mesopotamia (Iraq). Indeed in parts of these areas – in the Lebanon and Cilicia for France, in southern Mesopotamia for Britain – the agreement laid down that the two countries should be allowed to establish any form of administration or control they wished. Finally, on 2 November 1917, Mr Balfour announced that Britain supported the establishment in Palestine of a national home for the Jewish people. These pledges were mutually compatible provided the special meaning of the words used such as 'independence' was understood by all participants and it seems clear that the subsequent claims of Feisal, Lawrence and their admirers that the Sykes-Picot agreement was an underhand betrayal of the understandings with Hussein cannot be sustained.[42] The British and French negotiatiors took for granted that British or French advice and interference was perfectly possible in an 'independent' country; by 'independence', they meant independence from the Turks, not independence from themselves. On the other hand, the spirit of the pledge to the Arabs and of the Sykes-Picot agreement was a different matter: the one implied British backing for Arab aspirations towards unity and nationhood and British backing for the claims of a particular Arab dynasty to leadership of all Arabs, while the Sykes-Picot agreement assumed a Franco-British partition of the Arab lands, regardless of Arab wishes.

The French insisted on the agreed partitions; nearly all the British on the spot and many in London were prepared to try to keep the French out of Syria, to go back on the Sykes-Picot understanding and to support Feisal's attempt to create an united Arab kingdom centred on Damascus. From the British point of view this latter scheme had great attractions, for Feisal seemed certain for the future to rely on British support and advice so that his kingdom would ensure British control of the entire Middle East without any need for a partnership with the French. The claims of the French that they, too, could reasonably advise and support Arab rulers was regarded as absurd by the British in the Middle East, who, encouraged by Feisal, were ready to believe that British control of Arabs meant Arab independence while French control meant Arab subjugation and that therefore for the French to control Syria was something wholly different from and morally less sound than, for instance, British control of Iraq.

What was at stake for Britain and France in the Middle East? It does not appear that either country was thinking primarily of securing direct control of oil resources; thus Clemenceau and Lloyd George appear never to have discussed oil in 1919 and Lloyd George was surprised when he discovered that their subordinates had drafted an agreement on oil.[43] The Mosul area, which was expected to become an important oil-producing area, was first allotted to the French sphere and later transferred to the British without undue difficulty; the British and French were fairly readily able to agree on division of the proceeds of oil-wells. This is not to say that the importance of Middle East oil was not coming to be recognized, even though in 1920 only about one per cent of world oil production came from the area, but that other issues mattered more to Britain and France.[44] To Britain it was above all the old concern for India, the desire to secure control of the Suez Canal, the Red Sea, the Persian Gulf and the approach to these areas that dominated her policy and also the wish to win favour in the Moslem world by advancing Moslem interests, for the British Empire was, as its officials often reminded each other, the greatest Moslem power; to France it seems to have been a matter of prestige coupled with a genuine concern to protect and extend French culture outside France, a concern that British statesmen could not understand.

This quarrel between Britain and France broke out in the Council of Four with a violent attack on British policy by Clemenceau on 21 May 1919; Clemenceau reminded Lloyd George that he had, in December 1918, modified the Sykes-Picot arrangement according to British wishes – 'I said to you "Tell me what you want in Asia, so as to suppress all causes of misunderstanding between us" ' – and now the British were preventing the French army from occupying its share of Syria. Clemenceau was right, the British were doing as he said, for Allenby was reporting that Feisal would 'raise the Arabs against the French and ourselves' if the French army came to Syria and that in such case he would be 'totally unable to handle the situation with the troops at my disposal'.[45] Lloyd George was faced with a clear-cut choice between supporting Allenby, Lawrence, Feisal and his followers on the one side, and honouring the British obligations to France on the other. After some weeks in which he tried to evade the issue, by bringing together Feisal and the French, he made up his mind. Between 9 and 11 September 1919, he held four conferences with Allenby. On 13 September, disregarding Allenby's sympathies, he told Clemenceau that British troops would withdraw from Syria, leaving the towns of Damascus, Homs, Hama and Aleppo to the forces of Feisal and the area west of that line to the French army.[46] This was capitulation, for it meant leaving the French free to deal with Feisal in Syria, and by the summer of the next year they had turned him out, without comment or protest by the British, in spite of Feisal's and Allenby's appeals.[47] Thus Lloyd George and the British government chose France and co-operation in Europe rather than the probably delusive hope of a satellite Arab Empire.

The British were left with various embarrassments: a resentful Feisal, whose existence aroused feelings of guilt among nearly all British students of the Arabs, the territories comprised in Iraq,

Palestine, and the area between them, a diminishing army and a tight-fisted Treasury.[48] The result of the shortage of money and men was that the London government became anxious to control the Middle East with a minimum effort and therefore to avoid direct administration. Thus Arab governments were hastily set up in Iraq and in Transjordan, the name given to the area between Iraq and Palestine, the first under Feisal as king, the second under Feisal's brother, Abdulla, as emir. Palestine could not be disposed of so easily for no Arab rulers could be left to preside over the establishment of the Jewish national home there, nor could the administration be put into Jewish hands if the British were to remain on reasonably good terms with the Arabs, and the Jews themselves be safe. Palestine had to have direct government and, as a result, Palestine came to have an efficient modern administration with standards well in advance of those that came to prevail in the areas of British influence as distinct from British rule.

This settlement of the fate of the former Ottoman Empire outside Anatolia was a settlement imposed by the allies; the final settlement in Constantinople, Thrace and Asia Minor was not. Here, allied intentions were frustrated by the Turks who, in the process, emerged into full national self-consciousness. During the war the allies arranged the partition of Turkey amongst themselves; at the end of the war it was assumed that indigenous Turkish attempts at reform had been irrevocably discredited by the misguided pro-German policies of the pre-war Committee of Union and Progress and that Anatolian Turkey should be treated, like Syria or Iraq, as an area requiring more or less colonial methods of rule by outside powers. The last thing that occurred to anyone at Paris in 1919 was that the Turks might stand up for themselves. However, even before the Council of Four came to agree on the outline of its plans for Asia Minor and the Straits, it had taken the decision that precipitated the Turkish national revival.

On 5 May 1919, when the Italian representatives were absent in Rome, Wilson, Lloyd George and Clemenceau agreed that there were signs that the Italians, who had already landed troops in southern Anatolia, were preparing further expeditions and might well be planning to take Smyrna (Izmir). At this time relations with the Italians were at their most strained and the three leaders both genuinely resented unilateral action on the part of Italy and believed that this action would make it yet more difficult to curb Italian territorial ambitions in Europe. Lloyd George had a solution ready: 'We must let the Greeks occupy Smyrna.'[49] Thus the Italians would be frustrated and the other Allies would have at their disposal an obedient Greek force to control

Italians and Turks as a substitute for the forces they were neither able nor willing to send themselves. On 7 May, Veniselos, the liberal Greek Prime Minister, who intended to revive a Greek empire round the Aegean, was told to send troops to Smyrna – the Italians were informed on 12 May and given the pretext that massacres of Greeks were imminent in Smyrna, which may well have been true.[50] On 15 May the Greeks landed; on 19 May the distinguished Turkish general, Mustafa Kemal, arrived at Samsun, in northern Anatolia, under orders to supervise the disbanding of the rest of the Turkish armed forces, as required by the allies. He did nothing of the sort. Instead, he began to raise an army and to build up a movement to regenerate Turkey.

Progressive Turks, including Mustafa Kemal himself, had already been cast into deep dismay by the events of 1918 and early 1919 and had become increasingly suspicious of allied intentions and increasingly contemptuous of the Sultan's government in Constantinople. In parts of Anatolia, nationalistic resistance groups had already been formed, but it was the arrival of the Greeks that brought the support and enthusiasm for Mustafa Kemal and his aims that enabled him to win Turkish independence by force of arms. The folly of Wilson's remark of 13 May, made during the discussion of the partitioning of Turkey, that the Turk was 'docile' and would 'obey without difficulty the power acting as his guide' was quickly demonstrated.[51] That remark, however, shows the direction in which Wilson's mind was beginning to move, that is to say towards the notion of a Turkish government for Anatolian Turkey supervised and advised by one of the great powers without a formal mandate. For this role Wilson suggested France, while Lloyd George and Clemenceau urged Wilson to take Turkey on himself. This Wilson thought the United States Senate would probably refuse to permit him to do but he supposed that it would approve a mandate for America to rule in Constantinople and at the Straits and in Armenia.[52] The Turkish settlement was therefore held up while the powers waited to hear how much of Turkey the United States would take over – the answer, none at all, took a long time to come, or rather, an answer which the governments could officially act on. A consequence of this delay was to exacerbate the discomfort of the allies over Turkey for it became more and more evident that the sort of settlement that the allies had in mind in 1919 would have to be fought for against the nationalists. As neither Britain nor France could spare troops, the Greek army would do the fighting and in return the allies would accept their installation in and around Smyrna and in eastern Thrace. Unfortunately using the Greeks meant that Turkish anger and resistance became stronger and more unanimous. The Italian occupation of parts of southern Anatolia came to an end in the summer of 1919, when Nitti succeeded Orlando and introduced a less adventurous Italian foreign policy so that the Greeks were left on their own.

Thus the Treaty of Sèvres of 1920, imposed on the impotent Constantinople government and ignored by Mustafa Kemal and the nationalists, proved to be a provocation to defiance rather than a settlement, with its clauses involving the Turkish loss of eastern Thrace and Smyrna and the close allied control of Turkish government finance. A curious fact about the Treaty of Sèvres is that it was regarded by all those in touch with Turkish affairs as implausible and unenforceable well before it was actually signed. Only M. Veniselos disagreed. He was, in March 1920, 'anxious that the British government should know that in his deliberate judgment the contention that Mustapha Kemal commanded any kind of formidable force was pure bluff.' By then, it was evident that both France and Italy, which was hostile to Greek expansion, might take up appeasement of the nationalists.[53] The British representative in Turkey, the British general staff, the Viceroy of India, the Foreign Office and the Foreign Secretary, all took the view that the terms of Sèvres could not be upheld against the nationalists and that, in particular, Greek demands must be curbed.[54] One man, almost alone, fought against these views and for those of Veniselos, Mr Lloyd George. In June 1920, he seemed to be justified by the success of the Greek offensive against Kemal. By the end of that year, however, things began to go wrong. The publication of the Treaty of Sèvres consolidated nationalist feeling in Turkey; the death of King Alexander of Greece, followed by the fall of Veniselos and the return of King Constantine, notorious for his pro-German attitude in the war, meant that France became even less enthusiastic about supporting the Greeks; above all, Soviet Russia began to intervene.

In April 1920, Mustafa Kemal sent a note to Moscow which led to the arrival, in November, of a Soviet representative in Ankora, Kemal's capital; meanwhile Armenian independence was destroyed by Turkey and Soviet Russia acting in, at least, tacit co-operation. By this time, the Soviet leaders had given up hope of an immediate general revolution and were ready to take empirical measures to strengthen Soviet Russia and weaken the West. Thus Kemal's elimination of the Turkish communist leaders in January 1921 (by throwing them into the sea) in no way hindered the conclusion in March 1921 of a Soviet-Turkish treaty which enabled Russia to appear as the enemy of imperialism in the Near East.[55] Thus fortified, the Turkish nationalists were able to resist another Greek offensive in 1921 while the differences between Britain and France, which had always been suspicious of British patronage of the Greeks, became open with the signature of the Franklin-Bouillon treaty with the Ankora government in October. By this treaty France abandoned substantial territorial claims in Asia Minor, promised French help to the Turks and secured concessions for French capitalists. By 1922, nationalist Turkey was receiving munitions from Russia, France and Italy, munitions used by Kemal in the final expulsion of the Greek forces from Asia Minor in August 1922. This expulsion was accompanied by blood-thirsty massacres and followed by the total ruin of what was left of the Greek population around Smyrna.[56]

Mr Lloyd George stuck to his position to the last; he praised Greece and the Greek army in the House of Commons in August and prepared to resist, at the risk of war, the Turkish advance on the Straits. At Chanak, where Turks and British met, the French contingent of the allied forces of occupation withdrew, the Italians stood aside, Lloyd George appealed to the Empire for armed men and made it clear that Britain would fight alone if need be. Poincaré, the French Prime Minister, who had ordered the desertion at Chanak, relented and agreed to join with the British in pressing on Kemal an armistice which denied him immediate control of the Straits while conceding to Kemal the handing over of eastern Thrace which the now defunct Sèvres treaty had allotted to Greece. These events show something of the curious working of the Anglo-French alliance in these years; both wished it to continue – France, in order to secure British support against Germany, Britain, in order to be able to restrain French oppression of Germany. As a result, neither power pursued its own Near Eastern policy consistently and logically – the British were prevented from giving whole-hearted support to their Arab and Greek protégés; the French were prevented from a determined search for a dominant position in Turkey based on collaboration with the nationalists and outright opposition to Britain; both powers regarded the German problem as far more important than the Eastern question.

Peace with Turkey was made, at last, on 4 July 1923, after two conferences at Lausanne; Turkey kept eastern Thrace, so that Turkey retained a foothold in Europe. Turkey was completely sovereign except that the Straits areas (and both sides of the borders of European Turkey) were to be demilitarized; freedom of passage of the Straits was stipulated. When the treaty was ratified in August, the treaties of peace were complete. Unlike the treaties with Germany, Austria, Hungary and

Bulgaria, the Treaty of Lausanne was a truly negotiated treaty based on discussion and consent. As a result, the new reformed republican Turkey of Atatürk, as Mustafa Kemal came to be named, was not a revisionist country, striving for international change, but a source of stability in south-eastern Europe.

The Middle Eastern settlement of the post-war years brought French and British power in that region to its height. In spite of difficulties and disturbances in Syria, Iraq and Egypt all these countries were held firmly under French or British influence between the wars. Yet at the very moment when western influence and power reached furthest, it was checked by an indigenous nationalist anti-Imperialist movement. Nationalistically-minded Arabs, themselves victims of the arbitrary decisions and partitionings of the great western powers, contemplated the success of their former Turkish overlords with relish and even with hope.

4

The Consolidation of Peace: Russia

Peace with Turkey was negotiated, not dictated, for the allies were not strong enough to impose peace by force; the conditions of the settlement, or, rather, of the truce arrived at between Russia and the western powers were equally not at all what the western powers ardently wished them to be. Above all, quite contrary to the hopes and intentions of the allies, Bolshevism survived. The frontiers of the Soviet Union, moreover, were fixed by processes little influenced by the meditations and directives of allied councils and conferences. Britain and France were not strong enough to impose their will, or rather, their will was not strong enough for it to be imposed on Russia; it is possible that the British and French armies, with quite a small proportion of the effort they had mounted in 1918, could have suppressed Bolshevism in Russia, but it was completely impossible for the British and French governments to put forward this effort. The mass armies of the First World War could not be treated as mercenary armies, they would fight only for a cause in which their soldiers believed, to liberate France, to end war, to free Belgium, to make the world safe for democracy and they had been told, often enough, that the defeat of Germany would bring about these desirable ends and that all men could then live in happiness and peace. It was difficult to persuade them that a new evil was to be overthrown in a remote country and that the peace they had longed for had not, as they had supposed, arrived in November 1918, but was to be indefinitely postponed. What is more, the Bolsheviks claimed, with some reason, to be on the side of the toiling masses, the workers and peasants, while there was much evidence to show that their opponents in Russia represented landlords and capitalists. In such a conflict it was by no means certain that public opinion in either Britain or France would be sufficiently unanimous to support a continued war effort or that British and French soldiers could be counted on to fight if they arrived in Russia; on the contrary, they might well become 'infected with the Bolshevist virus' themselves. In short, a serious attempt to crush Bolshevism using British and French troops in Russia seemed in 1919 as likely to produce revolution in the west of Europe as to prevent it.

Thus the numbers of allied troops in Russia declined in 1919, leaving the Japanese, who had separate objectives, out of account. In 1918, the allies had dispatched troops to Russia as a means of preventing accumulated stores from falling into German hands and in an attempt to recreate, with Soviet or anti-Soviet forces, an eastern front against Germany. By the end of 1918 there were allied forces at Murmansk and Archangel in the north, in the Caucasus in the south and at Vladivostok in the east. At the end of 1918 large allied forces, eventually amounting to 25,000 men under French command, including strong units of the French army itself, arrived at Odessa while smaller forces landed in the Crimea. Two things quickly became clear, firstly that the anti-Bolshevik forces available on the spot were meagre and disorganized, secondly that French troops and the sailors on board French warships in the Black Sea could not be relied on to fight. Active communist propaganda was carried on among the French rank and file and the withdrawal of the demoralised French and allied forces was carried out in April amidst mutinous outbreaks on some of the warships.[57] This was the only large-scale post-war attempt at armed intervention – the other allied forces in Russia which had arrived during the war with Germany were left stranded there, holding defensive positions and contributing nothing to the outcome of the Russian civil war.

The significant allied intervention against the Soviets took the form, therefore, of money, weapons and supplies. Three major campaigns in 1919 were financed and supplied, largely by British funds: those of Kolchak, attacking westwards from Siberia, Denikin, northwards from the Black Sea, and Yudenitch towards Petrograd. The French became sceptical about the White Russian armies before the British did (even though their support, as it turned out, lasted much longer). On 25 March 1919, the Council of Four discussed Russia. Wilson urged his policy: 'To leave Russia to the Bolsheviks – they will stew in their own juice until circumstances make the Russians wiser and to limit ourselves to preventing Bolshevism from invading other parts of Europe.' The French view proved remarkably similar. Marshal Foch spoke firmly,

What is sent to Denikin is lost. I do not attach great importance to Denikin's army because armies do not exist by themselves. They must have behind them a government, a body of law, an organized country. Better a government without an army than an army without a government. That is why I tell you,

'Build on Rumania, because you have there not only an army but a government and a people'.

And two days later, Foch spoke of a 'cordon sanitaire' – 'it is not a question of an offensive but of a defensive barrier'.[58] Thus French effort in 1919 was largely, though not exclusively, devoted to building up the strength of Poland and Rumania, rather than supporting the anti-Bolshevik Russian armies. By the end of 1919 the policy of the barrier seemed to have succeeded and that of intervention had certainly failed, but the success of the first was made possible only by the maintenance during the critical months of 1919 of forces strong enough to keep the Red Army fully occupied. Similarly, in 1920, the narrow escape of Poland from extinction at the hands of the Red Army was helped by the last flaring up of the civil war in European Russia under Denikin's successor, Wrangel.

Arming the Poles meant encouraging the revival of memories of the Poland of 1772 with its frontiers far to the east of ethnographical Poland. In September 1919, the Poles offered to send half a million men to march on Moscow, if the allies would pay expenses at the rate of £600,000 or so per day. Clemenceau and Lloyd George quickly squashed this scheme for they were meditating a quite different use for the Polish army – the ejection of German forces from the former Baltic provinces of Russia. The armistice with Germany had provided that German troops on former Russian territories should be withdrawn only 'as soon as the Allies shall think the moment suitable, having regard to the internal situation of those territories'. In consequence, General von der Goltz remained in the Baltic provinces with formed units of the German army. This concentration of German troops acted as a magnet for disreputable extremists of a right-wing kind partly encouraged and financed by reactionary industrialists, partly attracted by the prospects of colonisation in the Baltic area.[59] The objects of the leaders of the varied groups that found themselves in the Baltic area included securing German control of that area, restoring the Russian monarchy, and crushing the German republic. When all these objects were secured, then a Russo-German alliance could destroy Versailles.

The allies were presented with the choice in 1919 between accepting the aid of these armed bands against Soviet Russia and letting the Poles march on Moscow on the one hand, or of curbing, on the other hand, the revival of nationalistic German militarism in the Baltic and keeping the Polish army in check to use against these Germans if need arose. The choice was made without hesitation, to get these armed Germans back to Germany and to compel the German government to disarm them. In 1919, in fact, the German danger loomed larger in allied minds than did the Red Peril and though the destruction of Soviet Russia would be welcome, German nationalists, then as in 1941, could not safely be trusted or permitted to carry it out. In June Wilson, Lloyd George and Clemenceau decided to get them out. In September the Germans were in the Baltic states in larger numbers than ever and the allies carried out the one measure to deal with this or any other situation that was within their power without someone else's assistance, that is to say they threatened the German government. The German government's control over the forces in the Baltic was minimal and it was reduced to issuing an appeal to the Germans in the Baltic to come home in order to forestall allied invasion and blockade; a month later the Germans were still there meditating the formation of an independent 'Eastern Germany' in East Prussia, Lithuania and Latvia; in October, they were attempting to subdue the Letts and not until December did the German forces withdraw, leaving a trail of havoc and devastation as they went, looting and bullying the local population.[60] Their departure was dictated by the end of support from Berlin where the civilian government, anxious from the very beginning to control these forces and unable to do so, was backed by those elements in the higher ranks of the army who took General von Seeckt's view that open defiance of the western powers would delay and not advance German recovery. With the armed Germans removed, the Baltic states, which were uninterested in conditions in Russia, provided Russia would leave them alone, were able to reach understandings with the Soviet government based on their independence – a treaty with Esthonia in February 1920 came first followed by treaties with Latvia and Lithuania.[61] Like so much else in eastern Europe between the wars, the independence of these countries rested on the simultaneous weakness of Germany and Russia – a precarious basis for survival; in 1920, the Germans were held down by the allies, the Russians had to face Wrangel and Pilsudski and solve increasingly urgent economic issues at home. The Russian withdrawal was under way; the belief that European revolution would solve the Soviet government's economic and political problems was waning; the New Economic Policy at home went with the search for peaceful co-existence abroad, for a breathing-space in which to stabilize the Russian government and economy.

The object of Pilsudski, the head of the Polish state, was to detach the Ukraine, White Russia and Lithuania from Russia and to link these territories with Poland in a federation, while leaving them enough independence to secure the support of national movements such as that led by Petlura in the Ukraine. These ambitions made it impossible for Pilsudski to co-operate with Kolchak and Denikin, who upheld the notion of restoring the unity of the territories of former Russia; nor were the Russian counter-revolutionaries men of a type to commend themselves to Pilsudski, whose career had been one of conflict with Tsarist Russia and who had, until 1916, endeavoured to co-operate with Austria-Hungary and Germany against Russia. He was prepared, indeed, eager, to invade Russia in 1919 but not to make it possible for Denikin to win control of Russia. Hence his offer to the allies in September to destroy Bolshevism for them; he would attack if he could be certain of full western support and certain therefore that *his* voice rather than that of Denikin should dictate the final Polish-Russian settlement; when this support was refused, the Polish government sought in 1919 to strengthen its position to the east without distracting the Red Armies from the defeat of the counter revolution in Russia. The strange result was that secret negotiations took place between Polish and Soviet representatives through whom Pilsudski promised not to attack while the Soviet armies were struggling with Denikin. In return, the Soviet government agreed to the Polish occupation of further territory. Meanwhile Pilsudski was preparing to enforce his wishes by war – but only after Denikin was overwhelmed. Lenin and the Bolsheviks may have owed their survival to Pilsudski.[62]

At the end of 1919 the Soviet government offered a final peace to the Poles, hinting at the maintenance of the existing line between the Polish and Russian armies. Pilsudski tried to secure an opinion from Britain and France. Would they help Poland to make peace? Would they help Poland to make war? He got a cloudy answer: the allies would not advise Poland not to make peace but would enter into no diplomatic relations with the Soviet government themselves; they would not advise Poland to attack Russia, but if Russia attacked Poland within her 'legitimate frontiers' they would help Poland.[63] Pilsudski, faced with growing Soviet military concentrations, determined to attack, pressed on his own preparations and the Polish offensive began at the end of April 1920. On May 8, Kiev was taken. Early in June, the Red Army counter-attacked and within a week forced the Poles to abandon Kiev. During the following two months the Soviet armies continued a rapid advance and at the beginning of August, with Russian armies closing on Warsaw, the extinction of Poland seemed at hand and with it, the collapse of the Peace of Paris and perhaps the overthrow of German and European capitalist society. In the middle of August, Pilsudski struck back and the Soviet armies collapsed. This time, the Poles used victory as a means of reaching a settlement with Soviet Russia, for Pilsudski felt obliged 'by the lack of moral strength of the nation' to limit the Polish advance eastward.[64] The Soviet government, equally, was ready to compromise, faced as it was with famine at home, and with the need to deal with Wrangel, the last of the White Russian campaigners in European Russia. The result was the agreement reached at Riga in October 1920, embodied in a formal treaty in March 1921, by which a frontier between Poland and Russia was agreed on which ran well to the east of the so-called Curzon line, drawn up by the allies in 1919, but which gave to the Poles substantially less than the Poland of 1772.

The Soviet defeat was the result, above all, of the weakness of Russian equipment and lines of communication. Against Poland the Russians deployed about 360,000 men, with only 50,000 taking part in the decisive battle even though, in October 1920, the Red Army had a total strength of over five million men. Secondly, the two lines of advance of the Red Army into Poland were too widely separated to be mutually supporting and the Russian armies in southern Poland did not co-operate strategically with the northern armies advancing towards Warsaw. Thirdly, as a Polish revolution failed to materialize, the notion of exporting revolution with bayonets proved fallacious. Fourthly, Wrangel's counter-revolutionary offensive from the Crimea distracted Soviet attention in July and August, though, on the other hand, the end of the Polish war ensured the speedy destruction of Wrangel's forces.[65] The consequences of this brief campaign were of transcendent importance in the post-war world. Within Russia, the war with Poland consolidated the Bolshevik regime, for the conflict with the Poles raised a spirit of patriotic fervour in its support, but, on the other hand, it demonstrated the weakness of Soviet Russia and checked ideas of a grand westward advance of Soviet communism. It made it plain that Soviet Russia was compelled to seek survival in a basically hostile world which could not yet be overthrown and that this survival imperatively required a solution of Russia's economic problems. In the early 1920s the output of Russian large-scale industry fell to less than a fifth of the pre-war figure, peasants refused to part with agricultural produce without receiving something in return and famine descended on the towns. The energies of the Soviet regime were fully absorbed for the rest of the decade and much of the next in the search for rapid economic growth and, as a result, Russian foreign policy after the Polish war was defensive, designed to hold off the rest of the world, rather than to change it. The Soviet Union, like the United States, though for quite different reasons, became a great absentee from

European and from world politics, and the increasingly artificial dominance of the western powers, Britain, France, Italy and Germany, in
world affairs was protracted until the 1940s. A renewed confrontation
of Russia with Germany was postponed and, as we shall see, until
Hitler chose a different course, Germany was able to deal with Russia
as a friend and an ally. The Treaty of Riga, then, ranks with the Treaty
of Versailles in determining the fate of the world between the wars;
the one rested on German defeat, the other on Russian weakness, so
that the stability of the settlement of Europe was almost certain to be
provisional and precarious.

The Russo-Polish war compelled the other European powers to consider with some urgency what their policies towards the Soviet Union
should be and the results showed that the prospect of an effective
European anti-Bolshevik coalition was even more remote in 1920 than
it had been in 1919. Britain and France continued to be linked by their
alliance, kept going by the concern of each to influence the other's
German policy, which acted as an irksome restraint for both powers but
one their governments dared not break, because of self-interest but also
because in both Britain and France there existed a genuine sentiment
in favour of mutual co-operation. The alliance worked through conferences and discussions in which each power tried to persuade the other
of the validity of its own policy; in only three of the months of 1920 was
there no meeting between Mr Lloyd George and the French *Président
du Conseil* – Clemenceau, Millerand or Leygues. At these meetings,
there were often present representatives from Italy, sometimes from
Japan, and occasionally American observers, but full allied conferences
were usually preceded by Anglo-French confabulations in which, with
varying degrees of success, a joint line of action was sought.[66]

Towards Russia, a common policy proved increasingly difficult to
attain. Lloyd George had never been convinced of the usefulness of
intervention in Russia, and, from the beginning of 1920, he urged a
settlement with the Soviet government and the resumption of trade with
Russia, and as the year went on he sought obstinately to escape from
the limitations on his actions imposed by France. Thus in January, he
suggested in Paris that steps should be taken to re-establish trade with
Russia, arguing that dependence on American grain caused by the
absence of Russian exports distorted the foreign exchanges and led to
high prices in Europe, and that 'the moment trade was established with
Russia, communism would go'. Conveniently, commerce could be
carried on through the Russian co-operatives who were (in theory)
independent of the Soviet regime, and thus the blockade of Soviet

47

Russia be lifted without, so it was alleged, any 'change in the policy of the Allied governments towards the Soviet government'. In March, Lloyd George demanded that peace be made between Russia and her neighbours – one month before Poland attacked; British anxiety to bring about a revival of world trade by ending political conflicts was coming to override all other concerns. At San Remo, in April, he secured allied agreement to the idea of negotiating with the Russian representatives on trade and at the end of May conversations opened in London between Britain, represented by Lloyd George himself, and a Soviet delegation. At this point, the French backed out and no French delegation took part. In June, Millerand objected to any political negotiations with the Bolsheviks unless the Soviet government recognized the engagements of Russia towards foreign governments – that is to say, unless it agreed to honour Russian debts to foreign investors, a high proportion of whom were French. The result was agreement to differ and the London talks went on.[67]

By this time, the French seemed to have been, once again, hoping that Bolshevik Russia might be overthrown. Though, officially, the French had adhered to the allied line that Poland should not be encouraged to attack, unofficially, France encouraged Poland to go to war and to continue it after the Polish victory. At the same time, France assisted General Wrangel, and went so far, in August, as to recognize him as the legitimate ruler of Russia, while Britain washed her hands of Wrangel.[68] Indeed, France seems to have pinned greater hopes on Wrangel than on Poland, and until Soviet successes threatened Poland's existence French help to Poland was given grudgingly. Pilsudski's conduct in 1919 had probably fostered French suspicions of him. In the summer of 1920, the one thing about Poland that Lloyd George and Millerand were able to agree on was that the Polish state was fundamentally unsound and that Pilsudski himself was very likely a traitor who might well be preparing to make a compact with Lenin and to preside over a Bolshevised Poland. Lloyd George drew the conclusion that the Russian advance should be halted by buying off the Soviet government at the expense of Poland – that peace should be made with the Russians on the best available terms – while Millerand drew the conclusion that Poland should be made to fight whether Pilsudski wished to or not.[69]

This divergence between Britain and France became evident after the Russians produced their terms in the middle of August when the British urged acceptance on the Poles and the French suggested refusal. It is true that Lloyd George was misinformed by Kamenev, who was still in London for the trade talks, of the full extent of the Soviet demands, but those which he himself passed on to the Polish government with his approval would have meant that Poland would henceforth be unable to defend herself. Naturally, too, the difference between British and French views expressed itself in a difference on the provision of help to Poland. Agreement between the two countries went no further than the dispatch of an Anglo-French mission, which would report on the situation in Poland. On the British side, the mission included Lord d'Abernon who sent back disheartening statements about Polish morale and efficiency and Sir Maurice Hankey who tried to induce Poland to accept the British system, which he had devised, of a Cabinet Secretariat, while both sought to make the Poles 'reasonable', that is to say, to persuade them to settle with the Russians. On the French side, the mission included General Weygand, Foch's Chief of Staff, whose reputation in the west was such that it was assumed both in Paris and London that the allegedly unreliable Pilsudski would be unable to avoid handing over the command of the campaign in Poland to him. This Pilsudski did not do and the Polish victory, as Weygand himself pointed out, was Pilsudski's alone, yet Weygand was exalted as the saviour of Poland by Pilsudski's opponents in Poland and by Millerand's supporters in France.[70]

Over the actual supply of munitions for the war to Poland, Britain and France acted quite differently. France supplied equipment and even, on 30 July 1920, told the Polish government that immediate payment would not be required. The British did not. At the end of July the Belgian government decided to send arms to Poland but only if both Britain and France did so, and inquiries from the Belgian ambassador were made in London which secured the answer that as long as attempts were being made to secure an armistice from the Russians the British would not risk doing anything that the Soviet government 'might regard as direct co-operation with Poland'. Accordingly, the Belgian government did not allow arms to be sent, and faced strong protests from France, which accused Belgium of acting contrary to the decisions of the Allies. Again, the French ambassador in London asked Lord Curzon, the British Foreign Secretary, to secure the agreement of the British government to allow the Poles to have war material which was surrendered, under the treaty of peace, to the allies – the question was put on 2 August and it was not until 13 August that Curzon replied that 'until the Polish-Russian negotiations have definitely broken down, His Majesty's Government regret that they do not feel able to support this proposal'. The British attitude towards supplying Poland was of great importance for Danzig was at this time under British control in the sense that the temporary administrator of the future free city – Sir Reginald Tower – was appointed by the British government, and, though, strictly speaking, the nominee of the allies, he took his orders in practice from London and looked to London for military support.[71] It was through Danzig that supplies for Poland must come, since Germany and Czechoslovakia refused to allow munitions destined for Poland to cross their territories. Over Danzig the conduct of the British government was ambiguous and evasive. The population of Danzig was overwhelmingly German and that population was bitterly hostile to Poland and to the Poles, who, indeed, showed no inclination to avoid provocations to German nationalist feelings.

Pacifism, sympathy for Soviet Russia, and, above all, dislike of Poland caused German workmen to refuse to handle munitions destined for Poland. When Lloyd George threatened decisive action, the workers' movement gave in – but that was only after the battle of Warsaw. For nearly a month at the end of July and the beginning of August, Danzig was closed to military supplies. During these weeks the British authorities wavered impotently and the British Foreign Secretary, Curzon, behaved with casual indifference, while insisting that he himself, rather than d'Abernon, who was in Warsaw, and whose interventions secured the unloading of one ship, should handle the problem.[72]

All in all neither the British, who hindered the Polish fight, nor the French greatly endeared themselves to Pilsudsky and his associates during their great crisis and this fact helps to explain the later tendency of these men to follow an assertively independent policy and to rely, unwisely enough, on Poland's capacity to survive alone.

The London negotiations on trade with Russia were broken off after the failure of the armistice moves in August and were not reopened until December. An Anglo-Russian trade agreement was signed in March 1921. Small though the economic results may have been, the treaty represented, as the Russian Foreign Minister said, 'a turning-point in Soviet foreign policy' – it meant British de facto recognition of the Soviet regime and signalized the Soviet acceptance of peaceful relations with the capitalist countries to make possible Russian economic reconstruction. The Soviet government promised to abandon revolutionary propaganda in all British territories, and though this pledge, disingenuously enough, was not held to bind the Communist International, the treaty showed clearly that Russian foreign policy no longer relied on revolution abroad.[73]

The most striking encouragement to the Soviet government in these years came from Germany. Three attitudes to the Bolsheviks were canvassed in Germany after the war. One was to attempt to offer Germany's services to the West against the Soviets in return for the sacrifice of Polish claims; a second to attempt to destroy Bolshevism in Russia and to form an alliance with an anti-Bolshevik Russia against the West; a third to strengthen Germany by co-operation with the new rulers of Russia. The first line of policy was urged by General Groener in the spring of 1919.[74] Allied hostility to Germany was too great for anything to come of it – Lloyd George's concessions to Germany over Poland were designed to make an eventual German reconciliation to the treaty possible rather than to secure immediate German co-operation against Russia and did not go far enough to make the shape of the new Poland acceptable to German generals. Allied demands for German withdrawal from the Baltic showed that the allies would rely on Poland rather than on Germany as their European bastion against the Soviets. The clearance of German forces from the Baltic checked but did not end the aspirations of men like General von der Goltz, rather it altered their timing: first republicanism in Germany should be destroyed, then the allies and the Bolsheviks resisted. Their aspirations were brought to an end by the failure of the Kapp *Putsch* in March 1920 which meant the defeat of the wildest and most hot-headed of German nationalists. Cooler and more rational minds were able to reassert their control over German foreign policy, those who recognized the fact of Germany's weakness and who saw the need for delay while Germany became strong enough to challenge the post-war settlement. The attitude of the German army towards questions of foreign policy was important for it was impossible for the post-war German government to ignore its wishes.

This important fact was the result of the internal dangers that threatened republican governments in Germany from the left and from the right: from communists on the one side and from the reactionary monarchists and authoritarians on the other. The former could not be held in check without the help of the army and in return for its resistance to Bolshevism in 1918 and 1919 the army successfully asserted its independence of the German government. Under these conditions the democratic republic could not survive without the army's consent, and the army's obedience to republican government was, at best, uncertain. Thus, when the Free Corps and the forces which had returned from the Baltic, led by hot-headed generals, attempted to seize power in March 1920, the regular army, the *Reichswehr*, stood aside, remaining neutral, while the strike of trade unionists brought about the defeat of the *Putsch*. The *Reichswehr's* support had to be negotiated for, it could not be counted upon by the German government – thus after the *Putsch*, General Reinhardt, who had been ready to support the government against Kapp and General von Lüttwitz, the leaders of the *Putsch*, was dismissed from command of the army and replaced by General von Seeckt who had successfully insisted on neutrality.

This capitulation to the independence of the army was followed by the acceptance by the government of a full-scale campaign launched by the *Reichswehr* against the government's own supporters, notably in the Ruhr region, where strikes, which had begun as a counter-measure to the Kapp *Putsch*, continued as a challenge to militarism in Germany and in support of genuine republicanism and democracy. The workers believed, rightly, that the *Reichswehr's* attitude towards the *Putsch* had been less than loyal to the republic, and so they fought against it and to create a truly republican army. The government was compelled to treat the movement as purely communist, which it was not, and thus to accept the *Reichswehr's* view of it, for the Kapp *Putsch* had shown that with the full support of the army, a coup d'état might succeed.[75]

The effect of the Kapp *Putsch*, then, was to reinforce the influence in Germany of the army and to reinforce the influence within the army of General von Seeckt and those who thought like him. Seeckt, himself a monarchist, was prepared to tolerate the republic as a temporary expedient, a screen behind which German strength could revive. That revival must be based on the army and the army must be kept free from republicanism and free from outside interference. The Treaty of Versailles, with its restrictions on German strength, must be quietly evaded until it could be openly overthrown, and Poland destroyed. Help from outside Germany was needed; Russia could provide it. This thought was common enough in post-war Germany; Seeckt was one of the first to believe that its validity did not depend on the nature of the Russian regime. As early as January 1920, Seeckt declared a political and economic agreement with Soviet Russia to be 'an irreversible purpose of our policy' and he believed this purpose to be perfectly compatible with the rigorous suppression of Bolshevism in Germany. Others were interested in Russia, for different reasons, among them Walther Rathenau, who was soon to become German Foreign Minister (son of the founder of the great electrical firm, the AEG), who was said to have organized the industrial mission which left Germany in the middle of 1919 and who formed in Berlin early in 1920 a group of industrialists to study Russian affairs.[76]

The Russo-Polish war aroused intense interest in Germany. It occurred to no one in Germany to help Poland, that disreputable state with its iniquitous frontiers and absurd pretensions in Silesia; but should Germany help Russia? Seeckt hoped that Poland would be swallowed up[77] but what would Russia do then? 'Neutrality' in the Polish war was formally announced by Simons, the Foreign Minister, in July 1920. This was the price offered by Germany to Russia in return for Soviet abstention from interference in East Prussia and, it was hoped, in return for the acceptance by Russia of Germany's pre-war boundaries. This neutrality was of critical importance to the Soviet government, since military supplies for Poland could not be transported across Germany and detachments of the Red Army were duly withdrawn when they crossed into East Prussia. Thus an effective though unsigned Soviet-German alliance came into being as the Red Army advanced on Warsaw; but it naturally fell apart when the Russians were thrown back. However, even though hopes of an immediate partition of Poland and the destruction of Versailles were dashed, economic reasons – and military reasons – for German interest in Russia remained. On the Soviet side, the eclipse of the hope which the Polish war had revived of immediate export of revolution meant that, as Lenin put it,

our existence depends, first, on the existence of a radical split in the camp of the imperialist powers, and secondly, on the fact that the victory of the entente and the Versailles peace have thrown the vast majority of the German nation into a position where it cannot live ... the German bourgeois government madly hates the Bolsheviks, but the interests of the international situation are pushing it towards peace with Soviet Russia against its own will.[78]

While German anxiety to develop steel exports to Russia might or might not lead to the development of a special Russo-German relationship, the Russian policy of Seeckt made certain a degree of co-operation between the ruling powers in the two countries which must produce a close working understanding. For while the Russian market could be exploited in association with other western countries, the assistance from Russia for secret German rearmament that Seeckt looked for could only, of course, be secured behind the backs of the British and French governments. In December 1920, talks began between Kopp, the Russian representative in Berlin (who had arrived in November 1919 to negotiate exchanges of prisoners and who had remained to discuss wider issues) on the one side, and the German military authorities and certain industrialists on the other, talks designed to make possible the reconstruction of the Russian armaments industry with German help in return for Russian help for the *Reichswehr*, and Seeckt set up a secret department within the Defence Ministry to handle the negotiations. Agreement was reached in the early spring on a project for manufacturing (in Russia) arms forbidden to Germany several months before the German Chancellor was even informed that the talks were going on.[79]

On the economic side, the Anglo-Soviet trade agreement encouraged the German government to conclude a similar agreement in May 1921 and to agree to exchange official representatives between Germany and Russia. However, the problem arose in acute form for Germany at the end of the year of whether to work with other powers in developing trade with Russia and in the development of Russian economic resources through investment and technical supervision or whether to act alone. The issue had wide implications – Germany could seek alleviation of Versailles through co-operation with the west or work with Russia towards the overthrow of Versailles, and until the international scene changed in 1924 the possibility of pursuing both policies at once did not exist. Thus every step which suggested that the co-operation of France was impossible, like the outcome of the Upper Silesian plebiscite and the emergence of Poincaré as French Prime Minister, strengthened the tendency towards Russo-German co-operation. Again, the issue divided German businessmen, heavy industry being anxious to regain its predominance in the Russian market of pre-war days, other sections of German producers being relatively more closely linked with the West.[80]

In the autumn of 1921 the French Minister of Finance, Loucheur, evolved a scheme for Franco-German co-operation to expand German industry and thus make more realistic French claims to reparations. His scheme broadened into a plan for allied co-operation in the common exploitation of Russia. At the allied conference at Cannes in January 1922 Lloyd George proposed a general 'economic and financial conference' with Germany and Russia to be represented.[81] At that point, Poincaré came to power as French Prime Minister, an event which wrecked the Genoa economic conference in advance since Poincaré had no intention of co-operating with Germany. The outcome was that the Genoa conference of April-May 1922 produced, instead of general economic agreement and co-operation, a formal Soviet-German understanding, the Treaty of Rapallo. This treaty came from the fears of its authors – each partner desired to prevent the other from hostile actions. The Russians were deeply suspicious of any scheme for international co-operation in economic contacts with Russia since part of the basic fear in Soviet policy was the formation of a politically hostile bloc – they greatly preferred to face western businessmen who were competing with each other rather than joining together to dictate terms. On the German side, fears of a Franco-Russian understanding, fears carefully fostered by the Russians, brought the German signature to the Rapallo treaty. The Germans were encouraged to believe that the Russians had received large offers from Poincaré, that France would make loans to Russia and even abandon Poland if Russia would join in upholding the Treaty of Versailles and join in the suppression of Germany, from which country Russia's right to receive reparations had been thoughtfully reserved in the Versailles treaty. The German delegation, even so, was divided, Rathenau, who had become Foreign Minister in February 1922 being especially concerned not to risk a clear break with the western powers – only when the course of the preliminary discussions at Genoa suggested that Britain and France were on the point of making a separate understanding with Russia, did he agree to sign.

The course of discussions at Genoa makes it clear that Rapallo was not the direct outcome of pressure from General von Seeckt, who was surprised when he heard the news, but rather the result of skilful exploitation of circumstances by the Russians. Indeed Rapallo was, in the short run, at least, more useful to the Russians than to the Germans; to the Russians it meant that there would be no anti-Russian European coalition, to the Germans it meant that Russia would not join in holding down Germany – but France was in any case ready and able to do that on her own. Indeed, Rapallo was more likely to bring about French action than to restrain it. The real gain for Germany was long-term – Rapallo produced an atmosphere of confidence between Russia and Germany which Seeckt exploited to secure Russian help in building the *Reichswehr* as the basis for a future great German army. To bring that about, the *Reichswehr* must be highly trained, and thoroughly familiar· ized with modern weapons and their tactical possibilities – a thing impossible to achieve without an evasion of Versailles and an escape from allied supervision. Probably in the summer of 1922, the Russians agreed to put military bases at the disposal of the German army for the training of members of the *Reichswehr* in flying, tank tactics and gas warfare.[82] Even in the military field, however, it is possible that Russia gained more than Germany – German military and technical advice enabled the Red Army to modernise itself more rapidly than it could have done without it; German soldiers helped to train their own most formidable future foes. Nothing shows more clearly the gap between Seeckt's ambitions and those of Hitler; Seeckt's activities assumed that Poland was Germany's true enemy and Russia therefore Germany's natural ally whereas Hitler put the matter the other way round. Seeckt thought of Bismarck's Germany which could co-exist with a powerful Russia; Hitler of a great Germany which could not.

5

The Consolidation of Peace: Great Britain, France and the German Problem

1

The Anglo-French alliance survived dissension over Poland, Russia, Turkey and Syria because both powers cared, above all, about Germany. Each country feared that the other, if left to itself, might recreate the German problem, might produce a situation in which a renewed expansion of German power and ambition would require curtailment by force. For France, safety seemed to lie in enforcement of the Treaty of Versailles while British policy tended to seek for the reconciliation of Germany through a revision of the treaty or, at least, through mildness in its application. Thus French statesmen were faced with an awkward choice between enforcement of the treaty on the one side and British friendship and support on the other. It is, in general terms, correct to say that until 1924 French policy chose to uphold the treaty and after 1924 chose British support. Before 1924 those dominant in the making of French policy sought, it is true, to obtain British co-operation but were ready to do without it, or to take it for granted, rather than yield in essentials. After 1924 French governments proved increasingly reluctant to take any action towards Germany without asking Britain first.

The determination of French governments to enforce the treaty was supported by the Chamber of Deputies elected in 1919 which was further to the right in its opposition than any French assembly since 1871; indeed this chamber was ready to enforce its wishes on governments and ministers suspected of lack of firmness towards Britain and Germany. Clemenceau's defeat, by Paul Deschanel, in the election for the Presidency of the Republic was in some part due to suspicion among the right of the assembly that Clemenceau was too ready to compromise with Lloyd George and that he had failed to insist vigorously enough on the conditions of peace demanded by Marshal Foch and Poincaré. Briand's resignation at the beginning of 1922 came about entirely because he was thought to be ready to make concessions to British views on the German problem in return for an Anglo-French defensive alliance. For the French right, safety for the future lay in the maintenance of the strength of France and in readiness to use it as a means of keeping Germany in check and as a means of preserving the support for France of those other countries in Europe, notably Belgium, Czechoslovakia and Poland, who might be expected to share French fears of Germany and to follow the lead of a determined and powerful France. Only on the left were men to be found at this time ready to believe that disarmament, conciliation towards Germany and reliance on the new international organization of the League of Nations might ensure peace.[83]

Dissensions between Britain and France arose over four issues: the enforcement of reparations payments by Germany, the measures to be taken to ensure German disarmament, the Upper Silesian question, and the guarantees to be provided for the maintenance of the frontiers of Germany, especially those with Poland. French governments in these years were ready to invade German territory to coerce Germany and to insist on specific British commitment to the integrity of Polish territory. In the 1920s the German-Polish frontiers were the most clearly contested by German opinion so that while France made a firm defensive alliance with Poland in 1921, it was not until 1924 that a similar but much looser agreement was made with Czechoslovakia.[94] Czechoslovakia, indeed, at this time, feared Hungarian hostility rather than German, a fear shared by Yugoslavia and Rumania, whose frontiers also included territories claimed by Hungary. In 1922 these countries came together in the so-called Little Entente, designed to keep Hungary in check; the Franco-Czech treaty of 1924 linked France with this combination and there emerged a group of powers – France, Poland, Czechoslovakia, Rumania and Yugoslavia, committed to the defence of the Paris treaties. It was to this group that France wished for some pledge from Britain, and especially to Poland, the country most directly threatened, but Britain, while ready to defend France and Belgium, was reluctant to undertake more far-reaching pledges in the east of Europe than those involved in the covenant of the League of Nations.

The first open clash between Britain and France came over the military clauses of the Treaty of Versailles. Under the treaty, a de-militarized zone bounded by a line drawn fifty kilometres to the east of the Rhine was created, in which Germany was to have no troops or military installations. Provisionally, the German government had been allowed to maintain some forces in this zone to maintain order; in March 1920 it asked to be given permission to send more troops into the Ruhr area to suppress the left-wing rising there that had been precipitated by the Kapp *Putsch*. Millerand first proposed that the allies should themselves restore order and then that they should seize other parts of German territory as a guarantee that German troops would eventually withdraw from the Ruhr. These proposals the British declined and while heated debates were going on, German troops moved in; in reply, French troops seized Frankfurt, Darmstadt and three smaller towns on 6 April, defying British objections and protests. It is clear that Millerand, urged on by Foch, had in mind not merely to reply to the German violation of the demilitarized zone, but more generally to make it clear that France would use force, if necessary alone, to make Germany carry out the whole of the Treaty of Versailles. When Millerand justified his action to the British government, he wrote of the 'higher and permanent interests of civilization' and more particularly of German failure to surrender war criminals, deliver coal or disarm. 'Do not [the] British government measure [the] danger of these successive and systematic violations? When will they call a halt to Germany? If they do not do so France must.' The affair was concluded when Millerand promised not to act in future without the previous consent of the allies.[85]

The Upper Silesian issue was equally significant. It will be remembered that Lloyd George had insisted on a plebiscite taking place to determine the wishes of the population of this important industrial area rather than that it should simply be handed over to Poland as the first draft of the Treaty of Versailles had arranged. The plebiscite took place on 20 March 1921. By that time the British were firmly and rightly convinced of the complete lack of impartiality of the French chairman of the allied plebiscite commission, General Le Rond, who tolerated or even helped the dubious activities of Korfanty, the Polish agent in Upper Silesia, and the armed bands at Korfanty's disposal. The British tried, and failed, to secure the recall of Le Rond and the expulsion of Korfanty before the plebiscite – British influence was limited by the absence of British troops in the area and the consequent dominance of the allied forces there by the French.[86] The plebiscite itself, as plebiscites are liable to do when they are held in areas where the wishes of the population are truly uncertain, produced a cloudy answer to the question of the political destiny of Upper Silesia. Over the whole plebiscite area, the voting was about 700,000 for Germany and about 480,000 for Poland, and the Germans therefore demanded the whole territory; the Poles, on the other hand, insisted that those parts of the area in which there was a Polish majority should go to Poland and that in order to make this possible some communes with a German majority must be included in Poland, too. These communes happened to contain the major industrial regions – in general the towns in the industrial region voted for Germany but the surrounding countryside for Poland. The British and Italian plebiscite commissioners reported in favour of leaving the entire industrial area to Germany; Le Rond, the French representative, advocated a solution largely along the lines claimed by the Poles. When Korfanty took the lead of a rising designed, apparently, to underline Polish claims and the German government offered troops to suppress the revolt, the French denounced the offer; Lloyd George suggested its acceptance. While Poles and irregular German units fought in Upper Silesia, the fate of the territory was disputed between Britain and France until August. Then Briand and Lloyd George, who had tried to save for Germany as much of the industrial area as possible, agreed to submit the issue to the League of Nations – a sympton of the flexibility with which Briand, while he remained in charge of French foreign affairs, continued to keep Anglo-French co-operation from total extinction. The League's award of October 1921 partitioned the crucial industrial area between Poland and Germany.[87]

At the end of 1921, Briand, indeed, sought to establish a solid basis for Anglo-French harmony by negotiating a formal defensive alliance with Britain. The Anglo-American pledge of 1919 to defend France against Germany, in return for which France had abandoned her demand for permanent military occupation of the left bank of the Rhine, had fallen to the ground as a result of the failure of the United States Senate to ratify the treaties. Briand sought a British guarantee – but a guarantee of wider scope than that of 1919. Above all, the French wished for two things, a promise of British help to defend Poland and a British commitment to support France in maintaining the demilitarized zone. As for the first, the French argued, in the words of their ambassador in London, the Comte de St Aulaire, that without this pledge 'such an alliance, at the best would cover us, if not against another Charleroi, at least against a Sedan, but it would not cover us against a Polish Sadowa, which, for Germany, would be the best preparation for another Sedan'. In other words, Germany might seek to destroy Poland as a preliminary to an attack on France, so that if Britain wished to defend France, she should join France in defending Poland, too.

The British reply, as communicated by Lloyd George to Briand, deserves lengthy quotation, for it embodied British policy towards Poland, and eastern Europe in general, until March 1939.

So far as the western frontier of Germany was concerned, it would be possible to give France complete guarantee against invasion. The British people were not very much interested in what happened on the eastern frontier of Germany; they would not be ready to be involved in quarrels which might arise regarding Poland or Danzig or Upper Silesia. On the contrary, there was general reluctance to get mixed up in these questions in any way. The British people felt that the populations in that quarter of Europe were unstable and excitable, they might start fighting at any time, and the rights and wrongs of the dispute might be very hard to disentangle. He did not think, therefore, that this country [*i.e.* Britain] would be disposed to give any guarantees which might involve them in military operations in any eventuality in that part of the world. On the other hand, he repeated, public opinion would readily give a guarantee against German attack on the soil of France.

In fact, Britain would not defend the peace settlement of 1919 as a whole; if France wished to do so, she would be obliged to do it without British help. But the British government refused even to agree 'to concert together' with the French on questions calculated to endanger peace and to commit themselves 'to examine in common the measures necessary to ensure speedily a peaceful and equitable settlement.' The independence and integrity of France were regarded as British interests, the defence of anything east of Alsace and Lorraine was not. France might or might not seek to curb an aggressive Germany; she would receive no encouragement from Britain if she tried.

In the treaty which was proposed by the British, the parties were to 'consult together should any breach be threatened' of the clauses of Versailles establishing the demilitarized zone. Briand insisted that Britain should be bound to treat a violation of the demilitarized zone by Germany, and indeed any breach of the military, naval and air clauses of the Treaty of Versailles as equivalent to a direct act of aggression against France. Poincaré, who now became Prime Minister after Briand had resigned in face of criticism of his alleged weakness towards Britain, naturally held to this line. In reply, Curzon produced another important statement of policy:

This was an obligation which I did not think the British people would be likely to accept. Moreover, was not the proposal to assume it entirely inconsistent with the new theory upon which it was generally believed that the policy of Europe was to be based after the war? Everywhere it had been preached that the old policy of rival groupings of great powers was to disappear and to be replaced by a concord of the nations.

Britain, once again, would not combine with other powers in the defence of the treaties against a potentially resurgent Germany: concord not coercion was what Britain sought.

When the British refused to give way to French demands, Poincaré expressed to the British ambassador in Paris a complete lack of interest in further discussion of a defensive alliance

to which, in the form presented to him, he added, he attached no importance whatever . . . He considered it as a mystification without any real value, since if circumstances arose such as had occurred in 1914 . . . England, in her own interests, will be obliged to take the same action as then.[88]

It was over the reparations to be paid by Germany that a definite breach opened between Britain and France. After the coming into force of the Treaty of Versailles, which laid down the categories of damage for which the Germans were to pay compensation, notably pensions and separation allowances paid during and after the war by the victorious powers and the physical destruction of allied property caused by German military operations, attempts were made to reach agreement between the allies and Germany, or failing such agreement, between the allies themselves on an assessment of what the amount was that Germany should produce in exchange for the abandonment of the exactions to be worked out, according to the treaty, by the reparations commission. The British were anxious for voluntary German acceptance of a figure that Germany might then seriously devote herself to paying and which Germany might be able to pay; the French, until Poincaré came to power, felt it essential to have British support in making Germany pay and therefore to compromise with British views; the British, on their side equally desired a compromise with France in order to avoid driving the French into extreme measures.

Endeavours to reach an agreement between the allies and Germany on the settlement of reparations failed completely. Indeed, as Lord d'Abernon, a friend to Germany, wrote,

in the numerous conferences which took place in 1920, 1921, and 1922, the German negotiators did not give the impression of any exaggerated anxiety to put their own finances in order, nor did they appear to make a serious effort to meet the reparation claims of the allies.

However anxious the British government was to reach agreement with Germany, the Germans made it impossible. In July 1920, at Spa, the first mutual confrontation of German and allied delegates took place. There, the Germans were unwise enough to allow Stinnes, a combative

61

industrialist, to speak, with the result that the worst allied suspicions of their attitude of mind were confirmed. Most of the discussion was taken up with a sharp controversy over the size of coal deliveries to be made by Germany which was settled only after the allied military commanders had been summoned to Spa and instructed to prepare an invasion of Germany. However, the German government, through Simons, the Foreign Minister, presented a scheme for reparation payments. This led to discussions between allied and German experts who met in Brussels in December 1920 and who in January 1921 produced a plan, covering the next five years, that Germany appeared ready broadly to accept – but only on the condition that Germany should keep the whole of Upper Silesia. This conditional and hesitant acceptance by the German government enabled, or rather compelled, M. Briand, the new French Prime Minister and Foreign Minister, to abandon the Brussels scheme and to start afresh at the allied conference held in Paris at the end of January 1921.[89] Here Briand sought to secure British agreement to reparation demands formidable enough to satisfy French opinion; Lloyd George was ready to agree in order to keep Briand in power and so to keep the uncompromising advocates of severity towards Germany out of power, but his agreement was conditional on further negotiations with Germany and the Paris agreement was presented to the Germans as a set of propositions capable of modification. Lloyd George, however, was compelled to agree that sanctions should be applied to Germany, notably that more of Germany should be occupied if an understanding with Germany could not be reached – a legal pretext for bullying Germany could always be found amongst the various German evasions of Versailles. At the London conference in March 1921, the Germans, once again, confounded their friends. Dr Simons, in Keynes' words, 'instead of stating in plain language what Germany thought she could perform, started from the figures of the Paris decisions and then proceeded by transparent and futile juggling to reduce them to a quite different figure.'[90] The result was that an ultimatum was presented to Germany, which extracted no more than that Germany would accept the Paris decisions for the first five years provided she retained Upper Silesia. On 8 March allied troops occupied Duisburg, Ruhrort and Dusseldorf. Still the Germans refused to accept the Paris terms.

Thus, in the spring of 1921, the atmosphere was tense; troops marched, ultimata were drawn up. Briand promised to occupy the whole of the Ruhr region, if a settlement were not reached. The outcome was paradoxical; under threat of invasion, the mildest scheme yet devised by the Allies for reparation was imposed on Germany on

5 May 1921 after another conference in London. How did this come about? Firstly, Briand was well aware that Germany could be made to pay only what she was able to pay but he could not openly say so. He could act on his beliefs only if he could appear not to be doing so. On 27 April 1921, the reparation commission announced that Germany was liable to pay 132,000 million gold marks.* If Briand could seem in theory to arrange to collect this sum, he could arrange in practice not to do so. Lloyd George had probably genuinely desired to reach a negotiated settlement with the Germans and was quite certainly anxious that Germany should be able to recover economically; only the difficulties of negotiating with the German government had persuaded him to accept the barrage of threats and sabre rattling that Briand required to make it possible for him to fall in with his views.

The schedule of payments of May 1921 divided the bill presented to Germany into three parts: A, B, and C. Part A was 12,000 million gold marks, B was 38,000 million, C was 82,000 million, the total being the 132,000 million prescribed by the reparation commission. Germany was to issue bonds for all these classes and to pay five per cent interest and one per cent for amortization on the whole sum. However, interest on the C bonds, of more than half the total, was not to become due, nor was the capital, represented by the C bonds, to be repaid, until receipts from Germany were adequate. Those receipts were fixed at 2,000 million gold marks per annum to be paid in cash and 26 per cent of the value of German exports. From these figures any payments made in kind were to be deducted. In other words, the amount that Germany was asked to pay was evolved quite separately from the stipulated total of her obligations. The C bonds, the bulk of the theoretical total of German obligations would probably, it was clear from the start, never be discharged or at least not be paid until, in the remote future, the A and B bonds had been extinguished.

However, the reparations problem was far from solved. Cash payments by Germany were fixed in gold marks; the German currency was paper marks, and the value of paper marks fell steadily in 1921 and 1922, even before the catastrophic fall of 1923. The number of paper marks equivalent to one gold mark is shown in the following table:

	1921	1922
January	15	46
February	15	50
March	15	66
April	15	69

* 1 U.S. dollar equals approx. 4 gold marks; 1 pound sterling, approx. 20 gold marks.

	1921	*1922*
May	15	69
June	16	75
July	18	117
August	20	241
September	25	348
October	36	718
November	62	1618
December	46	1757

This situation meant that reparation payments represented a sharply increasing figure in paper marks. For the German government to be able to raise the sums required in paper marks, taxation rates inside Germany would have had to be moved upwards as rapidly as the mark fell: an administrative feat difficult to achieve. Paper marks, if assembled in sufficient quantity, would themselves have to be converted into gold or foreign currencies in order to make reparation payments; to attempt to sell the quantity of paper marks involved on the foreign exchange market would certainly precipitate a further fall in the external value of the mark and so render the problem even worse. Two linked causes made the payment of reparations first difficult and then impossible in 1922: the fall in the purchasing power of the paper mark inside Germany and the even more rapid fall of the value of the paper mark in terms of other currencies. What brought this situation about?

The opinion of German governments, bankers, industrialists, journalists and some economists at the time and afterwards was that the cause was external, that a fall in the foreign exchange value of the mark resulting from Germany's paying more to foreigners than she received from them in payment for German goods and in loans, led to German imports costing more in terms of marks and therefore to a rise in prices in Germany which caused an increase in issues of paper marks which brought about internal inflation. On this interpretation, payments to the allies could be blamed for the fall of the mark. Helfferich claimed in 1924 that 'the depreciation of the German mark in terms of foreign currencies was caused by the excessive burdens thrust on to Germany and by the policy of violence adopted by France'. It is true that in the years 1919–22 Germany imported 1,000 million gold marks worth of goods more than she sold abroad, and payments to the allies must be added. However, in 1922 the balance of payments was actually favourable, yet the depreciation of the mark continued and accelerated in the remaining month of the year even though reparation payments in cash were suspended after August 1922. Lack of confidence in the long-term future of the mark resulting from the continued threat of reparations explains this phenomenon in part but cannot explain its extent. A fall in the value of the mark made German goods and services cheaper for foreigners and increased the price of foreign goods and services for Germans – so that unless some factor was present other than external payments the fall in the external value of the mark would necessarily have come to a halt relatively soon.

A much more plausible explanation both of the origins and of the extent of the collapse of the mark lies in the financial policy of the German government. During the war government expenditure was not met by income and in 1917 and 1918 expenditure was nearly 100,000 million marks while income was about 67,000 million marks, a figure including the proceeds of loans. The gap was filled by the issue of treasury bills. In so far as these were taken up by banks and other institutions they, too, represented borrowed money, but about half of these bills were discounted by the *Reichsbank*, that is to say turned into paper currency. A gap between expenditure and income remained after the war. Once again, the gap was covered by an increase in floating debt, that is to say by loans from banks and other institutions and by money printed by the *Reichsbank*. This situation could lead only to a collapse of the mark which a balanced budget alone could prevent. For reasons already referred to, once the collapse had got under way, it was extremely difficult to raise enough in taxation to balance the budget, yet the German government missed the opportunity of doing so. Between April 1920 and March 1921 the value of the mark remained almost stable and the government could, therefore, have escaped from the problem of taxes which no longer had the value they were expected to bring in by the time they were collected. It did not seek to use this respite to increase taxation or to curb government spending sufficiently. It is not true that the gap between expenditure and income was caused by payments to the allies.

INCOME AND EXPENDITURE OF THE *REICH* IN MILLIONS OF GOLD MARKS

	Income	Expenditure	Expenses under Versailles
1919	2559	8560	—
1920	3178	9529	1851
1921	2928	6651	2810
1922	1488	3951	1136
1923 (to Oct.)	519	5278	—

It is true that to meet reparations the German governments would, of course, have had to raise taxation to a higher level in order to balance the budget than would have been required in the absence of reparations but this is not to say that reparations caused the collapse of the mark. Did the German governments deliberately destroy the value of the mark in order to evade reparations? There is no evidence to suggest that they did. It is much more likely that the theory that the fall in the mark was entirely a consequence of the adverse balance of payments prevented German authorities from making any serious attempt to balance the budget. The effect was the same and the failure to carry out the financial reforms persistently demanded by the reparations commission strengthened the belief abroad that the Germans were cheating the allies of their due.[91]

In 1921, Germany carried out the obligations laid on her by the schedule of payments, but in December, the government announced that it could not pay the instalments due in January and February 1922. It was agreed that German obligations should provisionally be reduced to 31 million of gold marks to be paid every ten days. In March this was reduced to 50 million a month in return for promises from the German government that the floating debt would not be increased and that the reparations commission would be informed of and consulted on measures to balance the German budget. (On 24 June 1922, Walther Rathenau, the German minister for foreign affairs, was murdered and with him disappeared one of the few German statesmen, who, in spite of his tireless work for German interests, inspired both confidence and respect among Allied negotiators). On 12 July 1922, Germany asked for a suspension of payment in cash for the rest of 1922, and for 1923 and 1924. This was refused in August, though for the year 1922 the Germans were allowed to pay in treasury bills, that is to say, payment for 1922 was deferred. On 14 November the German government asked for a suspension of payments for three or four years except for payments in kind for reconstruction of devastated areas, payments which could be made without increasing the German floating debt.[92]

This request produced an open breach between Britain and France. Poincaré had already refused to abate French demands on Germany and had threatened unilateral action to secure guarantees that Germany should pay if the allies could not agree. This could be done by seizing German productive resources and exploiting them under allied, or French, control.[93] The British held that the essential need was to make the mark stable and that interference with German industry would finally ruin the German currency.

What were the motives of British policy towards France and Germany? A simple, and unconvincing, answer is frequently produced: that Britain was seeking to maintain the European balance of power by supporting a weak power, Germany, against the preponderant European great power, France. It is said that British foreign policy had been, perhaps since the sixteenth century, certainly since the beginning of the nineteenth century, determined automatically. British statesmen discovered which European power, at any given moment, was the strongest and sought to strengthen its opponents. This view obscures more than it explains. Thus Bismarckian Germany, which clearly dominated Europe after 1871, met with no hostility from Britain, and, indeed, as late as 1901 a formal Anglo-German alliance was seriously contemplated in London. Britain came into conflict with Germany in the early twentieth century not because Germany was powerful but because of the ways in which it was supposed that Germany was likely to use her strength. Similarly, British policy towards France after 1918 was determined not by French strength, which the course of the war had shown clearly enough to be far inferior to that of Germany, but by the ways in which that strength was employed. British statesmen were aware that French preponderance in post-war Europe was an artificial consequence of Anglo-American support in the Great War. Some spoke and wrote of a balance of power against France, but only because the repeated assertion that British foreign policy always sought a balance often caused commentators to fit their interpretations of international affairs into this conventional mould. Evidence that shows that the British military authorities were speculating about the effects of war with France should not be taken to mean that any such war was expected, for soldiers construct defence policy only with great difficulty without a hypothetical enemy – France provided that role for the British defence staff in the 1920s just as in the United States plans were made in the early 1930s to meet a ludicrously improbable simultaneous attack from Britain and Japan.

Another hypothesis is that British policy was dictated by fear of communism. Germany might herself go communist if she were treated too harshly or, under any government, might work with the Soviet Union to destroy the new order in Europe, or might, alternatively, help to provide a barrier to the westward advance of Russian Bolshevism. It is clear that fear of a possible communist Germany influenced Lloyd George in 1919. The events of 1920 and the Rapallo treaty emphasized the possibility of Soviet-German co-operation against the west. On the other hand, the Polish victory of 1920 and the Russo-Polish treaty of 1921 established that an armed incursion westwards by Russia was not an immediate danger. Furthermore, Lloyd George's policy towards Soviet Russia in 1920, 1921 and 1922 was to pacify the Soviet government by establishing trading links with Russia rather than to counter the Soviet Union by constructing a defensive western league. Nor did the British take the prospect of political and military collaboration between

Russia and Germany too seriously. What is probably true is that British statesmen feared communist disorder and revolution in Germany. This fear together with the desire to avoid sowing the seeds of a new German war sufficiently explains British policy towards Germany in 1919 and 1920.[94]

Thereafter there is a mass of evidence to suggest that the dominant motive of British policy became economic. In 1921, British industrial production fell, exports diminished sharply and unemployment increased to an extent unequalled since accurate records had been kept. The violence of the slump came as a surprise. The fall in industrial activity in 1921 compared with 1920 surpassed in its extent any contraction in the century before 1914. Upon this sudden decline in production attention became concentrated. What was wrong? The answer was unanimous: international trade had not revived after the war. Let pre-war trading be restored and all would be well. During and after 1920 Lloyd George's foreign policy sought economic recovery before all else and in particular he tried to open Russia to trade and to permit a prosperous Germany. Hence Lloyd George's sponsorship of the abortive conference of 1922. In December 1921, he had insisted on French co-operation in the 'reconstruction of Europe' as a condition of an Anglo-French security pact in a memorandum handed to Briand at Cannes, a memorandum which noted that 'nearly two millions of the British working class are unemployed'. In April 1922, he told the British House of Commons that 'before trade can be fully restored you must be able to establish everywhere the convertibility of currency with gold or its equivalent' in other words that the value of currencies must be stabilised, notably, of course, the mark. In December 1922, Bonar Law, who succeeded Lloyd George as Prime Minister, was consulting Keynes on reparations, an economist whose views were well known – 'on the prosperity of Germany the prosperity of the rest of the Continent mainly depended.' In August 1923, Bonar Law's successor, Stanley Baldwin, declared,

you must either have a broken country that will pay no reparations, which will leave the trade of the world in such a state that it will become the work of a generation to make good and find new fields of industry, or you must have a Germany that will be powerful industrially and that will pay adequate reparations,

and in November,

I think we must all of us be convinced that, owing primarily to the occupation of the Ruhr, and the effect which that has had on the economic position of Germany, the economic restoration of Europe has been postponed for years . . . Had all the old markets in which we used to sell been available, we should not have been suffering today from unemployment as we are.

These views were shared by the opposition. In February 1923, Snowden, for the Labour Party, declared,

the Prime Minister said the other day that we are paying one hundred million pounds a year to support the unemployed. That, I assert, is mainly the result of French policy, and the hindrances they have put in the way of the reconstruction of the European market,

and in November, Charles Buxton summed the matter up: '*the* international issue is the problem of unemployment'. In the House of Commons, in fact, debates on unemployment and on international affairs merged because the two topics were regarded as inseparable.[95] In December 1922, an allied conference was held in London to consider the German request for a suspension of cash payments for reparations. At the same time, the question of debts between the allies themselves was considered. During the war, the United States had lent large sums of money to all the European powers, including Britain, and by the beginning of 1923, the allies (Russia, who was highly unlikely to pay anything, left out of account) owed the United States the equivalent of 42,000 million gold marks, of which Britain's share was over 19,000 million, the French share about 14,000 million and the Italian 8,000 million. Britain had also been a substantial lender and was owed by France 12,000 million and by Italy 10,500 million. The British government had consistently urged that inter-allied debts should be wiped out – that is to say, in practice, that the United States should abandon its claims on the allies, who would then give up their claims on each other. The ultimate effect would be to lighten the burden on France and Italy, who might then be ready to give up some of their demands on Germany. The scheme was, in fact, a plan for American aid to Europe, which did not commend itself to public opinion in the United States. The United States Congress, and President Harding, insisted, on the contrary, in the spring of 1922, that arrangements should be made for repayment of capital and interest to begin. In August, the British government announced that it would demand from its European debtors as much as should be demanded from Britain by the United States.[96]

In London the powers stated their positions. Bonar Law declared that Britain would consider modifying her demands on her allies, irrespective of the attitude of the United States, if Germany were given a moratorium. Poincaré insisted that no moratorium could be accepted unless productive resources were seized in Germany, including the occupation of Essen and Bochum, and that inter-allied debts could be dealt with by transferring reparations bonds C, that is to say those which were unlikely ever to be worth anything. Mussolini argued for productive pledges of a less drastic sort than those demanded by Poincaré. When the conference resumed in Paris in January, Britain and France merely reproduced their positions in greater detail. Poincaré argued that the financial condition of Germany was the result of the deliberate action of the German industrialists and that Germany was voluntarily evading her obligations. He proposed, once again, to seize German productive and fiscal resources in order to extract reparations by direct action and as a means of putting pressure on Germany to produce viable plans for reparation payments in the future. The only reduction in German debts he would accept was the abrogation of the dubious C bonds in return for Britain's receiving C bonds of the theoretical value of the debts due to her from the European allies. In reply, Bonar Law objected that the French plan would ruin German commerce and credit and bring about a major political and social crisis. He proposed that Germany should pay nothing in cash for four years, then 2,000 million gold marks for four years and 2,500 for the subsequent two years and that thereafter an impartial tribunal should fix the amount. Britain would renounce the bulk of the debts due to her from Europe. In spite of the advantages thus offered to France, Poincaré would have none of it. He claimed that the British plan underestimated what Germany could pay and, above all, that the British plan meant a speedy restoration of German hegemony in Europe. Poincaré was determined to uphold the treaty and the reparations settlement of 1921 by force. The conference broke up in open dispute.[97]

On 26 December, the commission of reparations, by three votes (France, Belgium, Italy) to one vote (Britain), declared that Germany was in default with respect to reparations deliveries of timber and on 9 January the same majority declared that Germany had defaulted over deliveries of coal. Immediately the French and Belgian governments informed Germany that they would despatch a mission of control into the Ruhr which would give orders to the local coal syndicate and to the transport authorities and demand information from all business organizations and would ensure the payment of reparations in kind and in cash. On 11 January 1923, French and Belgian troops moved into the Ruhr and, after the proclamation of passive resistance by the German government, extended the occupation to virtually the whole of the Ruhr basin. The Italian government supported the operation by attaching engineers to the *mission interalliée de contrôle des usines et des mines* (MICUM) probably because it was anxious to continue to secure a share of German coal deliveries, and because Mussolini had conceived the strange notion that the Ruhr operation could lead to a continental bloc directed against the British empire.[98] The French and Belgian authorities proceeded to extract what they could by the following methods: securing coal from the German producers, levying a tax on coal production, arranging for timber deliveries by direct management of woodlands and by establishing customs barriers to the east and west of the occupied territories. On both the western and eastern boundaries exports were permitted only under licence and on payment of taxes; on the western side and, after June 1923, on the eastern, imports, except of food and raw materials, were equally subjected to licences and taxation.

The effect of the passive resistance was that Germans refused to work the mines and the railways. MICUM endeavoured with difficulty to work a few mines directly, and secured some coal by seizure of stocks, and with more success worked the railways under Franco-Belgian direction. The German government forbade Germans to co-operate with the French and Belgian administrators in any way so that licences for exports and imports were not applied for – the result was that passive resistance turned the customs barriers into a blockade of the occupied areas, from which deliveries to the outside world, including unoccupied Germany, ceased, as did imports other than those of food and raw materials. The period of passive resistance generated feelings of bitterness and resentment towards France. Though the French army in the Ruhr faced much less resistance than that offered to the *Reichswehr* in 1920, some violent incidents occurred, notably at Essen where thirteen German workers were killed in March 1923. There were many attempts at sabotage of the railways – on 25 May, Leo Schlageter was shot for taking part in an attempt, but next month twelve Belgian soldiers were killed in an explosion on a bridge over the Rhine. About 150,000 railwaymen and officials were forcibly expelled by the Franco-Belgian authorities during this period. Inside the occupied area, industrial activity soon almost completely ceased, outside, industrial products had to be imported from abroad; the German government took upon itself the burden of financial support of the population of the occupied area – a process financed, once again, by resort to the printing presses rather than by reform of the taxation structure. This flood of paper marks, together with the worsening of Germany's balance of foreign payments caused by the blockade of the Ruhr, finally ruined the mark, which, after a pause at the beginning of 1923 when the *Reichsbank* used its reserves to halt the decline, moved rapidly downwards to worthlessness.

In September 1923 the average exchange rate of the dollar was of the order of a hundred and twenty million paper marks; Germany had to give in. Passive resistance was ordered to cease on 26 September 1923.

Here, at last, was victory for Poincaré, in one sense at least. The Ruhr operation was designed to do two things: first to secure reparation at once, secondly to make Germany carry out the treaty and the payments schedule of 1921. Now Poincaré began to get the first; but instead of the second he got, as we shall see, international intervention. It was only a short term victory, followed later by total defeat, but it enabled the collection of reparations to the net value of nearly 900 million of gold marks, of which France received 313 million, Belgium, as a result of her priority in cash payments, 458 million and Italy 63 million.[99] For after the end of passive resistance, coalmines began to produce again, the railways worked smoothly once more and the frontier barriers began to produce income instead of enforcing a blockade.

The summer of 1923 was enlivened by elegant and acid diplomatic exchanges between Lord Curzon and the British Foreign Office on the one side and Poincaré on the other. Poincaré insisted on the maintenance of the schedule of payments of May 1921, and asserted that the Ruhr would be evacuated only when Germany began effectively to pay reparations, that the commission of reparations would be the only body entitled to judge Germany's capacity to pay, and, above all, that only force would make Germany carry out the Treaty of Versailles.

Since the signature of the peace, England has always tried to seek a basis for conciliation on which Germany could negotiate as an equal with the allies . . . We are persuaded, on the other hand, that if Germany, so far from making the slightest effort to execute the treaty of peace, has only sought to evade her obligations, it is because she has not yet been convinced of her defeat . . . In fact, the allies have never got anything from Germany, except when, together, they have threatened to use force.

Curzon argued that the Ruhr operation was illegal, that reparations would only be secured by a plan regarded as practicable and acceptable by all parties concerned, that the commission of reparations was not impartial and that impartial experts should consider Germany's capacity to pay.[100]

The acceptance of the Dawes plan of 1924 represented the triumph of this British policy. How did this come about? The turning point came in November 1923. In that month, Poincaré proposed that a committee of experts should be set up by the commission on reparations to consider Germany's capacity to pay and that these experts should come from the allied and associated powers – that is to say that they should include

Americans. Publicly, Poincaré insisted on limitations on the experts, that they should consider only what Germany could pay for three years and that they should not regard the occupation of the Ruhr as within their terms of reference; privately, Louis Barthou, the French representative and chairman of the reparations commission, made it clear that there were no limitations on their activities. This was a significant retreat: in the summer, Poincaré had flatly refused the notion of expert consideration of reparations. The principal reason may have been that France could no longer count on support in the reparations commission from Belgium and Italy, whose votes had been decisive in December 1922 and January 1923 in making possible the Ruhr occupation. Italian conduct had been ambiguous in 1923. Italian engineers worked in the Ruhr but no Italian troops were sent there, and by November it was clear that Italian policy had moved towards the British view. On 16 November 1923, indeed, Mussolini, publicly called for a moratorium, a reduction of the German debt, and substitution of other guarantees of payment for the occupation of the Ruhr. The Belgian government, always embarrassed by dissensions between Britian and France, urged in October that a solution of the reparations questions agreed among the Allies, should be sought. Evidently it became clear to Barthou, at least, that France must compromise in order to avoid complete isolation. Poincaré seems by now to have been uncertain what to do with his own success in defeating passive resistance; he had always said that the Ruhr occupation would compel Germany to make serious proposals for the payment of the reparations laid down in 1921 but no such proposals came. Poincaré had played his trump card and coerced Germany, but by the end of 1923, Germany was beginning to recover from the disasters of that year and was showing no sign of any intention of meek acquiescence in French wishes.

In January 1924, the experts began their work. The principal committee was to consider how the German budget could be brought into balance and the German currency stabilized. It included two Americans, General Dawes, a lawyer and banker, whose military rank came from his appointment during the war as chief of supply to the American army in France, and Owen D. Young, another banker and businessman, whose importance in the final outcome was greater than that of Dawes himself. In April the plan, usually called the Dawes plan, was submitted to the commission for reparations. It proposed that Germany should pay 1,000 million gold marks in the first years after the plan should be put into effect, of which 800 million should be raised by a foreign loan and that over the five following years the figure should rise to 2,500 million which might be subsequently supplemented by a figure worked out according to an elaborate index of German prosperity. To prevent inflation, the new *Reichsbank* should be forbidden to discount treasury bills, and should maintain resources in gold and foreign exchange of at least forty per cent of the note issue. To guarantee the payment of reparations, the German railway revenues, the revenues of German industrial concerns, certain excise duties and customs were to be assigned as security. All these measures were to be supervised by foreign experts and a committee was to supervise the transfer of German payments abroad and to ensure that it did not place undue strain on the external value of the mark. The economic and fiscal unity of the *Reich* must be restored and measures such as the Ruhr occupation should not be taken except in case of flagrant default by Germany and only then by agreement among all Germany's creditors: that is to say the French government was invited to abandon its present policy and renounce any repetition of it for the future. The plan was presented, it was expressly stated, as a whole, from which no one part could be subtracted.[101]

On 17 April the German government accepted the Dawes plan in principle, on the 24th the agreement of the British, Italian and Belgian governments followed, and on the 25 April Poincaré accepted. Fear of isolation and uncertainty about what to do next continued to move Poincaré to retreat but by this time a more compelling and urgent motive was increasingly operative: the franc was on the point of collapse. In 1923, one dollar, worth about fifteen francs in January, was worth about nineteen in December. Thereafter the fall accelerated and on 8 March 1924, the dollar reached twenty-six francs. In order to reinforce its capacity to support the franc by buying operations the Bank of France borrowed both in London and New York and it seems probable that the lenders insisted on a reversal of Poincaré's foreign policy.[102] The origins of the fall of the franc were analogous to those of the fall of the mark: reliance by the government on borrowing rather than taxation to finance its expenditure. The French tax-payer was unwilling, in fact, to pay for the coercion of Germany and the Ruhr operation did not produce a large enough return to ensure French financial stability.

The Dawes plan, whatever Poincaré claimed, did not produce more for France than the Bonar Law proposal which France had summarily rejected at the beginning of 1923.[103] In that sense France gained nothing from the Ruhr operation. Furthermore the loss of goodwill was incalculable – not merely in Germany, but elsewhere. France came to be considered as a misguided, selfish, reckless bully. On the other hand, it can be maintained that the occupation of the Ruhr brought benefits to France and even to the world, though not of the kind Poincaré had anticipated. The seizure of German territory, coupled with the disasters of the inflation, forced the German government to attempt a serious effort to make reparations work and to stabilize the German currency. The result was that Germany's creditors secured regular payments as long as the Dawes plan lasted and, at the same time, that Germany's international credit was restored and a sounder basis for German economic growth established. Without the disaster of 1923, it is unlikely that a German government could have been found to accept the limitations of German financial and budgetary policy contained in the Dawes plan and without these limitations confidence in the mark was unlikely to have returned. The relative prosperity in Germany and stability in Europe of the years 1924–29 was partly due, then, to Poincaré. When, however, that prosperity collapsed, German hatred of France could easily be revived by memories of 1923. In any event, however beneficial the Dawes plan was even for France, its acceptance meant a surrender, a surrender of France's claim to interpret the treaty at will and to impose her interpretation by force. Nor was it evident at the time, even though it may have been true, that France derived any benefit from the consequences of the Ruhr occupation that she could not have had without it. In the French election of May 1924, the majority of the French people rejected unilateral force and espoused conciliation and international co-operation; this was an expression of a disillusionment which influenced French thinking until 1939. In London, at the end of July and the beginning of August, a conference first among the allies, and then with a German delegation present, agreed on the application of the Dawes plan: it was the last time that German representatives were kept out until the allies had agreed among themselves. The French delegation fought for the right for France to act separately against Germany in case of future defaults – it secured the shadow in complex formulae, having already surrendered the substance, and France agreed to evacuate the Ruhr within a year, together with the towns occupied in 1921.[104]

2

With the London conference, and the acceptance of the Dawes plan, a new note began to dominate in international exchanges; words such as peace, understanding, conciliation became everyday slogans. In

Britain the emollient Ramsay MacDonald expressed a consistent British policy – the stabilization of Europe; Herriot represented the French retreat from Poincaré and his precise insistence on French rights; the German foreign minister was a man very well able to harmonize his utterances with the new pacific melodies: Gustav Stresemann. In London, Stresemann met Herriot in secret. He persuaded Herriot that he was a reasonable and trustworthy statesman, who, to his own regret, was compelled by a nationalistic public opinion at home to seek concessions from allies. Such concessions would ensure the continuance of a moderate, conciliatory policy in Germany so that the self-interest of the allies required compromise and flexibility. Stresemann, on his side, believed that his readiness to reach agreement with the former allies would induce in them a relaxation of hostility and suspicion towards Germany. Thus the Dawes agreement was the first general reparations settlement voluntarily accepted by Germany, yet Stresemann never took it seriously – to him it was something that must and could be revised when allied sympathies for Germany had successfully been evoked. He wrote of it as an economic armistice, whose terms would be unendurable for Germany as early as 1927, that is when payments under the plan would begin to mount.[105] Its significance was political, it should mark the end of the era of coercion of Germany and the beginning of an era of co-operation which should bring about the slow disintegration of Versailles.

A sharp set-back took place at the end of 1924 – in December, the allied conference of ambassadors announced that the evacuation of the northern zone of the Rhineland by allied troops, due under Versailles in 1925, would be postponed. The reasons were given in an Allied note in January; they were based on a report of the inter-allied control commission for German disarmament which complained of the reconstruction of the great general staff, of the training of volunteers enlisted for short terms of service, of failure to convert armaments work to civilian production, of the retention of excess military equipment, of failure to prohibit import and export of arms and of the tolerance of armed right-wing organizations. Stresemann's effective reply was embodied in his notes to the British government of 20 January 1925 and the French government of 9 February 1925 in which he offered a pact of security which would guarantee the frontiers between France, Belgium and Germany established at the peace. Stresemann saw that France wanted above all to be safe and that for France the Treaty of Versailles and its enforcement were means to this end; if France could be made secure (by means acceptable to Germany) then her conduct towards

Germany would become more tolerant and she could accept a recovery of German economic and even military strength. Enforcement of the treaty, including its disarmament clauses, might cease to be oppressively pursued. Stresemann's policy led to the treaties of Locarno of 1925. The idea was not new, Stresemann himself had spoken of it in August 1923, as had Cuno's government before that.[106] The notion had met with the contempt of Poincaré, but with the Dawes agreement and the fall of the Poincaré government in 1924, French policy no longer rested on the armed enforcement of the peace against Germany. The Locarno treaties, the results of Stresemann's offer, like the Dawes plan, rested rather on the search for German co-operation in upholding peace. The formal substance of the Locarno treaties must first be outlined and then the policies of the countries involved can be analysed.

The Locarno agreements consisted of a treaty of mutual guarantee between Germany, France, Belgium, Britain and Italy; arbitration conventions between Germany and Belgium and between Germany and France and arbitration treaties between Germany and Poland and between Germany and Czechoslovakia. The final Protocol of the Locarno conference included a statement by France that agreements between France and Poland and France and Czechoslovakia had also been concluded at Locarno. The treaty of guarantee laid down that Germany and Belgium and Germany and France would not attack or invade or make war against each other except in pursuit of a decision of the League of Nations or in resisting a violation of the clauses of Versailles providing for the demilitarisation of the Rhineland (of a sort requiring immediate action). These countries pledged themselves to accept arbitration in case of disputes between them in a manner prescribed in the separate conventions. The French and Belgian frontiers set up by Versailles were formally recognized. If one of the signatories launched an armed attack on another or flagrantly violated the demilitarized zone, the other powers would immediately come to the assistance of the victim. The effect was that Britain and Italy guaranteed Germany against Belgian or French attack and Belgium and France against German attack. The German arbitration treaties with Poland and Czechoslovakia provided procedures for conciliation or arbitration in case of disputes, but the Versailles frontiers were not recognized by Germany nor were any guarantees provided to ensure fulfilment of these treaties. On the other hand, the treaties between Poland and France and Czechoslovakia and France concluded at Locarno, but not included in the general protocol, pledged mutual support, under articles fifteen and sixteen of the League Covenant, in case of German breaches of the Locarno obligations. The treaties were to come into force when Germany became a member of the League of Nations. This provision raised difficulties. The first arose because Germany insisted on permanent membership of the League Council, a claim which aroused a similar demand from other powers, especially Brazil, which produced a delay of some months in German entry into the League. The second was more important – Germany declined to accept all the obligations of article sixteen of the League on the pretext that her disarmament made it impossible to do so. The solution was found with the adoption as an agreed interpretation of the League Covenant of the idea that a member was obliged to co-operate in resistance to aggression only 'to an extent which is compatible with its military situation and takes its geographical position into account'.

At Locarno, Germany had been treated no longer as a defeated enemy but as an equal partner in negotiations. Stresemann hailed the agreement as 'the beginning of a period of life together full of confidence among the nations'. This sort of nebulous and uplifting utterance, characteristic of many of Stresemann's public speeches, induced among his admirers the belief that Stresemann was seeking to construct a European or world unity which should override and make obsolete petty national ambitions and rivalries, while it confirmed among Stresemann's nationalist and *völkisch* opponents at home the conviction that Stresemann, like so many other distinguished and intelligent Germans, was a 'traitor', an advocate of renunciation of Germany's rights and of fulfilment of the demands of her enemies. Neither of these views of Stresemann was correct. He was a highly patriotic German, with a strongly nationalist past, who was sensible enough to understand, unlike his opponents, that the aims of German foreign policy could not, in a period of German weakness, be shouted defiantly to the world or advanced except by patient manoeuvre. What were those aims? On 7 September 1925, Stresemann wrote to the former Crown Prince, and with brevity and precision set them out. Reparations must be made tolerable and peace must be assured so that Germany could recover her strength. Germany must seek to protect Germans abroad, 'those ten or twelve millions of our kindred who now live under a foreign yoke in foreign lands.' The frontiers with Poland must be changed and Danzig, the Polish corridor to the sea, and part of Upper Silesia recovered for Germany. 'In the background stands the *Anschluss* with German Austria.' Foreign occupation of German territory must be brought to an end. Though these are not the aims of a man striving above all for some 'European' idea, they are relatively moderate: Stresemann seems to have accepted that Germany should pay some reparations – after all, as he told the Crown Prince, the burden of debt borne by the German citizen was substantially lower than that in France or England. He thought that the return of Posen should not be claimed by Germany: that is to say he did not propose to recreate the German eastern frontier of 1914. The Germany Stresemann wished to create, an independent, prosperous, powerful Germany was certainly a Germany whose influence would be dominant in Europe, but whose ambitions would not be intolerable for other European powers – except perhaps for Poland.[107]

What were the means he employed to this end? The central element in his policy was Franco-German reconciliation. France must be soothed, made to feel safe, and so brought to regard as acceptable a revival of German strength. To do this, Stresemann was ready to accept any guarantees, any international safeguards, that could be devised to prevent a German attack on France and was ready to abandon German claims to Alsace-Lorraine and even to accept the demilitarized zone. If France could thus be brought to trust Germany, even to regard Germany as a friend, then France might accept an end to the occupation of German territory and further modifications to reparations, might tolerate German rearmament and, above all, might abandon Poland, and perhaps even connive at German union with Austria. Hence the terms of Locarno, which elaborately guaranteed the frontier settlement between France and Germany while providing no guarantees for Poland not already provided by the machinery of the League of Nations. Locarno established a sort of hierarchy of frontiers: the German-French frontier was sanctified; the Polish-German frontier given a less elevated status. A start was thus made with the division of the frontier settlement of Versailles into two parts; a part accepted and a part brought into question.

In April, 1925, Stresemann wrote, 'our policy with regard to the security offer was undoubtedly correct, it secures the Rhineland against a continuance of a French policy of persecution, has broken open the Entente and it offers new possibilities for the East.' Here was a revival of a Bismarckian policy: France should be encouraged into neglect of eastern alliances directed against Germany. Locarno, furthermore, guaranteed Germany against France – this making impossible a repetion of the occupation of the Ruhr. This, together with the Dawes plan, was calculated to make Germany credit-worthy, a country to which foreign loans would be made on a large scale. As for the Entente, one purpose of Stresemann's Locarno policy was to prevent any revival of an Anglo-French co-operation from which Germany was excluded. In particular, at the end of 1924, it was suspected that the new British Foreign Secretary, Austen Chamberlain, was prepared to renew former British offers of a direct guarantee to France against Germany, without insisting on any security for Germany against France – Stresemann's offer of January 1925 was designed to forestall a new Anglo-French pact of this sort. New 'possibilities for the East' were offered by Germany's entry into the League of Nations. The Crown Prince was told that

Poland, Czechoslovakia, Yugoslavia and Rumania who are all bound by international treaties to care for their minorities, i.e. especially for German minorities, will not be able to disregard so shamefully their obligations if they know that Germany can bring all these failures before the League of Nations.

Indeed, when Germany became a member, the League began to hear a great deal of the alleged sufferings of Germans under foreign rule, especially of the sufferings of those ruled by Poles. Thus Stresemann sought to undermine the Versailles frontiers by creating doubts about their rectitude and by arousing feelings of sympathy towards German demands for revision.[108] Towards Poland still stronger measures were taken, of a kind not easily to be reconciled with the fictitious picture of Stresemann as a great European. In April 1926, Stresemann wrote to the German ambassador in London directing him to persuade Britain not to help Poland economically because a change in Poland's frontiers could not come before 'the economic and financial catastrophe of Poland reached an extreme degree.' If Poland were reduced to a sufficient degree of economic ruin, she would be compelled to turn to Germany, who would then make conditions before offering economic assistance. From the summer of 1925, Germany launched a tariff war against Poland while Stresemann and Schacht, the President of the *Reichsbank*, urged on American and British financiers that Poland's economic difficulties could only be solved by Polish co-operation with Germany.[109]

What did Stresemann's western policy achieve? It had two major objects: to reduce allied, especially French, insistence on the literal execution of the treaty of Versailles and to separate France from her eastern allies, especially from Poland. Stresemann succeeded in modifying the treaty in three ways. Firstly, German disarmament ceased to be effectively supervised, secondly the period of Allied occupation of German territory was curtailed, thirdly reparations demands were further reduced. Two events took place towards the end of 1926 which suggested, to anyone who did not wish to be blind, that Germany was evading important military clauses of the treaty. Firstly, the allied military control commission, in its last report, showed that 'Germany had never disarmed, had never had the intention of disarming, and for seven years had done everything in her power to deceive and "counter-control" the commission appointed to control her disarmament.' Secondly, on 16 December 1926, Scheidemann, speaking in the Reichstag for the Social Democratic party, the only major party in German politics which sincerely and whole heartedly looked forward to a peaceful future for Germany, denounced illegal rearmament in Germany, the *Reichswehr's* support of armed right-wing organizations and the military co-operation between Germany and Soviet Russia. The western allies did wish to be blind, for short of reversing the policy of trusting Germany, there was nothing they could do. It is true, too, that German evasion of the disarmament clauses of Versailles meant only that the bases for the reconstruction of a great German army were kept in being, not that the creation of such an army was imminent or that Germany, at the moment, was capable of any serious military operations. In January 1927, the allied military control commission was withdrawn, and a Leage of Nations control was substituted, a control intended from the start to be fictitious.[110]

Immediately after the formal signature of the Locarno treaties, the evacuation began of the northern zone of the Allied occupation of Germany, which had been postponed at the beginning of the year and was completed by January 1926. It was, however, only in August 1929 that Stresemann was informed that the remaining Allied occupation of German territory would be brought to an end in 1930.[111] Over the occupation, then, Stresemann's success was long delayed, because of hesitations on the part of France in applying Briand's policy of under-standing with Germany. The accelerated end to Allied occupation came, in the end, as part of a bargain of which the counterpart was German agreement to the 'final' reparation settlement embodied in the Young plan.

Though Stresemann had frequently expressed the view that the Dawes plan for reparation must be revised, the initiative for its revision came not from him but from the agent-general for reparations, Mr Parker Gilbert, and, paradoxically, from Poincaré. The former took the view that the Dawes payments, when they reached their full extent, would be more than Germany could pay; the latter, concerned now with the defence of the franc, was influenced by the payment of French debts to Britain and the United States. These had been settled in 1926 on the basis of sixty-two annuities, but in addition France was due to pay to the United States four hundred million dollars in 1929 for American stocks in France bought on credit at the end of the war. In order to deal with this the French government sought a new arrangement linking the modification of reparations with a modification of inter-allied debts, which the American government refused to consider, or, failing that, a new arrangement of reparations payments on a basis permitting a portion of German reparations annuities to be capitalized and used for repayment of French debts due to the United States. This could not be done unless at least a part of German payments was compulsorily transferable across the exchanges whereas under the Dawes scheme it was possible for the transfer of German payments into other currencies to be deferred. The outcome was a new expert committee under the chairmanship of Owen D. Young, the American banker.

The Young plan, unlike the Dawes plan, fixed a limit to German payments, to be made in annuities ending in 1988 (it may be well to notice at once that the plan worked in practice for little more than one year). The size of the German payments was based on the war debt payments that the allies themselves would have to make, plus an allowance towards the costs of repairing war damages, especially in France. The result was figures rising in thirty-six years from about 1,600 million marks to about 2,300 million marks and, for the last twenty-two years, in which payments would cover war debts alone, from about 1,600 million marks to about 1,700 million. A part of these annuities must be transferred into foreign currencies at once; the remainder could be deferred if the state of the mark required it. The overall figures for German payments under Young represented a considerable reduction from those proposed under the Dawes plan.[112]

A weakening of the international position of Poland was a major object of Stresemann's policy towards France which, if successful, should lead to a slow disintegration of the Franco-Polish alliance. There were signs of success in the years after Locarno. In 1927, Stresemann found from Briand no criticism of the idea of a revision of Polish frontiers, and Berthelot, the Secretary General in the French ministry of foreign affairs, seems to have been equally ready to accept change. The development of French foreign policy after Poincaré's resignation in 1924 was contemplated with gloom and dismay in Poland. In 1926 Pilsudski seized power in Poland, and began to follow a policy based on a mistrust of France which he had probably already acquired in 1920. Though avoiding precision on frontier matters, Pilsudski began to seek an improvement in relations with Germany, a search expressed most vividly in an interview with Stresemann at the end of 1927.[113] The process was moving forward which led from Locarno to the Polish-German understanding of 1934. It was emphasized by that dramatic symptom of French isolationism: the construction of a great fortified barrier behind the frontier with Germany, the Maginot line, which was begun after Locarno.

German friendship with Soviet Russia, embodied in the Rapallo treaty of 1922 and in military understandings between the *Reichswehr* and the Red Army, had been based on a shared hostility to the western powers; Stresemann eliminated, or at least disguised, German hostility towards France and Britain and yet he succeeded in keeping the Russian connection in full working order. He avoided making a choice between east and west. Of course, this was not entirely a result of Stresemann's skill. The French, and still more the British, were so eager for a reconciled and co-operative Germany that they were ready to overlook the German-Russian link and to hope, against the evidence, that it would fade away; the Russian government was so afraid of Germany's committing herself to an anti-Soviet western bloc that it was ready to work for understanding with Germany on almost any terms. Even so, however, Stresemann was obliged to avoid creating undue doubts in the west about the extent of German reconciliation to the new Europe, meanwhile he had to avoid creating the impression in Moscow that he was thus so linked with the west as to make it necessary for Russia to improve her relations with her neighbours, especially Poland, and to cease her important contribution to German military potential. It was done by timing: Stresemann kept the Russians waiting with encouragements and reassurances until France was committed to the Locarno policy; then Stresemann reinforced the wire to Moscow by definite concessions to Soviet fears. With the Soviet government using every available device to bully or cajole Germany into an abandonment of the Locarno policy, Stresemann needed and showed a confidence and perceptiveness which Bismarck himself could hardly have equalled.

After the agreement of 1924 on the Dawes plan, the Soviet government became deeply alarmed by the trend of Stresemann's foreign policy, his tendency towards a rapprochement with the western powers, and by his readiness to enter the League of Nations. All this might point to an anti-Soviet western bloc and to the possibility of German co-operation in actions sponsored by the League against Russia. In December 1924, the Soviet commissariat for foreign affairs proposed discussions between Germany and Russia to bring about a definite understanding on the Polish question and on political issues in general and proposed an agreement binding both governments not to enter into any political or economic alliances or agreements with third parties directed against the other. This proposal was repeated and amplified in the following months. It was accompanied with more or less veiled threats: that Russia might seek to work with France, which had recognized the Soviet regime in October 1924, and that Russia might guarantee the frontiers of Poland. Stresemann refused any new committment as long as the Locarno negotiations were in progress, but at the same time repeatedly explained that his policy contained nothing inimical to Russia. Chicherin, the Soviet commissar for foreign affairs, was assured that any obligations Germany might incur to Poland on entering the League of Nations would be purely theoretical, that Germany was determined to insist that she could not take part in any League sanctions and that this neutrality would serve, in fact, to protect Russia from the League. Stresemann insisted to the Russians that the proposed arbitration treaties with Poland and Czechoslovakia were no more than a meaningless gesture to France and that Germany had never recognized the frontiers of Poland. He pointed out that he was trying in the west only to create a defence against France, to free German territory from allied occupation and in general to induce the French to remove their stranglehold on Germany. Stresemann fulfilled his promise to reject the full obligations of League membership by securing at Locarno the formula already quoted. Negotiations for a trade treaty between Germany and the Soviet Union continued during the Locarno preliminaries and a commercial treaty was signed in October 1925. After the formal signature of the Locarno treaties, Stresemann resumed political discussion for a new understanding with Russia. The Soviet government helped matters on by simultaneous negotiations with France, which came to nothing, based on French credits for Russia and a resumption of interest payments on Russia's pre-revolutionary debts, and by threatening to conclude a non-aggression pact with Poland. The treaty of Berlin between Germany and the Soviet Union was signed on 24 April 1926. It provided that if either country was attacked the other would remain neutral. Neither country would take part in an economic or financial boycott against the other. In an exchange of notes, Germany promised to oppose energetically any anti-Soviet tendencies the League might develop. The German interpretation of the League Covenant was set out: that a League decision to declare any country an aggressor could not be binding on Germany without German consent and that therefore

Germany could not be compelled to act against the Soviet Union. Two months later a substantial credit was given by Germany to Russia. Meanwhile Soviet-German military co-operation continued, undisturbed by the Locarno policy.[114]

By the time of Stresemann's death in October 1929, he had secured a series of triumphant successes. Germany was now an equal and even trusted participant in European diplomacy with the other great powers – there remained, it is true, restrictions on German rearmament and on the use of the demilitarized zone in the Rhineland, but Stresemann had won the removal of effective foreign control of the German armed forces, which were able, with Russian help, to establish the foundations for a full reconstruction of German armed might. In the West, the Treaty of Versailles had been thoroughly revised; the premature end to allied occupation of German territory was in sight, reparations had been established at last on an apparently permanent and tolerable footing. A repetition of the Ruhr occupation of 1923 had become impossible. Political stability had brought economic progress and a prosperous Germany, which Stresemann had anticipated as one of the results of Locarno, albeit based on the unreliable foundation of foreign loans. French control of the Saar remained the single failure of the 'Locarno spirit' to secure Germany's aims. In the east, the link of Poland with France had been weakened, the moral basis of the Versailles frontier settlement had been undermined; it was far less probable in 1929 than it had been in 1923 that Poland could count on French help to defend her frontiers against German demands and still more likely that England would be completely indifferent to territorial revision in the east. Russian friendship had been retained with its military advantages, and the Soviet Union remained uncommitted to support of the post-war territorial arrangements. Hitler inherited Stresemann's achievements: without Stresemann's work in undermining belief in the validity of Versailles, Hitler's militant search for revision would almost certainly have been challenged sooner than it was.

What of French policy? France was torn between appeasement, the conciliation of Germany by concessions, by modifications of Versailles, and the search for a pacific contented Germany with whom France could live in peace and, on the other hand, a policy of coercion, of holding Germany down, of pursuing peace through French strength rather than through German acquiescence. It is probable that Briand was a convinced advocate of appeasement, but the development of his policy towards Germany was checked and delayed by a continued fear that a powerful Germany could not be trusted, a fear fully justified by subsequent events. In practice, it usually needed the stimulus of financial difficulties to push France into accepting appeasement. The acceptance by France of the Dawes plan and the end of the Rhur occupation was dictated by the need for American and British support for the French franc. Poincaré's defeat in 1924 was, in part, brought about by the refusal of the French electorate to pay the price, in higher taxation and balanced budgets, for the policy of force. Locarno was the consequence – French security must be sought by means acceptable to Britain and America. The franc remained unstable in 1925, after the temporary relief brought by the Dawes settlement, and this emphasized the need to continue a foreign policy acceptable to the financial great powers, Britain and the United States. If French safety could no longer rest on French strength, then guarantees from Britain, hitherto rejected as limiting French policy, must now be accepted. It emerged that Britain would still not commit herself to maintenance of the treaties in eastern Europe, and indeed would not now even accept a unilateral defensive pact with France of the sort Lloyd George had offered and Poincaré rejected. Stresemann's offer of a pact of guarantee which would restrain France as well as Germany was too attractive for the British government for it to accept any alternative means of support for France. Locarno was as much as France could get from Britain. Of course, there were many in France, among those politically to the left who welcomed, as things good in themselves, conciliation, arbitration and the notion of working through the League of Nations; and their views were uppermost in the French governments of 1925 – so that the connection between financial strain and appeasement is less decisive for French policy in the year of Locarno than in the preceding and subsequent years. In July 1926 the government majority changed because of the inability of the parties of the left to agree on financial matters and Poincaré returned as Prime Minister, with the support of the radicals and all the moderate conservative parties, with the mission to save the franc. Briand remained the minister for foreign affairs and Poincaré was chastened by the experience of 1924 and no longer the man of coercion and intransigence that he had been. Still, Poincaré and even more the right-wing element of the majority on which his government rested were certainly not convinced appeasers. Furthermore, the inclination to the right of the government was accentuated after the elections of April 1928.

Under these circumstances the Locarno policy seemed to come to a halt in France, and after the autumn of 1926, Briand substituted, as he was well qualified to do, emotional oratory for action. With the exception of the withdrawal of the inter-allied military control mission from Germany, no further conciliatory measure was offered to Germany until concern at inter-allied debts induced France to accept the Young plan and to buy German acquiescence in it. Yet Stresemann expected and demanded at least the end of allied occupation of Germany as an immediate consequence of Locarno. Briand seems to have been prepared to end the occupation at once. At Thoiry, in 1926, Stresemann and Briand talked with only one other person present – Hesnard, who acted as interpreter. Here a programme of action to serve as the basis of a Franco-German entente was evolved. Germany would assist the French franc by payments of capital on account of reparations, capital which would be raised by offering bonds on the money market whose interest would be secured on the revenues from the German state railways assigned to reparations under the Dawes plan. France would agree to the ending of military supervision over Germany – provided Stresemann kept the development of armed organizations in Germany in check – to the end of military occupation and to the end of the regime in the Saar (where Germany should buy out French treaty rights in the coal mines) and co-operate in securing the recovery by Germany from Belgium of part or the whole of the Eupen-Malmédy region. Here was a grand design for the ending of Franco-German hostility.

The scheme came to nothing. Two days after Thoiry, Stresemann publicly asserted that German membership of the League of Nations had wiped out the notion that Germany had been to blame for the war, demanded colonies for Germany and an end to foreign occupation of German territory, including the Saar. This unwise pronouncement aroused the suspicion in the minds of Poincaré and other members of the French government that Briand had gone too far. On 26 September, Poincaré spoke at Bar-le-Duc and proclaimed that Germany *was* responsible for the war and that though France was, as always, ready for attempts at rapprochement, she would only take measures compatible with the treaties and with France's alliances and which could be justified by preliminary proof that Germany had disarmed both morally and materially. An official communiqué declared that these words had been approved by the French council of ministers, both in form and in substance and that they represented government policy. Thus Thoiry was repudiated. In any case, Poincaré contrived to restore the franc without help from anticipated German reparations – an anticipation that would have been impossible anyway since American bankers would have refused to take up a new issue of German bonds to raise money for reparations unless France first ratified the agreement on war debts to the USA.[115] Stresemann was doomed therefore to wait for tangible results from the Locarno policy – apart from the end of military control and the allied withdrawal from the first zone of occupation – until the agreement over the Young plan, which involved the total end of allied occupation of Germany. Briand's policy triumphed thus, belatedly, because France was compelled to seek means of mobilizing German reparations debts under pressure of her own immediate obligations to the USA and in order to make sure that German reparations should cover future repayments of war debts by France.

It must be said, however, that this interpretation of Briand's foreign policy is open to question. It is possible, in the present inadequate state of documentation of these years, to take the view that Briand was, as much as Poincaré had been, an exponent of the policy of securing peace through strength and that the difference was one of method rather than aim – that Briand sought to conceal this endeavour behind a smokescreen of pacific verbiage and sought to secure as much backing from Britain for French security as could be had. Certainly, Briand made no objection to the maintainance of the strength of the French army – but this is not in itself incompatible with the attempt at conciliation suggested above. More important is the doubt about what he, in fact, promised to try to do at Thoiry.

The only contemporary source on the conversations at Thoiry, other than Stresemann's account, are the notes prepared by M. Hesnard for Briand. These are distinctly different in tone from Stresemann's record. Hesnard shows Briand not at all as the exuberant advocate of conciliation that Stresemann represents. Again there is not recorded any clear promise on the part of Briand; rather the initiative in suggesting concessions to Germany is reported as coming from Stresemann. Briand, on his side, is shown as insisting on solutions of the problems of reparations and German disarmament, nor is there open mention of the prospect of a premature end to Allied military occupation. Even from these notes, however, it is clear that Briand was ready to discuss general solutions [*solutions d'ensemble*] of questions in Franco-German relations. Briand, of course, knew perfectly well what these questions were – he did not need from Hesnard any reminder of their nature. It is understandable that M. Hesnard should produce a document stressing Briand's conditions for Franco-German conciliation rather than a statement of Germany's familiar demands. Briand needed no reminder of them; nor did he need a reminder of his own customary tone of casual amiability – indeed Hesnard's notes, which are in indirect speech, are clearly a working summary of the Thoiry talks and not a verbatim account. In short, Hesnard's account of Thoiry is not incompatible with the conclusion which is explicit in Stresemann's report that the conversations there produced a bargain based on French withdrawal from the Saar and the Rhineland in return for advance payments to France from Germany. It was not Briand's fault that his efforts to arrange concessions, in order to conciliate a pacific republican regime in Germany and to see the 'diminution of the strength of certain parties' in Germany – the nationalist and racist parties – were not fully successful until 1929. It was not his fault that they tended to degenerate into meaningless verbal manifestations culminating in the Briand-Kellogg pact of 1928 to aboilsh war.[116]

Briand's hope that the strength of nationalism in Germany might decline was bitterly disappointed as early as the *Reichstag* elections of 1930. The hope of a real successor to Stresemann faded fast; a Germany anxious to recover her strength, but ready to do so by means that would keep the peace of Europe soon became a thing of the past. In that sense, Briand's policy was a total failure. This is not to say that it was a foolish policy for what went wrong was rather that the conditions for stability and moderation in Germany, prosperity and internal contentment, began to disappear in 1929. Briand's policy was never tested in the only circumstances that might have brought it success.

3

Italy had little influence in these years on major developments in Europe. The peace treaties had by no means satisfied the full aspirations of Italy as expressed in the war-time treaties of London and St Jean de Maurienne. The Italian governments that preceded Mussolini's advent to power in October 1922 had tended to accept the post-war settlement, without enthusiasm, but with a resignation induced by a prudent understanding of Italy's weakness. Between France and Britain, Italy had taken a middle course though tending to support British policies of conciliation rather than French policies of force. Mussolini might be expected to follow a different path. Insofar as any coherent line of policy could be extracted from his numerous post-war writings and speeches, it was that Italy should not tranquilly accept the new ordering of the world but should seek to change it, and should seek to express the greatness of Italy by extensions of territory and by diplomatic assertiveness.[117]

In 1923, the Corfu incident seemed to show that Mussolini might, in practice, prove a danger to European peace. The Italian general, Tellini, was presiding over a commission, dispatched by the conference of ambassadors in Paris, to demarcate the frontiers of Albania, when, on 27 August 1923, he and his Italian assistant were murdered by assassins of uncertain nationality. Mussolini chose to believe that the Greek government was behind the murder, and put into effect violent measures against Greece, which must have been planned before the convenient excuse of the murders. A peremptory ultimatum gave the Greek government twenty-four hours to accept demands for a large indemnity, death for all the assassins, and various apologies and homages to Italy. When the Greeks accepted the substance of the ultimatum but rejected the more dishonouring demands, Mussolini ordered Italian warships to seize Corfu. On 31 August, after the preliminary bombardment of an old fort containing Greek refugees and orphans from Asia Minor, the island was occupied. The Greek government promptly appealed to the League of Nations and Mussolini threatened to leave the League if the issue were discussed there. Faced with the danger of intervention by the League, however, Mussolini climbed down, gave up his probable intention to remain in Corfu and accepted a means of escape offered by the skill of the Italian ambassador in Paris. With French support, brought about by concern to maintain Italian connivance in the Ruhr occupation, the League of Nations was persuaded to hand the matter over to the conference of ambassadors, which drew up a reasonable settlement of the incident, and saved Italian prestige by sparing to Italy the need to climb down before the League.[118]

The Corfu incident, though trumpeted in Italy as a great success for Italian forcefulness and fascist energy, in fact pointed to the difficulties of Mussolini's quest for grandeur. Without British and French connivance, Italy could not engage in a foreign policy of expansion because Britain and France were overwhelmingly powerful in western Europe and in the Mediterranean. There was, as yet no force in Europe to counterbalance Anglo-French predominance – French fears of Germany were prospective, not actual. Nor were Anglo-French differences sufficient to make it possible for Italy to hope to use the force of one of them against the other; for those differences were not based on any direct clash of interest between the two countries but only on divergences on the best way of ensuring European peace. Italy, therefore, could not risk conflict with France nor with Britain; expansionism could only be verbal, or, at best, be limited to the futile killing of defenceless Greeks, and the receipt of gifts from Britain in the form of a few deserts and co-operation in securing economic advantages in Ethopia. Only when German power revived, could Mussolini's irresponsibility be given full expression. There are signs that Mussolini recognized this, and that, unlike sensible Italian professional diplomatists, he wished to encourage German nationalism and aggressiveness in order to be able to escape from an enforced and regretted international respectability. It is almost certain that some prohibited armaments were dispatched from Italy in 1923 to Germany, probably for the *Reichswehr*, and certain that contacts were made with right-wing groups in Bavaria, including the Nazis. Some evidence suggests that the Nazis, the only section of German nationalists prepared to abandon the south Tyrol to Italy, received financial help from Mussolini.[119]

However much, as this evidence suggests, he disliked the fact, Mussolini was compelled in the 1920s to live in an increasingly stable Europe. Though Locarno, with its implications of an end to Franco-German tensions, was not at all welcome to him, it was clear that the agreements would be made irrespective of Italy's attitude towards them, so that Mussolini joined in, consoling himself by stressing that the pact implied an equality of status between Britain and Italy as twin guarantors of the Rhineland pact, and by insisting, correctly enough as it turned out, that Locarno was a truce, not a final end to conflict in Europe. Some day things would start moving again, territorial demands could be made and in readiness 'we must make ourselves warlike, we must have a powerful army, a strong navy, an air force which dominates the skies, and above all a spirit in every class of the people disposed to sacrifice'.[120]

Meanwhile in the 1920s, with France moving after 1924 towards reconciliation with a Germany increasingly committed to peace, and faced with an amiable enough, but fundamentally conservative Britain, Mussolini could achieve little. By the end of 1928, fascist Italy had secured only Fiume, in return for a short-lived friendship with Yugo-slavia, an effective protectorate over Albania, embodied with British connivance in treaties with Ahmed Zogu, insignificant territories on the borders of British Kenya and British controlled Egypt. The way in which Mussolini's more ambitious designs could be frustrated by Britain and France was shown clearly enough. In 1926, Italian designs on Turkish Anatolia seemed to be reviving, notably when Arnaldo Mussolini spoke of Italy's claims to Smyrna and Adalia; the only result was that Turkey abandoned the attempt to contest with Britain the possession of Mosul and signed a treaty of security and friendship with Britain. No more was heard of Italian demands. In the same year, Balbo, one of the potentates of fascism, visited the Italian community in French-controlled Tunisia, and stirred up its hostility to France. The French replied with naval manoeuvres off Bizerta, which induced a prompt retreat on Mussolini's part.[121] Indeed, one aspect of Mussolini's activities militated against any willingness on the part of France to concede Italian demands – for guarantees for the Italian population in Tunisia, for the colonial compensations promised by the Treaty of London of 1915, for a share in the control of Tangier – that is to say, his attitude towards Hungary. Reversing the policy of 1922–4, Mussolini began to express open support for Hungarian demands for revision of the post-war settlement; this rendered nugatory his search for influence in the Balkans expressed through treaties of friendship with every Balkan country and identified him with the enemies of the Little Entente (Yugoslavia, Czechoslovakia and Rumania) which was designed to oppose Hungarian claims. The result was that Mussolini appeared in the role of would-be disturber of the peace settlement in south-eastern Europe; a role that could only arouse the suspicions of France. However much the Hungarians welcomed the support of Italy, that support had no practical effects for the moment. Yugoslavia, drawing tighter its links with France, could not be threatened effectively by Italy, though it was disturbed by Italian help for anti-Serb revolutionists; Rumania had nothing to fear; Czechoslovakia could hardly be threatened by Italy. In effect, then, Mussolini's diplomatic activities, for all the rant and boasting with which they were expressed, did nothing except arouse the suspicion that he could not be trusted to work for peace in Europe. In the 1920s this was of no significance: France, safe from Germany, could defend her own interests and those of the Little Entente; Britain, undisturbed by European complications, could defend Egypt and her own mandates and colonies and could protect Greece and Turkey. In the 1920s, in fact, Mussolini did not matter, and his frivolous search for glory did not prevent Europe moving towards an apparently securely peaceful future.

The end of 1928, and the beginning of 1929, indeed was the last moment at which Europeans could look forward, with any confidence, to peace in their time. The Soviet Union was fully absorbed in ruthless modernization under Stalin and the communising of the rest of the world had been postponed indefinitely. No one talked of war except Mussolini, and his utterances could safely be ignored. France was secure. In Great Britain governments could reasonably lay down that defence planners could take it for granted that there would be no major war for the foreseeable future, a period defined as ten years. No one had any possible reason for fear of the United States. Above all, and this was the commanding fact, Germany seemed to have accepted peace. Even a section of the German nationalist party had recognised that Stresemann's policy could not be challenged and had begun to participate in republican governments. No doubt, Germany had not accepted the Treaty of Versailles, but at least outwardly, she had renounced war as an instrument of revision of that treaty in favour of persuasion. Germany was now prosperous and those who were anxious to attack notions of collaboration in a peaceful Europe were declining in strength inside Germany. Negotiations on the reduction of armies had begun, albeit slowly. The pact of 1928 by which the powers renounced aggressive war as an instrument of national policy was a more plausible instrument than it could have been in any previous era. The foundations of peace having, as it appeared, been solidly established with the agreements on the Young plan and on the end of allied occupation of Germany made at The Hague in 1929, began to crumble in the same year.

6

Europe between the Wars: Economic and Social Trends

The most striking change in the appearance of the world economy in the years after the First World War compared with the years before 1914 was the decline of the European share of international trade. In the years 1909–1913, exports from Europe to the world outside made up thirty per cent of all exports, while from 1925–38 they represented only twenty-five per cent. Before 1913 only twenty-five per cent of world exports were sent by countries outside Europe to other countries outside Europe; in 1925–38, the figure was forty per cent. This change was a symptom of a wide range of difficulties affecting European economies some of which had shown themselves before the war, all of which were made more acute by the effects of the war.[122]

The basic pattern of world trade before 1914 lay in the exchange of the manufactured articles of Europe for primary, or unprocessed, products of the outside world – food and raw materials. The war interrupted a fairly stable development of this trade. Until 1914, European economic growth led to rising demand for primary products which in turn enabled primary producers to buy more manufactures and thus further to stimulate the development of European industry. European investment in the primary producing countries made possible a steady expansion of the productive resources of the countries supplying food and raw materials. The war had two important effects on many of these countries outside Europe. In the first place, war-time difficulties of supply of manufactures from Europe encouraged the development of industry at home; in the second place, war-time demands from Europe, with a temporary decline in Europe's own production of primary goods, especially in agriculture, led to rapid expansion in their own production. At the end of the war, therefore, European industry found some of its markets less ready to accept its goods, while the primary producing countries were faced with a fall in prices of their own exports,

94

especially of food, as European agriculture revived. Failure of European exports to recover meant reduction of European demand for imports which in turn weakened the exporting capacity of the primary producing countries, and by cheapening the price of food and raw materials encouraged their own tendency towards developing their industrial self-sufficiency (often behind protective tariffs) and further weakened the position of European manufactures.

The table below gives examples from three countries It will be seen that a rapid expansion of imports between 1899 and 1913 was checked after the war and reversed after 1929. The figures are for imports of manufactures, from twelve exporting countries, in millions of dollars at constant (1955) prices.[123]

	1899	1913	1929	1937
Argentina	218	744	1064	725
Brazil	174	429	489	372
India	704	1219	1159	796

Another reason for the weakening of Europe's position in world trade lay in the growth of competition from outside Europe, especially from the United States, but also from Japan. The table below shows the proportion (in percentages) of total exports of manufactures produced by five countries, 1913–37, as compared with total manufacturing exports of western Europe, Canada, the United States, and Japan.[124]

	1913	1929	1937
U.S.A.	12	21	21
U.K.	32	22	20
Germany	26	20	16
France	12	12	6
Japan	2	3	10

The following tables show movements in exports of manufactures to three countries at constant prices (1938) in millions of dollars.[125]

To Argentina

from:	U.K.	Germany	France	U.S.A.	totals
1913	131	87	40	48	306
1928	121	77	32	127	356
1938	80	57	16	76	229

To Brazil

from:	U.K.	Germany	France	U.S.A.	totals
1913	72	65	19	45	200
1928	55	42	15	65	177
1938	21	58	7	50	135

To India

from:	U.K.	Germany	France	U.S.A.	Japan	totals
1913	466	46	11	10	16	549
1928	336	48	11	34	49	478
1938	160	42	3	26	52	283

E.—4*

The growth of Japanese and American competition occurred partly during the war, when Europe was to some extent unable to supply its normal customers, but it continued after the war for other reasons. In the case of Japan, it was a matter of success in the earlier stages of industrialization; Japan's exports rested on the sale of cheap and relatively simple manufactures, notably low-quality textiles. United States exports depended on the special readiness with which industrialists there had developed new techniques of production, especially mass-production, and new types of product, so that not merely was United States' industrial production advancing as a whole, but the demand for its exports was increasing more than proportionally. The most obvious example is the motor car industry; in 1929 the United States exported over three times as many passenger cars and commercial vehicles as the United Kingdom, Germany, France and Italy taken together. Only in the 1930s did European countries begin to develop a motor industry capable of competition with the United States in mass markets. Exports of machinery from the United States in 1929 were two-and-a-half times what they had been in 1913 while exports from western Europe had increased only by about one-fifth.[126]

The USA however, did not fill the same role in the world economy as the western European countries had done before 1914, for the United States was largely self-sufficient in food and relatively self-sufficient in raw materials and, unlike Britain, was protected by high tariffs. Thus exports from the primary producing countries to the United States did not increase at the same rate as their imports from the United States increased.

The demands of war in Europe encouraged the rapid expansion of heavy industry and the demands of peace-time were insufficient to keep fully occupied the capacity thus created. This tended to generate, in the major industrial powers, sectors of unemployment of resources and men whose diminishing incomes restricted their own demands on other sectors of the economy and so tended to bring about a general stagnation. A good example is shipbuilding, inflated in capacity before and during the war by demand for warships, war-time transports and replacement of lost merchant shipping. This swollen capacity met a restricted demand because of the failure of international trade to resume its pre-war growth. Here it was not a question of United States competition, for European shipyards maintained their economic advantages, but of overcapacity leading to unemployment. In the years before the war, building of new merchant ships had averaged two and a half million tons a year, which fell to less than two million tons between the wars, while at the same time naval construction fell off sharply. As in some other industries, however, it was the oldest established producers who were worst hit – especially in Britain – while newer yards specializing in building motor ships and employing the latest techniques, such as those in the Scandinavian countries, improved their relative position.[127]

Overcapacity showed itself after the war in another major western European industry: coal mining. There were two kinds of reason; first the expansion of industries using coal was slower after the war than before, or non-existent, and secondly technical progress caused rival fuels to be used, oil and hydro-electricity. Shipbuilding combined both – construction consumed less coal and the ships themselves increasingly used oil. Once again some coal-fields were worse affected than others, especially those coal-fields in Britain which depended on exports.

While trade between Europe and the outside world failed after the war to resume its pre-war rate of growth, so too trade among European countries did not recover. Contraction of exports from one European country to countries outside Europe and consequent checks to production led to falling off in demand which affected other countries in Europe. The weaknesses of British exports after the war in particular, by indirectly reducing British demand, affected other European countries, especially Germany and France. Trade among the three major industrial countries of western Europe, Germany, France and the United Kingdom, did not regain the level of 1913.[128]

In international trade the experience between the wars of the greater industrial countries was not shared by the smaller industrial countries. These countries developed exports based on industrial specializations or on higher average levels of technical accomplishment. Thus, for example, exports of manufactures from Belgium and Luxembourg increased sharply between 1913 and 1929 and fell only slightly between 1929 and 1937, while such exports from Sweden increased in both these periods.[129] There were differences, too, in the experiences of the main agricultural countries in Europe. All were faced with difficulties because of the low prices of farming produce on the world market, especially in the 1930s, difficulties aggravated by the protective policies for their own agriculture pursued by the major industrial countries, but some regions suffered more than others. The more highly developed countries of western Europe, such as Denmark, exported mainly animal products while importing a proportion of the necessary feeding stuffs – thus gaining some benefit from low cereal prices; while eastern European countries such as Bulgaria, Rumania and Yugoslavia whose exports were mainly of grain suffered grave hardship from falling prices.[130]

The industrial countries of Europe, then, especially the larger, ceased their pre-war growth in industrial production, and, particularly in those industries dependent on exports, suffered from unemployment of men and resources. The agricultural nations suffered from low prices for farming products, especially in countries producing corn for export. Several changes were needed: above all, measures to encourage international trade, a change in emphasis in the balance of production and investment in the larger industrial countries towards more advanced and complicated forms of manufactures and away from the pre-war staples such as cheap cloth and steel rails and a growth in investment by the richer countries in the economies of the less developed countries, both in Europe and abroad. Instead, international trade was hampered, especially in the 1930s, by tariffs and quotas designed to protect national economies and to monopolize colonial markets. The redeployment of resources inside the main industrial countries was hindered by administrative rigidities, such as controls of home rents and still more by the pursuit of deflationary policies designed to maintain the exchange parities of individual currencies. International lending was curtailed by the shortages of foreign currency suffered by Britain and Germany while French investors were understandably suspicious of long-term foreign loans after the loss of the whole French investment in Russia. The USA provided no satisfactory substitute for these countries since American financiers lacked the lending experience of European financial institutions and were inclined to lend before 1929 on short-term for non-productive projects, and after 1930 not to lend abroad at all. *Laissez-faire* economics had broken down, or, rather, the hardships that the application of *laissez-faire* would impose in the establishment of a new economic equilibrium were too great to be tolerable to populations and their governments. As we shall see, however, when we examine the fate of individual countries, governments were not always successful in the attempts they made to help their populations by interference in economic processes.

Though in general the European economy of the years between the wars was less encouraging and hopeful than it had been before 1914, not everything was gloomy. Some countries and some industries did well. The industrial countries, and individuals within them who were actively employed in industry, benefited from the falling prices of food on the world market, especially in the United Kingdom. By 1929, furthermore, it appeared that the progress of pre-war years had recommenced. As in international relations, so in economics, that year opened full of hope and confidence. It ended amidst the beginnings of disaster.

The account of the world economy above deals with long-term trends discernible throughout the period between the wars. These trends were, however, sometimes strengthened, sometimes weakened, by causes and economic movements of briefer duration, especially those associated with the trade cycle. The pattern of the world economy between the wars was roughly this: a sharp boom in 1919 and 1920 gave way to a slump in 1921–2; a steady advance followed from 1922 until 1929, with interruptions in 1924 and 1927. In 1929–32 a drastic slump occurred followed by slow and painful recovery from 1932 to a new peak of activity somewhere about 1937 after which date war, and preparations for war, supervened. These general trends merged with the longer-term trends already discussed and with the circumstances or policies of individual countries to produce widely divergent effects. In Britain, for instance, the slump of 1921–2 was felt severely, while in France, where easier credit and more relaxed governmental fiscal policies kept demand high, prosperity based on inflation continued, and in Germany this phase of the trade cycle was totally overridden by the beginning of an inflation which went unchecked to its end. These economic fluctuations can best be examined in their effect on individual countries, whose political life they frequently dominated. But the slump which began in 1929 had consequences so wide that it calls for separate analysis.

The great depression began in the United States. An unparalleled rise in prosperity in the 1920s was followed by collapse. Between 1921 and 1929 gross national income rose from 62·5 billion dollars to 93·6 billion dollars, at constant prices. By 1932, industrial production in the United States was down to almost half the level of 1929 and national income down to 58 billion dollars.[131] The causes of the American slump remain matters of dispute. It is fairly clear, however, that the first weakening of the boom came in building: private and public construction taken together began to fall off in 1929. At the same time the rate of increase of consumption fell with a consequent check to investment. In July 1929, the volume of industrial production began to decline. These processes were accelerated by the stock market crash in October, which shook business confidence and further reduced readiness to invest. These reasons for falling demand were reinforced and protracted by a crisis in American agriculture which contributed largely to the banking crisis of 1930–3. Agricultural prices had remained at a low level in the latter part of the 1920s, and with the industrial slump, they collapsed. Farmers, generally indebted, found it difficult to maintain interest payments, or were forced into outright bankruptcy. The result was a series of failures of banks, mainly of small local banks, which led to a spreading lack of confidence which by March 1933, threatened the ruin even of the major banks when emergency legislation warded off the danger.[132]

The slump in the United States had effects throughout the world, except within the completely insulated economy of the Soviet Union. Firstly, United States demand for the exports both of primary producing countries and manufacturing countries declined sharply. The effect was most damaging on the producers of food and raw materials: although American imports had not expanded as rapidly as the United States economy had done in the 1920s, the size of the American market was such that the curtailment of its imports damaged the already weak economies of the countries supplying raw materials and food. Between 1929 and 1932 world prices for raw materials fell by more than half, for food by nearly half. Hence the demand for European manufactures declined in turn. A further effect of the American depression was the curtailment in American lending overseas: above all to Germany and to the primary producing countries.

In 1929 the U.S.A. made available to the rest of the world through imports and investments, the sum of 7,400 million dollars (world imports amounted to 35,601 million dollars); this sum contracted in 1932 by 5,000 million dollars to as little as 32 per cent of what was made available in 1929.[133]

Those countries which had been borrowing from the United States were faced with a danger to their balance of payments which forced them to reduce imports through the erection of tariff barriers, through devaluation of their currencies or through import controls, measures which in their turn struck further blows at world trade. The United States took the lead in tariff increases with the Smoot-Hawley tariff, designed to protect domestic producers, and other countries, including Great Britain, followed suit sooner or later. In 1929 and 1930 some important primary producing countries were compelled to accept a reduction in the external value of their currencies – thus making their exports cheaper and their imports dearer, and so bringing their payments into balance by stimulating the first and checking the latter. This process was accelerated by the consequences of the European banking crisis in 1931. This brought international lending, which had revived in 1930, to a complete standstill.

The crisis began in Austria, whose financial position had been weak since the end of the war. In May 1931 it was announced that the *Creditanstalt* had suffered grave losses and was in danger of being unable to meet its commitments. The announcement, which may have been precipitated by French interests, who were anxious to frustrate the customs union then proposed between Austria and Germany, but which was probably not a result of French withdrawal of funds, set off fears for the stability of German banks.[134] Withdrawal of foreign balances followed from German banks. A moratorium on international governmental payments, that is to say German reparations and payments of war debts to Britain and the USA, was reinforced by international and German measures to restrict the exit of funds from Germany. With foreign assets, including British balances, thus tied to Germany, fears developed for the safety of foreign holdings in London. Doubts developed too, about British determination to make harsh economies in government spending, to maintain the value of the pound, and these doubts led to a run on London, as foreign creditors hastily sold pounds in exchange for assets in currencies which seemed more stable. This action brought about the crisis it was designed to anticipate and in September 1931, Britain left the gold standard – that is to say, it ceased to be possible to exchange pounds for gold at a fixed rate and the value of the pound was allowed to fall.[135] Many other countries followed suit; others which did not, notably Germany, were driven to desperate measures to maintain the exchange value of their currencies by restricting imports and by curtailing internal demand to keep the prices of their exports from rising too far above the export prices of those countries whose currencies were devalued. These restrictions on imports, by direct control or by tariffs, led to retaliation from other countries so that trade became subject to a great variety of restraints and obstacles. In 1932 world trade in manufactures was only sixty per cent of its 1929 level.[136]

The crisis meant the end of the hopes of the 1920s for a restoration of a liberal world economy. Then it had been hoped that general prosperity could be based on a growing international trade fostered by stable currencies with fixed values, freely interchangeable one with another and that free movements of capital between countries would automatically produce sound and productive investment and steady economic growth. Now the failure of liberal international economic policies seemed complete and individual countries sought their salvation by national policies without much regard to their wider impact. The failure of the self-regulating mechanisms of classical economic theory induced reliance on national governments as the instruments of the economic security

101

of their subjects. Acceptance of state regulation advanced; doubts of the merits of free economic systems inside the national units were fostered by the collapse of the free economy of the world.

Some measure of the relative success or failure of the major industrial powers in the defence of their economies is given in the table below.[137] (It should be remembered that the apparent failure of the United States is partly the result of their unusual success in the 1920s.) The table provides, too, an indication of the relative economic strengths of the great powers, who had, between them, four-fifths of the manufacturing capacity of the world. The figures are percentages of world output of manufacturers.

	U.S.A.	U.S.S.R.	Germany	U.K.	France	Japan	Italy
1929	43·3	5·0	11·1	9·4	6·6	2·5	3·3
1932	31·8	11·5	10·6	10·9	6·9	3·5	3·1
1937	35·1	14·1	11·4	9·4	4·5	3·5	2·7
1938	28·7	17·6	13·2	9·2	4·5	3·8	2·9

The instability and weakness of the European economies between the wars, and the political disturbances which they helped to generate, hindered, but did not prevent, important advances in human welfare. By 1939, the average length of life in peace-time Europe was about ten years greater than in 1914. Europe (and areas of European settlement outside Europe) retained its lead over Latin America, Asia and Africa, where life was shorter and more precarious with people born more freely and dying more quickly. Around 1930 the annual death rate in Europe (excluding the USSR) was 14 per 1000; in Africa it was 35.[138]

Europe was, however, far from homogeneous in its social and population patterns. There was a clear contrast between the economically advanced countries of the north and west and the more backward countries of the east and south. It was a contrast between relative riches and poverty, in expectation of life, and between a low and a high birth rate (with, curiously, an exception to be made of the Netherlands, which had a relatively high birth rate). These disparities went together with others: a greater or lesser dependence on agriculture, with a higher or lower level of education, with low or high death rates and infantile mortality rates. Thus, about 1930, a newly born Dutch child could be expected to live twenty-five years longer than a newly born Rumanian child. Out of a thousand Dutch infants 51 would not survive their first year; the figure for Rumania was 178. Nearly all Dutch children of ten years old could read and write; probably nearly one-half of Rumanian children could not. About one-fifth of the Dutch population was dependent on agriculture, nearly four-fifths of Rumanians. The Netherlands death rate was 9·4 per thousand; the Rumanian 20·1. These correlations are shown on a wider scale in the following table (some of the figures are approximate).[139]

			NORTH AND WEST EUROPE		
	Birth Rate	Death Rate	Infant deaths under 1 year per 1000	% Illiterate at age 10+	% Dependent on agriculture
Belgium	18·5	13·3	88	6	15
Denmark	18·4	11·1	77	0–5	30
Norway	16·7	10·7	46	0–5	27
Sweden	15·1	12·1	56	1	31
Switzerland	17·0	11·9	50	0–5	22

			SOUTH AND EAST EUROPE		
	Birth Rate	Death Rate	Infant deaths under 1 year per 1000	% Illiterate at age 10+	% Dependent on Agriculture
Bulgaria	30·4	16·5	147	31	75
Greece	31·2	17·1	117	41	46
Poland	31·6	15·6	142	27	60
Portugal	29·8	17·0	143	60	46
Yugoslavia	34·6	19·4	159	45	76

The high standards of social welfare maintained, as the table shows, in Denmark and Sweden demonstrate that a fairly high degree of dependence on agriculture could be combined with such high standards. Other variables are involved. Agricultural productivity in these countries was far greater than in southern and eastern Europe. Taking the average net production per person dependent on agriculture, fishing and forestry in Europe as 100, the Danish figure was about 275 and Swedish about 159, while for Bulgaria the figure was 66, for Greece 68, for Poland 50, for Portugal 83 and for Yugoslavia 56.[140] The explanation is that in the latter countries too many people were employed in an unduly inefficient agriculture.

A major phenomenon of nineteenth and twentieth century Europe was the 'vital revolution'. First death rates fell, as epidemic illness was checked, then, after an interval of time, birth rates fell and a new balance based on greater longevity resulted. By the inter-war years, northern and western Europe had moved through both phases; southern and eastern Europe had largely completed the first phase but was still far from the end of the second. The result was rapid population growth, though, during these years, the rate of growth was declining.[141] Lack of alternative opportunity of employment, together with the preponderance of small peasant family holdings, kept this increasing population on the soil, deriving a meagre return, often barely sufficient for subsistence. Industrialization had not proceeded far in southern and eastern Europe.

GROSS VALUE OF MANUFACTURING PER HEAD, 1930-8, IN
DOLLARS AT 1926-9 PRICES.[142]

Sweden	260	Hungary	60
Denmark	200	Poland	30
Netherlands	170	Rumania	20

Progress was not easy to achieve for the situation was self-perpetuating. An impoverished population dependent on agriculture, whose markets were weakened by the results of the First World War, could not provide capital for industrial development without resort to the drastic measures of forced saving, involving misery and hardship, of the sort taken up by the rulers of Soviet Russia in these years. Equally, lack of capital held back advance in agricultural productivity. In some countries, especially in the Balkans, the small size of holdings combined with over-population to produce a situation in which capital was both scarce and unprofitable to apply. The table shows the percentages of agricultural land in holdings of various sizes.[143] (One hectare equals about 2½ acres.)

	1–10 Hectares	10–50 Hectares	Over 50 Hectares
Bulgaria	56·4	32·0	1·6
Rumania	48·1	19·7	32·2
Yugoslavia	55·0	35·3	9·7

In Hungary, and in Spain and Italy (two countries which combined features of both underdeveloped and developed Europe) large holdings were common but, especially in Spain, absentee landlords often failed to attempt more than to maximise their current income and neglected capital investment for the sake of their own current consumption. Outside the Soviet Union, political development of the inter-war years tended to accentuate these trends: in areas with a high proportion of small peasant holdings, measures of land reform increased their number, while in countries where large estates were numerous, as in Hungary, socially conservative regimes emerged which maintained them, without enforcing high standards of estate management.

In standards of housing, feeding and education, the contrast between 'advanced' and 'backward' Europe can be identified and, to some extent measured.

DENSITY OF OCCUPATION IN SMALL DWELLINGS IN CERTAIN TOWNS WITH A
POPULATION OVER 100,000 ABOUT 1920–1.[144]

	% of dwellings with 1–4 rooms with more than 2 persons a room	% of dwellings with 1–4 rooms inhabited by more than 3 persons a room	% of dwellings with 1–4 rooms in relation to all dwellings
England and Wales (London & County Boroughs)	9	2	n.a.
Sweden (Stockholm)	15	n.a.	n.a.
Denmark (Copenhagen)	12	n.a.	86
Norway (Oslo and (Bergen)	15	4	77
France (towns over 100,000)	5	1	85
Belgium (4 towns)	6	1	79
Czechoslovakia (Prague)	32	13	n.a.
Finland (Helsinki)	39	20	87
Austria (Vienna)	20	5	92
Poland (5 towns)	45	24	91
Germany (towns over (100,000)	5	1	n.a.

Overcrowding was by no means confined to large towns. In Poland, figures for 1921 show that 48 per cent of the dwellings in towns with under 20,000 inhabitants housed more than two persons per room. In 1931, more than half of the Polish dwellings in rural areas consisted of one room inhabited by an average of 4·8 persons, while a further 35·5 per cent of rural dwellings contained two rooms with an average of 2·7 persons per room. In 1921, the average number of persons per room in Polish towns with over 20,000 population was 1·9 and in towns below that size 2·1. The contrast with, for instance, the Netherlands is striking. In 1930, only about 10 per cent of dwellings in the Netherlands housed more than two persons per room while the average number of persons per room in the whole country was about 0·96. Italy came in between: in 1931, in communes with more than 20,000 inhabitants, dwellings contained an average of 1·4 persons per room. In Poland in 1921 only 36 per cent of the population in towns lived in buildings which had running water; in Italy (1931) about 58 per cent of the dwellings in communes with more than 20,000 inhabitants had a supply of drinking water.[145]

Standards of nutrition varied between the advanced countries in northern and western Europe and the relatively backward areas of southern and eastern Europe. More bread and other cereals were eaten in the poorer countries; less meat, fish, milk, milk products and eggs. The following table illustrates these contrasts.[146]

105

QUANTITIES (KILOGRAMS) OF FOODSTUFFS CONSUMED BY WORKERS' HOUSEHOLDS PER
YEAR PER UNIT OF CONSUMPTION

	Sweden	Germany	Poland	Bulgaria
Cereals and Bread	106·5	134·0	219·21	290·46
Meat, fish etc.	64·9	52·9	51·22	38·68
Margarine, fats etc.	12·3	16·3	3·29	9·77
Milk, milk products and eggs	284·1	174·0	94·84	43·73
Vegetables and fruits	160·0	227·2	267·09	n.a.
Sugar	37·5	16·6	20·78	9·60

In some parts of south-eastern Europe actual famine was possible. A
League of Nations report of 1936 printed these words:

according to the statistics for 1932, out of 343 districts in Yugoslavia with
14,049,738 inhabitants, there are 129 districts with 4,566,985 inhabitants in
which more than 50 per cent of peasant families have not sufficient food to
await the next harvest and, in which, therefore, nutrition is very inadequate.[147]

Standards of primary education are most easily illustrated by using
statistics of illiteracy. Census returns of about 1950 give the following
figures for illiteracy among those aged 25–34 at the time of the census.[148]

Belgium   = 1·1 %
Yugoslavia = 19·0 %
Greece   = 20·3 %
Portugal   = 36·7 %

Another indication comes from figures for school attendance, together
with the ages for which attendance was compulsory, at least in theory.[149]

	Year	Ages	Percentage in School
Germany	1932	6–14	99
Netherlands	1932	6–13	99
Norway	1931	7–14	97
Poland	1934	7–14	94
Bulgaria	1934	7–14	85
Rumania	1933	7–14	80

Extensive contrasts can be found in secondary education: thus the
Swiss census of 1960 showed that 32 per cent of the population then
aged 45–54 had attended secondary school while the Rumanian census
of 1956 recorded about 7 per cent for the age group 35–44.[150]
Educational comparisons between different nations are, however,
extremely difficult; for higher education, they are virtually impossible,
though one notable fact is reliably established by the available figures:
in relatively backward countries female educational standards were
especially low. The following table illustrates this point.

COMPARATIVE PERCENTAGES OF ILLITERACY[151]

	Census date	Age group	% of males illiterate	% of females illiterate
Belgium	1947	25–34	1·4	0·9
Greece	1951	25–34	6·0	20·6
Portugal	1950	25–34	28·2	45·0
Yugoslavia	1948	25–34	8·3	27·9

The next table shows the proportion of women attaining certain levels of education compared with the proportion of men (the proportion of men equals 100). Figures for the USA are inserted for comparison.[152]

	Census date	Age group	Secondary Education	Higher Education
U.S.A.	1960	45–54	Males 100	100
			Females 107	96
Switzerland	1960	45–54	Males 100	100
			Females 88	59
Netherlands	1960	45–54	Males 100	100
			Females 76	16
Italy	1961	45–54	Males 100	100
			Females 71	20
Rumania	1956	35–44	Males 100	100
			Females 67	36
Bulgaria	1956	35–44	Males 100	100
			Females 55	21

Recent social history has seen a steady movement towards equality of education between the sexes. In the inter-war years equal provision of primary education was made for boys and girls in the more prosperous European countries while in the less prosperous marked inequalities in the levels of male and female education survived. In secondary education the same phenomenon is evident. In higher education, though, it seems that those sections of the population in the more backward countries who were able to secure reasonable education for their daughters were as ready as the more educated sections of the populations of the advanced countries to encourage them to proceed to higher education.

Variations between nations in average standards of living did not, of course, mean that everyone in one country possessed so much more or so much less of the amenities and necessities of life than those in another. Within each country there were wide variations between different classes and, often linked with them, between different regions. Thus, about 1930, the infantile mortality rate* in Catalonia was seventy-four (Spanish average 117) while that in County Durham was eighty-four (English average sixty-three). Within Britain there were sharp contrasts between the extreme figures of ninety-one (West Central Scotland) and thirty (Isle of Wight) and inside Spain, the figure for Catalonia can be

* Mortality rate: the death per thousand infants in their first year.

compared with the figure of 156 for Extremadura.[153] Class differences in levels of nutrition and standards of housing can also be documented. In the province of Salerno, Italy, in 1929, family budget studies produced the following figures for food consumed, in kilograms per year.[154]

	Workers and lower salaried employees	Persons engaged in agriculture	Higher middle class
Cereals and bread	240·89	278·85	201·47
Meat, fish etc.	24·57	20·50	37·01
Margarine, fats etc.	14·48	16·13	16·60
Milk, milk products and eggs	40·36	29·05	68·72
Vegetables and fruits	74·82	108·39	90.15
Sugar	5.11	2·19	9·49

Figures from Germany in 1927–8 also shows consumption patterns varying with economic status.[155]

	Households with an annual income in Reichsmarks per consumption unit of	
	less than 800	1500 and over
Cereals and bread	138·5	131·8
Meat, fish etc.	39·2	68·3
Margarine, fats etc.	18·1	13·8
Milk, milk products and eggs	123·6	203·2
Vegetables and fruits	197·1	252·8
Sugar	14·1	17·7

Differential standards of housing can be illustrated by figures drawn from the Italian census of 1931.

NUMBER OF PERSONS PER ROOM IN COMMUNES WITH 20,000 INHABITANTS AND OVER[156]

Farmers	1·8	Armed forces, religion, professions and liberal arts	0·8
Workers	1·7		
Salaried workers	1·0	Property owners and rentiers	0·6

The association of overcrowding with poverty and ill health is demonstrated by studies of Glasgow and Amsterdam in the 1920s. In Glasgow, the infant mortality rate in the more crowded areas was nearly four times that of the richer districts as the table shows.[157]

	City of Glasgow	Mile End	Gorbals	Langside	Cathcart
Density of population: persons per acre	57	136	207	45	22
Death-rate per 1000	14·2	17·6	17·2	9·2	8·7
Infant mortality rate	104	163	128	44	52
Death rate per 1000 from infectious diseases	0·81	1·69	1·86	0·11	0·12

The same kind of disparities appear in Amsterdam, though they are less extreme.[158]

	Amsterdam	Jordaan	Vondelpark and Boerenwetering
Wealth in 1915 according to the % of incomes over 2200 florins		1·4	31·8
Death-rate per 1000, 1920–1	10·5	12·4	8·4
Infant morality rate, 1929–31	36·5	58·4	22·6
Deaths from tuberculosis of the lungs per 10,000, 1920–1	11·1	12·7	7·0

Over a wider area, figures for infantile mortality in England and Wales show the connection between social class and welfare levels.[159]

Social Class:	I	II	III	IV	V
1921	38·4	55·5	76·8	89·4	97·0
1929	26·8	34·4	44·4	51·4	60·1

There was great variety, too, in the education available to different social classes. The primary level was generally free. But secondary education and higher education usually had to be paid for. Thus progress beyond an elementary standard tended to be the prerogative of the middle and upper classes.

Advances in welfare in European countries in these years took the form of measures, mostly of a tentative and hesitant kind, to secure for the economically weaker sections of the population some of the conditions of environment, nutrition and education that the richer members of society could buy for themselves. Even in medicine, progress involved to some extent the application to wider sections of society of principles and techniques already established by 1914 rather than in the discovery of completely new procedures (although, for instance in the introduction of new methods of inoculation against diptheria and with the discovery of the sulphonamide drugs, major innovations were made). Improvements in the average standards of living of European populations were, then, in great part, a consequence of moves towards greater equality, towards redistribution of income, towards the provision of supplements in cash or goods or services to the poorer sections of society as additions to what economic conditions enabled them to acquire for themselves.

Two different methods of redistribution can be identified. In the first the state provided services or benefits in cash or kind paid for out of general taxation. This meant some closing of the gap between rich and poor, most markedly in countries where taxation was progressive, that is where the rich were taxed proportionately more heavily than the poor. In the second, individuals or the state made arrangements for mutual insurance within more or less broad categories of the various strata of society. This meant a redistribution of income within classes, or occupational groups, in which the more secure and fortunate members of the group paid for help to the more needy members of the same group. The second method, of course, did not reduce over-all inequalities between separate classes. It was, therefore, less worrying to those who were anxious to defend inequalities of wealth and it is not surprising that in countries where social conservatism was strong, this method was politically more acceptable. Commonly the two methods were combined: insurance schemes or mutual assistance schemes were supported by subsidies from the state. Then the equalitarian effect depended on the extent of the subsidies and on the nature of the taxation structure which financed them. In Britain, where the social services were financied in as redistributive a way as in most of the advanced countries, it was calculated that about two per cent of national income was transferred through them in 1935 from the rich to the poor.[160]

Such methods were not new. Help for the destitute, financed out of some form of taxation, had been organized for many years by public authorities in most European countries. Before 1914, some governments had begun to provide social assistance going beyond the mere relief of complete destitution. In 1883, Bismarck's imperial German government set a major precedent for the organization by the state of insurance schemes applicable to certain categories of workers. Changes between the wars brought changes in the geographical extent and in the scope of welfare schemes rather than radical innovations of method or principle.

It is difficult to generalize about the motives leading to extensions of welfare schemes. Probably the main impact came from socialist movements. Outside Russia, governments feared full-scale socialism and to weaken the force of demands for the abolition of private property, were ready to reduce the hardships imposed on the weaker sections of the countries they ruled. Thus advances in social security were not much less marked in countries with conservative governments than in those with left wing governments. The rapidity of such advances seems rather to have been determined by the resources available in the various European countries; where there was not much wealth to redistribute, not much redistribution was done. Socialist movements contributed, too, to what was probably the most powerful factor in social progress: the development of humanitarian concern for the fate of the poor. This was fortified by the increase in information provided by social investigators. The League of Nations and, still more, the International Labour Office, sponsored extensive enquires into social conditions.

Their studies and reports made social welfare schemes a source of international prestige. The First World War, like the Second, contributed to the acceptance of social provision; universal military service produced some sense of solidarity within communities while the high levels of taxation reached in the belligerent countries made government spending seem possible on a far larger scale than had ever been contemplated before. By 1945, it was almost taken for granted in all the advanced European countries that states should act to secure a minimum standard of welfare for all their citizens. Indeed an International Labour Office report of March 1942 asserted that the 'idea of social security' was 'one of the great purposes of the nations now fighting for freedom and for a civilization based on respect for human personality' and concluded that social security

can only be planned as part of a larger programme which includes measures promoting employment and maintaining it at a high level, for increasing the national dividend and sharing it more equitably, for improving nutrition and housing, multiplying facilities for medical care, and widening opportunities for general and vocational education.[161]

Some examples will show the methods by which social provision was made between the wars, and some measure of their effects in education, health and nutrition, and housing.

Spending by governments on education produced more primary schools, permitted an extension of the period of compulsory schooling and reduced the number of pupils per teacher. Thus between 1913 and 1933 the percentage of national income devoted to spending by the state on education rose from 2·8 to 4·4 in Germany, from 2·1 to 5·0 in the Netherlands and from 1·6 to 2·6 in the United Kingdom (the UK figures represent only part of such expenditure).[162] In 1938, the following amounts (in dollars) were spent on education per head of the population in the countries listed.[163]

United Kingdom	13	Denmark	11
Germany	13	Finland	5
Norway	12	Italy	3
Netherlands	12	Portugal	1
Sweden	11		

The next table showing illiteracy rates by age groups in certain countries gives another indication of the advance in primary schooling.[164]

Age-groups	45–54	35–44	25–34	20–24	15–19
Belgium (1947)	3·3	1·8	1·1	1·0	0·9
Yugoslavia (1948)	35·8	28·3	19·0	12·8	12·5
Greece (1947)	46·5	32·6	20·3	16·9	18·7
Portugal (1950)	50·3	46·6	36·7	32·2	31·6

The extension of secondary and higher education in European countries was, however, selective – most of the population ceased its education at the end of primary school, but public money was laid out in some countries to secure for pupils more or less rigorously selected by competitive academic examination the chances that were bought in payments for fees and maintainance for pupils with richer parents. The effect of this tentative increase in equality of opportunity was, however, even less than was perhaps expected, for the children of the worst educated and generally poorest classes, irrespective of intelligence, tended to be weaker performers in competitive examinations than those from less restricted home backgrounds. The effect, and the limitations, of these measures is suggested by the results of a sample survey conducted in England and Wales.[165]

	Percentage with secondary education		Percentage with university education	
Date of birth	Status categories 1–4	Status categories 5–7	Status categories 1–4	Status categories 5–7
Males:				
Before 1910	27·0	4·0	4·4	0·9
1910–29	38·9	9·8	8·5	1·4
Females:				
Before 1910	25·6	3·5	2·1	0·1
1910–29	35·7	9·3	4·0	0·2

In the advance of health and nutrition, social policy took various forms: direct provisions of services or direct provisions of cash grants to the needy financed out of taxation, and encouragement, sometimes with state subsidies, of insurance schemes providing services or cash benefits to those whose incomes might fall below the level that made possible an adequate standard of living. Direct provision was made principally for infants and children, for the old and for the destitute. In Britain, which probably possessed the most extensive range of services financed from taxation, ante-natal clinics, maternity hospitals, infant welfare centres and the advice at home of health visitors were provided out of public funds, though charges graded according to means were sometimes made. Subsidised or free milk and meals were provided to school children while a school medical service furnished regular health checks. In many countries hospitals (especially isolation hospitals for infectious diseases) were provided at public expense giving free treatment or making nominal charges. In Britain and Denmark non-contributory old age pensions were payable to those below certain prescribed income levels, while in Britain cash assistance to the unemployed was paid under a separate mechanism from that of the unemployment insurance scheme. For the totally destitute, most countries had long made provisions through poor laws, with stringent conditions of eligibility for benefit.

The characteristic of social welfare schemes in Europe between the wars, however, was the spread of the insurance principle, by which workers, employers and, sometimes, the state, contributed to a fund from which benefit was due, by right, to those suffering temporary disability (sickness or unemployment) or who had retired from work. Insurance was politically more acceptable than welfare schemes based on general taxation but there were other reasons for its predominance. It was held that the working man would not be corrupted by receiving benefits to which he had a right, paid for by contributions of his own, as he would be, it was alleged, by direct charity from the state; it was believed too that state assistance must mean inquiries into the means of support of its beneficiaries and that potential beneficiaries would therefore be discouraged from thrifty and prudent self-help. By 1939 there were insurance schemes organized under the aegis of the state, to assist workers whose incomes were reduced by sickness or old age in nearly every European country. Unemployment insurance was less common and in many countries help to the unemployed came from poor laws. The insurance schemes varied in coverage and in the scale of benefit. Most were compulsory for defined classes of wage earners, some were voluntary.

Unlike social insurance, family allowances were an innovation of the inter-war years. During these years schemes of comprehensive scope were introduced only in France and Belgium and partial schemes in Italy (through collective agreements). In France and Belgium the whole cost was borne by employers so that, in effect, they provided a structure of differential wages. (In Italy, the cost was shared by the workers.) Through family allowances the burdens of child rearing which could lead to hardship for parents and children, especially in larger families, were partially relieved.[166]

Some rough indication of the scale of social security provisions in the middle of this period is given in the following table, which shows the amount spent on social security quoted in dollars per head of the whole population (1954 prices) in selected countries in 1930.[167]

United Kingdom	59	France	17
Germany	54	Belgium	12
Denmark	26	Italy	5
Switzerland	24	Finland	5
Sweden	22	Spain	1

113

The improvement of housing required state intervention since in the period between the wars, especially in the 1920s, economic conditions made it impossible even for many regularly employed workers to secure reasonable homes in the open market. One measure, which was almost general in the 1920s, was the imposition of rent control, which kept the rents of cheaper dwellings below the level that free dealings would have established. However, this served to create a privileged class: those who were fortunate enough to have possession of such dwellings. To provide cheap housing and make possible the clearance of slums further state intervention was needed. Financial support was made through subsidies, either in lump sums or annual payments, or by the provision of credit through direct loans at reduced interest rates or through state guarantees of interest payments. The construction of cheap dwellings was carried out by the state directly or by housing associations or by commercial builders acting under state supervision. The table shows that about a quarter of the houses constructed in the periods in question in selected countries were built on a non-commercial basis.[168] Intervention by public authorities on this scale was wholly unprecedented.

Countries	Dates	Total dwellings constructed	Proportion constructed by (percentages)		
			Public authorities	Housing societies	Private enterprise
England and Wales	1919–29	1,476,648	36	–	64
Germany	1927–29	976,078	11	31	58
Netherlands	1921–29	426,427	11	18	71
Denmark (all towns)	1920–29	74,114	16	31	53
Czechoslovakia (78 towns)	1928–29	62,884	10	16	74
Finland (all towns)	1924–28	30,235	2	21	77
Poland (Warsaw)	1922–29	12,412	5	15	80

It is difficult to measure the effects upon the average standard of health and welfare of these measures and of such economic growth as took place in Europe between the wars. Averages conceal, too, the extent to which the position of the poorer classes was improved. One consequence has already been mentioned: the average increase in the duration of life of about ten years between 1914 and 1939. The best guide is probably to be had from infantile mortality rates, which reflect a wide variety of social conditions including nutrition, housing, education, medical care and general health.

Comparison with the 1963 figures shows that European social progress accelerated after the Second World War. Significant medical

DEATHS PER THOUSAND OF INFANTS UNDER ONE YEAR OF AGE[169]

	1920–24	1925–29	1930–34	1935–39	1963
Austria	141·6	120·2	100·2	85·9	31·3
Belgium	108·5	101·3	91·6	83·4	27·2
Bulgaria	156·8	149·8	144·1	146·4	35·7
Czechoslovakia	160·0	145·8	128·5	111·4	22·0
Denmark	82·4	82·2	73·1	64·2	19.1
France	97·1	91·4	80·1	71·1	25·4
Germany	127·2	98·1	77·8	66·3	n.a.
Hungary	192·2	175·1	156·7	135·6	42·9
Italy	128·8	122·2	105·6	102·7	39·5
Netherlands	74·4	57·9	46·7	37·4	15·8
Norway	53·3	50·4	45·2	40·4	n.a.
Poland	n.a.	148·6	139·6	136·0	49·1
Portugal	152·8	142·2	144·7	139·4	73·1
Rumania	206·9	195·2	179·3	180·6	55·2
Spain	148·2	127·8	118·0	124·5	40·5
Sweden	61·4	57·7	51·9	43·2	15·4
Switzerland	70·3	55·5	49·0	45·3	20·5
United Kingdom	79·2	73·3	65·5	58·5	21·8
Yugoslavia	n.a.	149·3	154·9	138·8	77·5

advances, faster economic growth and more radical policies have combined to produce this acceleration. The advances of the inter-war years were more sluggish, but the record shows that peace-time life was more tolerable for more people at the end of the period than at its beginning.

7

Britain 1919-39

The years between the wars in the United Kingdom, were, above all, the years of mass unemployment. Neither before nor since has unemployment on so large a scale been recorded. Government policies were usually of a kind that made unemployment more severe and which involved attacks on the living standards of those who were employed and even sometimes on those who were unemployed. The most remarkable fact of these years is the lack of the political disturbance that might have been evoked, the stability of the parliamentary régime, the absence of violence, the weakness of extremist parties, the presence of a degree of cohesion, which prevented class war and revolution or extremist reaction. In this respect, British history in these years presents a sharp and illuminating contrast with the history of the major European industrial countries and even with the United States where economic depression led at least to the radicalism of the New Deal. It is this paradox that this chapter seeks to illustrate and explain.

GREAT BRITAIN: PERCENTAGE UNEMPLOYED[170]

1921	16·6	1927	9·6	1933	19·8
1922	14·1	1928	10·7	1934	16·6
1923	11·6	1929	10·3	1935	15·3
1924	10·2	1930	15·8	1936	12·2
1925	11·0	1931	21·1	1937	10·6
1926	12·3	1932	21·9	1938	12·6

(The average unemployment rate in the 30 years before the war was about 6%).

The principal cause of this disastrous situation, with never less than one million unemployed, was the weakening of British exports after 1920. Great Britain was affected to an exceptional extent by the stagnation of demand for European manufactures already described, because the major British exporting industries of the pre-war years were precisely those which were most seriously damaged by changes in the types of goods demanded by importers or by the weakening of their demand as a whole. Coal, iron and steel, machinery, vehicles, ships and textiles made up two-thirds of all British exports before the war.[171] Most of these staple exports suffered decline. Exports of coal remained at a high level until 1924 because the effects of war-time dislocation in reducing production abroad were protracted by strikes and, above all, by the occupation of the Ruhr in 1923. Thereafter Britain faced the full effects of competition from the technically more efficient European coal fields while world demand for coal fell because of substitution of other fuels and because of industrial depression, especially after 1929. Thus British coal production fell from about 270 million tons before 1914 to about 230 million tons in the years immediately preceeding 1939, while the number of men employed fell from over one million to about 700,000.[172]

Net annual exports of iron and steel before the war were about 2,750,000 tons, by 1921-2 about 1,250,000 tons and in 1927-9 750,000 tons. During the war and immediately after, steel-producing capacity had expanded beyond what was justified by demand after 1920 so that on average the British steel industry between the wars operated at less than two-thirds of its capacity. Furthermore, the British industry had lost competitive advantages; its slower growth of output before 1914 compared with Germany and France, for example, had caused its modernization to fall behind, while modernization on the continent had made it possible for ores readily available on the continent to be exploited. The absence of tariffs until 1932 left the British market itself open to foreign competition while British competitive weakness led to a fall in the British proportion of world exports of steel products from thirty-eight per cent in 1912-3 to thirty-four per cent in 1927-8 and twenty-five per cent in 1936-8. Cyclical fluctuations affected demand at home and abroad for iron and steel with peculiar violence, so that workers were retained in the industry by the temporarily-increased needs of boom periods who became unemployed in large numbers in depression; thus the unemployment rate among producers of iron and steel was twenty-one per cent in 1924, twenty per cent in 1929, forty-seven per cent in 1932 and ten per cent in 1937.[173]

The fate of the British shipbuilding industry between the wars illustrates most of the causes of Britain's economic weakness. Once again, a British industry was damaged by a general fall in demand – but it was more harmed than its competitors abroad. Before 1914, British yards produced about seven times the tonnage of ships made in Italy, Belgium, the Netherlands, Sweden, Denmark, Norway and Spain combined; in the 'twenties three times as much, and in the 'thirties only twice as much. British shipbuilders were slow to adopt major innovations such as electric welding and slow to adapt their yards to the production of motor ships and to new categories of ship such as oil tankers. Nor did they succeed in keeping costs of production down – labour costs, for instance, were kept up by one of the most damaging features of British trade unionism, the existence of several unions with membership drawn from workers engaged on the production of a single article. Each union insisted on the maintenance of the monopoly of its members in the exercise of their special crafts and skills, so that a task that might require the work of one man in Norway or Sweden might need contributions from four or five in Britain. Average costs of production were kept up, too, by the under-employment of capacity and consequent pressure on profits which checked investment and attempts at modernization. In consequence, though many workers left the industry – about a quarter of the 250,000 or so employed in it in 1924 – unemployment rates in shipbuilding and ship-repairing were thirty per cent in 1924, twenty-four per cent in 1929, sixty-three per cent in 1932 and twenty-four per cent in 1937.[174]

In textiles, the British cotton industry contracted sharply – not because world demand for cotton cloth was falling but because the needs of Britain's major pre-war customers were being met either by new industries of their own or by imports from newly developed industries outside Britain. The table below illustrates these points.

COTTON PIECE GOODS IN THOUSANDS OF TONS

		1913	1925	1938
Exports from:	UK	576	377	135
	Japan	3	103	234
Imports by:	India	249	116	67
	China	181	127	2

Before 1914 more than half the products of the cotton industry were exported; the decline of exports, therefore, struck this industry a hard blow. The cause lay in the dependence of British exports on the sale of cheap cotton cloths, which could relatively easily be produced by the nascent industry of countries such as India and China, and which could be made more cheaply by the Japanese who progressively reduced the share of British cotton in a declining international trade. Though the labour force declined by about one quarter between 1924 and 1937, unemployment rates were high, thirteen per cent in 1924 and 1929, twenty-nine per cent in 1932 and twelve per cent in 1937.[175]

Machinery and vehicles were both expanding industries between the wars; unfortunately British specializations before 1914 did not fit the evolving pattern of world demand. British manufacturers had been especially successful in exporting non-electrical power-generating machinery and railway equipment, both of which were in decline, while the United States held the lead in the expanding trades in office machinery and road vehicles and Germany and the United States between them dominated the growing trades in metal-working machinery and electrical machinery. Thus the value of British exports of machinery actually fell between 1913 and 1929, in contrast to the experience of every other industrial area. Similarly, while exports from Britain of transport equipment increased in the same years, roughly doubling in value, this compared unfavourably with the more than ten-fold increase in United States exports. In short, in contrast to France, Germany and the United States, Britain failed to increase the value of her exports of manufactures between 1913 and 1929 and after 1929 shared in the general fall of world exports.[176]

This stagnation in the main British export trades was clearly the principal cause of British unemployment between the wars, because of its direct effects and because of its indirect effect in curtailing demand for the products of other industries. The reason for the difficulties faced by British exports was that British industry had developed and prospered in meeting demands which were now stagnating or declining and that it was less well equipped to seize its share of expanding trades. What was required to restore health to the British economy was a shift in resources of investment and labour from declining industries to the growing manufactures and probably, too, some increase of production for the home market as against production for export. These objects were difficult to achieve against a background of unemployment and weak demand. Nor did government policy help – it was designed, as we shall see, principally to maintain the external value of the pound sterling which meant policies of deflation which hastened the decline of weak industries but slowed down the progress of the strong.

British efforts to meet post-war economic difficulties were based on the assumption that a revival of the expanding world trade of the years before the war was the essential solution and that the principal barrier to this revival lay in the instability of currencies and consequent lack of confidence among traders and producers. Abroad, therefore, British policy was devoted to restoring political stability and, above all, to efforts to curb French demands on Germany for reparations and to prevent French governments from injuring the German economy by enforcing those demands. At home, British governments devoted themselves to a restoration of a stable value for the pound sterling and the return to convertibility of the pound into gold. The assumption was made that this return to the gold standard should be carried out at the pre-war parity, that is to say, in practice, that the value of the pound in terms of U.S. dollars should be stabilized at the pre-war level. It was believed that a British return to the gold standard would be both a condition and a cause of a general return which would ensure the stability of the major currencies of the world. The self-regulating mechanism of the gold standard was believed to be the surest guarantee of stability.

In highly simplified terms, the mechanism worked in this way: any country whose balance of foreign payments became adverse, would find the value of its currency in terms of other currencies tending to fall and holders of that currency would exchange it for gold. The country whose currency was thus affected, generally because of importing more than it exported, would therefore be faced with a loss of gold, which would bring about a contraction of the lending of its banking system and so lead to a curtailment of credit and a falling off in internal demand which would bring about a reduction in its internal prices. This would stimulate exports and solve the original difficulty. Conversely, if a country exported more than it imported it would face an inflow of gold which would lead to a rise in bank credit and a consequent increase in internal prices which would stimulate imports and reduce exports. Currencies would therefore automatically remain stable in value and international trade could confidently flourish. Few economists in Britain doubted the validity of these arguments, and few believed that Britain should return to the gold standard at less than the pre-war parity. Indeed, the latter assumption was hardly questioned until it had actually taken place. There were both moral and practical reasons for this; it was thought to be a duty to maintain the value of money lent to the state by British citizens or by foreigners and so to restore the value of the pound and it was held that this restoration was essential to the establishment of the confidence in sterling needed to permit the revival of London as the financial and banking centre of the world.

In 1920 the value of the pound fell below 3·5 dollars, the pre-war parity was 4·86. The assumption that the pound should be made equal in value to 4·86 dollars required governmental policies of deflation, a return to so-called sound finance. The general world slump of 1921, following the end of the post-war reconstruction boom, caused a fall in the British price level, as a result of a general reduction in demand. This reduction, due to world trading conditions, was accentuated by government action to restrict demand further. Government spending was curtailed notably in 1922 on the recommendation of a committee of businessmen headed by Sir Eric Geddes, which cut down spending on the armed services and social expenditures, especially on education, so that in the years 1920–4 a substantial budgetary surplus was maintained. At the same time, the treasury kept up the long-term rate of interest to a level of over 5 per cent in 1920–1 and about 4½ per cent for the rest of the 1920s, compared with less than 3½ per cent in 1913, by the issue of long-term loans designed to enable a reduction in the short-term floating debt. The effect was to make it more difficult to raise capital for productive investment.[177]

These measures caused British prices to fall, but, compared with prices in the United States, they had not fallen far enough to bring the pound back to its pre-war value in terms of the United States dollar when the decision was taken to return to the gold standard, in April 1925, at the pre-war exchange rate. British prices, by then, justified an exchange rate of about 4·5 dollars to the pound; the rate of 4·86 meant that prices and wages had to be forced down still further to maintain this artificial value. The result was the General Strike of 1926 and the continuance of restrictionist credit policies, with high interest rates to encourage foreigners to hold sterling rather than to take gold out of Britain, high interest rates which also restricted demand within Britain. The new exchange rate meant that British export prices were too high in terms of foreign currencies, especially since other countries, including France, Belgium and Germany, linked their currencies with gold at lower values, thus giving their exports a competitive advantage. British exports were held back which perpetuated unemployment; the difficulty – this situation of maintaining the external value of the pound – led to high interest rates at home which hindered the transformation of British industry needed to meet new types of foreign and domestic demand. Britain largely failed to share in the world boom of 1925–9. Average British manufacturing production in these years was slightly less than in 1913, while for the world as a whole it was more than one quarter higher, and the British share in the exports of manufactures of the twelve major industrial countries fell from thirty per cent in 1913 to twenty-five per cent in 1929.[178]

In the 1920s, then, British unemployment, generated by export difficulties, was made worse by concern for the value of the pound sterling; the British working man was sacrificed to the City of London. After 1929, Britain was hit by the world slump, and export industries still further damaged by falling world demand. In 1937, British exports were only two-thirds in value of their 1929 level.[179] After 1931, it is true, Britain, having been driven off the gold standard, was no longer weakened economically by policies designed to maintain an artificially high value of the pound, and tariffs came much more substantially to protect home markets, but the fall in world trade was such that British unemployment remained at an even higher level than in the 1920s until war brought it to an end.

Here, then, appeared to be assembled the conditions for class war and for the emergence of extremisms of right or left to challenge British parliamentary democracy. Instead, democratic government survived unscathed, and as far as the great majority of the population was concerned remain unquestioned, and indeed, British governments of a socially and politically conservative kind ruled in these years on the basis of genuine mass support.

It must be said in the first place that there were some economic reasons for the relative lack of unrest in Britain. High unemployment was limited to certain industries and certain areas, to the industries built up to meet pre-war export demands and to the areas in which those industries had been established: Scotland, Wales, and the north of England. Other parts of England where industries were developing to meet post-war demands for new products were prosperous throughout the inter-war years. In 1937, unemployment in Wales was twenty-four per cent; in the midlands of England it was six per cent. By 1937 the electrical wiring and construction industry was employing nearly three times as many workers as in 1927 and the motor and aircraft industry half as many again, while coal mining employed less than three quarters of the numbers of 1927. Again, not all those who were unemployed were condemned to lose hope of finding a job in any foreseeable future: in September 1929 of about one million unemployed only about 50,000 had been without work for a year or more. The slump made matters worse and after 1932 a permanent army of unemployed emerged which did not fall below 250,000 until the approach of war.[180]

Malnutrition and consequent ill-health were certainly widespread among the unemployed, but they were not left to starve. Most workers participated in a compulsory scheme of insurance against unemployment and when an individual exhausted the benefits to which he was entitled, payments continued to be made by the central government or local authorities though after examination of the needs of an applicant, a condition which, when strictly enforced as it was after 1931, led to considerable resentment. It remains surprising that the unemployed did not become a threatening political force. One attempt was made by the Communist Party to organize them into a revolutionary army in the National Unemployed Workers Movement. Attempts were made with occasional success in the early 1920s, to use the organized unemployed to intervene in wage disputes by seizing factories and forcing stoppages of work. Demonstrations were organized which produced occasional riots and, above all, a series of 'hunger marches' was arranged when unemployed men from Wales, Scotland or the north of England marched on London. These were led by the communist NUWM, but included non-communists and were usually peaceful in character. The actual membership of this communist organization did not rise above 40,000 or so.[181]

Whether or not the British left would turn revolutionary depended above all on the trade unions. Their membership stood at over eight millions in 1920, declining to about four and a half millions in 1933, and recovering again to over six millions in 1939. Most of these were members of unions affiliated to the Trades Union Congress. Here was a potentially revolutionary force which was not revolutionary in practice. A contributory factor was that the standards of living of those men at work were tending to rise.

REAL WAGE RATES $(1930=100)$[183]

1920	94·7	1932	106·1
1924	91·9	1937	105·2
1929	96·7	1938	107·0

This was because of an increase in output per man-hour and, most important, because of a fall in British import prices, notably food prices. Thus those in employment derived benefit at the expense of primary producing countries and at the expense of the old exporting industries, whose markets were weakened by the falling incomes of food producers. This was particularly true of the deepest years of the slump, 1929–32. However, during the post-war years of inflation when workers sought to keep their wages in line with prices and during the years in which government policy was seeking to reduce prices in order to return to the gold standard at the pre-war parity and employers were obliged to reduce money wages, strikes became frequent:

AVERAGE ANNUAL NUMBER OF WORKING DAYS LOST BY STRIKES
IN EACH YEAR (EXCLUDING THE GENERAL STRIKE).

1919–21	49,100,000
1921–27	38,800,000
1927–39	3,100,000

Immediately after the war the government feared that the trade unions might use their power for political purposes, to challenge capitalist democracy. In August 1920, indeed, the unions and the Labour Party set up a Council of Action, and hundreds of local councils were

123

created to prevent British intervention against the Soviet Union in the Russo-Polish war. In the same years the unions worked towards using threats of generalised strike-action to coerce the government and general public into forcing the owners of particular industries into concessions to their own employees. The first attempts, through the formation of the Triple Alliance of miners, railwaymen and transport workers, came to nothing when mutual misunderstandings led to the withdrawal of a promised strike of the allies of the miners in April 1921. The government, however, made preparations to meet a general strike by a dictatorship backed by military force, euphemistically described as a 'state of emergency'. The Emergency Powers Act of 1920 empowered the government to govern by decree in such a situation. The great clash came with the general strike of 1926 when Britain faced a situation which might have been, but was not, a prelude to civil war.

British coal miners were the vanguard of the workers' struggle. The industry depended for the maintenance of its pre-war prosperity on demand from abroad. After the effects of the French occupation of the Ruhr ended, it became clear that foreign competitors threatened British exports. The return to the gold standard meant that British export prices were raised in terms of foreign currencies. British prices must be reduced. Wages formed a high proportion of the costs of coal mining. In 1925, the coal owners demanded a reduction in wages and a lengthening of hours worked by miners. The miners prepared to resist and the Trades Union Congress promised, if necessary, to call a general strike in support. Much was at stake. The miners were the most highly organized of all workers, their feelings of solidarity unique, their discipline unequalled. If they could be compelled to accept reductions in wages it was hard to see how any other body of workers could resist. On the other hand, if the government were compelled by a general strike to intervene against the coal owners, it was hard to see any limits to the power of the unions. The government bought time to make its preparations for a struggle by giving a temporary subsidy to enable wage reductions to be postponed. In the next few months large stocks of coal and food were assembled by an emergency committee under the permanent head of the Home Office, Sir John Anderson. The country was split into divisions to be ruled by civil commissioners with wide powers to maintain law and order. Road transport was organized, and plans were drawn up for naval personnel to man the docks and for armed convoys for food deliveries.[184]

The government subsidy would end on 1 May 1926, and unless mine workers and mine owners reached agreement, no further subsidy would be given. Such agreement was impossible since the workers would not accept reductions in wages. The employers gave notice that existing contracts would end on 30 April, and on 1 May work ceased in the coal-fields. On that day the general council of the Trades Union Congress secured the consent of its constituent unions to conduct the dispute. At midnight 3–4 May, the strike began. On 3 May, the Prime Minister, Stanley Baldwin, told the House of Commons that the union leaders were 'going nearer proclaiming civil war than we have been for centuries past.'[185] But it takes two sides to make a civil war and neither the unions nor the government had any intention of doing anything of the kind. It is clear, indeed, that to the leaders of the TUC the threat of a general strike was a means of compelling negotiations, not something they wished to carry out. After the general council had received powers to call a strike it immediately wrote to the Prime Minister to offer negotiations. Discussions began and were broken off by the government itself on 3 May on the pretext that strike action had already begun with the (spontaneous) refusal of the printing workers of the *Daily Mail* to print an article attacking the unions.[186] The government had decided to face a strike and defeat it. It rightly calculated that the risks were negligible and that it was not facing a threat of revolution or even of serious outbreaks of violence. It is true that ministers differed about how the government should handle the unions, how far by a show of force, how far by conciliatory gestures, but this was a difference of tactics, not of objective, for all expected the unions to capitulate.

The union leaders were forced into a strike they did not want. Their desire was to negotiate, not to fight; to secure the best terms they could for the miners, not to set off a revolution, or overturn the constitution. On 3 May, J. H. Thomas, the railwaymen's leader who was on the TUC general council and a Labour member of parliament, spoke in the House of Commons in a somewhat emotional way: 'In a challenge to the Constitution, God help us unless the Government won.' During the strike, W. M. Citrine, who was acting general secretary of the TUC, noted in his diary his fears of what might happen as a result of displays of armed force by the government and the use of volunteers to replace men on strike.

The principal danger is the effect such displays may have on the morale of our men. When some of them see their jobs filled by scallywag volunteers they may get desperate and resort to forceful means. That means disorder; and that in turn means an excuse for police and military intervention.[187]

The strike leaders did their best to avoid violence: the TUC general council insisted that picketing should be peaceful, that is that force should not be used to prevent volunteers or non-union men from strike-breaking and it firmly refused to agree to suggestions that Workers' Defence Groups should be set up. The council wondered how workers on strike should pass their time and suggested the organization of sports and entertainments. Indeed, the strike, known then and since as the general strike to everyone except the TUC, was not general at all; at first only workers in transport, building, printing and in iron and steel were called out and further workers – in the metal using industries – were called out only on the day before the entire strike was abandoned. What is more, the strike organizers, so far from exploiting their position to the full, offered to arrange for the delivery of essential food supplies, and allowed the issue of permits to enable workers on strike to transport food – the government was quite able in any case, with the help of volunteer labour, to handle food supplies effectively enough, but the TUC policy here shows yet again the lack of determination of the strike leaders.[188]

The TUC general council sought to escape with all speed from the unwelcome strike. The government would not negotiate unless the strike were ended, the TUC could not end the strike, without deserting the mine workers, unless the government promised to coerce the mine owners into compromise, which the government would not do. The TUC took the only way out: it decided to desert the miners, on whose behalf the strike had originally been called. Lord Citrine's diary of the general strike (Citrine was made a knight in 1935 – which caused him to feel 'a strange exhilaration' – and a peer in 1946) shows how the general council came increasingly to resent the intransigence of the miners' leaders, and even came to regard the government as a less hostile body than the mine workers' unions – the government could be negotiated with, the miners could not. On 12 May, the strike was ended on the flimsy basis that the government, which made no promises, might accept a compromise solution of the coal dispute, worked out by Sir Herbert Samuel. This was, in fact, a complete surrender by the TUC; the miners remained on strike for nearly eight months longer, when their resistance at last ended.

No strike on this scale has been attempted in Britain since. Indeed, the union leaders became even less revolutionary and militant after the strike than they had been before it. In 1927, twenty major employers, led by Sir Alfred Mond, invited the co-operation of the TUC in discussing 'industrial reconstruction' and the so-called Mond-Turner conversations began with the approval of the union leaders. Why were union leaders moderate, so little inclined to challenge capitalist democracy? It is not enough to reply with general assertions of the existence of an inborn British love of compromise and discussion and hatred of violence and conflict. The reasons must be sought rather by asking why reform and peaceful change seemed to be practicable to the men who led the organized British working class. The answer is clearly historical, that a cautious policy had been successful in the past. The trade union movement in Britain in the later nineteenth and earlier twentieth century was the strongest in the world. Its right to speak for the working class and to seek advantages for its members were fully recognized and accepted before 1914; so far from governments seeking to curb its power, it had been recognized by the law and even put into a position of privilege. From 1824, trade unions had ceased to be illegal organizations, in 1875 they were safeguarded from criminal prosecution. When it appeared, in 1901, that the law courts would uphold civil prosecutions brought against unions to secure financial compensation for damage done in strikes, legislation followed in 1906 to protect the funds of unions and to reinforce their rights. Even in the years between 1901 and 1906 when the unions were vulnerable and the British economy depressed, most employers did not try to destroy the unions but preferred to try to work with them.[189] It is understandable, therefore, that union leaders should be moderate and ready to remain within the bounds of legality.

The ordinary members of trade unions continued, for the most part, to elect and to follow such leaders for similar reasons: the unions seemed to have secured for them tangible advantages and might be expected to continue to do so. However, this belief was clearly conditional on a rising standard of living for the working class in general and union members in particular. In the years 1900-10 rising prices of British food imports checked and even reversed the nineteenth century tendency towards increased real wages. At the same time, increasing suspicion is seen on the part of union members towards their leaders.[190] It was important, therefore, that, as we have seen, the living standards of men actually employed were rising in the years between the wars. For, in these years, a serious challenge to the leadership of the unions by moderate reformists developed under communist inspiration, in the so-called minority movement in the unions. This sought to secure control of existing trade unions for its nominees or to create new unions to weaken the established organizations. The latter policy probably did more harm than good to the communists, since tactics of splitting unions were too evidently designed to weaken the union movement as a whole. The former policy secured occasional successes, the most notable being the election of A. J. Cook who was not a communist, but who could be used to further the party line, as general secretary of the miners' union. This appointment may help to explain the futile obstinacy with which the miners' strike of 1926 was protracted. However, such victories were rare, for, as the industrial organizer of the British communists admitted in 1931, workers were more interested in improving their living conditions than in any struggle for power, and regarded the minority movement as an outside imposition.[191]

The communists failed equally to secure mass support in national politics. The membership of the party probably never rose as high as twenty thousand between the wars.[192] The record of communist parliamentary candidates still more clearly displayed this failure. In 1924, with eight candidates, one seat was secured, in 1929 and 1931 not one of twenty-five and twenty-six candidates secured a seat, in 1935 one of only two candidates. In 1929, all but four of twenty-five candidates forfeited their deposits (that is, failed to secure more than one eighth of the total votes cast in their constituencies) and in 1931 all but five of twenty-six candidates lost their deposits. The constituencies chosen by the communists were nearly always those in which they were most hopeful of success, where there was an overwhelming preponderance of working class voters. British workers did not feel that the state could be counted on to be hostile to their aspirations, and therefore did not wish to overthrow it. In the first place, governments before 1914, especially the Liberal government of 1905–15, had shown themselves ready to legislate in favour of the poor and of the working class. Secondly, the rise of the Labour Party offered the prospect of an eventual accession to power, by democratic and constitutional means of governments still more committed to social reform. Indeed, the Labour Party formed two governments in these years, in 1924 and 1929–31. Those governments were weak, and depended for their parliamentary majorities on Liberal tolerance, so the changes they produced were extremely limited, but they strengthened hopes for the future, which were fulfilled in the Labour victory of 1945. The evolution of British politics between the wars can best be summarised by setting out the results of parliamentary elections and by listing the governments that were established or confirmed in power by those elections. A table showing these facts is printed at the end of this chapter.

By 1922, the Labour Party had displaced the Liberal Party as the strongest anti-Conservative party, and by 1935 it was clear that the Labour Party was the only possible source of a non-Conservative government. In the general election of that year, 154 Labour members were returned, to oppose the so-called 'national' government – but only twenty-one opposition Liberals. The Labour Party gave an effective means of self-expression to those anxious to accelerate social change and made it plausible for the British working class to choose reformism rather than revolution.

Another important reason for the moderation of the British working class was that the Conservative Party, at least since Disraeli's time, had taken care to avoid coming to be regarded as a party representing only the sectional interest of the possessing classes. It claimed always to be pursuing the interests of the nation as a whole. A sufficient number of Conservatives sincerely believed this to make these claims acquire plausibility. Stanley Baldwin, leader of the Conservatives between 1923 and 1937, was peculiarly able to convey the impression that he was above sectional interest, and that he cared for Britain, and especially England, rather than for men of property. As Prime Minister during the general strike, Baldwin generated the belief, which was possibly a sound one, that the combative attitude of his government which forced the strike, was taken up against his better judgment and to his own regret. He specialized in emollient, assertively honest, apparently direct utterances. The effects were important. Baldwin contrived, sometimes only with difficulty, to prevent his party from appearing as one side in a class war. He succeeded in giving the impression that his governments did their best to grapple with social problems and that their complete failure to deal with unemployment was not the result of lack of concern for the welfare of the unemployed.[193]

The most striking demonstration of the feeling of unity thus engendered in British political life came in 1931. The Labour government headed by Ramsay MacDonald faced the European financial crisis when foreign countries began to lose confidence in the future value of the pound. As British currency was sold on the foreign exchange markets British reserves of foreign currency fell rapidly, and it became necessary, if devaluation were to be avoided, to raise a loan in the United States. It became clear that such a loan could not be raised unless the British government were to take sharp deflationary measures, in particular to cut government spending in order to reduce domestic demand and hold down British prices and thus to maintain the value of the pound sterling. American bankers believed that confidence in the value of the pound could not be secured in this way unless British public opinion and especially British bankers thought the proposed cuts sufficient. The Conservative opposition, no doubt relying on the views of British bankers, insisted that what the Labour government could agree to do was not enough and demanded a cut in the rate of payments to the unemployed. Over this issue, the Labour cabinet split into two; one section which included the Prime Minister and the Chancellor of the Exchequer, Snowden, was ready to accept this demand, the other group was not. The Labour government could not continue. The outcome was that MacDonald agreed to serve as Prime Minister of a 'national government' including those Labour members who would support him, together with Conservatives and Liberals, a government which would work to solve the financial crisis and which would produce a safe parliamentary majority for the reduction in spending alleged to be needed. Most Labour members of parliament refused to support a government pledged to reduce the incomes of the poorest section of the community and only four senior Labour ministers stayed with MacDonald. The remainder and the bulk of the parliamentary Labour Party went into opposition to the new government.[194]

This chain of events can be interpreted in two ways – as an act of self-sacrifice by MacDonald and his close associates who cut themselves off from their own party to create the widest possible support for economies they considered essential in the interest of the nation, or as a betrayal of the Labour Party, which was split and weakened by the desertion of men abandoning the working class. Whichever interpretation is adopted, the significance of the outcome for the present argument remains the same. The National government was formed in August 1931 and fought a general election in October. It secured a resounding vote of confidence in which its supporters secured 554 seats, mostly going to Conservatives, with only fifty-two seats going to the official Labour Party in opposition, and nine to others. This must be regarded as a sign of the approval of the mass of the electorate for the activities of the politicians thrown up by the British parliamentary system. It is clear, too, that many Labour supporters had voted for National government candidates – over thirty constituences in which Labour had had a majority of over 10,000 votes in 1929 were lost by the opposition Labour candidates.[195] It was a clear demonstration that many working class voters, in an emergency, put national unity before partisan politics.

Nor did those who took the view that MacDonald's actions were a betrayal of Labour turn to extremism or violence. The communists produced their usual miserable showing at the 1931 election when twenty-six candidates failed to secure a single seat. Nor did the remnant of the parliamentary Labour Party in opposition lose its faith in the régime: Baldwin's tribute in the House of Commons was justified, 'they have helped to keep the flag of Parliamentary government flying in the world . . . I know that they, as I do, stand for our Constitution and our free Parliament.'[196] This attitude was helped by two things. Hope for the future revived when the Labour Party, in the 1935 election, once again regained the parliamentary strength it had had from 1924–9 (with 154 seats). The second fact was the result of the National government's failure to fulfil its original purpose – to save the pound sterling. In September, Britain left the gold standard, and the pound fell by about one-third of its previous foreign exchange value. It was no longer necessary to enforce the deflationary curbs that the continued defence of an over-valued currency would have required. In 1934, for instance, the cuts in unemployment assistance rates made in 1931 were restored. The result was that Britain recovered from the great slump more rapidly and more fully than many comparable industrial countries and production increased while food prices were kept down by the fall in world prices. Unemployment rates, in contrast with both Germany and the United States, rose only slightly in 1932 over the level of 1931 and thereafter fell faster than in the United States. A boom in the building of houses developed, including building of houses by local authorities with state subsidies. In the 1930s over a million of the poorest classes were rehoused.[197] These tangible advances counter-balanced to some extent at least the bleak spectacle of unemployment on a scale unprecedented even in the 1920s.

From the extreme political right a threat to liberal parliamentary democracy appeared in the 1930s, under a leader at least as able as most of his continental counterparts and less unappetising. This threat, though disagreeable, remained far from success until the war finally destroyed the very slender prospects of the inauguration in Britain of a dictatorship under Sir Oswald Mosley after German or Italian models. At least part of the explanation for his failure lay in the fact that it was difficult in Britain to feel seriously alarmed by the Red Peril at home; the strength of the Communist Party of Great Britain was insufficient to provoke or justify violent right-wing reaction, and it was really impossible to treat the Labour Party as a force threatening subversion and ruin. There was nothing in British politics to make the middle class afraid. Certainly many of its members suffered directly from unemployment, or stagnating business or professional conditions, and many who did not suffer were distressed by the contemplation of the fate of others – though it must be said that the deflationary policies and the stability of prices between the wars helped that large section of the middle class with fixed or inflexible incomes. But the existence of obvious grievances and misfortunes did not necessarily induce the conviction that solutions could only be found within a completely new type of political order. The British constitution commanded, perhaps especially among those classes to whom a fascist movement might have been expected to appeal, a feeling of respect deriving partly from the antiquity of its origins, partly from memories of past successes that Britain had enjoyed under a system recognizably the ancestor of the twentieth century structure. At least, even if they did not inspire respect, these considerations caused the British political system to be taken for granted. The workings of British democratic machinery, moreover, produced something whose absence provided the most convincing grounds for criticism of some continental democracies: stable governments.

The British electoral system was based on the constituency, usually returning a single member to the House of Commons, in which the candidate was elected who secured most votes in a single ballot. This system worked against minority parties for it was possible for a party to secure the votes of large numbers of electors, which, if scattered over constituencies in each of which another party had more votes, would gain it no representation in the House of Commons. Thus, for instance, in a system of rigid proportional representation of the whole electorate the 74,824 communist votes in 1931 would have secured two seats for their twenty-six candidates (out of a total voting strength of about $21\frac{1}{2}$ millions electing to 615 seats) whereas no seat at all went to them. Thus the scattered voting strength of a minor party did not produce a corresponding influence in parliament and made it difficult for such a party to gain strength by appearing a serious political force, for it seemed pointless to vote for such a party at all. Again, against a minority party whose voting strength was evenly dispersed, the larger parties secured a number of seats out of proportion to their total voting strength. Thus where a system of precise proportional representation would have produced no single party with a parliamentary majority, the British system could do so. The general election of 1924 is a good illustration.[198]

	Total votes cast	MPs elected	Candidates	% of Total vote
Conservative	7,854,523	412	534	46·8
Liberal	2,931,380	40	340	17·8
Labour	5,489,087	151	514	33·3
Communist	55,346	1	8	0·3
Others	309,943	11	32	1·8
Electorate				
21,730,988	16,640,279	615	1,428	100·0

In this situation, strict proportional representation would not have produced a Conservative majority in the House of Commons; in fact, the Conservatives had a majority of about two hundred over all other parties. In this way governmental instability was checked and strong government could in some sense be achieved. Thus it did not seem essential to substitute some form of authoritarian rule for parliamentary democracy, because that democracy was limited and curtailed by the electoral structure.

Under these circumstances, Mosley's party, the British Union of Fascists, never became more than a sordid nuisance. Sir Oswald Mosley was a rich man, intelligent and highly ambitious. He became a Member of Parliament as a supporter of Lloyd George in 1918 but by 1924 had joined Labour and by 1926 was an increasingly prominent and brilliant member of the leadership of the party. In 1929 when Mosley was thirty-two he became a minister, though not a member of the cabinet, in the second Labour government with the mission to work with J. H. Thomas, a cabinet minister, to evolve a solution for unemployment. He became increasingly impatient with the incompetence of Thomas and set to work, with some assistance, on the draft of a scheme of his own. This scheme, which certainly represented in many ways the best and most advanced thinking of the day, was submitted to the Cabinet in January 1930 and rejected under the influence of the Treasury and the Chancellor of the Exchequer. In May 1930 Mosley resigned in disgust. His ideas, though sympathetically received, failed to secure the formal support of the parliamentary Labour Party or of the Labour Party Conference in October 1930. After this Mosley took the decisive step. Instead of using a very strong position within the Labour Party to convert it, he sought more direct means.

In February 1931, Mosley announced the formation of the New Party which produced twenty-four candidates at the general election in October, with complete failure. After this disaster, Mosley, who had already shown authoritarian leanings, abandoned orthodox democratic political methods, and after visits to Munich and Rome and a meeting with Mussolini, set himself the task of organizing a British fascist movement. There had come into existence in Britain in the 1920s some fascist groups of a fissiparous and not very effective kind. Mosley invited the members of these groups to join the British Union of Fascists which was launched in October 1932. The full panoply of fascism began to appear: black shirts, riding breeches, jack boots, parades and marches. Anti-Semitic, anti-socialist, anti-parliamentary propaganda was distributed on a large scale. As usual, it is difficult to say precisely where the money came from to finance fascist activities – certainly from Mosley himself and from industrialists and other sympathizers, possibly from Mussolini. By 1934 the BUF had over a hundred branches. In January 1934, a major national newspaper with a mass-circulation, the *Daily Mail*, came out in support of Mosley. Elements of the Conservative party began to show some sympathy. In June 1934, the Fascists held a great rally at Olympia in London. This was marked by the extreme violence used against interrupters, which caused dismay and probably began the decline in Mosley's support. Shortly afterwards the Röhm purge in Germany further discredited Nazism and increased distaste for a movement which openly copied Nazism. In July, Rothermere, the proprietor of the *Daily Mail*, ceased his support for Mosley, partly because of the increasingly anti-Jewish attitude of the BUF (though the *Daily Mail* remained sympathetic to Nazi Germany – an example of the way in which some Englishmen applied a double standard of morality in which foreign wickedness was treated more tolerantly than similar manifestations at home). However, the Fascists were taken seriously enough by some of the Labour party leaders, especially in the Socialist League, to make them ready to advocate a united front with the Communists, and to urge the need for a future Labour government to take dictatorial powers to meet a possible Fascist resistance. But the Socialist League did not secure the support of the majority of the Labour Party and in 1937 it was expelled from the Party.[199] After riots in the east end of London in October 1936, the government thought it necessary to propose legislation forbidding uniforms and limiting freedom of assembly and of marches and processions. Thereafter this measure, and an apparent weakening of financial backing, accelerated the decline of the BUF.

It is difficult to assess numerically the strength of the BUF, because it took no part in the general election of 1935 when Mosley urged his followers to abstain without any very impressive results. The only electoral successes the BUF could claim came in elections in 1937 to the London County Council when the Fascists, in three constituencies with a substantial Jewish population, secured from fourteen to twenty-three per cent of the total vote, without coming near to winning a seat. In municipal elections later in the year, the Fascists again showed signs of strength in the same restricted areas of London, but elsewhere in London and still more in provincial towns their showing was contemptible.[200]

It is fair to say, then, that British politics between the wars took the form of a peaceful and largely rational contest between a Conservative party ready to compromise and a moderately-inclined Labour party, with the Liberals as a declining third force between them. The Conservatives, largely financed by industry, represented the upper class of landowners and big business men, and the mass of the middle class, concerned for the defence of the existing social structure and the existing distribution of income and property, and a section of the working class which was ready to accept its place within the social and economic hierarchy. The Labour Party, largely financed by the trade unions, represented a progressive section of the middle class, especially among salaried workers such as school teachers, and the broad mass of the working class. The Liberals, facing increasing financial stringency, represented those discontented with the choice between two rich large parties whose ultimate basis was a sectional one, others who were Liberal from traditions and habits acquired over other issues which had become out of date such as the defence of non-conformity against the Anglican Church, or were becoming out of date such as the defence of free trade against protectionism. Despite extremist challenges and despite the feeling of some Conservatives that their party was unduly ready to surrender and compromise and the feeling of some Labour men that their party should express a more militant socialism, both great parties remained content to work within the established constitutional framework and to act with tolerable restraint towards their opponents. The result was that Britain in 1939, in spite of the difficulties and hardships of the previous twenty years, was a society more united in outlook and politically less turbulent than the Britain of 1914. Between 1919 and 1939 no single life was lost in Britain in political or industrial conflict. British history in these years is in marked contrast to the history of most countries on the continent of Europe.

PARTIES, ELECTIONS AND GOVERNMENTS IN BRITAIN 1918–40.

Election Date	Party	Seats in Commons	Government
Dec. 1918			
	Coalition Conservative	332	Coalition under D.
	Coalition Liberal	136	Lloyd George until
	Coalition Labour	13	Oct. 1922
	Conservative	27	
	Liberal	27	
	Labour	59	
	Irish Representatives	105	
	Others	8	
Nov. 1922			
	Conservative	344	Conservative under A.
	National Liberal	53	Bonar Law until May
	Liberal	62	1923, then under

Election Date	Party	Seats in Commons	Government
	Labour	142	Stanley Baldwin until
	Others	14	Jan. 1924.
Dec. 1923			
	Conservative	258	Labour under Ramsay
	Liberal	159	MacDonald until Nov.
	Labour	191	1924.
	Others	7	
Oct. 1924			
	Conservative	412	Conservative under
	Liberal	40	Stanley Baldwin until
	Labour	151	June 1929
	Others	2	
May 1929			
	Conservative	260	Labour under Ramsay
	Liberal	59	MacDonald until Aug.
	Labour	288	1931
	Others	8	
Oct. 1931			
	Conservative	473	'National' government
	National Labour	13	under Ramsay Mac-
	Liberal National	35	Donald until June 1935
	Liberal	33	
	Labour	52	
	Others	9	
Nov. 1935			
	Conservative	421	'National' government
	Liberal	21	(almost entirely Con-
	Labour	154	servative) under Stanley
	Others	19	Baldwin until May 1937, then under Neville Chamberlain until May 1940

Sources: D. E. Butler and J. Freeman: *British Political Facts 1900–1960*. London 1963, pp. 9–26, 122–4. F. W. S. Craig: *British Parliamentary Election Statistics 1918–1968*. Glasgow, 1968, pp. 1–11. Most of the Irish members elected in December 1918 did not take their seats. Irish membership ended with the departure of Ireland (except the six northern counties) from the United Kingdom. Liberal Nationals, in practice, can be regarded as Conservatives after 1935.

8

Italy 1919-40

In Italy the outcome of the struggle for liberal democracy that dominates the history of western Europe between the wars was quickly decided. Indeed the name of the Italian victors came to be applied to most of the west European opponents of liberalism and democracy whose backing came from groups of society other than the industrial proletariat: fascists. It is important to determine what fascism meant in Italy, to make it easier to see how far Italian fascism was typical of violent right-wing movements between the wars on the one hand, or a specifically Italian phenomenon on the other.

Did fascism represent any ideas? Governments necessarily influence events by taking or avoiding action and a set of ideas may be ascribed to them by examining this influence. The danger of this type of argument is that what governments do may simply result from the pressure on them of outside events or situations. So it is with the fascist government in Italy; it was controlled by events much more than controlling them. However, it chose two dominant lines of action: one of threats of violence abroad, the other of the defence of economic inequalities at home. How far were these policies the result of theoretical conviction or of intellectual analyses of Italian interests? It is easiest to answer this question in terms of what Mussolini thought; for fascists accepted that fascist rule meant verbal dictatorship by Mussolini. What emerges clearly is that Mussolini may have had certain nebulous convictions in foreign affairs but that he had no ideas of any kind on the internal ordering of Italy except that he should play an important part in it.

Mussolini came to prominence as an advocate of Italian intervention in the war; there is some evidence to suggest that his advocacy was strengthened by French money. There were two distinct types of interventionist: those who believed that Italy should take her place in a

137

crusade for the liberation of nationalities, the assertion of international justice and the creation of a new order of peaceful co-operation, and those who saw in the war an opportunity for the expansion of Italian power and greatness. Mussolini, after some hesitation, embraced the second position with vehemence, at a time when his later attitudes to internal issues were not yet formed. From verbal advocacy, at least, of Italian grandeur, expressed as a readiness for violence, Mussolini never departed. Though, it is true, such attitudes were calculated to win him popular support among those Italians who were disappointed by the results of the war and dismayed by the painful nature of the aftermath, it is difficult to deny that Mussolini in some way believed in them. If so, they represented the sum total of Mussolini's 'thought', for it is clear that he had no settled convictions at all on social and economic questions or even on political issues and that the positions fascism took up were imposed on Mussolini and on his movement by expediency.[201]

Mussolini began his political life as a socialist, and when he broke with the bulk of Italian socialists because of his advocacy of intervention in the war, he remained a socialist of a notably violent kind. In March 1919, when the *Fasci di Combattimento* emerged as a national organization at a meeting in Milan, most of those present were left-wing in outlook and the programme issued in June was decidedly revolutionary. In the elections of November 1919, Mussolini unsuccessfully attempted in Milan to produce a common list of candidates with other left-wing parties.[202] These socialist posturings were a miserable failure and at the elections not one fascist was elected and Mussolini himself met a sharp rebuff. The fascists could not hope to rival the appeal of the socialist parties (and of the new catholic *Partito Popolare*) to the working classes; working class aspirations had sufficient outlets already. Only in 1920 did Mussolini find his true rôle: to represent the fears of anti-socialists rather than the hopes of the left. In short, Mussolini represented nothing in himself; he was an ambitious demagogue looking for a political force to carry him upwards and if the working classes would not do it then the enemies of the working class would serve as well. Mussolini said in September 1920, 'I am reactionary and revolutionary according to circumstances'.[203] In so far then as Mussolini may speak for Italian fascism, and it is hard to deny his right to do so, it had as its basis no abstract ideas of any kind except perhaps a general penchant for nationalistic display abroad.

After Mussolini had secured control of Italy there appeared, of course, exponents of fascist 'thought'. Their contribution to political and social theory was trivial: their philosophical utterances were clearly derivative from various lines of nineteenth century thinking – notably from Hegel and his followers and from misapplications of Darwinian biology on the political side together with certain borrowings from catholic notions in social and economic matters.[204] Luckily, we need not concern ourselves with fascism as a philosophy for the success of fascism in Italy was not the result of the existence of a body of fascist 'thought', rather fascist 'thought' was a consequence of fascist victory; and if any such thing as fascist thinking can be supposed to have existed before Mussolini's advent to power there is no evidence to suggest that Mussolini had much acquaintance with it.

How did fascism, then, and Mussolini, who had no insights or ideas or programmes to offer, secure control of Italy? The answer must be that Mussolini and his movement gave expression to powerful social and economic forces. These forces came from those sections of Italian society which were afraid of social revolution, and even, paradoxically enough, afraid of violence and civil war. (Paradoxically, because the violence from which fascism saved Italy was generated by itself and the civil war it averted was a conflict which it alone could have caused itself.) Fascism drew its strength from fear of social change. Such a fear might have brought strength to a conservatism of a traditional kind, based on the dominance of landed proprietors in alliance with industrialists and bankers. There were difficulties in the way of such an outcome. Under a democratic régime, such a conservatism must secure votes; it appeared in the years 1919–22 that a majority against drastic social change could not be counted on. Democracy was new in Italy; until 1913 the franchise was restricted to a handful of the population and those with privileged positions to defend had not had time to acquire the skill and the confidence to do so with a mass electorate before the economic blows of the post-war period struck Italy. (At the elections of 1909, 8·3 per cent of the whole population had the right to vote; in 1913, 23·2 per cent.[205]) Whether a democratic framework survived or whether democracy collapsed, the privileged class would need a mass force to hold back the threat of red control. In either event a mass-support for reaction was needed; the fascists provided it, or rather, gave it expression. It would be an over-simplification to think of rich reactionaries buying fascists to give themselves numerically substantial backing. It is more accurate to say that the fascists unearthed a mass-support for reaction which they were able to exploit in a way that more traditional reactionaries could not: this is the great contribution of Italian fascism to political history – the stumbling on the discovery that anti-socialism could have mass-appeal, that in the absence of a flexible and subtle conservative party of the British kind and in the presence of an active and alarming socialist party there was available to be exploited a section of society hitherto neglected by political manipulators.

The British propertied classes had evolved, in the nineteenth century and before, into part of a governing class and, as democracy approached, so they acquired the appropriate techniques of conciliation, concession and persuasion which enabled them to defend established positions without the need to connive at the more direct and brutal methods of fascism. The directing classes of nineteenth century Italy did not possess this experience; they accepted, therefore, the support enrolled for them by political leaders of a new kind. These new political leaders were not usually drawn from the traditional upper classes and still less from the intellectually or professionally eminent. Mussolini himself was a typical enough specimen – a man of humble origins and of superficial education. His fluency, self-confidence and half-baked profundities reflected the prejudices and served to increase the sense of importance and individuality of many Italians who felt themselves to be something better than workers or labourers but who were uneasily aware of their lowly place in the conventional social hierarchy. Such sections of society, suspicious of the very rich, of the aristocracy of land and capital, were won to the support of the social status quo, in the absence of effective political leadership from its principal beneficiaries, by the new methods of fascism. Indeed, the more ambitious and assertive of such men could find new satisfaction in fascism; a black shirt brought prestige and power and the chance to transcend the tedious limitations of daily life.

On the other hand, the extent to which fascism secured mass-backing before the so-called march on Rome must not be exaggerated. Fascism owed its success not to overwhelmingly large voting support (which was much less than that acquired by the German Nazis in 1932) or from the physical force of a revolutionary shock army (the fascist squads were certainly militarily more insignificant than the German S.A. in 1932) but to its winning sufficient votes and assembling sufficient physical strength to make itself formidable to governments and politicians who were frightened enough of the left to wish to avoid fighting a new enemy on the right or even to seek to make that new enemy into an ally.

Fascism came to power in Italy because the post-war inflation stimulated an active and successful working-class agitation for higher wages in the towns and in the countryside and because over-population in the countryside caused a rural class war to develop. Support for fascism came from those who were afraid of red revolution, bolshevism, socialism and the classless society. That support was powerful enough to overcome the rather mild resistance of the liberal state whose representatives were themselves much more afraid of socialist revolution than of fascist subversion.

During the war the cost of living in Italy had risen faster than wages and working-class standards were depressed. In 1918 real wages were about one-third less than they had been in 1913. In 1919 and 1920 workers sought to recover these losses and were successful. In 1914 there had been 781 strikes involving about 170,000 workers and the figures had been lower during the war; in 1919 there were over 1,800 strikes with about 1,500,000 workers and more than 2,000 strikes in 1920 with nearly 2,000,000 taking part (these figures exclude national strikes). There was considerable violence involved: between April 1919 and September 1920 more than 320 workers were killed at the cost of a very small number of police casualties. In September 1920, the pressure from organized labour reached its peak in the 'occupation of the factories'. This began with a scheme by the FIOM, the federation of metallurgical workers, for a stay-in strike. When the employers retaliated with attempted lock-outs, the unions ordered the seizure of the factories. First in Milan and then elsewhere factories fell into the hands of workers' committees who tried to keep them in production, and who continued in control for the first half of September 1920.[206]

In the countryside land-hunger led to seizure of land belonging to great proprietors by landless peasants. The movement began in July 1919 in the Lazio around Rome, with the invasion of uncultivated land, but from August it became more general and in places intensively cultivated land was occupied. In 1920 the government recognized the resulting land reforms, while trying to insist on compensation for the former owners and on improvements in cultivation. Still more serious was the rural class war caused by over-population. This showed itself in some of the richest regions of Italian agriculture: in Emilia and the Po valley. Here cultivation was intensive and a large force of labourers was needed. But there were more men available than were required, except at the busiest times of harvest. To most labourers work was offered for only about half the year. Two consequences could follow: that wages would be held down to near starvation levels and that some of the workers would starve or emigrate or that work would be equitably distributed among the whole labour force and that collective bargaining would keep wages up to a tolerable level throughout the year. The latter outcome required organization among labourers and organization of a rigid and even dictatorial kind. The interests of the labourers could be defended only if all workers were compelled to obey the labour organizations and all proprietors compelled to hire their labourers through those organizations. Once this unity was achieved the labour organizations could dominate the whole economic life of their districts; some chambers of labour (*Camere del Lavoro*) fixed prices as well as wages and conditions of work and distributed farm produce through the co-operatives they controlled. This economic control was supplemented by political dominance: nearly all the communes of Emilia were in socialist hands. Small proprietors and tenant farmers as well as, and indeed more than, large landowners saw their property threatened, their profits curtailed and their status reduced by the organised labourers.[207]

These advances by the urban and rural proletariat did not form part of a great scheme evolved by socialists aiming at the destruction of private ownership, the extinction of capitalism, and the bolshevisation of Italy. On the contrary, they were the work, usually, of men concerned for immediate reforms within the existing social structure rather than its immediate overthrow, of practical leaders dealing with specific local situations. The alarming attitudes and utterances of the politicians of the official Italian Socialist Party, however, suggested that red revolution was imminent; these men imitated Lenin in their language, though they were quite incapable of imitating Lenin in deeds and had no notion of how an Italian revolution might come. This revolutionary attitude was surprising, given the considerable success of reformist activity immediately after the war. One explanation is possibly the split in the Socialist Party caused by Italian intervention in the war. In Britain, France and Germany, the war had induced a sense of national unity and so tended to increase the moderation of the left; though less markedly as the war went on; in Italy, most of the working class regarded the war as something that was none of their concern which had been imposed on them by the machinations of domestic pressure groups rather than by attacks from aggressive foreigners. Whatever the reasons, Italian socialists, with the exception of a minority led by Treves, Turati and Modigliani, struck attitudes of revolutionary intransigence and propounded the imminence of the dictatorship of the proletariat.

The success of the working class in pushing up wages in face of the rising cost of living aroused further resentment among the middle class. The years 1919 and 1920 saw a redistribution of income, enforced by strikes, away from those dependent on relatively fixed incomes towards wage earners. By 1921, the cost of living was rather over four times the figure of 1913 while the salaries, for instance, of state employees in the higher grades were only about 2½ times their level of 1913.[208] Many middle-class sufferers looked to the state to redress the balance. Further irritation, especially among the middle classes, from whom had come the bulk of wartime officers, was created by socialist opposition to the war. Socialist propaganda was held to have caused the great defeat at Caporetto in 1917, and after the war the open hostility to militarism and contempt for the armed forces of the Crown shown by socialists provoked dislike and resentment both from serving officers and ex-officers. This sentiment contributed to the failure of the army and police forces to resist fascist violence.

The governments that presided uneasily over the dissolution of the Italian state after the war were formed under the following Presidents of the Council:

Orlando to June 1919	
Nitti	June 1919 – June 1920
Giolitti	June 1920 – June 1921
Bonomi	July 1921 – February 1922
Facta	February 1922 – October 1922

The instability of ministries was itself a cause of the increasing discredit of parliamentary government and of the loss of confidence in its future felt by many of its exponents. Orlando and Nitti found themselves trapped between President Wilson and domestic nationalism. Neither was able to persuade Wilson to accept Italian demands for the full execution of the Treaty of London of 1915 by which Italy had entered the war and which promised Istria and a substantial proportion of Dalmatia to Italy, or that Italy should have Fiume. Britain and France failed to support Italian claims and Italian nationalists (including the fascists) denounced the consequent 'mutilation of victory'. The power of the state was further brought into question in September 1919 when a gang of nationalists, headed by the poet d'Annunzio, seized Fiume with the connivance of the Italian forces of occupation there. Nitti's government, because of the unreliability of the armed forces, was unable to dislodge d'Annunzio. In November 1919, general elections for the chamber of deputies took place, in an attempt to strengthen the hand of the government. In fact, there resulted a chamber whose composition made governmental instability certain.

The elections brought to an end the long years of 'liberal' dominance in Italy. The liberals were not a single party, but a collection of groups, all of which accepted representative government and constitutional monarchy as the political framework within which a directing oligarchy could rule. Among these groups there was sufficient in common to enable mutual compromises on which majorities could be based. Now, the elections brought national mass-parties, with clearly defined programmes, to a position of dominance in the Chamber: 156 socialists were returned and a hundred deputies from a new party – the *Partito Popolare Italiano* (PPI). The PPI represented what might have been thought to be a strengthening of the Italian state, for its basis was christian, that is, in Italian conditions, Catholic. It meant the acceptance by Catholic voters of the existence of the Italian state, a movement towards the end of the long conflict between Church and State. But to old-fashioned liberals, like Giolitti, it seemed a dangerous phenomenon. It stood on a national basis rather than for local interests and it claimed to be a party in the modern sense – monolithic and obedient to a central direction. It implied a threat to the old system, of which Giolitti had been a masterly practitioner, of politics as the art of compromise between individuals or groups and the end of parliamentary flexibility. Clearly such fears were misplaced, for the PPI was, in fact, far from homogeneous or united. It included men who were genuinely anxious for social change, who were concerned for the rights of labour and for the development of agrarian co-operatives, but also included men who believed in a mystical transcendence of class conflict, men whose notions in practice were reactionary. It is true that in the short run its existence made the formation of a durable parliamentary majority nearly impossible – for it was difficult for liberals to co-operate with it, given its insistence on its programme and especially difficult for liberals who shared Giolitti's suspicion of any sort of clerical interference in politics – to Giolitti, indeed, the political secretary of the PPI, Don Sturzo, a priest, probably represented the biggest challenge to the liberal state rather than the socialists and certainly much more than Mussolini.

Giolitti's ministry, formed in June 1920, was the turning point in the rise of fascism, for it was during his government that fascism developed from a feeble band of loquacious agitators into a serious threat to the Italian state. Giolitti sought pacification, the harmonizing of discords, the solution of the most acute divisions in Italian public life. He sought the triumph of an enlightened, socially progressive conservatism, which would bring within the bounds of the constitution the major social forces of Italy. Conciliation abroad and at home would restore peace to Italy and reaffirm the liberal state. In a celebrated speech, delivered at Dronero in October 1919, Giolitti demanded the restoration of parliamentary authority, challenged by the method of Italy's entry into the war and by the way in which the war was run, and the taxation of the rich – especially of war profits – through a progressive income tax and death duties together with an immediate capital levy. At the same time he announced that the privileged classes could no longer be the sole rulers of mankind.[209] In some respects Giolitti's ministry was highly successful. In June 1920 a mutiny of troops at Ancona against their despatch to Albania was followed by the decision to evacuate Albania and to recognize its independence. In November, the frontiers between Italy and Yugoslavia were settled at last by the Treaty of Rapallo, directly negotiated between the two countries, which left to Italy the whole of Istria, while leaving Dalmatia to Yugoslavia, with the exception of Zara. Fiume became a free city. The treaty was followed by the elimination of d'Annunzio from Fiume – a success achieved because of the growing unpopularity of d'Annunzio there. Thus Giolitti solved the major foreign problems of Italy, restored good relations with the war-time Allies and established a basis for the development of Italian influence in south-east Europe.[210]

Giolitti's greatest success was his handling of the occupation of the factories. In September 1920, 160 factories in Milan were occupied by the workers and this example was imitated in Turin and then elsewhere in Italy. Giolitti firmly refused to employ armed force against the workers, and instead sought to conciliate them by offering promises of legislation to secure some measure of workers' participation in the management of industry in return for the evacuation of the factories. When the workers in control of the factories discovered that it was impossible for them effectively to manage their production, they accepted this bargain and normal work began again in October. Giolitti had done nothing less than demonstrate that the bolshevik threat was mythical, that proletarian revolution in Italy was only the empty phrase of socialists bemused by Marx and Lenin. If the workers were treated with consideration they would not try to seize power or drown Italy in torrents of bourgeois blood; Giolitti explained in October that the occupation of the factories was simply the result of the underpayment of Italian workers.[211] Unfortunately, Giolitti's triumph was not recognized for what it was: instead, frightened industrialists blamed the government for refusing to intervene and for compelling them to make concessions and the disgruntled middle class felt that the weakness of the liberal state had permitted the socialists to secure yet another victory. Thus, instead of persuading the Italian propertied classes to follow a path of enlighten-

145

ment and conciliation, Giolitti's caution and good sense weakened progressive conservatism and provided more material for violent reaction to exploit.

At this stage, fascists, and Mussolini, found their true rôle: the exploitation of the fears of property owners in town and country and the alarm of the middle classes at their declining status compared with organized labour. Only when this force was enrolled and added to the existing vague nationalism and that nebulous search for something new, some sort of renovation and even (ironically enough) of purification of Italian life, which gave a faint and elusive tinge of idealism to the movement, did fascism become a serious political factor. The crucial moment was after the occupation of the factories – which Mussolini had approved – in the period in which the most dramatic event was the outbreak of violence in Bologna on 21 November 1920.

The events in and around Bologna towards the end of 1920 were inquired into by a parliamentary commission set up after assaults on two socialist deputies had taken place there. The reports of the commission provided evidence of the nature and origins of fascism and of the attitude of non-fascists towards the violence generated by fascism. They are conveniently printed by G. Perticone in an appendix to his *La Politica Italiana dal Primo al Secondo Dopoguerra* and the passages following are taken from these reports. The first report comes from the non-socialist members of the commission of inquiry.

Trouble broke out in Bologna on 21 November 1920 when the newly elected town council was installed. It contained forty-eight socialists and twelve opponents. The local fascists resented the socialists' display of red flags and both fascists and socialists thought that they must display their strength to maintain their prestige in the town. A fascist poster urged women and children to keep off the streets on the 21st. When the new *sindaco* appeared on the balcony outside the council chamber, shooting and bomb throwing followed in the square below, which was crowded with socialists and fascists. In the council chamber itself shooting took place in which one of the anti-socialist councillors was killed. The result was to bring to a head the hatred of socialism which had already been expressed in fights between 'patriots' and socialists, attacks on news stands selling socialist propaganda and attacks on socialist municipalities in the area, chambers of labour and trade union headquarters. The report pointed to the events of 21 November as the turning point in the growth of fascism in and around Bologna. Before then the *Fasci* of Bologna had had no great influence and less than a hundred members; now they had some thousands. They were recruited largely from young people and ex-service men (indeed, they claimed to be a romantic movement of youth). Fascism would not be important without the sympathy of great numbers of the citizens of Bologna.

The report sought to explain the origins of support for fascism. It pointed to the activities of the socialist administrators of Bologna and its province. They had done much good and struggled manfully for the benefit of consumers. In doing so they had harmed landlords by a system of special taxation and by hostile propaganda, they had injured shopkeepers through the increasing activity of consumers' co-operatives, and attacked farmers through the socialist leagues. Their actions had involved growing violence and challenged public authority and individual liberty. (In 1920, the province of Bologna was involved in a bitter conflict over the hiring of agricultural labourers. There were refusals to work and boycotts until the employers surrendered, after several months of struggle and protracted strikes, and accepted collective labour contracts in October 1920.) The directly injured classes provided the strongest supporters of the reaction. But they had been joined by many intellectuals, disturbed by socialist methods, by people offended by the anti-patriotic attitude of socialists and by some workers in conflict with the red unions as well as by more disreputable elements. It would be wrong to regard the fascists as hired thugs. Fascists insisted that they were not hostile to the working class and that they had not begun violence. The report added, however, that they did seem to have the character of violent defenders of the interests of the bourgeoisie. The government, the report continued, had in the past shown weakness towards the socialists, now governmental activity was not firm enough towards the fascists. Public forces, harassed for too long by extremist insults and violence had come, through a natural sentiment, to view with benevolence the fascist fighters against socialism. Instead, the public powers should be impartial and respect for the laws should be restored.

A striking fact about this report is the degree of sympathy shown by its authors for fascism. Though their analysis of the origin of the movement is convincing enough and though its dangerously violent nature is recognized, yet fascism is treated as a natural outcome of socialistic excesses rather than as a peril to the state. 'Impartiality' is recommended as between fascists and socialists, as if they were equally to blame for violence, whereas, by the beginning of 1921, fascists were clearly conducting a deliberate and aggressive campaign of organized brutality, with their victims – the socialists, and sometimes other left-wing groups, including *Popolari* – defending themselves unavailingly.

147

A socialist deputy took a rather different view in a minority report: to him the socialist preponderance in Bologna was the result of perfectly legal political activity. Fascist violence was a quite different thing from the methods of socialism. That violence could easily have been prevented if the authorities had seriously tried to do so. But it was not to be expected that the government would seek to curb fascism since the government was itself simply a class manifestation, an instrument of struggle against the proletariat. Happily, this recognition of fascism as a manifestation of class struggle enabled the reporter to see that it was doomed to fail, for the great struggle of the classes could only end with the defeat of the bourgeoisie. This utterance was characteristic enough of the majority view of Italian socialist politicians to whom the class struggle would somehow or other bring everything right in the end, and the predestined course of history inexorably roll forward, without, apparently, needing much assistance from its eventual beneficiaries.[212]

The years 1921 and 1922 saw the extension and development of fascist bullying, burning, beating, forcible expulsion of socialist local administrations, and murdering throughout central and northern Italy. At the end of 1920, there were 88 *Fasci*, with 20,615 members, at the end of 1921 there were 834 with 249,036. From 1 January to 14 May 1921 alone there were 207 killed and 819 wounded in fascist attacks.[213] The legal authorities failed to suppress this one-sided civil war, indeed, appeared to tolerate and even to encourage it. In October 1922, the fascists threatened to direct their civil war against the state unless the state was handed over to them: meekly the king appointed Mussolini prime minister. The most remarkable fact of these years is the extraordinary passivity of those who controlled the liberal state in front of organized subversion. The central question to ask about this passivity is this: was it voluntary or unavoidable, was it that the liberals and democrats could not suppress fascism or that they would not? What might have been expected to happen was firm action to repress violence, of the sort employed at Sarzana on 21 July 1921. There 500 fascists descended on the town to liberate some imprisoned comrades. They were dispersed and put to flight by eleven *carabinieri*.[214] In general no such incidents were seen. On the contrary, while the forces of the state acted with rigour against any socialist counter-attacks they gave the fascists a free hand. Indeed, on several occasions, the forces of 'order' themselves took part in fascist attacks, the fascists were able to use lorries belonging to the army or the *carabinieri* and arms were widely provided for fascists by police and military units.[215]

There is evidence to suggest that liberal governments would have found it difficult to suppress the fascists, even if they had wished to do so. As early as September 1920 the attitude of the army was shown by a circular sent to commanders by the general staff. This stated that the *Fasci* could now be regarded as forces capable of opposing 'anti-national and subversive elements' and that it would be useful for the military to keep contact with them. In the spring of 1921 the Inspector General of the PS was entrusted by the ministry of the interior with an inquiry into fascism in Tuscany and Emilia. He reported that forces of order regarded the fascists as engaging their own enemies. No prefect denied to him that attempts at the impartial repression of violence found an obstacle in the spirit of mind of functionaries who believed fascist activities to be a reaction against subversion. In September 1921, Bonomi himself, the Prime Minister, pointed to the impotence of the government faced with the fascist sympathies of the police and *carabinieri*, of the army and of the judiciary. In August 1922, the prefect of Milan told the ministry of the interior that the military authorities could not be counted on against the fascists in a crisis. There is evidence to suggest that governments did sometimes seek to curb fascist violence. In October 1920, the army circular mentioned above was modified by a circular sent out by General Badoglio at the request of Bonomi, then minister for war, in which the duty of the army to keep out of party strife was stressed. In April 1921, several prefects received a circular from Giolitti, the prime minister, who complained that the public forces had failed in several provinces in their duty of repressing violence, and demanded that the prefect should report to him the names of officials who should be moved. In December 1921, another circular was sent to the prefects condemning the indulgence of local authorities towards the carrying of arms, and ordering the breaking up of armed organizations and the prosecution of their members.[216] However, Bonomi was the last prime minister even to attempt to resist fascism. Count Sforza recorded that Bonomi contemplated a decree dissolving fascist squads, and, if need be, making the entire party illegal, but he found lacking 'certain necessary support', that is, some parts of his coalition government objected to a direct clash with the fascists. With the arrival of the Facta government, fascists accused of crimes were simply released by local authorities, or if this was not done were put into 'provisional liberty' on orders from Rome.[217]

The crucial period in the evolution of the attitude of Italian liberals towards fascism was that of Giolitti's ministry in 1920–1. If fascism were to be resisted, that was the time when it could best be done – when the movement began to be powerful – and if such resistance were to find a leader, Giolitti was the obvious choice. He was by far the most distinguished and experienced liberal statesman – his ministry of 1920 was his fifth – he had been the most successful exponent of the art of constructing governmental majorities and he, if anyone, might be expected to be attached to liberal constitutionalism. He did not provide anti-fascist leadership or attempt to use every resource at the disposal of the government to organize the destruction of fascism. Instead, he applied to fascism his general doctrine of absorption: that all political forces could eventually be fitted into the liberal constitution and that the process of encouraging this acceptance of the state was to be advanced by conciliation and flexibility and not by forceful resistance. In the end, he is reported to have argued, the fascists, and the republicans and socialists, would come to work under the 'common rule of the liberal state, which tolerates everything and survives everything'.[218]

No doubt Giolitti's belief that the fascists should not be treated as simple enemies was strengthened by his fear of the mass-parties – the socialists and the *Popolari* – whose parliamentary strength made governmental majorities difficult to construct, since socialists refused collaboration and the *Popolari* drove hard bargains. This, together with his faith in the normalization of fascism, explains his extraordinary conduct in the general election decided on by himself, in the spring of 1921. By this time the fascism of blood-thirsty reaction was fully evident, yet the fascists were included in Giolitti's national bloc which fought the electoral campaign against socialists and *Popolari*; a clear demonstration that Giolitti and those who felt like him (let alone 'liberals' further to the right) were not likely to launch an anti-fascist combat. The results were disastrous: a slight weakening of the socialists and strengthening of the *Popolari* was accompanied by the election of thirty-five fascist deputies. The chamber of deputies now contained about a hundred right-wing members (including the fascists) about two hundred 'democrats' in various groups, including the reformist socialists, over a hundred *Popolari* and about a hundred and thirty socialists and communists.

The pattern of the months that followed was that most liberals continued to think, like Giolitti, that fascism was manageable – a coalition and a suitable distribution of offices which satisfied the leaders would bring an end to violence much more easily than by risking a sanguinary clash with the fascist squads. (This belief was based on a fundamental underestimate of the degree of power and influence that would satisfy the local fascists.) Those liberals who were ready to resist fascism were too few to be able to make a government without an impossible junction with *Poplari* and socialists. Since, however, the liberals who were ready to compromise with fascism could not govern without some anti-fascist support, the result was governments that could neither bargain effectively with fascism nor combine to suppress it. The election results caused the fascists to conclude that violence was more effective than winning votes as the means to power and its tempo was increased, while, at the same time, the fascists encouraged liberal illusions by talk of governmental coalitions and parliamentary co-operation. This uneasy situation was brought to an end when the fascists – with the 'march on Rome' – faced the government with a direct choice between fighting or surrender. It surrendered, and the king summoned Mussolini to become president of the council of ministers.

Three events deserve attention: firstly the pact of pacification and its failure, secondly the increasing readiness of some *Popolari* and socialists to join in an anti-fascist government, thirdly the conduct of the ministry and of the king at the time of the march on Rome. The pact of pacification was a bargain made between fascist parliamentarians and socialists by which violence should cease. It was an attempt by Mussolini to make himself respectable enough for a coalition government. Its rejection by provincial fascists showed that Mussolini's 'leadership' meant only the provision of an oratorical screen for fascism and that he could not overrule the wishes of local fascist groups. Mussolini himself could not pacify fascism without arranging to satisfy the ambitions of the leaders of violence. Thus a political settlement with fascism would not work unless it amounted to a surrender of governmental power and patronage. There was no middle way between capitulation to fascism and firm resistance.

On 13 July 1922, the fascists of Cremona, led by Farinacci, devastated the houses of two deputies. On 19 July the Facta government was overthrown on a vote demanding energetic actions to maintain law and order. In the evening the directorate of the PPI declared that a government must be formed to maintain the law and internal peace. On 2 June, a majority of the parliamentary socialist party had declared its readiness to support an anti-fascist government, and even when the national council of the party (still dominated by maximalists) condemned this vote and objected even to socialist abstentions, sixty or so socialist deputies continued to be ready to support a bourgeois anti-fascist government. (This decision led to a formal break in the party in October.) Though the PPI directorate soon came to oppose co-operation with socialists, Sturzo, the political secretary, was ready for such co-operation. Thus there appeared a possibility of a government, equipped with the support of part of the *Popolari* and socialists, which would seek to restore order. Bonomi was ready to make the attempt. His failure to form a government under these circumstances, was not the result of socialist intransigence but a refusal on the part of liberal 'constitutionalists' to accept a clearly anti-fascist government of combat. On 20 July, Giolitti himself wrote from abroad 'what good can come from the country from an alliance of Sturzo – Treves – Turati?' (The latter were the most eminent of the collaborationist socialists.) Clearly the bulk of the liberals preferred to continue the futile attempt at the absorption of fascism in a combination dominated by liberals. It is therefore wrong to assert that the attachment of socialists to unrelenting class war made impossible a combined resistance. The outcome of this crisis was the reappearance of the feeble Facta as a provisional measure, while negotiations with the fascists for entry into the government continued. In October an emissary of Giolitti told Don Sturzo that it was improbable that Giolitti would attempt to form a government without the fascists and impossible that he would do so against them. Meanwhile Giolitti was negotiating with Mussolini.[219]

The march on Rome was the means of bringing to a head the negotiations for entry into the government that Mussolini was carrying on, not merely with Giolitti, but with Salandra (of the liberal right), Orlando and Facta himself. Indeed, it was not an armed seizure of power but the hastening of an entry to the government already made inevitable by the attitude of the liberals. In one important respect, however, the march on Rome produced a result different from that anticipated by Mussolini's dupes: Mussolini himself formed the new government rather than participating in a government formed by liberal or democratic politicians.

On 16 October in Milan, four men – Balbo, de Vecchi, de Bono, Bianchi – were entrusted with the execution of an armed descent on the capital. On the 24th Mussolini announced, 'either the government is handed over or we take it by attack on Rome: henceforth it is a matter of days and perhaps of hours'. On the evening of the 27th the *quadrumviri*, from their headquarters in Perugia, announced the opening of operations. Three groups of fascists – about 26,000 men in all – were assembled within easy reach of Rome, at Monterotondo, Santa Marinella and Tivoli. Would the government resist? From the strictly military point of view, victory was certain: Rome was defended by more than 28,000 armed men, under General Pugliese, who were far better equipped and disciplined than were the fascists. At first it seemed that the government would act; no doubt a majority within it was reluctant to move from negotiations with Mussolini to complete surrender to his threats. On the evening of the 27th, the King returned to Rome, and Facta, the president of the council, agreed with him to declare a state of emergency. The cabinet met at 5 a.m. on the 28th, General Pugliese was ordered to defend Rome, telegrams went out declaring the state of emergency and the ministers signed a proclamation announcing that they would maintain order at every point. At 8 a.m. Facta asked King Victor Emmanuel III to sign the decree declaring the state an emergency; the King refused.[220]

This was a great turning point. The whole-hearted support of the King for resistance to the fascists could have brought the loyalty of the armed forces to the government. Indeed, the great advantage of constitutional monarchy should be precisely that the monarch provides a focus for loyalty to the constitution and of opposition to its subversion. Unfortunately, the crisis revealed the great drawback of constitutional monarchy – that a monarch is normally associated personally with men of the political right so that while the monarch can usually be counted on to act with vigour against the left (if the communists had threatened to march on Rome, there can be no doubt that Victor Emmanuel would have been eager to order a strong defence) he cannot be counted on to resist right-wing subversion. As it was, the King's attitude left Italy defenceless in the face of fascism. Why did he fail? One reason lay in a dynastic fear. His cousin, the Duke of Aosta, was known to be ready to lead a fascist coup d'état against the monarch himself if Victor Emmanuel chose to resist. A second reason was provided by the King's advisers – not his governmental advisers, but those he consulted during the crucial night of 27/28 October. These were probably General Diaz, Admiral Thaon di Revel, General Cittadini and the nationalist leader Federzoni. All these men were likely to have told the King that compromise with fascism, on any terms, was better than conflict. There is, too, some evidence to suggest that Facta himself may not have shown any energy in his requests to the King to sign the decree.[221] There remained illusions that Mussolini could be persuaded to join a cabinet headed by a non-fascist: on the 28th the King asked Salandra, the right-wing liberal, to form a government. Mussolini refused to come to Rome except to form his own government, for the King's surrender had already made it clear that his demands would not be resisted. On the 29th, Mussolini was asked to form a government. He boarded a train to Rome that evening and arrived next morning. Meanwhile, the 'march on Rome' involved nothing worse than discomfort for the fascist bands who were brought to Rome by special trains on 30 and 31 October.[222]

During the next few years Mussolini secured sufficient complicity and co-operation from the liberals, democrats and *Popolari* to enable a steady evolution into a dictatorial single-party state. Those who might have combined to oppose this process failed to do so because a sufficiently large number of them believed that the appointment of Mussolini as president of the council would bring about an eventual 'normalization', that fascism would abandon violence and accept the renewed working of the liberal constitution. Others were gratified by the prospect of the final defeat of 'bolshevism'. Mussolini's first government, in addition to fascists and nationalists, included liberals and *Popolari*. It received Giolitti's support: 'a ministry under Mussolini is the only one which can restore the peace of society'. Capitalist society trumpeted its backing in a manifesto from the *Confindustria*. When parliament assembled in November, Mussolini faced the chamber of deputies with a characteristic mixture of insults, threats, promises and blandishments. Fascism would govern regardless of parliament, the revolution was all-powerful yet the government would restrict liberty and defend the law. The outcome was a vote of confidence in the government by 306 votes to 116. The opposition came almost entirely from socialists and communists. Meanwhile it became clear that illegal violence had not ceased with Mussolini's coming to power. In Turin, for instance, in December, at least eleven persons were killed by fascists in retaliation for the mortal wounding of two fascists. Such violence was now put formally under the aegis of the state by the incorporation of the fascist black-shirts in a 'voluntary militia', placed under the direct orders of Mussolini, who made it clear that he regarded fascist rule as permanent, irrespective of parliamentary consent.

At this point there were signs that the *Popolari* might oppose Mussolini – an opposition which their strength in the chamber could still have rendered formidable. The fading away of this prospect was the result, above all, of the attitude of the Church towards fascism. At the congress of Turin in April 1923 the party had followed Don Sturzo in qualifying co-operation with Mussolini's government by sharp criticisms of fascist conduct. Mussolini replied by forcing the *Popolari* ministers to leave the government, and by launching attacks on the PPI and other Catholic institutions. The influence of the Vatican, always decisive if exercised with sufficient energy, was brought to bear, and on 10 July Sturzo was compelled to resign as political secretary of the PPI. The attitude of the papal authorities, in fact, provided one of the major reasons for Mussolini's successful advance to dictatorship. To the Catholic hierarchy, of course, socialist and doctrinaire liberals must necessarily be enemies, and no doubt it preferred as a rival creed the intellectual rubbish propounded by fascism to the perilously persuasive arguments of marxism and liberal rationalism. Again, in the last analysis, the Church is concerned with the affairs of this world only to the extent that they have a bearing on the situation in the next and better facilities for encouraging mankind to follow sound doctrine might be had by co-operation with government rather than by opposition to it.

On the same day that Sturzo resigned the discussion of a new electoral law began. Its passage was a major step in Mussolini's advance towards dictatorship. Its principle was the giving of two-thirds of the seats in the chamber to the electoral list securing the highest number of votes – which, it was assumed, would be the fascist list. The usual fascist display of mingled threats and conciliation was deployed: the fascist press declared that if the law were rejected, a violent coup d'état would follow, while Mussolini spoke to the chamber in the guise of a virtuous parliamentarian. Confidence in the government was voted by 303 to 140, with the *Popolari* supporting the government, and the principle of the electoral law, the Acerbo law, was voted by 235 to 139 with the bulk of the *Popolari* abstaining. (The illusions even of determined and sincere democrats were demonstrated by the abstention of Amendola on the grounds that Mussolini was moving towards the hoped for 'normalization'.) Mussolini accepted the need for the majority list to secure a minimum of votes under the new law but insisted on twenty-five per cent as sufficient – a provision carried by 178 to 157 with, once again, the bulk of the *Popolari* abstaining.[223] When it is remembered that the chamber contained only about fifty openly fascist members, the importance of non-fascist connivance becomes clear yet again. The hopes of a return to the free working of the legal constitution were shown to be unsound by the continuance of fascist violence, notably by two incidents. On 29 November 1923, the house of Nitti, the former Prime Minister, was broken into and wrecked and on 26 December Amendola, who had emerged as the strongest non-socialist opponent of fascism, was severely injured by a fascist gang.[224]

Elections took place on 6 April 1924. In spite of the evidence that fascist violence had not ended after the Fascists had become a party of government, the Fascist electoral list, the *listone*, of 356 names, included 135 liberals and democrats, including two former prime ministers, Salandra and Orlando, while Giolitti produced a small separate list which he insisted was not to be regarded as an attempt at opposition.[225]

Otherwise the parties fought the elections in dispersed order, without coalition, and about twelve lists sought the support of non-fascist voters. The governmental list secured sixty-five per cent of the votes, which under the Acerbo law gave it 374 seats in a chamber of 535. When the chamber met, Amendola and Matteotti denounced the violence employed by the fascists at the elections and denied their validity. Matteotti was one of the most eminent of the members of the PSU, the reformist socialist group which had broken away from the maximalist PSI in 1922. He was fully aware of the risks he took in launching a full-scale denunciation of fascist violence and illegality. He spoke on 30 May; on 10 June he was murdered.

It was universally assumed that the attack on Matteotti had been approved by highly-placed fascists, perhaps by Mussolini himself. The government fell into discredit and for a time it seemed that it would not survive. Many fascists sought to disavow their connections with the party. Hopes grew that the King would recognize his duty to defend the law and dismiss Mussolini. This was the principal hope of the so-called Aventine secession. On 18 June, about 150 socialists, *Popolari*, democrats and communists withdrew from the chamber of deputies until the rule of law should be restored – Giolitti sneered at this secession, Orlando and Salandra refused to join. In spite of repeated demands by the Aventine and the presentation of proof of the misdeeds of the government, the King refused to take any action whatever, so providing his second great service to fascism, and Mussolini recovered his confidence. In January 1925, when Orlando and Giolitti had begun a cautious and belated opposition, Mussolini announced, 'I assume, I alone, the political, moral and historical responsibility for everything that has happened . . . If fascism is an association of delinquents, I am the chief of this association of delinquents'.[226] (The full recovery of fascist vigour was expressed in a second assault on Amendola in July 1925 – he died eight months later, probably as a result of this attack.)

In 1925 and 1926, the fascist régime developed into a complete and open dictatorship. Freedom of the press disappeared, what was left of parliamentary interference was ended when the deputies of the Aventine were declared to have forfeited their seats and 'anti-nationalist' parties were suppressed. A special tribunal for the 'defence of the state' began operations early in 1927 and the powers of the police were strengthened. The special tribunal dealt with cases referred to it by the chief of police. There was no appeal from the decisions of the tribunal, whose members were appointed by Mussolini himself. Any person denounced to it was arrested at once and imprisoned. Over five thousand people were brought before the tribunal in the years 1927–43, of whom all but a few were convicted. Nearly all were imprisoned, the average sentence being rather over five years. There were seven cases of life imprisonment and twenty-nine death sentences. The police could submit someone suspected of anti-fascism to restrictions on movement, residence and employment and could inflict *confino* for up to five years, which meant deportation to islands or remote villages. About ten thousand people were at one time or another deported in this way. In 1927 a secret police, the OVRA, was set up.[227] Mussolini's régime was certainly a police state and a harsh one, but it was not murderous to an extent remotely approaching that reached by the Nazi government of Germany. Until Mussolini fell under German influence, fascism avoided racialism – it struck at its opponents, not, deliberately at least, at innocent and passive human beings.

In 1928, all pretence of representative government was abandoned, with a new electoral system under which a single list was to be nominated by the fascist Grand Council from names presented by the fascist trade unions and other organizations. The fascist Grand Council, a Party body, was to name ministers and future heads of government and to express an opinion on questions of a constitutional kind, and, if asked, on other issues. The Grand Council was a body without effective power which had no significance until it brought about Mussolini's fall in 1943.[228] In 1929, the régime was consolidated by its greatest success: the agreement with the Church embodied in the Lateran pacts. At last the question of the Pope's territorial sovereignty, open since 1870, was closed, and the relations between Church and State settled. The treaties gave substantial concessions to the Church, especially over religious education in schools, but the readiness of the Papacy to reach understanding with Mussolini's government gave inestimable benefit to the fascist régime. It contributed to the attitude of passive acquiescence which characterised the majority of the Italian people in the 1930s.

With a compromise thus arranged with an organization fascism could not crush, the régime could seek to mould Italians into conformity to its model of active, disciplined, regimented beings. A characteristic implement was its youth organizations. The *Opera Nazionale Balilla* was given a monopoly except for certain purely religious associations. It presided over various semi-military groups of children: from eight to fourteen years old, the *Balilla*; from fourteen to eighteen the *Avanguardisti*. The children had uniforms, marched in threes and were to be taught discipline, culture (i.e. fascist doctrine), and given

157

pre-military training. From 1937, the organization was extended to include girls and boys from six to twenty years of age. Six year old boys became 'sons of the wolf', at eleven they had wooden rifles, from fifteen real rifles. Their motto was a familiar slogan of fascist Italy: 'Believe, Obey, Fight.'[229] Schools were affected: the minister of education announced that

the government . . . requires that the whole school, in all its levels and all its teaching, shall educate Italian youth to understand fascism, to ennoble itself in fascism and to live in the historical climate created by the fascist revolution.

Under fascism uniforms symbolized uniformity. Mussolini himself, after a period of sartorial hesitation in which he was addicted to morning coats and spats, decided that uniform was the appropriate wear for a dictator. Silly slogans expressed the requirement to conform: 'Mussolini is always right' was only the most patently absurd. At a higher level of sophistication, fascist 'thought' came to justify the régime. It consisted in the limitless exaltation of the state, accompanied by the assertion that deeds were better than words, that only action mattered, that violence was superior to tranquillity. In 1932, there appeared a statement of doctrine signed by Mussolini, the *Duce*, himself.

The fascist conception of life stresses the importance of the state and accepts the individual only in so far as his interests coincide with those of the state . . . fascism reasserts the rights of the state as expressing the real essence of the individual . . . fascism does not, generally speaking, believe in the possibility or utility of perpetual peace . . . War alone keys up all human energies to their maximum tension and sets the seal of nobility on those peoples who have the courage to face it.[230]

All this was largely based on that strand of European political thinking which drew quite unwarrantable conclusions from the sound enough proposition that human beings acting as a co-ordinated team may be able sometimes to do things the same human beings acting as unorganized individuals could not. The effect of fascism on Italian intellectual life was, of course, lamentable. But it was more superficial and has proved more easily eradicable than used to be feared. Italian schools and universities continued, especially in fields not related to current politics, to maintain acceptable standards and the fascist indoctrination of youth proved to be shallow and transitory.

The fascist régime claimed loudly to have discovered a new order of society and a new way of organizing economic life in the corporate state. Productive processes need not generate wasteful class struggle; fascist thought showed the way to the harmonizing of the rival demands of capital and labour in the pursuit of national ends. Mussolini asserted that working-class aspirations must lead either to the abolition of private property or to some form of fascist corporate state.[231] It is certainly true that a capitalist society must contain some means of solving controversies between employers and labourers. The usual method is by bargains struck between representatives of working men and employers, with the workers in possession of the weapon of strike action to give force to their claims. Fascists argued that this method was wasteful and unnecessary and their régime sought a different method of compromise and conciliation. The corporate state, it was claimed, meant the abolition of class conflicts, and an end to the struggle between labour and capital. Representatives of the workers and representatives of employers, helped by officials of the state, were to work together in the interests both of production and of social justice. Essentially, the corporate state involved the setting up of an elaborate mechanism to bring about compromise and co-operation among producers, whether wage earners or proprietors. In spite of fascist boastings, however, machinery designed to bring about these ends are familiar phenomena in capitalist societies and it is the distinctive feature of the corporative structure that is significant, not its existence. Behind a pompous facade, that special feature was quite simply this: that genuine representation of working men through powerful autonomous organizations was eliminated. Strikes were legally forbidden and to take part became a criminal offence. Only fascist unions were permitted to take part in negotiations on behalf of workers and all who belonged to an industry represented by a fascist union were obliged to pay dues to these unions. The election of officials in the unions required the approval of the government before it became effective. For all practical purposes bargaining over wages and conditions of work became a matter of a dialogue between the state and the employers. This was the syndical system of 1926, elaborated into the corporate structure of 1934. The corporations of 1934, with representatives of employers and fascist unions in each industrial category, and of the state, were supposed individually and collectively to direct economic life. In practice they were little more than advisory bodies whose recommendations had no power to compel action on the government.

In October 1924 Mussolini declared,

the economic objective of the fascist régime is greater social justice. If modern science has solved the problem of multiplying wealth, science, spurred on by the state, must now solve the other great problem, that of the distribution of wealth, so that the illogical, paradoxical, and cruel phenomenon of want in the midst of plenty shall not be repeated. Toward this great goal all our energies and all our effort must now be bent.

This sort of thing must not be taken too seriously; fascist Italy was not egalitarian in its social policy. Indeed, one of Mussolini's first acts in 1922 was effectively to prevent the introduction of death duties. Furthermore, the increasingly heavy burden of taxation required by the régime involved a relatively greater reliance on indirect taxation, which inflicts most hardships on the poorest consumers.[232] It is true, though, that the régime was not one of unmitigated reaction – after all, Mussolini was well aware of the need to avoid determined opposition from the working class. Italy shared in the general western European movement towards the provision of welfare services – insurance against unemployment, old-age and illness. Maternity benefits were energetically developed, for the régime believed, on irrational militaristic grounds, that Italy's population should be expanded. Workers dismissed by employers through no fault of their own became entitled to indemnities. It is not very probable that the poorer Italian would have been much better off materially under any other sort of régime in the 1920s or 1930s, for his welfare was principally determined by economic forces to which the government reacted in very much the same sort of way that liberal governments did elsewhere. One exception, which was economically beneficial in periods of market weakness, was the régime's partiality for public works, largely in pursuit of prestige, a motive which had little influence on, for example, contemporary British governments.

Though Mussolini treated the restoration of the lira to the gold standard as a matter of prestige, the policy and its effects were little different from the similar policy followed by Britain in the 1920s. At the end of 1927, the lira was stabilized at just over 90 to the pound sterling, against nearly 145 in 1925. Until then, Italian industry had been reasonably prosperous, with production, profits and probably real wages rising. The deflation required to increase the value of the lira led to reduction in wages and increasing unemployment, and the over-valuation of the lira checked growth in Italian exports. The fascist syndical system enabled reductions in wages to be carried through with the minimum of fuss and it is probable that the fall in retail prices lagged behind falling wages, with at least temporary reductions in real wages. Unemployment rose from 111,000 in 1925 to 324,000 in 1928. A recovery in 1929 was reversed by the arrival of the world slump and by 1932 unemployment was over a million. The effects of the slump were protracted by the maintenance of the exchange value of the lira (until

1936) at the 1927 level. The result was that Italian exports became overpriced in terms of foreign currencies and their level remained below even that of 1931 until the year 1937.[233] To hold the value of the lira at this artificially high level, wages were further reduced, and while real wages did not fall to the same extent (and real wages of those fully employed may have risen) the benefits of falling world prices for food were reduced in Italy by the government's policy of agricultural self-sufficiency. This policy, which certainly succeeded in making Italy very nearly self-sufficient for wheat in good years, involved exclusion of cheap imported grain and so tended to prevent food prices inside Italy falling as far as they would otherwise have done. This was of benefit to the agricultural sector of the economy, but the real wages of agricultural labourers still fell in the 1930s principally because of rural over-population following the fall in emigration which set in after the war and became more marked in the 1930s. Thus during the fascist years of peace, the condition of the labouring classes probably declined in industry and certainly did so in agriculture. Fascism therefore, cannot be said to have insulated the Italian people from economic hardship.[234]

The distinctive economic policies of fascism were linked with military strength and prestige: the search for self-sufficiency in grain linked with the pursuit of high population growth and the reclamation of land together with large-scale public works. The attempt to increase the production of wheat, begun in the 1920s, was a success: the yield of wheat per hectare rose in a greater proportion in Italy between the period 1909–13 and the period 1930–4 than in any other area of western Europe.[235] This policy, however, tended to increase prices in Italy. The much advertised search for faster population growth was unsuccessful. Expenditure on public works was certainly useful economically in reducing unemployment. The most striking achievement was in the reclamation of land, especially through drainage and the building of aqueducts. Road building went forward as well as the construction of public buildings and the (artistically controversial) reconstruction of central Rome.

Otherwise the economic policy of the fascist government was no different from policies that might have been pursued by liberal democratic governments. Italian policy (the revaluation of the lira) was almost as harmful to the Italian economy in the 1920s as government policy was in Britain and the maintenance of an over-valued lira in the 1930s harmed Italy in the way that a similar policy harmed France. Indeed, while the Italian economy advanced until 1925, later years, especially the 1930s, were years of stagnation. While British production advanced rapidly in the 1930s, after the departure from the gold standard, Italian production did not, contained as the economy was by the deflation necessary to hold up the value of the currency. Thus Italian manufacturing production rose above the average level of 1925–9 only in 1936 while British production was about 37% higher in that year.[236] State interference in the economy, especially through protectionist policies and assistance in the reorganization of industry, were general in the 1930s, and not confined to Italy. Certainly, however, the fascist government involved the state in the financing of stricken industries to a much greater extent than was usual in liberal countries. The *Istituto Mobiliare Italiano*, the *Sofondit*, and the *Instituto di Ricostruzione Industriale* all involved the use of government credit to assist banks and industry. On the other hand, government help in the formation of *Consorzi*, or cartels for price-fixing and the distribution of market quotas, was familiar elsewhere. In short, it may be asserted that, while it is certain that democratic governments could have handled the Italian economy at least as badly as did fascist governments, the economic activities of the fascist régime did not provide adequate compensation for its suppression of political freedom and the degeneracy of intellectual life it brought about. The great hardships and unquestionable disasters inflicted on Italy by fascism came however, not from its economic policies, but from its foreign policy. The full consequences of the surrender of liberal democracy in 1922 revealed themselves only in Italy's unnecessary and disastrous participation in the Second World War.

9

France 1919-40

A retrospective aura of gloom has descended on the history of France in these years. It was a period with a sharply defined and painful end – the successful German invasion and occupation of France in the summer of 1940. Writing on the history of France in this period has been dominated by the defeat of 1940. This is often explained as the outcome of the workings of the democratic system of the Third Republic which, it is alleged, produced a debilitating political disunity and fatally weak and indecisive governments. Right-wing critics have added that the Third Republic permitted pacifists, socialists and communists directly to undermine the power of France, above all by preventing timely rearmament. Nostalgic reactionaries claimed that a drift from the countryside weakened France by reducing the number of sturdy peasants. Thus France was doomed to defeat before the war began. These views were naturally expressed by military men and those anxious to preserve the prestige of the army and to use that prestige for political purposes. Marshal Pétain, having presided over the destruction of the republic in July 1940, declared in October, 'the disaster is only in reality the reflection on the military level of the feeblenesses and vices of the former political régime'. The war in fact, was 'virtually lost in advance'.[237] In this chapter, an attempt will be made to examine this view and to consider how far the contrary view may be accepted that the defeat of 1940 is explicable in terms of the course of the battles of that year and of the strategic and tactical conduct of the campaign by the French and German commanders.

The question of the extent, causes and consequences of French disunity will be examined in this chapter, together with the argument that the French army was stabbed in the back before the battle began. The campaign itself will be analysed elsewhere. It may be suggested that there is much to be said for the contention expressed by General de

Gaulle in 1942: 'Before the war the French people refused no sacrifice to be ready to fight. But all this good will as well as all this money came to be lost in an obsolete military system.'[238] The defeat of 1940 has, indeed, caused French history between the wars to be interpreted in far too gloomy a way. It is hardly reasonable to judge a form of political and social organization by its suitability for preparing war, yet even by this criterion, the Third Republic did tolerably well.

Political history on the one hand and economic and social history on the other are inseparable. In the modern world, at least, political changes are at once causes and consequences of economic and social changes. French politics in this period can only be understood if the conditions of life of the French people are examined; economic fluctuations and their social concomitants cannot be explained unless the prejudices of political leaders are considered. The precise mechanism and timing of these varied interactions is not always clear; that they existed requires no demonstration beyond a recital of the facts.

In the 1920s, France did well economically. Since this success was secured largely as a result of a process everyone wished to prevent, the decline in the value of the franc, its full extent was hardly noticed. The economic history of France between the end of the war and the beginning of the world slump is in this respect in marked contrast to that of Britain where politicians succeeded in imposing their intentions. In Britain those with fixed incomes flourished while workers and producers suffered as the pound was restored to pre-war parity and uncomfortably stabilized there. In France the *rentier* and those with fixed incomes were ruined or severely damaged as inflation brought down the value of the franc until it was safely stabilized at one-fifth of pre-war parity, while workers and producers enjoyed a substantial rise in their incomes. During the war the franc was maintained artificially at its pre-war level of twenty-five to the pound. By July 1926 it was at about two hundred. Thereafter it recovered to about 124, where it was successfully held. This decline was caused by inflation at home and was accelerated on the foreign exchanges from time to time by speculation and occasionally checked by the intervention of the central bank in the market. Most important in its effects was the rise in prices inside France which was reflected in the exchanges: by 1928 retail prices had reached about 5½ times their pre-war level. Those who had lent money to the state before or during the war were deprived of the income they had counted on; the fixed number of francs they had arranged to receive bought them less and less. The average investor who had lent a hundred francs in 1914 to the state would possess the equivalent of about fifteen francs worth of 1914 currency in 1928 and his annual income would have fallen to less than one-fifth in purchasing power. Another way in which the holders of fixed interest securities suffered was through the default or evasion of foreign powers. Probably nearly as much had been invested abroad as in the French national debt before 1914; by 1928 only about one-quarter of the value of foreign investments remained. The investors in foreign bonds were not bold risk-takers; they had been deluded into a false sense of security by the great banks and sometimes encouraged by French governments anxious to influence foreign powers. The persons who suffered, above all, were the thrifty, prudent and respectable; not, typically, the very rich but men and women of modest means among whom rising prices after decades of stability caused misery and bewilderment. Inflation, in fact, produces the effect of an inequitable capital levy. Owners of rented houses and apartments found themselves in something like the position of fixed-interest bond-holders; by 1929 rents in Paris had risen only about three times since before the war.[239]

Sections of the community dependent on other sources of income did well. In 1929 real national income per head was about one-third higher than it had been in 1913. By the end of 1929 industrial production was over forty-eight per cent higher than in 1913. The benefit went to the economically strong: that is to those associated with industrial production, whether as part of management or as workers and to a much more limited extent to passive shareholders in industrial concerns. In spite of the general limitation to an eight hour working day imposed in 1919, the real income of members of the working class increased by up to a quarter between 1913 and 1930 while increasing prosperity enabled many working men and peasants to advance into the lower middle class. Managerial and entrepreneurial incomes are difficult to measure but there is every reason to suppose that they advanced while the average holder of industrial shares did not lose money in the years 1913 to 1929 – unlike the holders of fixed interest securities. An unproductive group, that of lesser government officials, gained most of all, perhaps because of their political importance. Unemployment was insignificant.[240]

These economic successes were obtained by an acceptance of inflation and a refusal, however reluctant, to resort to the rigorous measures that would have been required to 'save the franc', in the sense that the pound was 'saved' in England. The franc was stabilized at a level, in contrast to that of the pound in Britain, at which French prices were thoroughly competitive in world markets. The devastation caused

165

by the war was made good. Even the alarming decline in the numbers of the French population did not hold back economic growth, for the men killed and wounded during the war and the rising average age of the French population due to a long-established low birth-rate were made up by immigration into France and by a steady fall in the number of people employed in agriculture.[241] This great advance in the wealth and power of France and in the standard of living of most Frenchmen was achieved by accident; French governments would have stopped it, if they could, by imitating what most contemporaries thought was the British triumph of a restoration of the pre-war value of the currency by restricting demand to force down prices. Luckily for France the size of the French government debt was such that a full return to the pre-war value of the franc would have generated an impossibly large burden of interest payments which the post-war taxpayer would have had to meet. Even so, Poincaré, the 'saviour of the franc' was only with difficulty persuaded to 'save' one-fifth of it rather than to try to attempt more, because of pressure from industrialists and trade unionists who feared a check to production and the creation of unemployment.[242]

After 1930, the economic situation went wrong. In the first place France was affected by the world depression that began in 1929. In 1930 French exports fell by over one quarter. In 1931 the devaluation of the British currency removed at one stroke the help given to French industry on the markets of the world by the relative cheapness of its products caused by the undervaluation of the franc in 1926–8. The devaluation of the dollar in 1933 made matters worse. Between 1929 and 1933 French exports of manufactures fell by forty-two per cent. The collapse of world food prices damaged French food producers and reduced internal demand for manufactures. Government policy encouraged economic stagnation: until 1936 the franc was held at the level of Poincaré's stabilization. In order to do this the usual attempts were made to maintain balanced budgets; attempts made with more energy by the right-wing governments of 1934–6 than by their predecessors of 1932–4. Devaluation was excluded by the almost mystical sentiment in favour of a stable franc and the alternative of deflation increasingly imposed itself. Paul Reynaud's campaign in favour of devaluation was treated as an irresponsible eccentricity, or even as an example of treason.[243] Flandin's attempt in 1935 to stimulate the economy by injections of credit combined with planned restriction of production set off large-scale speculation against the franc which led to a drastic attempt at deflation under Laval in the second half of 1935. The major measure was a general reduction in all government spending, including even the service of debt, but excluding defence expenditures and social payments. The result was that though the depression hit France later than Britain, the United States and Germany, its effect, when it came, was a protracted period of stagnation. Industrial production fell:

INDEX OF INDUSTRIAL PRODUCTION (1929 = 100)			
1929	100	1933	81
1930	99	1934	75
1931	86	1935	73
1932	73	1936	78

Unemployment did not reach the dramatic heights found in Britain and Germany. This was because of the departure of many of the immigrant workers who had come into France in the 1920s and because of a widespread tendency towards a reduction in the number of hours worked. The figures for unemployment in France are unreliable, but there were probably four to five per cent of male workers unemployed in 1936. Wages fell, because of reductions in money rates and because of a decline in the number of hours worked. However, the fall in prices meant that the purchasing power of wages actually increased, by about ten per cent, between 1930 and 1935.[244] This was small consolation to those without work. Furthermore, as M. Sauvy has pointed out, the workers were much more impressed by the falling number of francs in their wage than by the fact that those francs could buy more. Their increased purchasing power was not large enough to prevent a sense of injury. This fact goes together with many other pieces of evidence from the period to suggest that deflation arouses more discontent than moderate inflation because of its psychological effects. The strikes of 1936 show that workers with jobs did not feel any sense of being a privileged class.

Industrial workers were not the only class of society affected. The incomes of those who lived by agriculture were drastically reduced. In money terms they had fallen by 1935 to less than half their level of 1929. In the same period incomes from commerce and industry fell by nearly one half with those businesses which were not in a monopoly position particularly hard hit. The falling cost of living partly compensated government officials for the reduction in their incomes imposed by deflationary governments, of between 13·6 per cent and 17·6 per cent in 1933 to 1935; the value of state pensions actually rose and owners of urban property held their own.[245]

The left-wing Popular Front government under Léon Blum, which came to power in the summer of 1936, abandoned deflation in favour of

167

a policy of increasing purchasing power, especially of industrial workers. Pushed forward by an outbreak of strikes, the government immediately arranged for increases in wages of about one-fifth. The strikes and the introduction of paid holidays in that summer, together with a flight of capital from France caused by fears of the policies of the government, forced devaluation in September 1936. The government failed to prevent export of capital by applying exchange control as a result of its fear of alienating its more cautious supporters. The effect of devaluation in stimulating production in France was restrained by the introduction of the forty hour week, and by its rigid application, which made overtime working impossible and by the reluctance of capitalists to engage in productive investment. The introduction of the rigid forty hour week, indeed, must rank as one of the gravest economic blunders any government had ever committed. It was designed to reduce unemployment; in fact it increased it. It created a shortage of types of skilled labour which had never suffered from unemployment, which led to bottle-necks in crucial sections of industrial production and rendered expansion impossible. The immediate effect of the devaluation was a startling rise in industrial production in the last months in 1936 followed by a return to the level of September 1936 as the forty hour week took effect in 1937.[246] Prices inside France increased rapidly and absorbed most of the gains of the working class of the summer of 1936, while industrial production after a short interval returned to a condition of stagnation.

In June 1937 Blum was replaced by Chautemps and a reversal of the policies of the first Popular Front government began. An end was made to the increase in purchasing power. At first the new course was pursued hesitantly as the government continued to rely on the Popular Front majority. Pressure on the franc continued and in July 1937 the franc ceased to be linked with gold and between then and April 1938 it fell from 110 to the pound to 179. With the Daladier government of 1938, which included members of the moderate right, the new course was followed more vigorously. The franc was stabilized in the spring of 1938. In November 1938 Paul Reynaud became Minister of Finance and launched an attack on the forty hour week by abolishing the five day week, and by reducing permitted overtime pay. At the same time he sought to restore business confidence by increasing indirect taxation together with a reduction of interest rates. An attempted general strike failed almost completely. Business confidence in fact revived, capital returned to France and in 1939 industrial production began to grow.[247]

INDEX OF INDUSTRIAL PRODUCTION (1929 = 100)

1935	73	1938	76
1936	78	1939 (7 months)	86
1937	82		

Blum's first government attempted to deal with the crisis in French agriculture by creating marketing organizations under the aegis of the state. The major instrument was the *Office du Blé* which fixed prices for all grains. The effect was to protect the weaker and smaller producers, who were worst affected by short-term market changes. Thus the 'drift from the land', already checked by unemployment in industry, was further reduced. Large numbers of peasants with uneconomically small holdings were assisted to continue to burden the French economy.

The gains in income secured for the working class by the first Blum government were short-lived. By May 1938 real working class income had only increased by about five per cent and by the time Reynaud's work was done the average working class income was less than it had been in 1935. The real gain was in leisure, which, apart from the paid holidays introduced by the Blum administration, meant less pay for less work. The forty hour week in a sense proved an equalizing measure as between members of the working class. It reduced the incomes of those who might have been able to work longer hours in the more prosperous industries. Reynaud's measures reintroduced a sharp differential in earnings between workers in progressive industries or in industries making arms as against those in industries for which demand was slack. Even so, the difference in France between sections of the working class was not as striking as that in Britain between the permanent unemployed and the workers in expanding sections of the economy.

After 1936 those with fixed incomes, especially from investments, suffered from the fall in the value of money as they had done before the Poincaré stabilization of 1926–8. By May 1938 the franc was equivalent to less than half the amount of gold compared with its value in 1928, and by the end of the 1930s it bought less than two-thirds of what it had done in 1935. Once again inflation effected a partial confiscation of economically weak forms of capital.[248]

France was much stronger economically in 1929 than she had been in 1913. Recovery from the effects of war was rapid and, as far as material things went, complete. The country had progressed beyond recovery in the later 1920s, to a position of increased industrial strength and a widely shared, though not universal, increase in prosperity. Between 1922 and 1929 French economic growth maintained an annual rate of

5·8 per cent compared with 5·7 per cent for Germany and 2·7 per cent for the United Kingdom. On the other hand, in the 1930s, France fell back absolutely and relatively. Growth ceased, indeed became negative, at a rate of minus 2·1 per cent per annum between 1929 and 1937 compared with a positive growth of 2.8 per cent per annum in Germany and 2·3 per cent in Britain. In automobiles, one of the major growth industries of the inter-war years, France was producing less in 1937 than in 1929 while Britain was producing nearly twice as many and Germany more than twice as many. Steel production tells the same story.[249]

PRODUCTION OF STEEL IGNOTS AND CASTINGS
(thousands of tons)

	France	United Kingdom	Germany (excluding the Saar)
1929	9,711	9,790	16,210
1938	6,221	10,564	20,099

The worse the economic situation the more active and disturbed the political life of France. Thus in the 1930s political conflicts were more urgent and violent than in the 1920s. In the 1930s, French economic developments produced an explosive combination of material impoverishment with injury to moral sensibilities. Moral disquiet, at least among the middle classes, was then, even more than now, aroused by a decline in the value of the currency. Inflation was wicked, deflation was virtuous. The foreign exchange value of the franc, therefore, became a moral gauge, a measure of the spiritual health of France. (This is why Reynaud's campaign for devaluation aroused among many people not so much disagreement as disgust; he was openly preaching immorality.) If the foreign exchange value of the currency declined the simplest explanation was self-indulgence and laziness or incompetence or corruption (all on someone else's part). One British pound would buy seven times as many francs in 1939 as in 1918. When this source of spiritual unease was supplemented by the direct impact of material hardship the sufferers might seek political outlets for their anger.

The decade after the end of the war was politically speaking one of the most stable in recent French history. The war had been accepted by all classes and parties in France and the republican democratic régime had presided over the victory. Republican democracy was now firmly entrenched and in the 1920s, the Republic was not seriously challenged either by the right or by the left.

On the right, the old monarchist and Bonapartist parties had virtually disappeared. Conservatism worked from within the régime, not against it from outside. The real social force behind political conservatism, the desire of the rich to defend their wealth, found full expression within parties whose leaders had ceased to fear democracy and political freedom even if they did not come to love them. Men like Tardieu, Germain Martin, Flandin, all thoroughly acceptable to the possessing class, could rise within the system. Among the Radicals, the great upholders of republican democracy, there were links with business. The *Union des Intérêts Economiques*, which deployed funds at election time, helped some Radicals, while some business groups such as insurance firms supported Radical party funds. It is true that especially during the years 1924-6, when a series of governments under Radical direction were struggling impotently with the falling franc, a number of organizations with a more or less marked fascist tinge, ready to use violence against the left, came into prominence. The *Camelots du Roi*, the violent league of the *Action Française*, the monarchist movement, became vociferous. In 1924, Pierre Taittinger founded the *Jeunesses Patriotes* which, early in 1925, set off riots against communists with fatal casualties in the best pre-march-on-Rome Italian style. It is unreasonable to deny the fascist element in this sort of activity even if the *Jeunesses* did not give themselves a bogus screen of anti-capitalism in the Mussolini manner. In 1925, a full-scale fascist group appeared complete with doctrines imported from Italy: the *Faisceau*. Yet another group, designed to attract ex-service men, the *Croix de Feu*, was formed in 1927, financed by the perfumer, François Coty. All these movements lost importance during the period of governments further to the right inaugurated by Poincaré in 1926. If the right could make its points by parliamentary means there was no need to resort to violence. Poincaré's stabilization of the franc, though it, in fact, confirmed most of the preceding devaluation, seemed to mark a return to 'sound' government.[250]

Poincaré's government was not, however, a government of combat against the left. It represented a compromise. It stabilized the franc but not, as in Britain in 1925, at a level which would create unemployment and compel a reduction of wages. There was no sequel comparable to the great British crisis of the general strike. Indeed, the socialists were moderate and restrained in their opposition to Poincaré. In foreign policy, Briand's activities secured virtually unanimous support – if only because of their ambiguity. Thus the reformist socialists of the SFIO, Blum's party, were not tempted to depart from democratic lines of action. When Tardieu, at the head of a clearly conservative government in 1929, adopted a policy of prosperity and proposed heavy government spending including spending on social purposes, Blum could do no more than complain that these were socialist proposals

171

which had been treated as absurd extravaganzas when socialists proposed them.[251]

From the revolutionary left-democracy was in no danger by 1929. In the immediate post-war period France, like other European industrial countries, had faced strikes and demonstrations caused by the need to push wages up to meet rising prices and by the example of the bolshevik revolution in Russia. The government reacted with a mixture of concession and coercion. In March 1919 a legal framework was provided for collective agreements between employers and unions and in April 1919 the eight hours day became law. When, however, a great demonstration was proposed for 1 May 1919, Clemenceau's government forbade it and when it took place in spite of the ban, serious rioting broke out in Paris with one man killed. There followed widespread strikes, precipitated by the cost of living, but conducted with openly political purposes: the French tradition of strikes as a means to a transformation of society had been reinforced by events in Russia. A further wave of strikes, even more clearly political in object, broke out in the spring of 1920. These failed, and their failure reinforced the influence of reformists within the general confederation of labour (CGT). In 1921, the communist element split the CGT and broke away to form the CGTU. The result was that the CGT became a respectable, cautious, almost middle-class, institution, especially since unions of government officials made up a substantial proportion of its membership. The CGTU on the other hand, adopted uncompromising intransigence, protracted strikes where it could and preferred a defeat which would heighten the workers' class consciousness to a victory which might weaken it. Significantly, the CGTU rapidly lost support in favour of the CGT.[252]

At the end of 1920, at the congress of Tours, the Socialist party split in two. A large majority, very nearly of three to one, voted for a junction with the Third International set up in Moscow and accepted the conditions prescribed by the International. This majority formed the French section of the Communist International (SFIC) while the minority seceded to become the French section of the Workers' (or Second) International (SFIO). The vote was the result of enthusiasm for a revolution which still seemed capable of world-wide extension. When it became clear, as it did very quickly, that the Soviet revolution was to be no more than a Russian revolution, the situation changed. The new French Communist party rapidly lost adherents, most of whom returned to the Socialists, a process accelerated by the dogmatic rigidity of Moscow. By 1925, the Socialists had more members than the

Communist party. The electoral strength of the Socialists remained considerably greater than that of the Communists: in 1932 the Socialists secured over twice as many votes as the Communists. Still, Communist voting support was substantial: 7·9 per cent of the voters in 1924, 9·3 per cent in 1928, 6·8 per cent in 1932 and 12·6 per cent in 1936, a year when the party had provisionally accepted the bourgeois republic. It is striking, however, that the time when the party was doctrinally most rigorous, most emphatic in its hostility to the régime, to anti-Communist parties, especially the Socialists, and most insistent on its revolutionary purity, coincided with its lowest level of voting strength in 1932. Again, it is evident that many, especially among the peasants, voted Communist simply because it was the party furthest to the left so that their votes were, in fact, affirmations of republican zeal rather than the expression of a desire for the inauguration of a proletarian dictatorship. Thus in 1932, when Communist voters were directed not to vote for the non-communist left-wing candidates (usually Socialists or Radicals) with better chances of success on the second ballot, most of them, on the contrary, voted for Socialists or Radicals.[253]

Thus there was political calm at the end of the 1920s; in the 1930s, on the contrary, France seemed, at times, to be on the edge of civil war. Two events stand out: the Paris riots of 6 February 1934 when, as some think, an attempt was made to crush the democratic republic by force, and the victory of the Popular Front at the elections of 1936 which brought fears of red revolution.

What seemed the most disreputable period of French governmental instability occurred between the elections of 1932 and the beginning of 1934. The elections of 1932 were a victory for the left. Left-wing parties secured 334 seats against 259 for the right, while the Communists secured twelve. The major elements in the new majority were the Radicals with 157 and the Socialists (SFIO) with 129 seats. Herriot, the Radical party chief, formed a government in June; the Socialists supported it without taking part in the ministry. The weakness of the new government emerged at once. The economic crisis caused a fall in tax receipts which threatened a budgetary deficit. This Herriot sought to extinguish in order to prevent a weakening of the value of the franc. Thus the government sought to increase taxation and reduce expenditure. The Socialists would not accept the measures put forward and the government was compelled to weaken its proposals. The left, in fact, were politically united but divided on financial policy. Herriot refused to preside over a weakening of the franc as he had done in 1925 and accepted defeat over the question of payment of war debts to the USA.

Herriot was succeeded by Paul-Boncour, whose government refused to accept modifications in its financial proposals, and was defeated by the chamber of deputies. In the spring of 1933, the next (Daladier) government secured the vote of financial measures only by lessening its original demands. When it tried again in the autumn it was overthrown. A few weeks later, the next government, under Sarraut, was rejected over an attempt to reduce the pay of government servants. Chautemps formed another ministry which secured only a portion of the financial provisions it called for. Thus, between the elections of 1932 and the beginning of 1934, five governments had tried and failed to secure measures to bring about a balanced budget. This caused alarm to those concerned with the stability of the currency and revived the belief that French parliamentary democracy produced only sterile talk, futile intrigue and inactive weakness.[254]

In 1933, therefore, the anti-parliamentary leagues revived. Apart from the *Action Française* little had been heard of them since Poincaré's stabilization of the franc. The *Faisceau* had vanished but the other leagues now revived and gathered strength while new leagues appeared. The *Solidarité Française*, based on Coty's money, appeared in 1932, and equipped itself with blue shirts; its numbers were small. In 1933, the *Parti franciste* appeared, with its members, again, dressed in blue, calling for a fascist revolution. Its supporters were limited in number. The most remarkable change was the rapid growth of the *Croix de Feu*. In 1933 this began to recruit outside the ranks of ex-service men. It possessed shock troops grouped in divisions in a semi-military organization capable of rapid movement and concentration. Here was a body apparently preparing for a coup d'état. It was led by Colonel de la Rocque, a man with a forceful personality and an effective public manner. His utterances and the doctrines of his movement were vague. Hostility to pacifism and communism, desire for 'order' and 'authority', desire for a union of 'good Frenchmen', such were the basic elements. What La Rocque thought he was doing remains obscure. There was talk of an H-hour when there would be action, presumably of a forceful kind, directed to what end was never known. Indeed, after 1936, the *Croix de Feu* evolved into a straight-forward right-wing party preparing for the next electoral contest. Until then, however, La Rocque introduced a cloudy menace onto the political scene.[255]

At the end of 1933 some of the activities of a dubious financier called Stavisky became known. Stavisky had secured control of the raising of loans for the town of Bayonne and had taken a large part of the proceeds for himself. It was clear that he could not have won the position which enabled him to launch his fraud without the support of persons of influence. Garat, the mayor of Bayonne, was a Radical deputy. One of Stavisky's lawyers was the brother of the Prime Minister, Chautemps, a Radical, and two other deputies, both Radicals, had worked on behalf of Stavisky. Deputies, especially on the left, were thus brought into even more disrepute. Chautemps sought to minimise the scandal. His attempt failed when Stavisky was found dead, allegedly as the result of suicide.[256] 'Suicides' are common form in matters of this kind in France and the belief is general – and it would be difficult to prove it wrong that they are arranged by someone in power to prevent embarrassing revelations. At this point, the right-wing leagues, especially the shock-troops of the *Action Française*, the *Camelots du Roi*, set off repeated demonstrations of protest in Paris. When a member of Chautemps' government, Raynaldy, was found to have been associated in the transactions of a shady bank, the government resigned in disgrace.

Daladier formed a new government on 29 January 1934. He announced that he would seek the acceptance of the chamber of deputies on 6 February. The violence and restlessness of the anti-parliamentary right now reached its climax. The leagues were joined by less specifically political organizations of ex-service men, including the communist group, and of disgruntled taxpayers, in separate but converging demonstrations of their strength. It is probable that some contact took place between the leaders of the leagues and the other groups before 6 February. On the morning of that day all of them, except the *Francistes*, called on their supporters to attend demonstrations of disgust against the iniquities of the chamber of deputies. Towards the end of the day, large-scale riots broke out, especially in the Place de la Concorde, as police forces sought to prevent demonstrators from reaching the chamber of deputies. Repeated baton charges, and mounted assaults had to be supplemented by outbreaks of shooting. Meanwhile the deputies voted their confidence in the Daladier government by a substantial majority and went home as unobtrusively as they could. The police held their ground and the chamber of deputies was preserved from incursion. The known casualties were high: among the demonstrators (and onlookers) sixteen killed and 665 injured; among the forces of order one dead and 1,664 injured.

There is no evidence to show that the riots were the result of a planned attempt to seize power and overturn the régime. The *Action Française*, who provided the most combative elements among the rioters, gave its men the slogan, 'down with the thieves' and told them 'to signify to the ministry and its parliamentary supporters that they have had enough of the abject régime'. The *Jeunesses Patriotes* were to shout their 'point of view' at parliament. The ex-service men were to 'manifest your indignation'. Characteristically, Colonel de La Rocque did not make clear for what purpose the *Croix de Feu* was to come out onto the streets, and kept their manifestations separate from the others. Indeed the *Croix de Feu* could have invaded the chamber of deputies. La Rocque explained in May 1934 that while revolutionary changes were indispensable he wished to accomplish them without violence and without excessive haste. The leaders of the small fascist group, the *Francistes*, complained precisely that the February riots, in which this group took no part, were no more than an expression of disgust and not an attack on the state.[257]

The morning after the riots, Daladier's government resigned, in spite of the majority it had secured the night before, probably to prevent more riots – perhaps with armed demonstrators. The president appealed to M. Doumergue, an ex-president of the republic, to form a government. Doumergue, an old man with a respectable left-wing republican past, formed a broad-based ministry. The Socialists would not participate, but all parties to the right of the Socialists were represented. Thus a government based on the support of the Socialists plus that of the Radicals was replaced by a government based on the support of the parliamentary right plus, once again, most of the Radicals. The Radicals, elected for the most part in co-operation with the Socialists, were once again, as after 1926, part of a government ruling against the Socialists. Léon Blum, and the Socialist party, denounced what they claimed to be a surrender of Daladier's legal government to illegal pressure from fascist bands. On the very night of the riots, Blum attacked the 'outrageous offensive of fascist reaction', which sought 'the brutal confiscation of the republican liberties which the working people have conquered... and which remain the pledge of their final emancipation.'[258] Fear of fascism was kept alive by the remarkable increase in Colonel de La Rocque's following after 6 February. His *Croix de Feu* continued to behave in a vaguely threatening way: La Rocque himself moved about in a powerful car surrounded by guards on motor cycles, mobilizations and concentrations of forces were carried out which led to nothing more than obscure speechifying but which gave an impression that an imitation of Mussolini's march on Rome was coming.

These events and these threats aroused a defensive reaction from the left. This culminated in the so-called Popular Front, an alliance of Radicals, Socialists and Communists, which acted together in the elections of 1936. It was not surprising that the Socialists should take up this anti-fascist posture: what needs explanation is the conduct of the Communists who had joined in the riots of 6 February 1934, and of the Radicals, who had participated in the Doumergue government which was the immediate result of the riots. The first sign of possible co-operation between Socialists and Communists came on 12 February .The Socialist CGT decided on a twenty-four hour general strike for the 12 February, accompanied by demonstrations. The Communist CGTU followed suit and the two demonstrations merged. Even so, the Communist party leadership did not abandon its hostility to the Socialist party. It sought still for unity of action 'at the base', that is, to win over the section of the proletariat deluded by social-democratic wiles. As the communist leader, Thorez, put it in 1932, 'we do not wish agreement with the socialist chiefs, we do not wish understanding with socialist organizations. We wish to lead the socialist workers to battle'. On 10 March 1934 Thorez declared that the Communist party 'would never tolerate a policy of understanding at the summit, a policy of withdrawal and abdication in front of social fascism' – the latter phrase referred to the Socialist leadership. At this point, Moscow seems to have intervened. An article appeared there in *Pravda*, which was reproduced in *l'Humanité*, the French communist party paper, on 31 May. This called for a common front with the Socialists without insisting that their leaders were to be by-passed. On 5 June 1934, the central committee of the Communist party opened negotiations with the leadership of the Socialist party and on 27 July a pact was signed providing for a common struggle against fascism, against the government, for democratic liberties and against war. This striking change in Communist tactics was determined by the success of Hitler and the Nazi party in Germany. There the refusal of Communists to work with 'bourgeois' socialists had helped Hitler's rise to power. It soon became clear that Hitler was not an ephemeral phenomenon, the last gasp of capitalist reaction, but a formidable threat to the socialist fatherland, the Soviet Union itself. Those who might collaborate with Hitler must be frustrated, those who might work against fascism at home and abroad encouraged.

Thorez recognized that a successful fight against fascism meant using middle-class help. At first, the Communists sought this support by attempts to undermine the hold of the bourgeois parties, notably the Radicals. They failed. The Communists turned to direct approaches to radical leaders, especially deputies. By June 1935, Thorez was to be found publicly expressing admiration for the Radical party. (By 1936,

Thorez had reached the point of appealing to catholics and even to members of the *Croix de Feu*.) In that month some Radicals (notably Daladier) joined with Socialists and Communists in proposing a great demonstration for 14 July 1935 and on 3 July the executive committee of the party approved this step. These moves, were, once again, helped by Moscow. One difficulty in the way of collaboration between Radicals and Communists was the latter's objection to national defence. On 15 May 1935 it was announced, after Laval's signature of the Franco-Soviet pact, that 'M. Stalin understands and fully approves the policy of national defence carried out by France to maintain her armed forces at the level required by her security'. On 14 July great crowds took an oath 'to remain united, to defend democracy, to disarm and dissolve the factious leagues, to put our liberties out of reach of the attack of fascism'. Negotiations went on for electoral co-operation and on 18 January 1936 a common programme was set out. This was limited to short term objectives and the individual partners could set out their own doctrines. It called for the defence of democratic liberties, of peace, and for a struggle against the economic crisis and fascist organizations. There remained the anomaly that Radicals were still supporting Laval's government as well as the opposition to it. Radicals were increasingly hostile to Laval's policy of appeasement towards Mussolini and disturbed by the hostility aroused by the government's economic measures. On 22 January 1936 the radical ministers resigned from the government. Laval himself was forced to give way to a centre government under a radical, Sarraut, which presided over the election of 1936.[259]

The radical party, as far as its leaders were concerned was an organization for winning elections. The French electoral system, with a multiplicity of parties, made success impossible for a party acting on its own. It was essential to make arrangements with other groups by which the voters of other parties would transfer their votes in a second ballot to whichever of the allied parties was best placed for victory. The failure of the Flandin government in 1935 had shown that an alliance with groups of the right-centre provided too narrow a base for electoral success. Radicals could not avoid a choice between right and left. They could maintain the co-operation with the right implied by their support of the Doumergue and Laval governments or they could work with the left, with the socialists, which now meant with the communists too.

Acceptance of the Popular Front signalized the choice of the left. The Radical party was historically the great republican party; it had acquired its strength by standing for the principles of the great revolution, for democracy, for freedom, for social (if not economic) equality, for reason, for opprtunity. It was hostile to Catholicism, big business, to great landowners, but suspicious of socialism. It represented the independent peasant and the lower middle class. According to Pierre Cot, the Radical party was, 'the party of the small independent proprietors, farmers, shopkeepers, artisans, civil servants, men of the liberal professions – that is to say, all those who live from their work, but work that is distinctively theirs'. It was politically progressive and economically conservative or even reactionary. It is striking that the classes represented by the Radicals were precisely the type of people from whom in Germany came mass-support for the Nazis. In France the same classes chose political freedom rather than rushing to the violent right to defend them against communism. This is the main reason why France got Blum while Germany got Hitler. Radical voters, whatever may be said of some of their leaders, took their nebulous principles seriously. The principles of liberty and equality seemed in 1935 to be threatened by violence from the right. Radicals responded by efforts to defend the democratic republic. They were historically conditioned. They had praised republicanism for decades and the republic had, until recently, brought stability. (In Germany, republican democracy was associated with disasters and disorder.) In 1935 they were faced with the threats of violence and disorder made by the *Action Française*, and, above all, by the *Croix de Feu*, whose activities, however meaningless, were highly alarming. In contrast to Germany in 1932, they were faced with a tamed, almost decorous, Communist party.[260]

The elections of April and May 1936 produced a Popular Front victory: it was supported by groups with 378 deputies and opposed by 220. The Radicals lost heavily – about fifty seats – but the Communists gained fifty and the Socialists (SFIO) sixteen. This was a rather more left-wing chamber than that of 1932 (though a Popular Front majority could have been assembled in the latter). The position of the Radicals remained, however, decisive. A substantial move of Radicals to the right could bring left-wing governments to an end. The Socialists became the largest party in the chamber and Léon Blum formed a government with Radical participation and Communist support.

Before the government took office, large-scale strikes broke out, taking the form of an 'occupation of the factories' or sit-in strikes. The workers evidently wished to make sure that their claims should not somehow be evaded by clever politicians; they had been promised a new age and they expected to get it. They did. For the first time in French history there was a government in power whose main concern was to make life better for the working man. Immediately representatives of French employers were induced, by government intervention, to accept large increases in wages. Jouhaux, the trade union leader, spoke a day later:

For the first time in the history of the world, a whole class obtains at one moment of time an amelioration of its condition of life . . . this is of high moral significance. That demonstrates clearly that it is not necessary to bring about a totalitarian and authoritarian state to raise the working class to its rôle of collaborator in the national economy, but the regular functioning and the heightening of democracy permit it.

The increase in wages was soon spoilt by increasing prices; some of the other work of the Blum government, like the forty hour week, was actually damaging. It was the spirit that counted – Jouhaux was right; the French working man could never again regard the democratic state as something irrevocably hostile. Indeed, the greatest success of the Popular Front government, the legal institution of paid holidays, exemplified with clarity the social overtones of its work, its concern to give the working man a chance to share in some of the decencies of life. Blum was fully conscious of what he was doing: 'I had the feeling that I had . . . brought an embellishment, a ray of light into difficult and obscure lives . . . There had been opened to them a glimpse into the future; hope had been created for them'.[261]

Blum's government aroused passionate hostility from the French right. The strikes of 1936 caused alarm and the subsequent devaluation of the franc revived middle class fears for their incomes. At the same time the outbreak of the Spanish Civil War generated a deep division in French opinion. Many, though not all, of Blum's supporters called for aid to the Spanish republicans against the rebel armies – Communists and some Socialists were for intervention, most Radicals against it. Many on the right sympathized with the Spanish nationalists because of their reactionary Catholic leanings while they claimed that aid to the Spanish government would mean an unnecessary conflict with Italy whose alliance they believed to be essential for France. In consequence journalistic attacks of unparalleled severity were launched against the Popular Front government in France. Blum feared that French intervention in Spain might lead to civil war in France. Blum's Jewish background provoked numerous outbursts of journalistic anti-Semitism. The outstanding achievement of the journalists was their campaign against the Minister of the Interior, Salengro. On 17 November 1936 he committed suicide.[262]

In the spring of 1937 the work of the Popular Front came to an end. The linked attempts of the Blum government to increase national production through a rise in purchasing power and to redistribute incomes for the benefit of the workers came to an end – largely in failure. The Radicals called a halt. They were alarmed by inflation and frightened by the Communists. On 16 March 1937 supporters of the *Front Populaire* launched a demonstration at Clichy to protest against a meeting of the *Parti Social Français* (the revised form of the *Croix de Feu*). The demonstrators clashed with the police: five were killed and many injured. The Radicals blamed the Communists and accused them of fomenting disorder. The Popular Front majority survived the resignation of Blum in June 1937 – if Socialists refused to support a Radical-led government they would simply drive the Radicals into full collaboration with the right – but it survived as a pretence. The open break in the Popular Front came towards the end of 1938 when the government headed by a Radical, Daladier, sought successfully, under the inspiration of Paul Reynaud, to reverse some of the legislation of the Popular Front – notably the forty hour week. Socialists and Communists now moved into opposition.

Thus the chamber of deputies elected in 1936 had supported two opposed systems of government – that of 1936 of social progress and reform and that of 1938 of social conservatism and financial orthodoxy. As in 1926 and 1934, Radicals, elected for the most part as men of the left, had come to co-operate with the right. In 1938, a firmer course came to be taken by the Daladier government against strikes and with the defeat of the general strike of November 1938, labour disputes died away, helped by the recovery in economic activity and by the end of Communist agitation over the Spanish civil war. By 1939 much of the domestic discord that reached its height in the years 1934–6 had gone. The working class had lived through a period when the state was on its side; the right had seen a return to domestic conservatism. The threat of fascism seemed to have passed. In June 1936 the government had decreed the dissolution of the *Croix de Feu*, the *Jeunesses Patriotes*, the *Solidarité Française* and the *Francistes*. The *Croix de Feu* instantly reappeared as the *Parti Social Français*. This was the most important of the leagues – now it claimed to be an ordinary political party, though one 'above' the other parties. In practice it began to behave like an ordinary parliamentary party, vigorously preparing for the next elections. Significantly, Colonel de La Rocque's movement gained immensely in support after this open transformation and after 1936 it came to have as many as two million supporters. The support secured by Colonel de La Rocque, for a nebulous new style conservatism, weakened the violent leagues. By 1938 indeed, the other leagues had sunk into insignificance. The *Action Française* continued its journalistic activity but with an influence well below that of its peak in 1934.

It is true, however, that new organizations devoted to violence were created. In 1936 Doriot, a former communist, started the *Parti Populaire Français*, a fully fledged fascist party. This acquired a considerable following in 1937, helped by subsidies from Italy, only to come near to extinction in 1938.[263] Then there was the strange group, the MSAR or *Movement Secret d'Action Révolutionnaire*, which became known as the *Cagoule*, with its directing committee (CSAR). This was devoted to resisting a non-existent Communist plan to seize power in France. It intended to provoke violence from the Communists and then to intervene against them, introducing at the same time some sort of authoritarian régime. The new element lay in the contacts developed by the *Cagoule* with sections of the army. Most army officers had long disliked politicians, and despised the democratic republic. The events of the post-war years, above all attempts at disarmament and the inflation which hurt the classes from which officers were mainly drawn, accentuated their distaste. The Popular Front with its acceptance of the Communist party as a party of government, brought some to feel that they must take deliberate steps to prevent subversion of the army and to maintain it as an ultimate defence against the reds. Within the army clandestine groups were formed around 1936, to watch for communists, and to arrange for the geographical distribution within the army of safely anti-communist officers. This activity was helped by senior officers, including Marshal Pétain, Marshal Franchet d'Esperey and General Georges. These groups in the army made contact with Deloncle, the chief of the CSAR. Nothing much came of it: in September 1937, the *Cagoule* arranged for bombs to go off in the headquarters of two employers' organizations in Paris – no doubt to demonstrate the existence of the communist menace. The affair rebounded and in the following months the police discovered stores of arms and arrested numerous *Cagoulards* in 1938, though the secret anti-communist cells in the army remained in being.[264]

Divisions of opinion on the internal ordering of French affairs were complicated in the later 1930s by profound divisions on foreign policy. Until 1936 the French right advocated firmness towards Germany and the maintenance to this end of military alliances and of the military power of France. Until 1935 the left advocated conciliation and disarmament and reliance on the League of Nations for French security –

1 Woodrow Wilson, President of the USA, 1913-21

2 Clemenceau in New York

3 Lloyd George leaving the palace after signing the Treaty of Versailles for Great Britain on 28 June 1919

4 Kemal Atatürk, President of the Turkish Republic, 1923–38, shown adopting western customs

5 Raymond Poincaré, French Prime Minister during the Ruhr crisis

6 Gustav Stresemann, German Foreign Minister, 1923–29

7 Signatories of the Locarno agreements at Victoria station: Aristide Briand (centre) and Austen Chamberlain (right)

8 The unemployment problem in Britain (*opposite, above*): a queue outside a labour exchange in 1924
9 (*Opposite, below*) Police clearing the street before the first tram left the depot at New Cross in London after the General Strike in May 1926

10 From left to right: J. H. Thomas, a member of the TUC general congress during the General Strike and cabinet minister in the second Labour government (1929–31), Stanley Baldwin, Conservative Prime Minister (1924–9) during the strike, and Neville Chamberlain who headed the National Government from 1937 to 1940
11 (*Opposite, above*) The fascist salute being given at a demonstration in London in October 1938
12 (*Opposite, below*) A floodlit meeting of Sir Oswald Mosley's British fascists in July 1939

13 New housing in Britain: a housing estate in Birmingham

14 Giovanni Giolitti
(1842–1928)

15 The March on Rome, October 1922

16 Mussolini with four
of his generals during
the March on Rome
17 King Victor Emmanuel
III of Italy

18 Fascist celebrations in November 1923: cyclists saluting Mussolini
19 Fascist youth passing in review for Mussolini

20 A barricade in Paris during the Stavisky riots of 6 February 1934
21 (*Opposite, above*) Léon Blum, the Socialist leader of the French Popular Front, arriving in England with his wife in July 1936
22 The Reynaud Cabinet (*opposite*), March 1940. In the front row from left to right: Daladier, Reynaud, Chautemps

23 Manuel Azaña (left), Prime Minister of Spain, 1931–3 and 1936 and President of the Republic, 1936–9, with the Catalan leader, Luis Companys
24 Gil Robles, leader of the coalition of Spanish right wing parties, the CEDA

25 Nationalist forces on a mountain road in the Sierra de Guadarrama during the advance on Madrid, 1936

26 General Franco addressing a crowd in Burgos after he had been proclaimed head of the 'Nationalist Government' in October 1936

27 The Spanish Civil War: nationalist troops, 1939

28 General von Seeckt, the principal architect of the *Reichswehr*
29 Alfred Hugenberg (*opposite*) who became chairman of the German
Nationalist Peoples' Party in 1928

30 (*Above*) Brüning, German Chancellor 1930–2 (right), and his foreign minister Curtius (centre), visiting London in July 1931

31 General von Schleicher: Chief of the *Ministeramt* in the German Ministry of Defence, 1929–32, and Chancellor, December 1932 and January 1933

32 Franz von Papen (left)
German Chancellor, June
to December 1932
33 Field Marshall
Hindenburg (*below*),
President of Germany,
1925–34

35 Hitler speaking at a rally in the Lustgarten, Berlin, 1935

34 (*opposite*) 1933: Adolf Hitler, shaking hands with President Hindenburg

36 Marshal Pilsudski, Polish head of state 1918–23 and 1926–35

37 Engelbert Dollfuss, Austrian Chancellor from May 1932 until
he was killed in the Nazi *Putsch* in July 1934

38 (*Opposite, above*) Pierre Laval, the French foreign minister, with
Maxim Litvinov, his Russian opposite number,
39 (*Opposite*) Pierre Flandin (right), French Foreign Minister in London
for talks on the Rhineland situation in 1936
40 (*Above*) Von Ribbentrop, German Ambassador to Britain, seeing off
Lord Halifax, on his visit to Germany in 1937

41 (*Right*) Beneš,
President of Czechoslovakia
in 1938
42 Neville Chamberlain
leaving London for his
meeting with Hitler at
Godesberg, September 1938

43 Bonnet (left), Daladier (centre) and Gamelin in London after Chamberlain's meeting with Hitler at Godesburg

44 The invasion of Czechoslovakia: (*above*) Germans entering Prague in March 1939
45 Colonel Joseph Beck (right), the Polish Foreign Minister, leaving the Foreign Office in April 1939.

46 Belgian soldiers retreating before the German advance, May 1940
47 German troops in Paris, June 1940

48 Part of the centre of Dresden after the allied bombing, 1945

though the Radicals, at least, never pushed this advocacy to the point of accepting unilateral disarmament. The Ethiopian crisis induced an evolution in the view of the left: if the League of Nations were to be viable then Italian aggression must be curbed. (The Manchurian crisis had made no serious impact on French opinion). The left opposed Laval's attempts to avoid complications with an aggressive Italy. The right began to suspect that the left was prepared, on ideological grounds, irresponsibly to alienate a possible ally of France.

The Spanish Civil War brought much graver complexities. Virtually the whole French right sympathized with the Spanish army's revolt against the Spanish Popular Front, while the French Communists used every means, especially demonstrations and strikes, to try to force French intervention on the side of the Spanish republican government. Intervention in Spain seemed likely to bring conflict with the backers of the Spanish rebels – Germany and Italy. The French right-wing concluded that French Communists were eager, on orders from Moscow, to risk a European war for the sake of advancing the cause of red revolution in Spain. The next step in the chain of reasoning was crucial though it was a step taken by only part of the French right: Communists, therefore, desired European war for the sake of assisting the Communist International to spread its power. If this were so, then those who proposed to resist European fascism and in particular to contain Hitler's Germany, if necessary by force, were communists or communist dupes acting whether consciously or not in the interests of Moscow. The French Popular Front demonstrated the dangers of communism and the way in which Moscow could gain a hold on French politics. Hitler was an anti-communist, determined to smash bolshevism. Instead of resisting German expansion, France should therefore accept it, should seek compromise with Germany and leave Germany to destroy Russia. France could defend herself against any direct German threat, if it ever came, especially if conflict with Italy were avoided. The Franco-Soviet alliance, originally the work of right-wing French governments in 1934 and 1935 should be abandoned; indeed France should disinterest herself in eastern Europe altogether and avoid being dragged into assisting Moscow's sinister designs by concern for Czechs or Poles.

Not all the French right took this view. Some stuck to the old-fashioned view that an aggressive Germany must necessarily seek to ruin France and that Hitlerian aggression should therefore be resisted and that anyone who would help to resist it must be a friend of France – even Soviet Russia. Among the right-centre and among the Radicals similar divergences opened. All had hoped that the post-war structure would preserve peace through the terms of the Treaty of Versailles and through France's alliances in eastern Europe or through the co-operation of the League of Nations. By 1936, after Germany had begun to rearm openly and had remilitarized the Rhineland, it had become plain that post-war arrangements had collapsed. Some drew the conclusion that this failure must be recognized and that France must make the best arrangements she could with Hitler's Germany. Others believed that, though some opportunities of curbing Germany had been lost, Germany must still be curbed in the future if France herself were to be safe from Nazi domination. The eastern alliances must be revived, Russia should be brought in, Britain should be encouraged to join in resistance to future German advances. This divergence of opinion was obscured by the fact that the advocates of French surrender were prepared to bluff: to talk of France's honouring her commitments, to maintain the 1935 alliance with Russia and to ask for British help in the hope that Hitler might be frightened into passivity. Superficially, therefore, supporters of both schools of thought could act in the same way until the bluff was called and the choice came between war and acceptance of German demands.

The Socialists, too, were divided. The Spanish Civil War and German and Italian intervention in it convinced most Socialists that fascism must be resisted by force. A minority took a different view. Some were simply pacifists believing all war to be evil. Others claimed that war would bring an end to hopes of socialism and that war could be avoided by negotiation for peaceful revision of the post-war treaty settlements in eastern Europe and by renewed attempts at disarmament. The first view was upheld by Léon Blum, the second by Paul Faure. In December 1938 a party congress supported Blum's views against Faure's by 4332 votes to 2837 with 1014 abstentions, and sixty voted for total pacifism.[265]

Divisions in the Communist party came only when war had broken out. Until then the Communists, since 1934, had called for resistance to fascism everywhere and for French aid to any foreign resisters – in Spain, in eastern Europe, even in China. When war came the party voted for military credits and Thorez went off to join his regiment. Then Moscow spoke and imposed the new line embodied in the Nazi-Soviet pact of August 1939: the war against Hitler was an imperialist war which Communists must oppose. This was too much for most Communist voters and sympathizers and the opposition to the war belatedly taken up by a reluctant leadership had little effect.[266]

It would be untrue to say that these divisions on what to do about Germany faded away once the war had begun. Those who had been against going to war at all tended to favour a compromise peace. What is untrue is to say that these people wished for a French defeat. One event strengthened this belated unity: the co-operation of Soviet Russia with Germany in the destruction of Poland. To the French right, Hitler, the ally of Russia, was something much more worth fighting than Hitler the anti-bolshevik. On 2 September 1939 Daladier secured unanimous votes for war credits (only Bergery in the chamber and Laval in the senate ventured to raise a voice of dissent). French mobilization was carried out calmly. As in Britain, and indeed in Germany, there was none of the enthusiasm for war in France that had appeared in 1914, but at least a gloomy acceptance. In domestic politics divisions between Frenchmen had declined by 1939 and the economy was making rapid progress; republican democracy had survived and France remained a country of liberty; in foreign affairs disunity, however, temporarily, was silenced by the outbreak of war. However, even if the defeat of 1940 was a military defeat, a defeat of the French army, the result of that defeat was the reopening of the divisions of previous years. The effect was to cause many Frenchmen to accept defeat more readily than might have been so in a more united society and to cause some Frenchmen to support a régime which was prepared to seek a 'regeneration' of France under the aegis of a victorious Germany. Pétain said in January 1941, speaking of the possibility that France might have continued to resist in 1940 in North Africa after the defeat in France itself, that the price would have been the 'final postponement of all the work of material and spiritual reconstruction'.[267] The spirit of acquiescence and surrender that expressed itself in the armistice and in Vichy can be explained by past conflicts in France, even if the defeat itself cannot.

It was alleged that governments under the Third Republic were unduly weak. The principal basis for this claim was that governments were frequently turned out by votes in the chamber of deputies and that ministries and ministers were therefore transient and embarrassed phantoms without time to make, still less to enforce, coherent decisions. There were forty-two French governments between the wars, or thirty-three if governments reformed under the same Prime Minister are excluded. The effects of this were less damaging than might have been expected. There was much continuity of personnel between governments. Here are some examples – Briand was in charge of the foreign ministry without a break from April 1925 to January 1932, as a member of fourteen governments; Chautemps held the ministry of the interior from June 1932 until January 1934 in five governments; Daladier was in charge of war or defence between December 1932 and January 1934 in four governments and again between June 1936 and May 1940 in six governments. There were broadly two sorts of situation in which governments were changed – when the majority changed, that is, when a change in the policy and attitude of the ministry was required, and the more frequent changes when the activities of the government in a particular sector met with resistance which compelled the whole government to withdraw and to reappear not with fundamental changes in policy or personnel but with, perhaps, one crucial minister changed. The former state of affairs was not a source of weakness at all. This type of change in majority and therefore in government policy appeared in 1926, 1934 and 1938. On each occasion it was the Radicals who moved from support for the left to support for the right. On each occasion (even in 1934) their movement represented a genuine shift in the opinion of the people they represented. Thus, without frequent elections, governments remained in harmony with majority opinion in the country at large, while some continuity was secured in personnel through the continuity of ministers drawn from or acceptable to the Radicals. Indeed, there was something in Sarraut's claim that the Radical party was a 'guarantee against civil war' precisely through its making possible easy transitions from one political pattern to another.[268]

A more damaging type of governmental instability was the type exemplified in the years 1924–6 and 1932–4 when numerous governments of a similar political composition based on the same majority followed in rapid succession as one after the other was overthrown when it proposed unpopular financial expedients. The reasons for this situation are complex, lying ultimately in the electoral situation of the constituencies. Many deputies, especially among the radicals, were in parliament because of their own carefully cultivated local influence not because their local supporters were concerned about the success or failure of a particular government. Such deputies, when forced to choose between the maintenance of a government and the defence of their own position chose the latter. Thus electorally unpopular measures were difficult to carry through even when the deputies themselves privately approved them. The solution was to enfranchise the executive government from the minute scrutiny of deputies – this was done through the device of voting to the government *pleins pouvoirs*, thus delegating legislative power to the government. This was a sensible solution – parliament could still control the general policies of governments in the field in question without need for individual deputies to go on record as approving every detail. It is wrong to suggest that such grants of *pleins pouvoirs* marked an end to democracy.

The thesis that the depopulation of the countryside had deprived France of the virtues uniquely found among country dwellers can be dismissed briefly. It is true that there was a reduction in the population engaged in agriculture in the twentieth century. Taking figures for males alone there were 5·5 millions in 1906; 4·4 in 1931 and 4·1 in 1936.[269] This was inevitable if French industry were to grow at all. Indeed it is much wiser to argue that the protection of French agriculture by tariffs and by the measures of the Popular Front weakened France economically (and militarily) by retaining too large a population on the land, where it was insufficiently productive. As for the notion that peasants make better soldiers than industrial workers, that is a prejudice unsupported by any shred of evidence drawn from modern armies.

We may now turn to the question of preparation for war. After 1940 it was claimed that French governments after 1936, and especially Blum's government, had ensured the defeat by spreading moral decay and by hindering rearmament. It was said that the forty hour week, paid holidays, and weakness in face of strikes had generated habits of selfish idleness, which ruined that readiness for self-sacrifice required for an effective army. This charge was brought forward, above all, in the Riom trial when the post-armistice government of Vichy sought to show that the defeat had been made certain by these measures. Blum replied that it was

impossible to defend republican liberties in France while excluding from this effort the working masses and the fraction of the working élite still grouped around the communist conception. And I thought that it was above all an immense result and an immense service to have brought back these masses and this élite to a love and sentiment of duty towards the country.

The working class had learnt again to sing the *Marseillaise*. 'That sort of unanimous agreement that was found in France at the moment of mobilization was in part the consequence of all that; and as a result, was to some extent our work.'[270] Again, ordinary French soldiers conducted themselves well in the actual campaign. On the whole, indiscipline and demoralization set in after defeat and enemy breakthrough; it was a consequence not a cause of defeat. There were exceptions, especially among lower quality divisions, notably in the crucial Sedan sector, but they were infrequent.[271]

So far from its being the intention of the Popular Front government to delay rearmament it is reasonable to assert that a serious French effort to rearm began only when that government had come to power. In the early 1930s a major proportion of French resources was devoted to fortification: in 1930–4, about 5,000 million francs were spent on the Maginot Line behind the Franco-German frontier. At the end of 1934 a programme established under the supervision of Marshal Pétain was put into effect. It did not match German plans and in the middle of 1935 Laval withdrew the necessary credits, though they were restored at the end of the year. In 1936 Blum's minister for war, Daladier, asked the general staff to produce a plan for re-equipping the army. The general staff proposed spending 9,000 million francs over the period 1937–40. Daladier thought this inadequate and, with the full agreement of Blum, encouraged the general staff to draw up proposals for spending 14,000 millions. No difficulties were made by parliament and the credits were subsequently increased to meet rising prices. Indeed, in the 1930s, parliament never rejected or modified any proposals for expenditure on national defence put to it by any government. This plan of 1936 had been executed in full by the time active operations began in 1940. Thus the requirements of the general staff as set out in 1936 were completely met. The proportion of various types of weapon available to the army in 1940 were those that the general staff had laid down – including notably the proportions between heavy and light tanks, and the numbers of anti-tank weapons. This programme could not be speeded up; nor could the additional orders of 1938, notably for modern anti-aircraft weapons, be met. Here the deficiencies of French industrial capacity showed themselves. In so far as governmental action affected productive capacity, neither left or right can escape blame. Right-wing governments weakened industry by deflation especially in 1934 and 1935; in 1937, the rigid forty hour week certainly reduced capacity (principally through curtailing the work of specialists); it was effectively relaxed for work on national defence only in 1938.[272]

The navy was in excellent condition and (assuming the British alliance) fully capable of carrying out any requirements of European war. The air force was a very different matter. Preparations for war began with the plan drawn up by General Denain in 1934 for one thousand aircraft plus two hundred reserves; this began to be put into effect in 1935. The Popular Front government expanded the plan to 1,500 plus nine hundred aircraft. Unfortunately, the air minister of the Blum government, Pierre Cot, made what proved to be two mistakes. He was faced with two choices – between continuing existing production or waiting for new prototypes of more modern design and between

188

making the best of the existing productive methods of French industry or waiting while mass-production methods could be introduced. He chose to go ahead with existing designs on the basis of the artisan type of industry still prevalent. This meant that he got more aircraft turned out in 1937 than could otherwise have been made. Unhappily by 1938 they were all totally out of date and very nearly worthless. In January 1938, when Guy La Chambre became minister for air, this process of slowly turning out planes that were obsolete even when they were completely new came to an end. La Chambre inaugurated an attempt to organize mass-production for fresh prototypes. This meant that production actually fell during part of 1938 below the already alarmingly low level of 1937 of about thirty-five aircraft a month. (Germany in 1937: 350 per month; Britain: 120.) Mass-production, however, began to produce results in 1939. About 220 aircraft a month were produced in that year and in the first five months of 1940, 313 per month. By September 1939 something like 1,200 modern aircraft had been produced and by May 1940, 3,300 (these figures include about 170 and 340 aircraft bought in the USA). These figures are not, of course, figures for 'first line' aircraft – those immediately available for action with fully trained crews, as distinct from reserves. In 1938, therefore, the French air force was nearly non-existent; General Vuillemin, the chief of air staff, declared in January 1938 that in any conflict that year the French air force would be annihilated in a few days. This fact had some influence on French foreign policy in that year. Even in 1939 the French air force could expect to face war with Germany on equal terms only by putting the whole of the British air force in the balance – and it was impossible for the whole of the Royal Air Force to abandon the air defence of Great Britain. Furthermore, as a result of the views of the general staff the French air force was not equipped with bombing planes adapted for tactical co-operation with the army.[273] Thus there were real weaknesses in the French armed services, but when war came in 1939 it was reasonable to suppose that France might hold her own.

The failure of France to defend Europe and herself against Nazi Germany should not obscure the successes of the Third Republic. France remained until 1940 a country in which an intelligent and free man might reasonably choose to live.

10

Spain 1919-45

The major theme of Spanish history in these years is to be found in the failure of the attempt during the Republic to create a reasonable and free political system and to attack some of the causes of the backwardness and misery of much of the population.

In 1918 Spain was, in theory, governed by a democratic monarchy. In practice, governments and the assembly, the Cortes, did not represent the major social forces in Spain. Elections were still rigged by a governing oligarchy drawn from the middle and upper classes. Workers, peasants and, to a lesser extent, the army, were outside the régime. Workers and peasants expressed themselves through socialism and anarchism and above all through socialist and anarcho-syndicalist unions. The army intervened in politics through fluid conspiratorial organizations of officers.

A socialist party had existed in Spain from 1879. It accepted the notion of working by constitutional means towards political power. Since the constitution, until 1931, was a sham, the socialist party did not get very far. Much more important was the socialist trade union movement – the UGT (*Unión General de Trabajadores*) founded in 1888. This was a reformist movement believing in the advance of the working class through peaceful strikes. What was necessary for progress along these moderate lines was to develop organization and to spread political consciousness through education (in 1901 about sixty-three per cent of the population was illiterate).[274] In the early twentieth century, the Socialists set up *Casas del Pueblo* to provide centres for meetings and discussions and lending libraries. After the war the Socialists were faced, like the other European Socialist parties, with a decision for or against the Third International of Moscow; narrowly the Spanish party rejected the twenty-one conditions posed by Moscow. A substantial number of Socialist leaders then seceded to form the Spanish Communist party. The rank and file did not follow and the Communist party remained unimportant until the civil war. The UGT became a powerful organization: by 1934 it had more than one and a quarter million members with its major basis of working class support in the Asturias, around Bilbao, in Madrid and Valencia and in the urban areas of western Spain.

Doctrines of anarchism secured wider acceptance in Spain than anywhere else in Europe. Anarchists sought freedom and therefore the destruction of any authority which limits liberty, especially the State. Free men would co-operate with other free men to produce small societies which would contract voluntary pacts with each other. Capitalist industrialist organization should be destroyed and associations of freely co-operating producers replace it. In a libertarian society the vices of mankind brought about by subordination, exploitation and the destruction of human dignity would tend to fade away. A revolution, starting spontaneously from below, would destroy existing authority and inaugurate the golden age of freedom and voluntary co-operation. In October 1910 a conference of anarchist groups created a trade union organization, the *Confederación Nacional del Trabajo* or CNT. This syndical organization was, of course, to be decentralized, without paid officials. It sought the moral emancipation of the workers. In unions formed under Marxist inspiration, unity for political struggle is essential and strong and authoritarian leadership is aimed at. The object is the conquest of state power, not its destruction. The anarcho-syndicalists of the CNT sought spontaneity, not discipline; their object was the destruction of oppression by the State, the atomization of power, not its possession. Violence from the oppressors of mankind should be met with violence until the great general strike enabled the coming of the millennium. In 1927 the *Federación Anarquista Iberica* or FIA was founded. This contained pure anarchists, and acted as an inner group designed to prevent the CNT from evolving into a Muscovite type of organization seeking a strong proletarian dictatorship. The CNT's major area of strength was in Catalonia, especially in Barcelona.

These organizations for social change gained the support of many peasants and agricultural workers. There were great differences in its extent because of geographical and economic distinctions between the various regions of Spain. In the south of Spain, especially in Andalusia, anarchism was strong. This was an area of large estates. They were worked by an agricultural proletariat of landless labourers. There was a superabundance of labour – industrial development in Spain was insufficient to absorb the excess population of the landed regions – and miserable wages were the rule. Even these wages were available only for part of the year, often less than half. The land was poor and dry and could not be cultivated intensively. Indeed, large tracts were often allowed to go out of cultivation altogether. Agricultural labourers therefore lived in conditions of permanent near-starvation. In the rather similar regions of La Mancha and Extremadura the UGT acquired a stronger hold. In Castile, where short leases on small farms were granted by landlords who fulfilled no economic function of any kind, the UGT had some influence but in many districts the Church maintained its grip: this was a region where Catholic agrarian associations assisted the peasantry. In Galicia with minimal peasant properties paying quit rents to absentees a similar rivalry prevailed. In the rural regions of Asturias, the Basque provinces and Navarre a relatively prosperous peasantry of small proprietors and tenant farmers (generally share-croppers) was found. Here, especially in the Basque country and in Navarre, the Church retained full influence. Indeed, in Navarre a prosperous society of peasant owners was the basis of the most conservative movement in Spain, that of Carlism. In Aragon the mountainous country was similar to Navarre, while an area of large estates was strongly affected by the CNT. In rural Catalonia peasants holding vineyards, under leases lasting as long as the vines, had grievances deriving from the shortened life of the vines. Here allegiance to the CNT or UGT was cut across by Catalan separatism.[275]

The army was an unusual institution. It was useless against any modern force. It proved incapable of holding down Spanish Morocco without French co-operation. It contained a swollen number of officers. They were not well paid, but the sons of the middle class who made up the officer corps found in the army security, social prestige and the sense of belonging to an élite group. The army was no use for foreign war; on the other hand it could intervene with decisive effect in internal politics. Its officers had nothing very serious to do (except in Morocco) and had leisure to brood over the iniquities of civilian politicians with minds irritated sometimes by their own poverty, sometimes by the grievances and fears of the class from which they came. The army had a tradition, in the nineteenth century, of intervention in political life, to restore 'order', to eliminate corruption, to embody the 'national will'. In this period the tradition revived.[276]

The upper elements of the Spanish middle class were closely integrated socially and economically with the landed aristocracy. Industrial development around Bilbao, in the Asturias, and around Barcelona had created a class of rich industrialists (though the wealth thus generated was in a very high proportion enjoyed by investors from abroad). These men worked with the landed oligarchy in controlling the financial institutions of Spain, while rich landed proprietors invested in industry. Thus clashes between a liberal industrial class and a conservative landed class were unlikely, for at the highest level land owners and industrialists formed a unified property owning group. There was no reason why this group should be opposed to efficient and even democratic government provided such a government did not lead to radical attacks on property rights. Among engineers, lawyers, doctors, journalists, members of universities, and school teachers were to be found the strongest supporters of parliamentary government by discussion and compromise. This group, confident in its skill and ability, feared change less than most – but many could be driven into reaction by fears of disorderly revolution. These fears took much stronger root among the lesser men of property: small business men, shopkeepers, petty land-lords were readily alarmed by threats to their wealth, especially from the anarchists, and ready to seek protectors however intellectually disreputable. The course of the Second Republic was largely determined by the shifting balance between the hopes of reform and renovation on the one side, and fear of subversion on the other, felt by these groups of the middle class.

The Spanish Church was a large, rich and powerful body. There were 80,000 priests, monks and nuns. No one knows quite how much property, landed, urban and industrial it possessed. The Jesuit order was believed to have far-flung investments. The Church retained control over education. In some parts of the countryside the Church continued to be revered by all classes. Middle and upper-class women in general were firmly devout. Some religious feeling remained among middle and upper-class men; more supported the Church as a bastion of order. That it certainly was, without reservation. Perhaps because of its wealth (not shared by the parish clergy) perhaps because of the threat from atheistic anarchism, the hierarchy of the Church was profoundly conservative.[277]

In the years 1919–23 a social war broke out in Catalonia. The world war had produced prosperity for the industrial regions in Spain and even for the agricultural areas. After the war European demand fell off and food prices fell. Falling wages and unemployment produced revolutionary strikes, especially in Barcelona. Employers (organized in a federation), damaged by diminishing profits, fought back. The employers attempted to subvert the CNT by setting up so-called free unions.

These resorted to terrorism to break the anarchist unions using gangs of gunmen or *pistoleros*. The anarchists, seeking the violent overthrow of bourgeois society through direct action, replied with bombs and *pistoleros* of their own. From November 1920 the civil governor, a general, used the police to help in the shooting of syndicalists. In 1918–19 strikes of agricultural workers broke out in Andalusia and were suppressed by troops. The strike movement petered out into a desultory private war of gunmen in Barcelona and by mid-1923 revolutionary unionism had clearly failed. These events caused panic among property owners, especially in the areas affected by strikes. As in 1936, these fears caused an eager demand for a strong government to extend to the whole of Spain the repressive methods of Barcelona so that the military dictatorship of General Primo de Rivera was set up in 1923 with the acquiescence of men of property.[278]

Meanwhile, in 1921 the Spanish army suffered a shattering defeat at the hands of a much smaller force of rebel Moroccans. Inquiries began in the Cortes which pointed to the partial responsibility of the King, Alfonso XIII. This fact added to the impatience the king was beginning to feel with constitutional government. Elections were showing signs of becoming real, of escaping from safe governmental control – if this process were allowed to develop the King would find his independence vanishing. As a result the King, like many property owners, was ready for a new governmental model. When, in 1923, General Primo de Rivera proclaimed his assumption of power, with the support of the army, the King readily appointed him Prime Minister.

Here was a partial rehearsal of 1936 with the army stepping forward to defend itself against criticism and to save Spain from subversion. The King's conduct made governmental resistance impossible. The CNT was weakened by the struggle in Barcelona, while the UGT, instead of trying to defend the constitution, was ready to co-operate with the dictatorship in order to extend its own influence at the expense of the CNT and in order to win advantages for those it represented.

The dictatorship of Primo de Rivera was not a period of pure reaction. The dictator himself was an amiable, sometimes drunken, and eccentric ruler. He did not seek to surround himself with any of the mystical trappings of dictatorial rule or endeavour to maintain an aura of remote dignity. He showed concern for the material welfare of the working class and, in return, his rule was accepted by the UGT, whose leader, Largo Caballero, became a councillor of state. In 1926, mixed committees with equal representation for workers and employers and a government chairman were established to settle wage disputes.

Extensive public works were set on foot, notably the building of roads and dams. These activities and the international boom of the later 1920s brought a relative prosperity to Spain.

Opposition came from various sources. Catalan aspirations for autonomy, based ultimately on the feeling that this rich province was exploited by Madrid in the interests of the poorer parts of Spain, were firmly squashed; an attempt was even made to suppress the Catalan language. The politicians of parliamentary days resented their exclusion from power and the contempt poured on them by the dictator. Hostility from the possessing classes followed from his social policies. An attempt was made to inaugurate an effective income tax and there were vague thoughts of agrarian reform. In 1929 the foreign exchange value of the peseta began to fall and this was regarded as a sign of economic ill-health. Above all, the army was alienated. In 1926 Primo de Rivera attacked the independence of the corps of artillery officers who maintained a separate promotion structure, and, when they resisted, the dictator suspended the entire body of officers. In spite of the dislike felt felt by other branches of the army towards the artillery, widespread resentment developed towards this high-handed treatment of army officers. The King had come to object to being disregarded by Primo de Rivera and he was anxious to detach himself from the mounting unpopularity of the dictatorship. In January 1930 Primo de Rivera, aware of the King's attitude, made inquiries as to whether his power was still supported by the army. The unenthusiastic replies he received induced him to resign – he died in Paris a few months later.[279]

The months after the fall of Primo de Rivera were filled with attempts by King Alfonso XIII to keep his throne. The dictator had ousted the King from power but the King was still held responsible for allowing him to come to power in the first place. The King's attempt to carry on with a new and less demonstrative dictator, General Berenguer, did nothing to restore his popularity among the politicians, in Catalonia or in the army. In the spring of 1931 Alfonso's last government allowed municipal elections to be held, hoping for a demonstration of residual monarchical sentiment. The elections, in April, demonstrated that this sentiment did not exist. Though the smaller towns voted monarchist, no one paid any attention to this expected result, and what mattered was that nearly every large town voted republican. Disorder threatened if Alfonso remained. The army showed no sign of readiness to support the monarchy; above all, General Sanjurjo, the influential soldier who commanded the gendarmerie, the *Guardia civil*, which was the major bulwark of order, refused to oppose the Republic. On April the King abdicated and departed from Spain.[280]

Thus the Republic, which was set up after the abdication, was supported or at least accepted, in the beginning, by the most important elements in Spanish society. The history of the years between 1931 and 1936 is that of the collapse of this measure of agreement; this collapse is the decisive event in the recent history of Spain.

With the departure of the King, power fell into the hands of a provisional government containing moderate republicans and socialists, under Alcalá Zamora, a Catholic republican. Azaña, an able radical intellectual of the middle class, became minister for war and Largo Caballero, the head of the Socialist UGT, minister of labour. Immediately the government began to deal with the great problems: the land, the Church, the army. Largo Caballero acted to protect smallholders against mortgage foreclosures, authorized municipalities to oblige land-owners to cultivate their estates and extended the law on industrial accidents to agricultural workers. The employment of migrant labour to break wage-strikes was forbidden. The government announced complete religious freedom, promised to introduce divorce, and produced plans for the development of a state-run non-religious school system, while announcing its intention of reducing the number of religious orders. Azaña worked out plans for a smaller, more efficient army; to this end the number of officers was to be cut by more than half. Aware of the dangers involved in meddling with the army, he tried to buy off discontent by offering terms of startling generosity to officers prepared to leave the army: full-pay, to be increased at the rates and at the times that normal promotion would have provided for a serving officer – terms which measure the fully justified fear of the enmity of the army felt by the government.[281]

At the end of June 1931, elections were held (free elections) for a Cortes to draw up a constitution. The result was a victory for the coalition of left-republicans and Socialists. In approximate figures, a hundred and twenty Socialists were elected, eighty of the members of the middle class republican groups of the moderate left, thirty Catalan nationalists, twenty Galician nationalists. In the centre were about a hundred Radicals, the group led by Lerroux, a party anti-socialist in economic matters but still expressing an anti-clericalism which was linked with the suspicious hostility towards rich catholic oligarchs felt by its middle class supporters. On the right were about eighty deputies, including thirty or so conservative republicans, twenty-five agrarians (drawn principally from the Catholic areas of Castile), ten from the conservative Catalan party and fourteen Basque nationalists (Catholics). The left did well partly because the electoral system adopted gave rewards to a coalition of groups, but within it the moderate followers of Azaña and those of similar tendencies, the real supporters of the democratic republic, were over-represented since CNT supporters appear to have voted for them rather than to have abstained or voted for the rival socialists of UGT affiliations. (There were, of course, no anarchist candidates.)

The Cortes voted for a democratic constitution of an up-to-date and progressive kind. Its most controversial part was Article twenty-six which prescribed that the State should cease to contribute to the stipends of priests, that religious orders could hold only the property necessary to their functions, that all religious orders that endangered the State should be dissolved (in practice this meant the Jesuits) and that religious orders should cease to engage in teaching. All this secured the determined hostility of the Church to the new régime – not merely of the Vatican and of the hierarchy in Spain, but of simple parish priests. The Catholic Prime Minister, Alcalá Zamora, resigned (he was soon to be elected President of the Republic) and Azaña succeeded him. The government made a determined effort to replace schools run by the orders and to create schools for those who received no education at all. By early 1933, almost 10,000 new primary schools had been put up under the republic. The policies of the dictatorship towards the peripheral provinces were reversed: Catalonia received an autonomous government and promises were given to the Basque provinces of similar treatment. Agrarian reform was legislated for in September 1932. In principle this authorized the expropriation of millions of acres belonging to large estates and their resettlement either by collectives or in individual holdings. In practice, shortage of money to pay compensation and difficulties in legal procedure limited the scope of reform: about 10,000 poor families received plots. Largo Caballero, as minister of labour, produced decrees on sickness benefits, paid holidays, the eight hour day and minimum wages. The laws of the dictatorship for the settlement of labour disputes were extended. Representation of the workers was strengthened on the mixed committees, and these worked under the supervision of delegates appointed by the ministry (usually Socialists). Azaña attempted to create an army on which the public could rely, without incurring the hostility of existing officers: this was an almost impossible task and Azaña's search for republican officers and his alleged manipulation of promotion aroused suspicion.

Azaña presided over the best government Spain had had in modern times. It suffered from one grave weakness, which was to prove the ruin of the Republic: its inability to prevent disorder. Already, in May 1931, anarchist feelings expressed themselves by burning churches and convents especially in Madrid and Andalusia. In July and August 1931, the CNT set off a series of violent strikes, the most formidable being in Barcelona and Seville, where the government used artillery against a general strike – thirty people were killed. These strikes were political as much as economic in motive, designed to maintain the revolutionary consciousness of anarchist-inspired workers and peasants. At the end of 1931 the civil guard in the small agricultural town of Castilblanco were mutilitated and killed. In January 1932 anarchists seized control of the Llobregat valley near Barcelona. In August 1933 a first attempt was made by a section of the army to intervene, not to restore the monarchy, but to overthrow 'the anti-clerical dictatorship of Azaña'. General Sanjurjo, who had been removed from the command of the Civil Guard, raised the standard of military revolt in Seville. The plot was poorly organized, the government was warned in advance, and most army officers felt that their time had not yet come. The rising was squashed without much difficulty and Sanjurjo was sentenced first to death and then to life imprisonment. In spite of this warning that armed reaction was alive, the anarchists did not relax their hostility to the government. In January 1933 some anarchist militants attempted a rising in Barcelona. At the same time a group of anarchists seized control in the village of Casas Viejas in Andalusia. The local civil guard were beseiged before being relieved by a detachment of *Asaltos* (the *Guardia del Asalto* – a body set up as a republican gendarmerie). In their turn, the anarchists were beseiged and troops moved towards the spot while aeroplanes flew overhead. The anarchists were overcome and about twenty-five were killed, including fourteen shot by the *asaltos* in cold blood. This pattern of events discredited the Republic among conservatives and Catholics while arousing the resentment of workers and peasants. The republicans found themselves moving along a narrow path between violence from the right and from the left.[282]

In the summer of 1933, Azaña resigned, faced with increasing obstruction from Lerroux's Radicals. Elections were held in November. They expressed a clear turn to the right. A new right-wing grouping, the CEDA (Confederación Española de Derechas Autónomas), led by Gil Robles, secured a hundred and ten seats, the Carlist traditionalists and the monarchists forty seats, while in the centre the Lerroux radicals won a hundred seats. The left-republican parties suffered a severe reverse, with about thirty-seven seats instead of over a hundred and thirty, while the Socialists lost nearly half their seats, falling to fifty-nine. The CEDA was a party based largely on Catholics, who, stimulated by an expensive campaign, had turned out to vote in large numbers. Its success was helped by its electoral coalition with the monarchists and Carlists. The Radicals gained as a result of the fears of the non-Catholic middle class inspired by the history of Azaña's government. On the left, the parties behind Azaña suffered as a result of the refusal of the Socialists to make an electoral agreement; the Socialists were anxious to detach themselves from the unpopularity – among workers and peasants – involved in co-operation with middle class republicans. In consequence they lost seats too. The anarchists directed abstention from voting, a move which weakened the parties in Azaña's orbit compared with 1931.

The CEDA presented an ambiguous aspect. Many of its supporters, and most of the rich men from whom its funds came, were suspicious of republican democracy and all were hostile to the anti-clericalism and disorder of the first years of the Republic. It is possible to argue, however, that Gil Robles was eager to win the right to the support of the Republic and that the CEDA accordingly represented a stabilizing force which, in sound liberal fashion, would strengthen the Republic by seeking parliamentary victories while peacefully accepting electoral defeats without rushing to arms. Certainly Gil Robles accepted parliamentarianism at least to the extent of trying to win power within the system. It has been claimed that it went no further than that: that Gil Robles and the CEDA would secure Spain for conservatism by winning votes if that would suffice, but would encourage right-wing revolt if they failed. In any case, the argument is academic: when the time came it was not Gil Robles or the CEDA supporters who decided for or against revolt. On the whole it seems likely that Gil Robles, a man whose success had come from peaceful politics, preferred to continue playing this game which he had mastered, rather than to try to join in the rougher sport of armed revolt in which his special talents would cease to be required.[283]

Progressive government ended with the elections in 1933. The Radicals were even less radical than their French colleagues and would not work with Socialists. The government could rest only on CEDA and radical votes. This coalition presided over the rapid destruction of the changes of 1931–3. The laws and decrees of those years were reversed, suspended or ignored. The religious orders were left to carry on as before 1931 and such property as had been taken away from them was restored. Building of new schools ended and church schools

199

functioned undisturbed. Two-thirds of the cost of the secular priests was taken over again by the state. The mixed tribunals to fix wages were converted, by changes in their chairmanship, into machines for reducing wages; agricultural labourers' pay fell by about one half. Landlords and employers took full advantage of the new course. Gil Robles thought that things went too far – later, he said: 'there were many, who, as soon as the right came to power, revealed a suicidal egoism by lowering wages, raising rents, trying to carry out unjust evictions and forgetting the unfortunate experiences of the years 1931–3.'[284]

The anarchists continued to act as before; the government of Lerroux and Gil Robles was certainly no less worthy of overthrow than that of Azaña. In December 1933 a rising broke out in Aragon; troops quickly suppressed it with the killing of sixty-seven members of the CNT. In March 1934 a general strike lasted for four weeks in Saragossa. Meanwhile a notable evolution went forward in the UGT and among the Socialists. Under the lead of Largo Caballero, they turned revolutionary. The UGT attempted to organize a workers' alliance but the CNT refused to join. Even so, the rural strikes in southern Spain in June 1934 included both the UGT and the CNT. The Socialists determined that the actual entry of the CEDA (which they assumed to be bent on the final destruction of the progressive gains of 1931–3) into the government should be the signal for revolt. The government of Catalonia had its own quarrel with the Madrid government over the latter's destruction of an attempt at agrarian reform within Catalonia. On 4 October Lerroux formed a new government which included three members of the CEDA. Revolt broke out in Barcelona, Madrid and the Asturias. Companys, the leader of the left-republican Catalan *Esquerra* declared Catalonia independent within a Spanish federation. He acted without the support of the CNT and was therefore deprived of mass backing and the revolt was suppressed by the local army garrison and its leaders arrested (together with Azaña, who had been trying to prevent the outbreak). In Madrid the rising was a complete fiasco. In Asturias, on the contrary, a full-scale social war broke out. Here was an area of miners and ironworkers. Their unions had long been highly organized, and there were affiliations both with the UGT and the CNT. There were also some communist syndicates, established since 1931. The CNT members here were less affected by the rigid purism of the FAI than those in Barcelona, while the Communists were now under orders from Moscow to seek a united front. Thus in the Asturias, combined action became possible between the various left-wing factions.

For two weeks the mining area of Asturias was governed by workers' committees and a Red Army set up.

To deal with the rising, Generals Franco and Goded, who were placed in charge of the suppression of the rebellion, brought troops from Morocco – the Foreign Legion (*Tercio*) and some Moorish *Regulares*. A full-scale campaign was launched. Few prisoners were taken in the fighting. After the campaign, the civil guards and the legionaries shot those suspected of participation in the revolt. A torture squad sought information on the whereabouts of hidden arms. The numbers of those who lost their lives in the Asturias will never be known: the figure was somewhere between one thousand and five thousand. About forty thousand people were imprisoned. Among the prosperous the prestige of the generals and of the army rose high: they were the saviours of society from a terrible fate, depicted with relish in the lurid (and almost entirely imaginary) stories of red atrocities. As the truth of the methods used by the 'forces of order' slowly leaked out, the movement towards unity among those opposed to brutal and indiscriminate repression gathered strength. The Asturias rising provided a rehearsal for the civil war.[285]

In 1935 a surprising intrusion of the French style in politics entered into the violence of Spanish life – appropriately enough through the so-called radicals. A promoter of gambling saloons turned out to have bribed several of the associates of the Radical prime minister, Lerroux. This made the continued lead in government by the Radicals impossible. Now, it seemed, Gil Robles must come to full power (already he had forced his way into the war ministry where he devoted himself to reversing Azaña's attempts at republicanizing the army). The obstacle was the obstinate conviction of the President, Alcalá Zamora, that government by Gil Robles was incompatible with the maintenance of the Republic. Rather than accept Gil Robles, the President preferred to dissolve the Cortes and order elections for February 1936, apparently in the hope that a new centre party would emerge to replace the discredited Radicals.

The elections were principally fought between two great coalitions. On the right, Gil Robles and the CEDA reached electoral agreements with the monarchists, Carlists and the Agrarians (or landowners' party); the left was united (for electoral purposes) in the Popular Front. This included the Socialists, the bourgeois democrats of Azaña's republican left, a group (under Martinez Barrio) which had seceded from Lerroux's Radicals when Lerroux abandoned all pretence of genuine radicalism, the left-wing Catalan separatists, and the Communists, the latter now keen advocates of the defence of bourgeois democracy. Thus the left stood to secure more seats, as a result of the electoral system, compared with 1933. Though the FAI, CNT, the anarchists and anarcho-syndicalists, were not in the Popular Front, it seems that most members of the CNT voted for the Popular Front because of the lesson of the Asturias rising and because the Popular Front promised an amnesty for the large number of CNT militants still in prison. The result was a clear victory in terms of votes and a decisive majority in terms of seats for the Popular Front, with 278 deputies against 134 from the right. The centre parties were reduced to fifty-five seats, with Lerroux's radicals virtually wiped out. Azaña's group secured eighty-seven seats, his moderate left allies seventy-five, the Socialists ninety-nine and the Communists seventeen.[286]

Azaña became Prime Minister and was succeeded when he became President in May, by his friend Casares Quiroga. Their governments were purely middle class, liberal and democratic in composition. The Socialists refused participation but the government rested on their support in the Cortes. This situation was a symptom of a split among the Socialists. After the Asturias rising, Indalecio Prieto had returned to policies of reformist moderation, while Largo Caballero, the UGT leader, called openly for a revolution from a united working class. Largo Caballero proclaimed that the Azaña régime was only a temporary forerunner of a proletarian dictatorship to be brought about by revolution. There is no evidence that he had any clear ideas as to how this revolution was to come, still less any plans for its conduct. Indeed, revolution was hardly possible, as 1934 had shown, as long as the government could use the army and the civil guard. However, Caballero's utterances and threats added to the alarm among the conservative classes already felt after the elections, and made it seem plausible to regard Azaña's régime, itself frightening enough to men of property, as the forerunner of worse to come. There were other grounds for fear. In south-western Spain peasants seized untilled tracts of land belonging to large estates, while the government resumed the more orderly process of settling peasant families on expropriated land. The conviction spread among the upper classes that the government could not defend order and property.[287] In June 1936, Gil Robles denounced the disorders that had broken out since the elections in February and alleged that, in four months, a hundred and sixty churches had been burned, two hundred and sixty-nine political murders had occurred, and 1,287 people had been injured in political brawls. Sixty-nine political centres had been wrecked, there had been a hundred and thirteen general strikes and two hundred and twenty-eight partial strikes and ten newspaper offices had been attacked. This statement calls for some reservations. No such statistical precision was possible, though the figures may have been approximately correct; 'general' strikes were usually short and always limited in geographical area. Violence came from the right as well as from the left. 'Church burnings' often amounted to little more than petty acts of incendiarism which did not cause much damage. Indeed, it was possible to travel widely in Spain without noticing the existence of the 'anarchy' denounced by the right.[288] What was important was the perfectly genuine terror felt by men of property – the fear that Spain was sinking into uncontrollable socialistic disorder was real enough.

The fears of the right generated a move towards violence. The ambiguous temporising policy of Gil Robles ceased to appeal and the clear anti-republican line embodied in Calvo Sotelo, an able monarchist, gained support. So did the *Falange*, the fascist organization led by the dictator's son, José Antonio Primo de Rivera. As usual with movements of this sort its doctrines were vague. They included corporatism, the notion of class co-operation, rather than class conflict, and an assertion of the unity of Spain. The *Falange* was, of course, strongly anti-liberal, anti-parliamentarian and authoritarian. The Mussolini-type social policy was probably taken quite seriously by José Antonio himself – a man of great charm and with many virtues, including honesty, who showed from time to time, in a way distressing to many of his backers, a certain sympathy with socialism of the moderate type exemplified by Prieto. His dislike of the conservative right was shown even after the elections: immediately afterwards, he instructed local leaders to,

see that no one adopts an attitude of hostility towards the new government or of solidarity with the defeated rightist forces . . . Our militiamen will utterly ignore all blandishments for taking part in conspiracies, projects of coup d'état, alliances with forces of 'order' and other things of similar nature.

This view was not shared by those who provided financial support for the *Falange*, a support which increased after the elections, or by the disappointed members of the CEDA youth movement who moved over en masse to the Falangists under their leader Ramón Serrano Suñer. These believed in violence and counter-terrorism and José Antonio could not prevent the evolution of the *Falange* militia into the shock troops of the reactionary middle class. In March, the *Falange* was declared illegal and its leaders arrested; thenceforward José Antonio accepted that a revolt was necessary, and hoped to direct it away from military narrow-mindedness or blind reaction – but he never left prison after his arrest in March and the loyalists executed him in November 1936. The Carlists and the monarchists were other civilians likely to try a rising some time against the republic. But what mattered most of all was the army.[289]

Azaña, on returning to the government, had recognized the danger from the army and had scattered those suspected of readiness to lead rebellion: Franco and Goded, the victors of the Asturias, were transferred to the Canary and Balearic Islands while General Mola, who was thought to be loyal, was brought back from Morocco to Pamplona, a garrison in Navarre. Sanjurjo, released from prison by the amnesty of the Lerroux government for those involved in the 1932 rising, was in Portugal. Though incontestably the senior conspirator, Sanjurjo left detailed planning to others, especially Mola. The plotters ran into difficulties due to the government's frequent transfers of officials who had earlier been assigned parts in the revolt which then had to be changed, and perhaps the new men won over to the conspiracy. Delays arose from the need to persuade the Carlists to give up their insistence on a commitment to monarchy in the revolt. Several times the rising had to be postponed, but about the end of June final arrangements were made and the commanders of the revolt were named for each military district and garrison town. On 11 July a private aeroplane left England, chartered for an unknown purpose – this was to fly Franco to Morocco. The monarchists and Falangists were informed in general terms and their co-operation secured. On 13 July, by coincidence, a remarkable climax came to the disorder which was by now the major excuse for the military rebels: Calvo Sotelo (by now effectively the leader of the opposition in the Cortes) was shot by officers of the *Asaltos* who were apparently inspired to murder some prominent man of the right by indignation at the murder (by Falangists) of an *Asalto* officer. It was about then that Mola sent out the final orders for revolt: to begin at five p.m. on Friday 17 July in Morocco, with revolts in Spain itself to follow within twenty-four hours.[290]

The rising began in the afternoon of 17 July in Morocco and key points there were in the hands of the rebels within twelve hours. On the 18th and 19th July Spain split into two as military risings broke out in numerous towns. In general, the military conspirators were able to secure the support of army officers, with hesitations which led to the failure of the rising in some areas. In Madrid many officers remained loyal to the government, either through conviction or through fear of the failure of the rising – the republican government's endeavours to find republican officers for senior posts had had some success there. The rising was generally supported by the civil guard and opposed by the *Asaltos*. Everywhere it was opposed by the organized workers. Above all, the revolts in Madrid and Barcelona failed.

The government made desperate attempts to avoid civil war. On the night of the 17th Casares Quiroga, the Prime Minister, refused to distribute arms to the working class organizations and on the 18th most of the civil governors in the large towns of the mainland similarly refused – a fact which often ensured the success of the revolts. After the events of 18 July Casares Quiroga resigned and Martinez Barrio was appointed to make a last attempt to prevent war starting. His telephone conversations with the rebels, the most important being an exchange with General Mola, failed to stop it. On 19 July, Martinez Barrio resigned in his turn to be replaced by a government of resistance under José Giral. On the same day arms were distributed to the people and civil war began. By 21 July the immediate outcome of the revolt was clear. The rebels held about one-third of Spain, roughly north of a line moving from the Portugese frontier south of the Tagus to the mountains north of Madrid, thence south-east to Teruel and north-east to a point about half-way along the French frontier. South of this area, the rebels held Seville and Cordoba and the area round Cadiz. To the north, loyalists held the Basque provinces, Santander and the Asturias, but were cut off from the rest of government-held Spain.

The rebels' conquest of Spain took nearly three years – the war ended at the end of March 1939. There were four main phases in this victory: (1) until October 1936 when the rebel armies from Morocco (the Foreign Legion and the Moors) conquered the area of south-western Spain adjoining the southern half of the Portugese frontier and advanced by way of Toledo on Madrid, failing to take the capital in the months thereafter. (2) April – October 1937, when the northern republican territories, the Basque provinces, Santander and Asturias were captured. (3) March – April 1938, when the rebels drove to the Mediterranean coast south of the Ebro, cutting off Catalonia from the government-held central and northern provinces. (4) December – March 1939, the conquest of Catalonia and the collapse of resistance in central Spain. The war was not a matter of unbroken victory for the rebels. The successful republican defence in Madrid in November 1936 – March 1937 culminated in the rout of the Italians at Guadalajara in March. In July and December 1937, the loyalists won battles at Brunete and Teruel and, in July 1938, on the Ebro, but their victories were either in defensive battles or were tactical successes in attack which had no strategical impact because of the inability of their forces to exploit a breakthrough.

The rebel armies were smaller in numbers than those built up on the government side, but better equipped and with many more professional officers to organize and lead them. The basis of General Franco's army was the regular army of 1936, of which the army from Morocco was much the most effective. About 20,000 troops from the African army were used in Spain. The peace-time army in the mainland was less useful since the conscript rank and file were politically unreliable. The bulk of the nationalist army came to be made up of militiamen enrolled in the *Falange* or Carlist militias and left in separate units or transferred into the army proper. In all, the nationalist forces probably reached about 400,000 – 500,000 in strength. Foreign support was crucial to Franco's success. (The motives for this support will be discussed elsewhere.) At the maximum in March 1937, about the time when Franco's African army was severely depleted and before new troops were adequately trained, there were sixty to seventy thousand Italian troops in Spain. Substantial amounts of equipment were dispatched from Italy either for the Italian forces or for Franco's troops, including over seven hundred aircraft. From Germany, there came the Condor Legion: specialized troops with modern equipment, numbering about five to six thousand men and including aircraft of all types, tanks and anti-tank artillery. This was a group of the highest military quality, with officers and men sent in rotation to Spain as to a training ground. Germany, too, sold (on credit) large amounts of equipment for Spanish use. Both German and Italian troops assisted in the training of Spanish forces. This assistance began to come soon after the rising broke out, but there is no sign that either Germany or Italy in any sense planned the rising, or even that they made extensive promises of help in advance. It is certain, however, that the rebels could confidently expect help of some kind from Italy. Mussolini had promised aid to a Spanish monarchist in case of revolt in 1934 – and it is possible that advance notice of the rising of 1936 was sent to Rome.[291]

On the government side, armies were created almost from nothing. In the early stages of the war the loyalist troops consisted of the *Asaltos*, a handful of civil guards and, above all, the volunteer militias of the working classes. These latter formed 'columns' each attached to a particular political or syndical group. They were not amenable to discipline or to the orders of the central government. Such units were virtually useless in battle, except in defence against frontal attacks or in defending towns, when enthusiasm for the cause was not made futile by lack of tactical knowledge. They were the materials for an army, not an army ready made. Even so, helped by a number of professional officers, they were largely responsible for the defence of Madrid in November 1936 against Franco's seasoned troops. An army capable of co-ordinated action in the field came into existence only after the end of 1936 as the party militias were persuaded or coerced into renouncing their independence. The most effective of the party militias was the communist 'Fifth Regiment'; the communists insisted from the first on the need for discipline in war. Aid from abroad came to the government in smaller volume than to its enemies. No formed foreign units came into Spain to fight for the government, but there came instead genuine volunteers, from Europe and America, anxious to fight against 'fascism'. For the most part, they entered the international brigades, organized under the aegis of foreign communists. These units were probably about fifteen thousand strong though larger numbers of men served with them at one time or another.[292] Otherwise, effective help from abroad for the government came only from Russia (France, after handing over a few obsolete aircraft at the beginning of the war, quickly took up 'non-intervention' and took it fairly seriously). Here it was a question of material, not men. There were Russians in Spain and their activities were very important indeed, but they were staff officers, advisors and instructors, with a few pilots and tank crews. There were probably no more than five hundred Russians serving in Spain at any one time. Their sales of equipment provided the most important external sources of supply for the government forces; the amounts remain matter for conjecture, for the Russians were extremely furtive about these deliveries and the Spanish government itself had no certain knowledge of their extent. But it seems that at least 240 aircraft and 730 tanks were despatched from Russia to Spain.[293] Out of these materials a republican army of about 600,000 men was made.

What was the war being fought about? There is not much difficulty in explaining the aims of the rebels. These were to defend the privileges of the army, the landlords and the church. This simple purpose was left uncomplicated by doctrinal window dressing. This was because of the emergence of General Franco as undisputed master of nationalist Spain. It happened by accident – General Sanjurjo was killed on his way to become head of the rebel state, Mola was unpopular, the ablest civilian rightists, Calvo Sotelo and José Antonio Primo de Rivera, had gone. On 29 September, the military junta elected Franco 'head of the government' and he started naming himself 'head of the state' on 1 October. Franco was an extremely shrewd and cautious politician, with

207

an ambition untainted by ideals or passions. He recognized the need (if only for the sake of showing that Spain was part of the modern Europe of Hitler and Mussolini) to have a party with coloured shirts and parades and confused social doctrines. (Many of these things disappeared when it became necessary to show that Franco could be part of the Europe of NATO and the Common Market.) He was able to allow the Falangists to make a noise without allowing them to be taken seriously. José Antonio would have compelled some attention to be paid to the *Falange*. Franco casually drove the *Falange* into union with the theoretically utterly different Carlists, placed this amalgam under himself and threw the then leader of the *Falange* into prison.[294] Thus narrow-minded conservatism, without ideological frills, became the inspiration behind the victorious rebellion even more clearly after it fell into Franco's grip than when it began. To defend the privileged classes, a régime of 'order', that is of suspension of the liberties of all those who fell outside those classes, was to be installed. Little attempt was made to win popular support for the rebels, instead terror was used to secure popular acquiescence. The 'Labour Charter' of March 1938 was the only exception. It promised machinery to determine wages in industry and protected the leases of tenant farmers; it did not cover labourers on large estates. The arrangements of April for land reform gave priority to the restoration of land which had been settled by peasants during or before the war to its original owners.[295]

On the side of the republican government the situation was more complex. The supporters of Franco consistently spoke of their enterprise as a 'crusade against the reds'. Clearly it is impossible to describe the government of Azaña and Casares Quiroga, against which the revolt took place, as 'red'. It was a mildly progressive liberal régime. It was certainly threatened with social revolution from the anarchists and from the left socialists who followed the lead of Largo Caballero. The revolt of the army set off this threatened social revolution. When the government was deprived of the army and much of the police, revolution could no longer be contained. In consequence it would be more correct to say that the revolt caused a social revolution rather than to describe it as a revolt against a social revolution. In the first months of the war, the authority of the central government virtually disappeared in loyalist Spain. Except in the Basque provinces, the functions of government were taken over by committees in which the syndicates were the dominating force. Regular courts of law ceased to function and were replaced by all kinds of improvised tribunals, judicial records were sometimes destroyed and prisoners were often freed. Some legal officials were imprisoned, others executed. Hundreds of churches and convents were burned or put to secular uses. Several thousand of clergy, monks, nuns and members of the richer classes were killed. The revolutionary committees controlled public utilities and services and created militia units to fight the enemy. In towns, especially Barcelona, industries and commercial businesses were taken over, including small ones. In the country, landed properties were seized, and either worked in collectives or split up among the peasants. In Spain, in the three months after the rebellion, there took place, in fact, the most extensive and most successful spontaneous revolution 'from below' ever recorded. It had many admirable features: in many places a rare combination of concern for human dignity and freedom with attempts at material equality. It had its disasters: above all bloodshed and violence (for there were, of course, many supporters of the revolt in government Spain), sometimes expressing the anarchists' concern to purge society of dross, sometimes representing simply the work of hooligans and criminals. Here certainly was a triumph for the 'reds'.[296]

This revolution inside the government-held areas of Spain began to be checked after Largo Caballero became Prime Minister in September 1936. He owed his position to the confidence he had secured from the working class, partly through his advocacy of revolution, and he used that popularity to help him to check the revolution. He soon discovered that it was impossible to fight a war against an increasingly well-equipped and well-trained army without discipline in the republican army and behind the lines. This meant a government that could govern. It was a conclusion reached by others: in November, four CNT anarchists joined the cabinet, a startling abandonment of their previous doctrines. Most of all, the Communist party worked to curb disorder and even to undo the revolution of the summer of 1936.

The Communists, with their own traditions of rigid discipline, understood the need for wartime restraints. Current Comintern doctrine recommended the formation of broad anti-fascist fronts, a recommendation which fitted Spanish conditions and required the conciliation of the democratic bourgeoisie. Abroad, the policy of the Soviet Union was to seek the co-operation of the western democracies against fascism, and to postpone the proletarian revolution in those countries. Republican Spain urgently needed the help of Britain and France; most people in those countries were liable to be alienated if the disorders of 1936 continued. Inside Spain, the Communists grew in strength and in influence partly because they were efficient, but still more because they worked in association with the providers of aid from abroad. In the last months of 1936, a police force was recruited and the squads of the working class organizations began to be incorporated into the armed forces of the government. The government, spurred on by vigorous Communist pressure, turned to the defence of the small and medium land-owners and of lesser capitalists. Thus the curious situation arose in which the Communists led the return to an effective liberal government, which came to be stronger than the governments before the war (since it rested on a firmer basis of popular adhesion). It has been argued that this liberal government was a sham, a screen behind which the Communists secured complete ascendancy, an argument put forward most powerfully for the period of government under Juan Negrin, who succeeded Largo Caballero in the spring of 1937 and remained until republican Spain collapsed.

It is true that the government was not in full control of the activities of the Communists themselves. They built up their own private machinery of terror and used it with vigour against their own special enemies (i.e. against dissident communists). The campaign against the POUM militia in Barcelona in 1937 was not organized by the government so much as by the Communists. The Russian advisers interfered with the carrying out of government plans if these were not approved by the Communists. Still, it is an exaggeration to say that Negrin was a mere puppet of the party. In any case, Communist influence rested not on acceptance of any long-term Communist aims, but on the fact that it was Soviet Russia alone who gave effective help. Most of the supporters of the Communists were supporters only for the duration of the war; Communist dominance was temporary. No one can tell what would have been the outcome if republican Spain had won; even so, it seems possible to suggest that its cause was not the cause of blood-thirsty 'reds', but that of democracy, freedom and ordered progress.

The war was costly in terms of lives lost, more because of murderous terror on both sides than as a result of losses in combat. All figures relating to the Spanish war are tentative approximations. Professor Jackson has suggested a total death roll of 580,000. This figure includes only 160,000 deaths directly attributable to the war. The other 420,000 are attributed to political actions (executions or disease incurred through life in prison). Professor Jackson allots the responsibility for only 20,000 of these deaths or executions to the republicans and no less than 400,000 to action on the nationalist side either during or after the war. Mr Thomas argues for a total of under 600,000 with a far higher proportion of deaths in battle and a far smaller total for executions on the rebel side (40,000 at most during the war).[297] All that is clear is that there were many executions on both sides. On the government side, most were the outcome of the revolutionary outbreak of the summer of 1936; on the rebel side, a high proportion came from the massacre in south-western Spain during and after its conquest in 1936. Franco had few troops and a large and unreliable population to control; the simplest method seemed to be to kill every potential leader of opposition that could be found. The same method was continued thereafter during the war in the nationalist zone, and after the war in the rest of Spain. Thus the executions and massacres of Franco's side had a different significance from most of those of the government side. In the former, it was mass-killing organized by, or at least approved by, the constituted authorities; in the latter, massacres were the result of revolutionary disturbance, opposed and eventually checked by the government, though never eliminated. On both sides, these killings were fundamentally the result of the war being one in which the population was divided by class and belief, rather than geographically, so that all areas contained many possible 'traitors' to the dominant group.[298]

The Spanish Civil War is still frequently described as the first stage in the Second World War. This may mean one of two things, that the Second World War was a war of ideologies and that these ideologies first came to grips in Spain, or that Franco's hostility to the Allies seriously affected the course of the Allied struggle against Germany and her satellites. The idea of the war as part of a great global struggle between right and wrong had a profound appeal to intellectuals and to many idealistic democrats – it largely explains the move towards Communism in such circles in Britain and the United States, to whom it seemed that only Communists sought seriously to resist fascism, as provisionally embodied in Franco. The weakness in this argument is that the 'fascists' of Germany were distinguishable from the 'fascists' of Spain and that the sort of society Britain and the USA were trying to defend was clearly distinguishable from the society of republican Spain during the civil war. As for the second kind of argument, it is true that Franco's Spain did much to inconvenience the allies but because he remained neutral, Franco did not present a decisive threat. In consequence it was not worth while on military grounds for the Allies to challenge his position in Spain. Franco was shrewd enough not to be persuaded into open conflict with Britain and the United States and so his rule survived the Second World War.

11

Germany 1919-39

The great question of these years is: how did Hitler secure control of Germany? Germany was the only advanced country, advanced that is in its standard of living and in its level of education, that fell into the hands of an irrational dictatorship. The most plausible explanation lies in the economic fluctuations of the period between 1918 and 1933 and their social and political consequences. It is clear that opposition to democracy rose and fell in harmony with movements in prosperity.

Two major economic disasters descended on Germany in these years: the runaway inflation of 1923 and the depression of 1930-3. The causes of the great inflation are discussed elsewhere. Until 1923, the inflation was associated with a certain prosperity. The amount of money in circulation created a high level of demand and, as it became clear that a drastic inflation was going on, holders of money became increasingly anxious to convert it quickly into goods of real value. Thus investment and consumption were further stimulated. Industrial production increased rapidly while unemployment disappeared. In 1922, the average number of registered unemployed was only 77,000. In 1923, the Franco-Belgian occupation of the Ruhr, itself partly a consequence of the inflation, and the passive resistance that followed, led to the economic isolation of the Ruhr region. The financing of passive resistance brought about the final collapse of the mark. As the mark tumbled down to worthlessness the economic stimulus of inflation ceased. When it became clear that the exchange of goods for money was almost certain to produce a loss to the seller, as the value of the money received vanished, normal transactions became difficult or impossible. Thus production fell in 1923 and unemployment increased rapidly. The years until the end of 1922 were therefore of some benefit to Germany as a whole; 1923 certainly was not.

Inflation leads to redistribution of wealth. Violent inflation leads to

212

violent redistribution, with a correspondingly violent sense of injustice as expectations are destroyed. The inflation brought benefit to producers and, above all, to the direct owners of the means of production, and losses to the holders of assets of fixed money value and to those dependent on inflexible salaries. Wage earners, relatively, held their own, with severe fluctuations in their real incomes as inflation accelerated. Frequent strikes, however, marked their endeavours to maintain their real wages: an average of twenty-three million working days was lost through strikes in each of the years 1919–22. Even so, there were times when wages lagged well behind prices – periods of extra profits for employers – and, except for a short time in 1921, real wages remained below the level of 1913. Salaried workers were much worse hit. For instance the salaries of higher government employees in 1923 were not much above one-third of their real level of 1913. Pensioners were reduced, during the inflation period, to conditions of extreme hardship. Above all, those who had lent money in return for fixed interest payments were ruined. Their loans could be repaid in money which had no value. Instead of a reliable income, they found themselves possessors of useless paper. The 'revaluation' legislation of 1924 and 1925 did not restore more than, at most, one-quarter of the original value of such loans. Lenders were ruined, borrowers gained. Anyone who, before or during the inflation, was able to borrow a fixed sum of money and convert it into solid assets effectively confiscated the resources of his creditors. Banks continued to lend money to businessmen on terms which did not take full account of the effects of inflation, until near the end. Thus inflation led to an upsurge of investment, sometimes at no cost to the proprietors. Manufacturers engaged in exporting made large profits since the fall in foreign exchange value of the mark proceeded faster than the rise in internal German prices. Together with exporters, pure speculators, especially in the foreign exchange market, made large fortunes. It is true that some of these fortunes proved fragile when the inflation was over; much of the productive investment of the inflation period was uncompetitive when normality returned and there were many bankruptcies. Still, the general effect of the inflation was to transfer wealth from the thrifty, prudent, cautious section of the lower middle class to industrialists and businessmen and to speculators and adventurers.[299]

At the end of 1923, inflation was brought to an end with the creation of a new mark. There followed, until 1926, an awkward period of transition. The immediate effect of stabilization was to end the limitless demand for goods of the inflation period. Immediately, economic

213

activity fell off and unemployment increased – to more than a quarter of workers by the end of 1923. However, after the putting into effect of the Dawes plan in the middle of 1924, international confidence in the mark revived and foreign loans began to come into Germany, attracted by high rates of interest. Still, with the end of the protection against foreign competition brought about in the inflation and by effect on the foreign exchanges, German industry faced two problems. One was to modify the balance of industrial production to meet the post-war pattern of world and domestic demand, a problem less acute in Germany than in Britain, but important in industries such as ship-building and coal. The other was the result of the nature of some of the investment of the inflation period, much of which proved uneconomic in normal competitive conditions. Hence the later 1920s was a period of 'rationalization' involving high levels of unemployment, which reached a peak in 1926. However, industrial production rose after 1926, in 1927 overtook pre-war levels, and continued to rise until early 1929. Workers' earnings rose by nearly a third between 1925 and 1929.

In 1929, the depression began. The economic growth of the later 1920s was based on foreign lending, especially from the United States. The stock exchange boom in New York caused the supply of funds to lessen in 1929 and to go into reverse as the slump developed. Thus in 1930 and 1931, capital flowed out of Germany. The effect was to reduce investment in Germany and create the prospect of a major crisis in the foreign balance of payments. The mark came under pressure. The government responded by violent measures of deflation, to hold down prices inside Germany and maintain the foreign exchange value of the currency. Devaluation was ruled out, and budgeting for a surplus imposed, by the fear that devaluation could bring a revival of inflation. Under the Brüning government, in 1930–2, official salaries were cut by one-fifth and wage reductions imposed of ten to fifteen per cent, taxes were increased and unemployment benefit curtailed. Demand for industrial products was therefore reduced by the outflow of capital, by the falling off of demand for exports resulting from the world slump, and by deliberate government policy. Industrial production fell to about fifty-eight per cent of its level of 1928–9. Unemployment reached six million or more – in July 1932, about half of all members of trade unions were out of work. Meanwhile German agriculture was near collapse. In spite of protective tariffs, prices for home-produced foods were low. In 1930, German agricultural products sold for about 13 per cent more than in 1913, while consumer goods were 60 per cent higher in price. Agriculturalists were heavily in debt again, in spite of the abrogation of old debt in the inflation, and embarrassed by the calling in of loans. By 1932 German agricultural production sold for only 65 per cent of what it had fetched in 1928.

These violent fluctuations and the hardships they brought would have tested the power of survival of any old-established and revered form of government. The democratic Weimar republic was new and was not revered. It was associated with a gloomy period which could be compared to its disadvantage to the confident progress of the years before the war. But there was more to its weakness than that. The defeat of Germany in 1918 is crucial. The democratic republic was the consequence of a revolution which had compelled the destruction of Wilhelmine Germany and the abdication of the Emperor. That revolution was brought about by the defeat. That defeat came as a surprise. Until the last months of the war, its organisers professed complete confidence in its outcome. In 1918, a victorious peace had been imposed on Russia and a superficially successful offensive launched in France. When defeat came, it appeared that something must have gone wrong. That something bore a different aspect to the German left than it did to the German right. To the left, it appeared that the German people had been misled and deceived by irresponsible soldiers and their upper-class allies; to the right, it seemed that the German army had not really been defeated at all, that the revolution had caused the defeat and not the other way round. To the left, the German people had been involved in suffering and loss of life in a war which had been kept going by unscrupulous liars. If anything was wrong with the revolution of 1918-9, therefore, it was that it had not been enough of a revolution. The hold of the old governing class on power, landlords, capitalists and regular officers, had not been uprooted. The founders of the republic had compromised with this class instead of destroying it. This view explains the strength of the German Communist Party during the Weimar period. It was fortified by the belief that the republic was run by businessmen for businessmen and that that was the explanation of economic disaster. By the right, a quite different pattern of explanation was evolved. Now the miseries of Germany were due to foreigners, to the iniquities of Versailles and, above all, to reparations. There was some plausibility in this view, especially for 1923. Thus those who had signed this treaty and those who were ready to work it or to seek the friendship of the victorious western powers were traitors, whose positions of influence were the result of the democratic revolution. All good Germans must be nationalistic supporters of a revival of German power, not weak compromisers and internationalists. Defeat had brought hardship to Germany; the consequences of defeat must not be passively accepted. Moreover, the original defeat itself was brought into question. Had the German army really been defeated at all? The answer was that it had not, that it had been stabbed in the back by democrats, socialists and pacifists, the sponsors of republican democracy. The collapse of 1918 was a collapse in the rear of the armies, who were fighting successfully until civilian subversion weakened them. Here was a comprehensive explanation. The 'November criminals' were to blame for the defeat of Germany and for the consequences of the defeat – the imposition on Germany of endless hardships by foreign foes. This hypothesis was in no way an invention of Hitler's, though he stated it most stridently; it was familiar among the German right from the beginning of the Weimar era.

The only whole-hearted friends of the democratic republic were the Social Democrats, together with the handful of intellectual bourgeois who formed the German Democratic Party (DDP). The Social Democratic Party (SPD) grew before the war into the largest single party: in 1912, they had secured 35 per cent of the votes for the *Reichstag*. In the process of growth, the SPD had changed from a revolutionary group into a reformist institution aiming to secure social change by peacefully winning votes rather than by agitation and violence. In 1914, the SPD voted in favour of war and accepted the war-time political truce. The leaders began to be treated at least as associates of the imperial government. However, within the party, opposition to the war grew in strength and led to the expulsion of its left-wing elements, in 1917, and to the formation of the independent social democratic party (USPD). The SPD participated in Prince Max of Baden's government of October 1918, set up at the behest of the high command of the army to secure an armistice. In November, revolution broke out in the cities, spreading from mutiny in the fleet. On 9 November, crowds of workers marched towards the centre of Berlin. In response, the SPD took over the government and proclaimed a republic. The party leaders, Ebert and Scheidemann, had not made this revolution. On the contrary they tried to curtail it. The next day, Ebert secured the support of the high command of the army in resistance to 'Bolshevism'. This limitation of the revolution was unwelcome to the left of the USPD, especially to that section which broke away in December to found the German Communist Party (KPD). In the next two months, the government devoted itself to the restoration of order with the help of the army. In return the army counted on being allowed to survive; to survive, that is, as a continuation of the old army, with the same social and political prejudices. It is difficult to say who got the best of the bargain; the regular army was virtually unusable against popular disturbance, given the attitude of the conscript rank and file, and Ebert was renouncing all possibility of creating a military force on which the republic could rely, but, on the other hand, the *Freikorps* of volunteers, mainly ex-soldiers most of whom were emphatically not socialist sympathizers, were organized by army officers and effectively crushed the radical revolution by the spring of 1919. The high command knew what it was doing – it needed a social democratic screen to shelter it from the enmity of the working class while an army was rebuilt.

The Treaty of Versailles laid down that the army was to consist of long service soldiers and to be limited to 100,000 in strength. The result was the new *Reichswehr*. It was made into a corps d'élite. Its makers devoted themselves to securing officers and men of ability, but men, and still more officers, carefully drawn from those elements of society which provided 'suitable' material. This meant depending on the upper and upper-middle class for officers and on political agnostics for the other ranks. In consequence the army reflected their social and political prejudices. General von Seeckt, the principal creator of the *Reichswehr*, spoke of parliament as 'the cancer of our time'. He strove to create an army which should be non-party, indeed 'above' party. What this seemed to mean was that the army was to act in support of 'national' interests, as interpreted by itself, rather than at the behest of 'non-national' politicians. Seeckt had the impertinence to tell Stresemann in 1923, 'Mr Chancellor, the *Reichswehr* will march with you if you will go the German way'.[300]

This attitude emerged with clarity in March 1920 during the Kapp *Putsch*. This was a revolt against the new 'system', which was supported by many of the *Freikorps* men, protesting against disbandment, by officers excluded from the *Reichswehr*, by those who had returned from the Baltic adventure of 1919, by disgruntled monarchists. It emerged that only a handful of officers was prepared to defend the republic and the government by force of arms. When the putschists were marching on Berlin, Seeckt announced firmly 'that he would never permit Berlin to be presented with the spectacle of their soldiers fighting each other with live ammunition'. It is clear that the alliance, embodied in Noske's activities as Minister of Defence, between the government and the army worked in only one direction. The government backed the army; the army would not back the government. Or, rather, the army would not fight for the republic against the right. Against disorder from the left it could be counted upon. The Kapp *Putsch* was defeated by a general strike – a virtually single-handed victory of the Social Democrats and their allies in the trade unions, then at the height of their strength. The *Reichswehr* stood aside. When, however, the strike was protracted in certain areas, especially in the Ruhr and in Saxony, and led to demands for the radicalization of army and government, the army suppressed the consequent disturbances with ruthless energy. Indeed, there was never any danger of subversion of the republic from the left during the whole Weimar period; social democracy and the army saw to that. In March 1921, when an attempted Communist uprising took place, the police alone suppressed the consequent disturbances in Prussia, Saxony and Hamburg with the help of only one *Reichswehr* artillery unit, though other *Reichswehr* forces were standing by. Communist appeals had no impact on the majority of the German workers.[301]

The year of the great inflation and occupation of the Ruhr, 1923, was the climax of the early years of republican struggle. Civil war and the break up of the German *Reich* seemed imminent. Separatists in the Rhineland, an assortment of forces on the right, and the Communists on the left threatened revolt. The *Reichswehr* and the Social Democrats dealt with the Communists; the separatists failed through lack of support in their own areas; the right through its own dissensions. In Moscow, the Comintern contemplated the misery and despair of Germany in 1923 and concluded that the proletarian revolution might be launched. It should be possible to unite the working class under Communist leadership. (A basis existed in central Germany, in Saxony and Thuringia, where Social Democratic governments were working with local Communists to create armed bands in order to establish a centre of resistance to any reactionary violence. In October, Communists secured participation in the government of these states.) The intention was openly proclaimed. The KPD newspaper published, on October 10, a letter signed J. Stalin: 'The approaching revolution in Germany is the most important world event in our time', it began. On 14 October, the KPD *Zentrale* called on the workers to prepare for 'a battle to establish a government of all working people in the *Reich* and abroad'. Under-standably, the government acted first. It could count on the full support of the army against such left-wing manifestations. The local *Reichswehr* commander in Saxony was instructed to demand full co-operation from the Saxon government. On 21 October, *Reichswehr* reinforcements began to march in from outside Saxony. The social democrats declined to join the KPD in resistance and by the end of the month, the President, the social democrat Ebert, invoking the emergency article forty-eight of the constitution, suspended the Saxon state government and substituted a *Reichskommissar*. A similar pattern was followed in Thuringia. All this was perfectly peaceful. The communist revolution was reduced to an abortive rising in Hamburg during 23–25 October. Once again the mass of workers gave no support and the rising was suppressed, with some bloodshed, by police, naval units and even some SPD formations.[302]

The first movement from the right was an attempt at a new Kapp *Putsch*. It followed the calling off of passive resistance in the Ruhr against the French, an action regarded as treason by the extremists. The *Reichswehr* had responded to the invasion of the Ruhr with attempts to strengthen the defensive potential of Germany by creating semi-clandestine forces, loosely attached to the *Reichswehr*, largely built up of old *Freikorps* material, and by increasing collaboration with the numerous para-military organizations of a 'national' kind. One of the officers of the 'Black *Reichswehr*' and a former Kapp supporter, ex-Major Buchrucker, took it upon himself to overthrow the republic. Two hundred men attempted to seize the government quarter in Berlin on 29 September but were easily disposed of by the *Reichswehr*. However, on 1 October, Buchrucker's forces seized Küstrin and the Spandau citadel. The Buchrucker *Putsch* was suppressed by local units of the *Reichswehr*. Seeckt deeply resented this irresponsible disturbance. However much he sympathized with the purposes of such plotters, he deplored the means. He recognized that patience and caution were needed in the pursuit of 'national ends'. Civil war could not help any national cause.[303]

A much more serious threat of disturbance came from Bavaria. Here the government of the state was right wing. The Catholic party, the Bavarian Peoples Party (BVP), was distinctly more reactionary than was the Centre Party in the *Reich* as a whole. In consequence, the Law for the Protection of the Republic, of the summer of 1922, against the encouragement or carrying out of acts of violence against the Republic, was not effectively applied in Bavaria. This was partly a manifestation of Bavarian separatism, partly the result of dislike on the part of the Bavarian right of the leaders of the *Reich* government and, in 1923, suspicion of developments in Saxony and Thuringia. The consequence was that Bavaria became a sanctuary for extreme and violent opponents of republican democracy. There were concentrated in Bavaria many ex-*Freikorps* men and various semi-military 'patriotic' groups, the most notable of which was Hitler's National Socialist German Workers Party (NSDAP or Nazis). This combined a violent nationalism with racist doctrines and amalgamated both with a cloudy anti-capitalism.

In Bavaria, the local *Reichswehr* forces, above all the 7th division, found themselves in a particularly weak position as against their own nationalist allies, especially since the army in Bavaria was itself strongly tinged, among junior officers, with Nazi sympathies. In September 1923, the Bavarian government, concerned by its loss of control and by Communist activities in Saxony and Thuringia declared a state of emergency and handed over full powers to Gustav von Kahr. At once the *Reich* government proclaimed a general emergency and gave full powers to the War Minister Gessler, which, in practice, meant to Seeckt as commander of the *Reichswehr*. In October, after a violent attack on Seeckt in the Nazi newspaper, the Munich *Völkische Beobachter*, an attack which accused Seeckt of being a tool of Jews, the Bavarian *Reichswehr* commander, von Lossow, was ordered from Berlin to suppress the paper. After consulting Kahr, Lossow refused. Lossow was dismissed and Kahr refused to accept the dismissal. Towards the end of October Lossow made it clear in a conference in Munich that he proposed to march on Berlin in collaboration with the patriotic bands and to proclaim a national dictatorship. Early in November, an emissary from Kahr, Colonel von Seisser, spoke to Seeckt in Berlin. He reported, 'I briefly described opinion in Bavaria and Kahr's greater-German objective: creation of a national dictatorship, freed from Parliament, able to take ruthless measures against the socialist mess.' Seeckt replied, 'This is my aim too, but for me things are much more difficult.' Seeckt's attitude is significant. He regarded Kahr and Lossow and the nationalists in Bavaria, not as enemies comparable to the Communists but as errant friends. On 5 November, Seeckt wrote to Kahr. He assured him that the Communists in Thuringia, on the borders of Bavaria, were being dealt with by the *Reichswehr*. As for the Bavarian situation, Kahr was asked to be good enough not to risk setting off a German civil war. Seeckt urged that,

the *Reichswehr* must not be brought into a position in which it has to fight, for a government which is alien to it, against people who have the same convictions as the army. On the other hand it cannot permit irresponsible and unauthorized circles to try and bring about a change by force.

Kahr and Lossow hesitated; perhaps the *Reichswehr* would resist a Bavarian march on Berlin.[304]

This was not good enough for Hitler who had no intention of remaining a subordinate agitator in Bavaria. On 8 November, a speech of Kahr's to a group of notables in the Bürgerbräukeller in Munich was interrupted. Armed with a pistol, Hitler announced that the national revolution had begun. He formed a national government.

Ludendorff was Defence Minister, Lossow commander of the *Reichswehr*, Kahr the Bavarian Regent. Hitler reserved the 'political leadership' for himself. Having escaped from Hitler and his pistol, the doubts of Kahr and Lossow revived. Later that night they denounced the *Putsch*. Next day the rebels marched on the centre of Munich, hoping that resistance would not materialise. It did, and the Bavarian police opened fire on the column. The rebels dispersed. The failure had a permanent effect on Hitler's tactics. Never again would he risk going against the authorities; he would intrigue and threaten but not risk a fight. Seeckt was now formally given powers to act under the *Reich* state of emergency and became temporary dictator. In the succeeding months, until the end of February when Seeckt gave up his powers, there are signs that elements of the conservative right were urging him to seize power outright and inaugurate a military dictatorship. Seeckt refused – it does not seem that officers like Seeckt were anxious to rule Germany directly, then or later. They would grumble from the side lines about how Germany was governed, they could not be counted on to support the republic against right wing threats but they were not a direct threat to republican democracy.[305]

The Bavarian problem was solved by Hitler's failure. Kahr and Lossow disappeared into retirement; the *Reichswehr* in Bavaria was reintegrated into the *Reichswehr* of Germany. The separatist movement in the Rhineland was simply an aspect of the problem of French policy towards Germany. In October a series of separatist declarations took place in various Rhineland cities and governments were set up. They secured minimal support from the local population. They were clearly an underhand French experiment which collapsed with the rest of Poincaré's policy of the firm hand towards Germany.

Thus a united republic survived into 1924, after years of suffering and bloodshed, some of it deliberate murder carried out by nationalist organizations or individuals. Erzberger was assassinated in 1921, Rathenau in 1922, both because of the 'treason' involved in any dealings with the west; no less than 354 murders of humbler men took place between 1918 and 1922.[306] After 1924, the republic moved into a period of consolidation and growing stability, which began to collapse after 1929, a movement closely linked with economic trends. The process is illustrated in part by the pattern of elections to the *Reichstag*.

For the years 1924–8, the most striking feature is the growing strength of the Social Democrats, the firmest supporters of republican democracy, and the growing weakness of the Nazis. On the conservative right the German Nationalist Peoples' Party (DNVP) declined between

PATTERN OF ELECTIONS TO THE REICHSTAG
Voting 1924–32 (in thousands of votes)[307]

Election on	4.5.1924	7.12.1924	20.5.1928	14.9.1930	31.7.1932	6.11.1932
Entitled to vote	38,375	38,987	41,224	42,958	44,211	44,374
Non-voters and spoiled papers	9,093	8,697	10,470	7,987	7,329	8,903
PARTIES						
NSDAP	1,918	907	810	6,383	13,769	11,737
DNVP	5,697	6,206	4,382	2,458	2,177	2,959
Agrarian and smaller parties of the Right	666	545	1,025	2,373	552	510
DVP	2,728	3,049	2,680	1,578	436	661
Economic Party	530	639	1,388	1,362	147	110
DDPI State Party	1,655	1,920	1,479	1,322	372	336
Centre + BVP	4,861	5,226	4,658	5,187	5,782	5,325
SPD	6,009	7,881	9,153	8,578	7,960	7,248
USPD	235	99	–	–	–	–
KPD	3,693	2,709	3,265	4,592	5,283	5,980
Regional Parties + Minority Groups	608	708	956	683	219	353
Splinter Groups	662	401	958	455	185	252

the end of 1924 and 1928. This was the party of purest reaction, the party of landlords and their peasant dependents, and of some elements of big business; the party that hankered, above all, for a return to pre-1914 conditions, and for the political rule of a social élite. It was supported by voters ready to look upwards with respect rather than to seek for equality and opportunity. More significant still as a symptom of consolidation of the republic was the tendency towards the acceptance of the republican régime by a section at least of this party. This was largely the work of the greatest German statesman of these years, Stresemann. He showed how German strength, prosperity and prestige could be rebuilt within the republican framework. Many Nationalists were incapable of understanding the subtleties of his policy; some were, encouraged in their realism by the support of German industry for Stresemann's pursuit of prosperity. The Dawes plan of 1924 required a constitutional amendment to enable its provisions on the use of German railways as security to be carried through. In the *Reichstag* fifty-two of the DNVP voted against, but forty-eight voted for. In January 1925, four Nationalists entered the government formed by Luther, after pledging themselves to the republic and to the maintenance of Stresemann's foreign policy. They remained until October 1925, when their party, failing to share their understanding of Stresemann's achievements at Locarno, forced their retirement. However, in January 1927, Nationalists once more joined the government, in Marx's fourth ministry, this time after an explicit acceptance of Locarno, and they remained until the break up of the coalition in the spring of 1928.

A further reinforcement to the republic came with the election of Field Marshal von Hindenburg to the Presidency of the republic in 1925. This was not the intention of his sponsors, but the presence at the head of the republic of this prestigious relic of monarchical glories, the saviour of East Prussia of 1914, was bound to encourage a rallying to the republic on the right, especially among the *Reichswehr*. Hindenburg had a sense of duty. As long as his duty was clearly to uphold the constitution, he did it. It was only because of the existence of Hindenburg that the government was able to get rid of Seeckt in 1926. Unfortunately, when Hindenburg found it difficult to work out what his duty was, as he did after 1930, his temperamental weakness and indecision, combined with his right-wing prejudices, made him a ready prey to anti-republican intriguers.[308]

The greatest recruit to support for the democratic republic was Stresemann. He was the most prominent member of the German Peoples' Party (DVP) which was the successor to the old National Liberal Party. This had always been more 'national' than 'liberal' and Stresemann was no exception. In 1920 he accepted the Kapp *Putsch*. By the time of his death in 1929, however, he was a major prop of the constitution. Partly, no doubt, this was because of the power the republic brought to him, partly because of the failure of many anti-republicans to understand his foreign policy, partly because a republican democratic Germany was more likely to win the sort of goals by the sort of methods that his foreign policy aimed for. With himself, Stresemann contrived, on the whole, to take his basically non-republican right-wing party. Until his death it could be counted as a republican party. This was important since this was the party of commerce and industry. Its influence was greater than its voting strength, which derived largely from that section of the middle class which identified its own interests with those of capitalist success. With Stresemann gone, however, the party increasingly reverted to right-wing anti-republican-ism.[309]

It is difficult to make generalizations about the Centre Party and its ally, on a *Reich* level, the Bavarian Peoples' Party. This party was based simply on Roman Catholicism. Its social composition varied in different regions. It contained its own right and its own left. Its essential purpose was to fight for the Church. Since Bismarck's time, this had meant co-operation with governments in return for concessions. In the Weimar period, the Centre continued along this path and was a party that tried to be with the government rather than against it. In fact, the Centre was represented in every *Reich* government from 1919 to May

1932. In Prussia the Centre ruled in coalition with Social Democrats. Thus the Centre Party found its position under the republic much stronger than it had been in Imperial Germany and was content to work within it. The Prussian coalition meant that it did not have any fear of social democracy and caused the *Reichstag* party to be anxious to prevent any violent conflict with the SPD there. However, the Centre could not be counted on to fight to the last in defence of democracy – in the last resort it would seek to compromise with whatever force was dominant.

The Economic Party, the other substantial non-socialist party, was a pressure group for small business. As far as its leaders were concerned, it would support the constitution while it lasted and, as far as its voters were concerned, abandon it if it seemed likely to fail.

In the later 1920s then, republican democracy seemed to be growing more secure. The first setback came from the DNVP. After their losses at the 1928 elections, some of its leaders concluded that a violent opposition to the 'system' was what was needed rather than co-operation within it. The principal spokesman for this view was Hugenberg. He was elected chairman of the party in October 1928. He was an ambitious man, very rich, who had done well out of the inflation. He controlled a chain of newspapers and a film-making concern. The difficulty Hugenberg faced was that he and his party were too clearly plutocratic and upper-class to command overwhelming mass support. They needed a demagogue. There was a skilled demagogue available. He needed financial support. Hitler and Hugenberg met, and, in September 1929, launched a joint attack on the Young plan for reparations payments. They drew up, for vote by plebiscite, a 'law against the enslavement of the German people'. Germany's war guilt was denounced, the end of reparations demanded and the punishment as 'traitors' of the Reich administration, if it accepted the Young plan. This move was not a great success, and the 'freedom law' failed; twelve DNVP deputies resigned in protest against Hugenberg's manoevres and Count Westarp gave up the leadership of the *Reichstag* party. Hugenberg gained little; Hitler gained much. The financial and publicity resources at Hugenberg's disposal enabled Hitler to appear as a national figure in 'respectable' company. From October 1929 onwards the Nazis began to win votes at state elections.[310]

This was the prelude to the great Nazi electoral triumphs of 1930–2, which turned the Nazis into the major problem of German politics. In September 1930, the Nazis became the second largest party in the *Reichstag* and in July 1932, the largest of all. Why? It was a matter of very large numbers; there were over thirteen million Nazi voters in July 1932 out of about thirty-seven million who voted. It is clear from figures given above that Nazi votes came principally from two sources, the non-socialist parties and new voters. Compared with the elections in 1928, the parties other than the left parties (SPD and KPD) and the Catholic parties (Centre and BVP) lost over eight million votes in July 1932, while there were six million who had not voted before, half of them electors who did not trouble to vote in 1928, half of them newly qualified, i.e. young, voters. The left parties maintained their voting strength, though there were considerable SPD losses to the Communists. (There was, too, some movement among voters in the numerous elections of 1932 to and from the Communist and Nazi parties, the two great receptacles for the discontented.) The Catholic parties were unshakable. The parties who lost votes to the Nazis were these whose electoral support (though not necessarily their leadership) came from the middle class in the towns and from the same class together with farmers and peasants in the countryside. Rural support for Nazism was important: in July 1932 the six electoral districts (out of thirty-five) which produced the highest percentage of Nazi votes all contained an above-average number of inhabitants dependent on agriculture.[311]

Indeed, the only electoral district to produce an overall Nazi electoral majority (before Hitler became Chancellor) was Schleswig-Holstein, a mainly rural region. Interesting conclusions have been drawn from an analysis of the voting pattern and social structure of this district. Here the greatest support for the Nazis came from areas where small owners and farmers predominated and in which class division between wealthy proprietors and farmers on the one side and hired labourers on the other were largely absent. Where the latter pattern existed, the richer man tended to remain attached to the older conservative parties while the labourers voted for the 'Marxist' parties. The Nazis seem to have been able to appeal above all to those who wished for the defence of private property within a classless, socially unified community. Above all, the small farmer or peasant owner faced ruin when agricultural prices collapsed at the end of the 1920s, at a time when credit was contracting. Sales of farm stock or small holdings forced by creditors or tax collectors were common after 1928. The Nazis expressed hostility to big banks and 'international-Jewish finance capitalism', a nebulous but convenient scapegoat for all ills. They promised easier credit, reduced interest rates, higher tariffs, lower taxes, and insisted that agriculturalists would be a privileged class within the third *Reich*.[312]

Clearly the economic depression was crucial. In urban regions, its impact was greatest on the mass of the unemployed – men of the working class. The German middle class suffered, too. Unemployment was not confined to industrial workers, but extended to white-collar workers of a sort who refused to identify themselves with the proletariat and the SPD. Falling demand hit shopkeepers, artisan manufacturers and small businessmen. Their position was abnormally exposed because of the effect of the great inflation in destroying savings. The deflationary policies of the government led to credit contraction which made small businesses still more vulnerable. This sort of person faced a peril not merely to his comfort but to his status; he feared reduction to the ranks of the working class. At the same time, he resented the Socialists and feared the Communists. Socialism was vaguely believed to be responsible for high taxation and for contributions to social insurance, which small employers had to pay without any prospect of benefit for themselves. Trade union attempts to defend wage levels were more than usually hated when pressures on profits were at their highest. KPD gains in voting strength were noted with alarm; the Communists, it was thought, would certainly proletarianize the middle class even more effectively than the depression. The vague anti-capitalism that the Nazis professed offered happier prospects. 'Interest slavery' would be destroyed and credit somehow become more freely available. Multiple shops, that terror of the small shopkeeper, would be dealt with. The worrying aspects of competition would be removed without pervasive socialistic state control: the Nazis spoke of the development of a guild-corporatism and stressed the beauty and importance of craftmanship – a thought appealing to the small manufacturer.

As for the threat presented by the 'Marxists', the Nazis made it clear that they would eliminate it. Yet a tender-hearted bourgeois need not feel that an attack on the socialists and the communists would be an attack on the workers. On the contrary, the Nazis proclaimed their determination to abolish unemployment and secure the welfare of the working man in a society freed from 'Marxist' delusions. The idealistic element in support for the Nazis must not be disregarded. They propounded a society of co-operation and harmony as against one of class conflict and individual selfishness. The offer of material advantage was coupled with exhortations on self-sacrifice and duty. Somehow Germany would become physically and spiritually healthy. There was a strong boy-scout element in the Nazi appeal. The petty squabbles of party politicians would be transcended in a greater whole.

Above all, the Nazis offered vigour and action. They would struggle, they would fight, they would bring something new and different. Their energetic and continuous political campaigns were designed to give this impression. This appeal Brüning's government could not counter (Brüning was chancellor, 1930–2). Heinrich Brüning himself was cold and unattractive, without any mass appeal. The political situation made him, in practice, dependent on SPD acquiescence but at the same time made it impossible for him to proclaim this dependence or to work together with the SPD to produce a joint programme for action. Against the Nazis, the non-Nazi parties fought in dispersed order. None of them could hope to form a parliamentary government alone and this fact made their proposals seem pointless. The SPD was forced into a defensive and highly conservative position, yet unlike the British Labour Party, which it greatly resembled, it insisted on a theoretical revolutionary Marxism in doctrine.

Then there was the Nazis' nationalism, effectively linked with denunciations of the 'system'. The Young plan referendum of 1929 had enabled Hitler to advertise the argument that the plan would bring suffering to Germany imposed by foreigners; suffering had indeed followed. Hitler claimed that acceptance of the plan by the government was spineless acceptance of foreign dictation. This sort of thing was widely believed during the depression; in 1931, for instance, the astonishing notion existed that the British devaluation was a deliberate device for ruining Germany, and in 1932 the government had to issue a public denial that the suppression of the Nazi SA had been dictated by the French. Brüning's concentration on foreign policy fortified the belief that Germany's miseries were imposed from abroad and French obstruction over the Austro-German customs union, the Hoover moratorium and the Lausanne conference confirmed it. Germany must awake, cut off her shackles and fight for freedom.

The Nazi vote can therefore be explained. Yet the explanations are not completely convincing. Many, perhaps most, of the Nazi voters were reasonable decent people. The Nazi party was neither reasonable nor decent and this fact was apparent in 1932. Anti-Semitism, going well beyond the vehemence that anti-capitalism might inspire, was openly proclaimed, though the extermination of the Jews was not suggested. Brutality and violence were openly praised and practised. In September 1930, at the trial of three Nazi officers of the *Reichswehr*, Hitler shouted, 'I can assure you that when the Nazi movement's struggle is successful, then there will be a Nazi court of justice too, the November 1918 revolution will be avenged and heads will roll'. Edmund Heines, a murderer, appeared on Nazi platforms.[313] The SA visibly contained disreputable elements and provoked outbreaks of street fighting. In Prussia alone, there were 461 political riots in June and July 1932 in which eighty-two people were killed and about four hundred seriously wounded.[314] Mass support for the Nazis can only be taken as a depressing sympton of the evil way in which frightened human beings can behave. A major contribution to this evil can be found in the conduct towards the republic of the respectable conservative German right, especially among that section of the DNVP which fell under the influence of Hugenberg, and, above all, from the violence of the diatribes repeatedly produced in the Hugenberg press. The idea of violence as a legitimate weapon against democracy had thus been advocated for years by many of the natural leaders of German opinion.

It was not only millions of Nazi votes and a phalanx of Nazi deputies in the *Reichstag* that governments had to face in 1930–3. The Nazis declared that they were revolutionaries. Though Hitler and the leadership insisted that they would gain power only by legal means, it was reasonable to suppose that the Nazis might try to seize power by force if they could not do so without. In the SA, the Nazis had a weapon to hand. During these years its strength seems to have been about 400,000. It was a force organized on military lines, with brown-shirted uniform, but designed mainly for street fighting and political brawling. Except in certain eastern frontier areas, it had no serious military training and it was lightly armed. Still, it was a force which governments had to take into account.

There were two methods of handling the Nazis; by attempting to win them for some kind of partnership in government or by an attempt to keep them out of government altogether and to resist any attempt by the Nazis to challenge this exclusion. The last government to attempt the latter course with any consistency was that presided over by Brüning, who was chancellor from 1930 to 1932. His appointment was one of the earliest consequences of the great depression. From 1928 to the spring of 1930 Germany was governed by a cabinet under Müller, a Social Democrat, which relied on a majority based on the so-called 'Great Coalition', which included Social Democrats (SPD) democrats (DDP) the Centre Party (and the Bavarian Peoples' Party or BVP) and the German Peoples' Party (DVP). It collapsed because of disagreements between the DVP and SPD about the correct method of dealing with the increasing numbers of the unemployed. Broadly speaking, the DVP wished to curb rates of benefit to the unemployed and to finance the increasing amounts that would, in any case, have to be paid, by methods of taxation or contribution which should not damage the rich taxpayers or employers of labour. The SPD, especially its trade union elements, was anxious to prevent greater misery being imposed on the unemployed or disproportionately heavy taxation being levied on the poorer classes. Compromises proved unsatisfactory to one side or another and the Müller government resigned in March 1930.

Brüning was the nominee of General von Schleicher. The latter was an intelligent, flexible, rather unstable soldier with a highly developed taste for politics. His influence was embodied in his position in the war ministry as head of the *Ministeramt*, a department created for him by his old friend and superior, General Groener. Groener had become Minister of Defence in 1928, as a result of Groener's own war-time connection with Hindenburg, under whom he had served as Quartermaster General. He relied on Schleicher for political advice and political contacts. Schleicher had some ideas about the nature and purposes of Brüning's government. It was to be 'non-party', which seems to have meant in practice that it was to rely less on the *Reichstag* and more on the President than previous governments had done, and its composition should not be determined by inter-party negotiations. It was to exclude the social democrats. This should make possible a firmer line towards the Prussian government, which had shown some objections to the (illegal) measures for strengthening frontier defence favoured by the *Reichswehr*. It should win back the confidence of the Nationalists for the President and end support for Hugenberg's out and out opposition to the present system. The *Stahlhelm*, the nationalist paramilitary force, which the *Reichswehr* regarded as essential for frontier defence, would be restored to a co-operative frame of mind. If necessary, the President would empower the new Chancellor to use his emergency powers under article forty-eight of the constitution to govern by decree and would give him the right to dissolve the *Reichstag*.

The Brüning government soon ran into the same difficulty that had brought down Müller's administration. In July 1930, it proposed a series of deflationary measures to increase revenues and curtail spending in national and local government including limitations on unemployment relief. When the *Reichstag* voted against a section of these measures, the cabinet brought the whole group of proposals into effect by presidential emergency decree. However the *Reichstag* had the legal right to nullify such emergency decrees; it promptly did so, by the narrow margin of fourteen votes. The majority against Brüning included the Social Democrats, voting in defence of the interests of their supporters, the Communists, voting against capitalist democracy, and thirty-two Nationalists who sided with Hugenberg against twenty-five who supported the government. The last factor was significant. In spite of Hindenburg's support and the exclusion of social democrats, Brüning had not succeeded in winning the support of the DNVP as a whole. Hugenberg retained control of the party, in spite of resignations, and maintained opposition to the 'system', partly from conviction, partly from fear of losing support to the Nazis. The *Reichstag* was at once dissolved and elections were fixed for the last possible date, 14 September 1930.

It was expected that the Nazis would increase their strength at the elections. What was not anticipated was the extent of their success; six million votes turned them into the second largest party in the *Reichstag*. In spite of this portent, Brüning was able to construct a mechanism of government with some prospect of stability – at least the 1930 elections meant that another new *Reichstag* could be delayed until 1934, by which time economic recovery might undermine support for the Nazis, although that support must be expected to grow in the meantime. The key to the new political situation was the revised attitude of the Social Democrats. The SPD leadership now grasped that the alternative to Brüning could only be the end of democracy, probably through a Hitler-Hugenberg government. Even Brüning's government, with its inequitable deflation, was preferable to that. Thus the SPD came to tolerate Brüning. They could escape direct responsibility for Brüning's economic measures, provided that they were carried through by presidential decree, while seeking to prevent Brüning's fall by rejecting attempts at the subsequent nullification of emergency decrees. In this way, Brüning was able to secure freedom to apply his deflationary policy, and to seek success abroad by securing the end of reparations (to please public opinion) and some degree of rearmament (to please the *Reichswehr*). There was a weakness in this structure – it depended on support from the President. So long as the alliance worked between Brüning, Groener, Schleicher and Hindenburg, all might be well, but if it broke down, Brüning's system would collapse. In 1932, with the economic situation at its worst, and Nazi strength at its height, the break came.

In the spring, Brüning won a last victory, which soon turned out to be unreal. Hindenburg's term as President would come to an end in 1932 and only his continuance in office could prevent the election of a Nazi nominee, probably Hitler himself. Brüning first attempted to persuade the parties to accept a renewal of Hindenburg's tenure without re-election, a step needing a two-thirds *Reichstag* majority. The Nationalists and the Nazis refused and Hindenburg was, with difficulty, persuaded to face an election campaign. It was a paradoxical affair. The aged monarchist reactionary became the candidate of the defenders of democracy, notably of the SPD, the *Staatspartei* (formerly DDP) and the Centre, with the DVP supporting him too, although they had moved into opposition to Brüning's government. After much indecision, Hitler himself stood, while the DNVP, anxious to keep its following separate from Hitler's, put up Duesterberg, second in command of the Stahlhelm. Thälmann stood as Communist candidate. Hindenburg failed to secure an overall majority on the first ballot and a second was necessary to secure his election. On the first ballot Hindenburg got about eighteen and a half million votes, Hitler nearly eleven and a half million; in the second ballot Hindenburg received about nineteen and a half million votes while Hitler won thirteen and a half million.

Hindenburg disliked the whole process. He had come to regard himself as the symbol of German unity and it is irritating for someone with this status to find himself voted against (on the first ballot) by half the electorate. Furthermore, Hindenburg was much upset by finding nearly all the 'national' forces arrayed against him, especially most of the *Stahlhelm*, of which he was an honorary member. He felt no sense of obligation to do what he had now been elected to do – to maintain Brüning in power. A breach soon opened. Provincial governments, notably that of Prussia, had been pressing for some time for action against the SA. The discovery of plans for an armed seizure of power by the SA precipitated events. The governments of Prussia, Bavaria and Württemberg insisted that if the *Reich* did not act against the SA, they would do so themselves. General Groener, the *Reich* Minister of Defence and of the Interior, therefore persuaded Schleicher, Hindenburg and Brüning that the SA should be banned. A decree went out on 13 April 1932. This involved a change in Groener's policy towards the Nazis. He had hitherto followed the defence ministry's view that the SA, as a 'volunteer patriotic movement', should be treated as an auxiliary force for the *Reichswehr* in case of a Polish attack and as a source of recruits for the *Reichswehr* itself – 'the best men would naturally find their way into the Nazi organizations'.[315] Hindenburg's and Schleicher's support for this change proved very brief. Hindenburg was faced with protests from his nationalist friends, Schleicher with doubts and questioning from *Reichswehr* officers throughout the country. The result was the resignation of Groener as Minister of Defence on 13 May; this was followed by the resignation of the Brüning government on 30 May. Schleicher was anxious to revert to the policy of co-operation with the Nazis, and when the difficulties appeared, preferred to make greater concessions rather than risk a civil war. He came to see the Brüning-Groener government as the main obstacle preventing compromise with the Nazis. There was another factor involved. Brüning's Minister of Labour had worked out a scheme for settling unemployed men on land to be expropriated from bankrupt landlords, east of the Elbe. Those landlords took the view, on the contrary, that the state should devote still more efforts to saving them from ruin. Their protests against 'agrarian bolshevism' received a sympathetic hearing from Hindenburg. Moreover industrialists were demanding a firmer line against socialists and trade unionists than the Brüning government displayed. Thus Brüning lost presidential support, which was essential to his political survival.

The fall of Brüning was the decisive moment in the history of these years. With government based on the readiness of the *Reichswehr* to suppress a possible Nazi rising ruled out by the policies of the Defence Ministry and the sympathies of some officers for the Nazis, there remained no other alternative to the Brüning system except an attempt to come to terms with the Nazis. Schleicher was in touch with Hitler in April and May 1932. The new Chancellor, von Papen, a Centrist deputy in the Prussian *Landtag*, who was known for his eagerness to bring to an end the participation of the SPD in the Prussian government, and who had adopted conciliation towards the Nazis, was Schleicher's nominee. Early in June, Schleicher reached agreement with Hitler; the dissolution of the SA would be repealed, which was done on 16 June, and the *Reichstag* dissolved. After the elections, Nazi participation in the government would be arranged. In the elections at the end of July 1932, the Nazis secured thirty-seven per cent of the votes. Given the numbers of the Communists in the *Reichstag*, and the indifference of that party to the republic, government with the *Reichstag* now became impossible without Nazi support. Meanwhile, on 20 July, Papen had suppressed the government of Prussia, and appointed himself as *Reichskommissar* for Prussia. Thus the great bastion of democracy in Germany was overthrown, without resistance or disturbance.

The elections were followed by a sharp set-back for Schleicher and Papen; Hitler insisted on the Chancellorship for himself as the price of Nazi collaboration in the government, without which the Nazis would oppose Papen. Papen was not unduly concerned; he was perfectly prepared to disregard hostile majorities. Schleicher, however, retained some hope of winning the Nazis over. The rapid dissolution of the new *Reichstag* on 12 September postponed the political crisis until the elections of 6 Nov. These provided some encouragement for Papen – a strengthening of the DNVP, now his only supporters, and a weakening of the Nazis who secured thirty-three per cent of the votes – but the fundamental situation remained. Papen could rule only on the ultimate basis of force – the Centre would not work with him, the Socialists regarded him as the very embodiment of bourgeois reaction, the Nazis would not accept his terms. Papen was prepared to rule by force. Schleicher was not. He was meditating about the danger of the *Reichswehr's* being compelled to maintain by force of arms a government resting on the narrowest possible basis of general support and he preferred not to take the risk. In November, an elaborate study was made in the Defence Ministry of the *Reichswehr's* situation faced with a simultaneous revolt from Nazis and Communists, with a general strike and a Polish invasion thrown in. Given these highly implausible assumptions, it was clear that the *Reichswehr* would be swamped.[316] Armed with these conclusions, Schleicher worked for a new experiment in attempting to win support for a government – from the Nazis and, if possible, from elsewhere. Rather than face the alleged risk of civil war, Hindenburg reluctantly let Papen go. On 2 December 1932, Papen was succeeded by Schleicher himself.

Schleicher intended to use his own greater flexibility to broaden the basis of support for the *Reich* government. He abandoned Papen's clearly right-wing domestic policy as part of an attempt to win over the left, especially trade unionists. He believed that he could secure support from Hitler on his own terms or else split the Nazi party. To this end he relied on his contacts with Gregor Strasser, a leader of the radical, anti-capitalist Nazis, and on the demoralization among the Nazis following their set-back in the November elections and the financial difficulties the repeated elections of 1932 had created for them. Either Strasser would win Hitler over to acceptance of Schleicher's government, or he would, so Schleicher hoped, successfully challenge Hitler's leadership of the party or create a rival movement of his own. Strasser failed in every respect. Furthermore, Schleicher's casting himself in the rôle of the 'social general', sympathetic to the working class, failed to win him the support of the SPD. Though the leaders of the Socialist trade unions were ready to work with him, the political leadership categorically rejected the idea of supporting a 'reactionary' general; this was a grave mistake. Even so, Schleicher could survive and could reduce the Nazis to acceptance of a subordinate position in power provided he had the support of the President. He could dissolve the *Reichstag*, postpone new elections and rely on force to maintain himself. He was in a stronger position to do so than Papen had been. Schleicher had won support from the Centre and the Catholic unions; the free unions were sympathetic; the Commander-in-Chief of the army, von Hammerstein, was a certain ally. The essential condition was absent: Schleicher could not rely on Hindenburg.

Those best able to influence the President increasingly turned against Schleicher. He had revived fears of 'agrarian bolshevism' by renewed talk of land settlement, and the danger of an inquiry into the use of funds for assistance to eastern landowners had convinced them that a friendly government was essential, he had alienated industry by his overtures to the unions, he had incurred the hostility of Hugenberg and his followers by keeping Hugenberg out of his government, and, above all, Papen, whom the President trusted, evolved an alternative solution to Schleicher's. Contact between Papen and Hitler was re-established early in 1933. By 22 January, Papen had accepted Hitler's demand for the chancellorship and the support of the President's son, Oskar, had been won. Hitler demanded only two other cabinet posts for Nazis, for Göring who should also be Prussian Minister of the Interior, and for Frick as *Reich* Minister of the Interior. It remained to persuade the reluctant President to agree. Nationalist support for Papen's plans contributed one means; Hugenberg though suspicious of Hitler, fell in with the notion of a 'national front' and Seldte, the Stahlhelm leader, was brought in. The other means was the emergence of a senior general, who had Hindenburg's confidence, who was ready to take over the Ministry of Defence from Schleicher and thus place it in apparently safe hands: General von Blomberg. On 23 January, Hindenburg rejected Schleicher's request for a dissolution of the *Reichstag* and for emergency powers. On the 28th, Schleicher resigned; on the 30th, Hitler was sworn in as chancellor.

Papen, Seldte and Hugenburg supposed that they had secured, through Hitler, mass support for a conservative government controlled by themselves; in fact, Hitler had secured a screen of respectability to delude the aged President and the army into accepting moves towards a Nazi dictatorship. The Cabinet quickly accepted a decree 'for the protection of the German people' providing control over political meetings and the press. Complaints against its application could go to the courts only if they were allowed to do so by the police (in Prussia, Göring was rapidly nazifying the police) or by the Ministry of the Interior (controlled by Frick). On 28 February, with the convenient excuse of the *Reichstag* fire, a decree went through suspending all constitutional liberties and empowering the central government to take over the individual states. The new *Reichstag* elections of March, in spite of widespread terror, failed to give the Nazis an absolute majority; they secured forty-four per cent of the votes. It made no difference. With the Communist deputies proscribed and some Social Democratic deputies arrested, Hitler could count on a two-thirds majority (with his Nationalist allies) for the passage of an enabling law transferring legislative power to the government. As it was, the Centre voted for it too, clinging to its position as a party of government, and the vote was 441-94 with the surviving Social Democratic deputies alone voting against. The next step was to subject the states to direct control through the appointment of *Reichsstatthaltern*. Then Hitler's right-wing allies were put in their place. The Stahlhelm was subordinated to Hitler and Nationalist meetings attacked and broken up by the SA. At the end of June the police and SA occupied many Nationalist offices and the party dissolved itself. The SPD was suppressed, while in June and July the remaining parties accepted the inevitable and disbanded. On 14 July a law constituted the Nazis as the only political party. The only forces left for Hitler to worry about were Hindenburg, the army and his own followers.

The seizure of power that followed Hitler's appointment to the chancellorship rested on the terror disseminated by the SA. Their violence was not wholly controlled from the top; some of it was a spontaneous expression of independent aims. Within the Nazi party, and especially within the SA, there existed aspirations towards a 'second revolution' with real social changes. The independence of the army should be destroyed and it should be merged with the SA; the civil service should be purged and nazified; the leaders of business and industry should be excluded from the power their economic position gave to them. If these things could be done, then the restless ambitions of the dissatisfied, frustrated men who dominated the SA could be fulfilled. These projects did not suit Hitler. They would arouse the hostility of powerful forces in Germany, above all in the army. The people the SA wished to challenge were those on whose knowledge and skill the rebuilding of German power must principally rest and for Hitler this was far more important than social change. Moreover the army remained formidable. If Hindenburg could be roused from the acquiescent apathy which old age, Hitler's flattery and the ease which came of being deprived of his powers had induced in him – and army resentments might do this – then Hitler could still be turned out of power. In 1933, the SA expanded to enormous dimensions – it now contained millions of men. Hitler faced this situation indecisively: for some months he attempted to curb the SA leadership by conciliation and persuasion – especially towards its chief, Röhm. Action was forced on him in the summer of 1934. On 17 June, in a speech at Marburg, Papen denounced the advocates of the second revolution, in words some of which reflected on the Nazi régime itself. This was followed by a threat from Papen that the conservatives would withdraw from the government unless the radicals were curbed. Worse followed on 21 June, Blomberg told Hitler that the President insisted that tension be ended at once, failing which he would declare martial law and hand over power to the army. On 30 June 1934, Hitler acted. Using the SS, the élite corps of picked men, which was still technically a branch of the SA, Hitler arranged for the murder of the leaders of the SA. At the same time, others were disposed of such as Schleicher, von Kahr and Gregor Strasser.

The result was the stabilization of Hitler's régime. The army and the conservative right henceforward accepted Hitler's rule and turned a blind eye to Nazi measures, however murderous they might be; Hitler forbade social revolution and permitted some independence to the army within its own spheres of activity. This partnership survived, with some questionings from the army and hesitations from the conservatives and some intrusions from the party, at least until July 1944, and for many of those involved, until the end. Thus the army fought and conquered and left a free hand to the SS, while itself keeping aloof, while men like Papen, Neurath and Schwerin-Krosigk served Hitler to the last days of Nazi Germany.

Mass support for Hitler's rule was maintained and extended by different means. The years after 1933 were years of economic revival and expansion. Above all, unemployment disappeared. The average number of registered unemployed was about five and a half million in 1932 while in 1938 it was less than half a million. In the first place it was done by extending policies first applied by the Papen and Schleicher governments – giving credit to businessmen by distribution of tax remission certificates, especially directed to industrialists prepared to take on additional labour. The Nazis added government spending on extensive public works, especially motor roads. Then, especially after 1936, and still more from the end of 1937, the government spent large amounts of money on rearmament. The result was sustained economic growth, first to pre-depression levels and then beyond. Civilian consumption was held back by the maintenance of the high levels of taxation of the depression period. Prices were controlled, while wages, fixed by the labour trustees appointed by the government instead of by bargains between unions and employers, were held down. Internal full employment and the relatively high price levels inside Germany (the mark was not devalued to avoid setting off a panic fear of the recurrence of inflation) weakened exports and stimulated imports. The process was checked by elaborate measures of exchange control and import restrictions. Associated with exchange controls were the measures taken towards the development of bilateral trade. These were notably successful in south-eastern Europe and with some of the countries of Latin America. By offering more than the world prices for food and raw materials and paying in blocked marks, which could be used only for purchases in Germany, German economic hegemony was peacefully established in south eastern Europe. By early 1939, more than half the exports of Bulgaria, Yugoslavia and Hungary went to greater Germany and more than one-third of the exports of Greece, Turkey and Rumania. Within this structure, civilian standards of living in Germany recovered to the level of the prosperous year of 1928, while the government was able to increase spending on rearmament from 4,000 million marks in 1933–5 to 8,000 million marks in April 1937— April 1938. Thus rearmament was combined with a high standard of living and security of employment for the German people; no doubt the standard of living could have been higher still if a smaller proportion of national resources had been taken by the state, but, as it was, most Germans were reasonably satisfied.

The economic situation became strained in 1938. Spending on re-armament rose to 18,000 million marks. An inflationary situation developed, partly repressed by controls on prices and wages, but showing itself clearly in serious shortages of labour both in agriculture and industry. Though high government spending and internal controls prevented the world depression, which began in 1937, from any direct impact inside Germany, it meant a falling off of German exports helped by the upward trend of prices and wages inside Germany which the government could not completely check; thus the German balance of payments moved into deficit in 1938. This was dangerous. Germany was not wholly self-sufficient in foodstuffs and years of bad harvests could add extra difficulties. Rearmament required imports of essential minerals. The labour shortage was partly alleviated by immigration – but foreign workers made remittances home with required foreign exchange. In 1938 and 1939 the German government was faced with pressing choices. It could slow down rearmament – but that was completely unacceptable to Hitler until his political aims had been won. It could curtail civilian consumption and introduce a true war economy, with severe rationing and even higher taxation. There were political objections to this course, too: the Nazi *Gauleiters* and the police were fully aware that the popularity of the régime depended on the maintenance of high living standards. There remained the choice of war. Speedy military successes might secure German dominance in Europe before economic processes made it impossible to sustain the war machine. Military conquest might itself strengthen the foundations of military power – raw materials, food and supplies of labour would become available without needing foreign exchange to procure them. Again, war could provide a justification for the introduction of a war economy, if it became necessary. Hitler seems to have recognized these pressures towards war: on 22 August 1939, he told his commanders-in-chief: 'because of our restrictions our economic situation is such that we can only hold out a few more years. Göring [in charge of the Four Year Plan] can confirm this. We have no other choice, we must act.'[317]

The Nazi régime drenched Germany in propaganda and intellectual rubbish. Its main aim was psychological preparation for war. There is no convincing evidence that it succeeded. Apart from the substantial number of Nazi enthusiasts, there does not seem to have been much desire among the German people for aggressive war. Nor is there any clear evidence that the anti-Jewish measures (as yet non-murderous) introduced before the war, commanded more than passive acquiescence: economic recovery removed most of what mass support there had been for anti-Semitism. Hitler was supported in spite of, rather than because of, the policies he had most at heart – aggressive war and the destruction of the Jews. Still, there can be no denying the general support Hitler's régime acquired by 1939, principally because it was associated with an apparently stable prosperity.

12

The End of the Peace: 1929-33

By the autumn of 1929 world peace seemed secure; by the spring of 1933 all was changed. A great hope had gone, a major illusion had been destroyed. The prospect of a peaceful, reasonable, moderate, Germany had vanished; the notion that the League of Nations could command peace by moral authority alone had been wrecked by Japan. The forces in Germany and Japan that brought peace into question were not new: militaristic nationalism was familiar enough in most countries. What was new about these years was the collapse of the world economy which both in Germany and in Japan brought nationalists to dominance.

In 1929 the policies of understanding and compromise of the Briand-Stresemann era secured a victory in Germany. The nationalist opposition arranged a referendum against the acceptance of the Young plan. The best efforts of the German Nationalist Peoples Party and of the Nazis secured the support (in the form of signatures to a petition) of only a little over ten per cent of the German electorate. Though this suggested that resistance to compromise with foreigners was still alive in Germany, the referendum made it clear that cautious policies had overwhelming support. In 1930 the situation was transformed; at the elections to the *Reichstag* in September the Nazis secured 107 seats with eighteen per cent of the votes cast – in 1928 they had won twelve seats with two and a half per cent of the votes. The Nazi view on foreign affairs was quite clear in one respect; that foreign oppression was to blame for Germany's suffering and that the sooner German power was restored and foreigners frustrated the sooner those sufferings would end. The 1930 elections made it certain that non-Nazi German governments would seek diplomatic victories to display their skill in dealing with foreigners in order to protect themselves against Nazi accusations of weakness and treachery. Of course, it would have been better still for

239

German governments and for everyone else to alleviate the very real sufferings of many of the German people; but economic orthodoxies denied this to them. Thus German demands for concessions grew ever more vociferous. The rulers of France, especially, were faced with a great dilemma. Should they abandon altogether the hopes of the Stresemann-Briand era and resist every advance of German power? Or should they cling to the fading hopes of Franco-German reconciliation? Brüning plausibly argued the latter policy; whatever his government demanded, the Nazis, if they got control, would demand more. The French, therefore, should be generous in order to help Brüning to keep the Nazis out. He was not convinced by the counter-argument deployed by Briand that his own influence in France was for moderation and that things would be worse still for Germany if he and his policies were discredited in France by vociferous German agitation. Brüning, and still more, Papen, whose government was the most unpopular ever seen in united Germany, had to look for triumphs abroad to defend themselves at home.

The French could not avoid facing the choice: conciliation or firmness. The stakes were high and rising higher. If the wrong answer were given France might be in peril. The result was the usual outcome: to compromise on a little of each. In retrospect it is clear that this policy made certain the ruin of France. In these years before Hitler became chancellor France failed effectively to resist German demands. Equally, France failed to give advocates of German moderation the chance to argue that moderation might pay.

The great themes of European diplomacy in these years were the economic crisis and disarmament. Both increasingly came to turn on German demands: for the end of reparations and for the rearmament of Germany. In 1930 attempts to secure and perpetuate the apparent stability and peace of the late 1920s continued; in 1932 Germany openly demanded the right to rearm, stopped paying reparations, and the Nazis became the largest German party. Schemes for the continuance, with slow modifications, of the post-war status quo were increasingly drowned by German demands for its outright destruction.

In September 1929 Briand called for a codification and extension of the 'Locarno spirit', in the form of 'some kind of federal bond' between the European nations and in May 1930 made definite proposals for a 'general pact, however elementary it might be, to affirm the principle of a European moral union and solemnly to consecrate the fact of the solidarity instituted between European states'. There was to be a European body, representative of governments, with a permanent committee to study European co-operation. Economic co-operation could be advanced once – and here French preoccupations appeared with clarity – everyone felt politically secure through the extension of Locarno-type guarantees to the whole of Europe. Thus a slow advance could be made to the final idea –

The time has never been more encouraging or more urgent for the inauguration of a constructive design in Europe. The settlement of the principal problems, material and moral, that followed the last war, will soon have liberated the new Europe from what burdened its mental outlook and its economy most heavily.

In reply, the Germans produced a glimpse of their plans for the 1930s; the British of their fears of the 1950s. A growl came from the new German chancellor, Brüning:

Assuming that the political idea underlying the memorandum meant that the European nations must agree, as a precondition of an economic federation of Europe, that the present status quo as regards frontiers must be accepted, he said quite definitely that no government in Germany, however socialist in composition, could subscribe to such a condition.

The British Foreign Office objected to anything which might weaken British relations with America or the Commonwealth.[318] The whole scheme petered out: in September 1930 the League of Nations set up a commission of enquiry for European union. This devoted itself to general discussions of tariff questions, enlivened by the proposals for an Austro-German customs union in 1931, and to discussion of methods of dealing with the agricultural surpluses of eastern European countries.

In 1931 Brüning continued to grapple with the problems created in Germany by the world depression: over 4,000,000 unemployed, growing support for extremist politicians, the breakdown of a reliable governmental majority in the *Reichstag*. He pressed on with drastic deflation, which made all his problems greater. He sought to win successes abroad to heighten his prestige at home. The British had a plan suggested by their ambassador in Berlin:

A visit to England would, I think give him [Brüning] an international prestige which would be helpful to him in Germany itself. I cannot imagine anything which would more impress and please the Germans than if he were to spend a weekend at Chequers, for instance.[319]

Brüning had something stronger in view, an idea devised by his foreign minister, Curtius. In March, a plan was announced for an Austro-German customs union. The proposal was produced without previous consultation with France. French suspicions were instantly aroused; the scheme looked like a preliminary to the *Anschluss* and the beginning of a further attack on Versailles. Diplomatic preparation had been non-existent and only the Soviet Union had been informed in advance. This added to the disturbance created by the proposal. The French insisted that the scheme was incompatible with the independence that Austria was pledged to maintain; the British deplored the emergence of an issue which might jeopardize the successful outcome of disarmament talks. For his part, Brüning announced a fervent determination to push the customs union through regardless of all objections. The position of French diplomacy in resisting the scheme was greatly strengthened by the financial weakness of Austria and by the fact that the French financial position was growing steadily stronger in 1931. In May the major Austrian bank, the *Creditanstalt*, had to be supported by the Austrian government. The Austrian government itself was forced to seek financial help abroad. In June, with the French demanding Austrian abandonment of the customs union, the Bank of England stepped in with a credit to Austria. Even so the Austrian Minister for Foreign Affairs, Dr Schober, admitted privately on the day of the British credit that the scheme was dead. This was a short-term loan and the Bank of England could do no more; only from France could long-term assistance come. This meant giving up the union. At the beginning of September its abandonment was formally announced.[320] Curtius was forced to resign; the impression in Germany that the Allies, especially the French, blocked reasonable German hopes was strengthened and the argument that Brüning and the 'system' were weak in enforcing German claims was made still more convincing to German minds.

French conduct over the Hoover Moratorium strengthened this view. In June 1931 losses of gold and foreign currencies from the German *Reichsbank* sharply accelerated. The extent of Germany's short-term indebtedness was generally known and the weakness of the Austrian *Creditanstalt* suggested to holders of German obligations that withdrawal might be prudent. As always such views were self-confirming and by the middle of the month it seemed likely that the *Reichsbank* would be compelled to suspend payments. A prospect of economic collapse in central Europe appeared, when the President of the USA, Herbert Hoover, intervened with a proposal for a suspension of payments on all inter-governmental debts, including reparations. Agitation in Germany against continued reparations had risen in volume; there was a general tendency to blame German difficulties on reparations and the Social Democrats were prepared to curb their dislike of Brüning's deflationary measures if he worked effectively against reparations. It was correctly assumed that Brüning would use his visit to England in June to raise the reparations question. The President's suggestion stole the German government's thunder. In France, the President was thought to be giving away too much. It was argued that if the Germans once stopped paying reparations they would never start again and resentment was expressed at the insistence of the Germans on continuing to spend money on arms. '*We* are paying for the *Deutschland*' [the pocket battleship] declared M. Herriot.[321] The French insisted that the Germans should be made to pay at least the annuities which the Young plan had declared to be payable under all circumstances as distinct from those whose payment could be suspended if the normal course of German economic life were interrupted. After delaying the coming into operation of the Hoover Moratorium by two weeks, the French negotiators secured a paper victory of the sort that French diplomacy was increasingly forced to accept. The unconditional reparations payments were to continue but the money paid was to be lent at once to the German state railways so that the money would never leave Germany at all.

In July 1931 a conference in London decided that creditors of Germany should be asked not to withdraw their funds and that an enquiry should be set in train to examine Germany's credit requirements. In August a committee reported that long term loans to Germany were impossible unless 'the international payments to be made by Germany will not be such as to imperil the maintenance of her financial ability'. Thus reparations were brought into question. The German government demanded the convocation of the Special Advisory Committee provided for by the Young plan to consider whether or not German economic life might be endangered by the payment of the Young annuities. It reported in December 1931 and its report meant that the Young plan would never be revived. The crisis was greater than the 'relatively short depression' which the Young plan took into account; the committee called for action by governments and it concluded that 'the adjustment of all inter-governmental debts (reparations and other war debts) . . . is the only lasting step capable of re-establishing confidence'.

The French government contemplated with dismay the failure of its attempt to keep the Young plan going, if only in theory, and resorted to measures designed simply to soften the blow to the French chamber of deputies and the electorate. It was clear that reparations were dead. One compensation might have been an agreement by the USA to abandon its claims for war debts. This was refused. Germany, Britain and Italy agreed that reparations must be wiped out first and the Americans urged to change their mind afterwards. Laval, the French Prime Minister, was reduced to securing the postponement of the interment of reparations until after the French elections in the spring. The Lausanne conference, when it came, was designed on the French side, as Laval put it in January, 'to calm the excitement largely due to the attitude of Germany which has very much strengthened the belief that she is bent on tearing up all treaties and engagements'. No more reparations could be expected from Germany – Berthelot, the permanent head of the French foreign ministry, told the British ambassador in February 1932 that he 'had never had any doubt that once payment was suspended last July reparations were dead'. Yet the French government sought to conceal this fact, whether Laval, Tardieu or Herriot was in power. In June Germain-Martin, the French Finance Minister, told the British Prime Minister that 'he doubted if any French government which accepted complete and final cancellation at Lausanne could survive'.[322] At Lausanne the French sought to conceal the fact that reparations were at an end while Papen, now German Chancellor, sought to secure a diplomatic triumph, by making it absolutely clear that reparations were finished. Negotiations were therefore difficult and a sham resulted. Germany was to make a final payment of 3,000 million gold marks. This was to be in the form of bonds on which interest and amortization was not to be paid by Germany until at least three years had elapsed. Until the Lausanne agreements came into force this payment and all German payments under previous agreements were to be suspended. On 8 July, the so-called gentlemen's agreement between Britain, France, Italy and Belgium prescribed that they would not ratify Lausanne until 'a satisfactory settlement has been reached between them and their own creditors' – which meant, in practice, until the USA had agreed to give up her claims on the former allies for war debts.[323] This did not happen. Indeed, in December 1932 the French government prepared to pay the instalment then due to the United States. The chamber of deputies intervened. The right and part of the centre were joined by the socialists in opposing this payment and the government was defeated.

This decision meant the end of payments by France and the recognition of the final end of all hopes of payments to France by Germany. The Lausanne agreements could not be put into force until negotiations with the USA had succeeded; they could not be denounced until these negotiations had failed. In fact, these negotiations remained in suspense so that the whole structure of reparations and war debts collapsed. In

December 1932, Britain paid an instalment of her debt to the USA; in June 1933 only a symbolic payment was made 'as a recognition of the debt, while waiting for a final settlement'. In June 1934, Britain stopped paying altogether and thereafter only Finland paid anything. Thus the situation had at last been reached that Britain had always called for that war debts and reparations were cancelled. In 1921 Germany's total obligations had been fixed at just short of 130,000 million gold marks. In fact, Germany paid slightly less than 23,000 millions. Of this France received about 9,500 millions, a sum which failed by a large margin even to pay for her expenses in the areas devastated during the war. The sacrifices and concessions made by France secured no gratitude. None was to be expected from Germany, but none was received even from the former allies or from the USA. M. Weill-Raynal concluded his magnificent work with one plausible explanation. French governments concealed from their own countrymen the concessions they made, covered them with a screen of vigorous verbiage, feigned resistance and denied that they had made any concessions at all. Thus France secured no moral credit and lost reparations without gaining support against resurgent Germany.[324]

Most plans and projects for disarmament in this brief period between the two largest wars that have ever taken place are of little more than antiquarian interest. Naval disarmament, or at any rate naval limitation, was more successfully pursued than land or air disarmament. This was because the powers involved were few in number – Britain, USA, France, Italy and Japan – because the weapons involved could be fairly easily compared and because all those powers had an interest in preventing a costly naval race. American governments were interested in naval limitation for its own sake. Britain wished to keep in check any expansion of United States naval strength in order to be able to deprive Japan of an excuse for growing too powerful, Japan wished to avoid a naval competition with the United States in which she would certainly be defeated. France and Italy wished to hold down each-other's naval power in the Mediterranean. In 1922 the Washington treaty imposed limits on the capital ship and aircraft carrier strength of these countries and on the tonnage and size of guns of these classes of ship. The ratios between them were to be 5 : 5 : 3 : 1·67 : 1·67 for Britain, USA, Japan, France and Italy. (The German navy was, of course, already restricted by the Versailles treaty.) For the first time, Britain accepted the notion that the Royal Navy should not be the strongest in the world. This was a symbol of the acceptance of the fact of United States power. Though Britain had no fear of this power there was more in its acceptance than that. The self-governing dominions of the British Empire, especially Canada, were determined that Britain and the United States should act together in harmony; the dominions, especially Australia and New Zealand, shared American suspicions of Japan and were eager to see definite limitations on Japanese strength. Japan would not agree to restrictions unless the USA were restricted; American admirals would not restrict the US navy to any strength lower than that of the British Empire. Lloyd George's government might have been prepared to act quite differently – to deny the United States' desire for equality and to rely on Japanese friendship to secure stability in the Far East. Instead, the British Dominions forced acceptance of American terms – including the abrogation of the Anglo-Japanese alliance. The Washington naval treaty is an important step in the process of the middle years of the twentieth century by which Britain came to be subordinate to the United States.[325]

In 1930 the Treaty of London extended the naval agreements between Britain, the USA and Japan to cover ships smaller than battleships. France and Italy did not come in. Italy insisted on a theoretical parity with France, even if she did not intend to achieve it in practice, and the French refused to give it. This represented another display of the frivolous nature of Mussolini's foreign policy. His irresponsibility was, indeed, strikingly demonstrated during the course of the negotiations. While attempts were being made to secure an agreement between France and Italy which should secure theoretical equality and leave France with more actual ships, Mussolini spoke thus on 17 May 1930: 'Words are very beautiful but rifles, machine guns, ships and aeroplanes are still more beautiful'. The Italian foreign minister, Grandi, was reduced to telling the British ambassador in Rome that Mussolini was not to be taken seriously. Before Mussolini spoke Grandi had made a conciliatory speech to the Italian chamber. Grandi told the British ambassador that he had asked Mussolini how he could reconcile conciliation with Mussolini's utterances. Mussolini replied, according to Grandi, 'What on earth have they got to do with it ? What does it matter what I say to my crowds ? Why do you think I made you Foreign Minister except to be able to talk here exactly as I please ?'[326] The French were not reassured and no agreement came. The Treaties of Washington and London were the only instances between the wars of agreement on arms limitations.

More general disagreement, including reduction of armies, was discussed at length but nothing came of all the talk. Into the discussion there intruded the central problem of the period – the problem of

Germany. Prospects of disarmament seemed real after Locarno, in the Stresemann era; they vanished in Hitler's time. The years 1929–33, once again, are years of transition between the winding up of one war and the preparation of the next. In 1925, the year of Locarno, the League of Nations set up a 'preparatory commission for the disarmament conference', in whose work Germany, the United States and the USSR were invited to join. It worked slowly, struggling with interminable technicalities, and the Disarmament Conference itself did not meet until February 1932. Soon after the opening of the conference, Brüning, the German Chancellor, raised the central issue. He claimed that Germany was entitled to equality of rights with all other members of the League of Nations and that this equality should apply to armaments. In the summer of 1932, a crisis was precipitated by Germany: when the Conference adjourned in July, the German representative announced that Germany would not take part in any future meetings unless the German claim to equality of rights was first accepted.

This made the matter clear. There would be no agreement on arms with Germany unless equality were promised in advance. The alternatives were to rely on Versailles and attempt to enforce it on Germany or to seek some new arrangement which Germany might accept. In July, General von Schleicher, then the most powerful individual in Germany, insisted that Germany would not accept a continuance of the Versailles limitations. Germany, he declared, could be made secure by the reduction of the armed forces of the other powers to the German level. No one could believe in such a miracle, he went on. The second method would be by increasing Germany's armed strength. Schleicher announced firmly that Germany would employ this second method if she continued to be refused the equality she claimed.[327] Here was a direct challenge to the existing balance of power in Europe. Schleicher was engaged in domestic political manoeuvres rather than in foreign policy – he wanted to be able to remodel the German military structure in order to incorporate into it, under the aegis of the *Reichswehr*, the paramilitary units, especially the Nazi SA. Thus the Nazis would be tamed without the need for direct resistance. However, the French saw only a German demand for rearmament. What should France do?

The British position, as always, was that Germany should be conciliated. In October 1932, MacDonald wrote to Herriot in these words,

Europe has been undoubtedly drifting recently into militarist hands, and a great part of the impetus has certainly come from the psychological reaction upon the German mind of Germany's economic and political position. I think this ought to have been foreseen some years ago so that resentment would have been prevented from accumulating . . . I do not believe that any of us could rigidly resist the German claim that the treaty of Versailles must in some respects be reconsidered.

Respect for treaties should be preserved by abandoning treaties that Germany would not respect and making treaties that she would. The more alarming Germany became, the stronger the case for conciliation. From Washington, the Secretary of State, Stimson, expressed resentment at German demands and urged resistance, but President Hoover, as usual, took a much less combative line. In September, Hoover declared: 'We are anxious that Germany shall continue to participate in the arms conference which has now such promise of progress for the entire world and that she shall lend her aid in this great purpose'.[328]

Herriot faced a difficult situation. Once again, the outside world refused to understand the nature of the German menace. To the French, discussion of 'disarmament', which turned out to mean simply an increase in the relative strength of Germany, was a mad enterprise when Europe was faced with an unstable Germany in which extreme nationalism was advancing. France could refuse to modify Versailles – but the Germans would rearm just the same. France might seek to enforce Versailles – but this line of action had been given up at Locarno. France might adopt a conciliatory policy, not with any hope that it would succeed, but in order to gain the friendship and the help of Britain and the United States for use in an uncertain future when the illusions about Germany in those countries would have disappeared. Herriot chose the last course.

In January 1932, plans had been evolved in Paris to deal with the disarmament question. They took the form of proposals for increasing security by placing at the disposal of the League of Nations elements of, or the whole of, the permanent national forces of each country together with the creation of regional pacts of mutual assistance against possible aggressors. In February 1932, Tardieu, then French Prime Minister, had presented to the Disarmament Conference the 'minimum plan' – of putting certain air-forces and heavy artillery and naval vessels at the disposal of the League. Now M. Herriot took up the 'maximum plan' – of putting virtually all permanent national forces under the orders of the League and leaving only militias to the free disposition of individual states. He did not take it very seriously or feel any affection for it – it was a device for winning goodwill for France. Herriot explained his views to the French military chiefs in October:

I have no illusions. I am convinced that Germany wishes to rearm . . . We are at a turning point in history. Until now Germany has practised a policy of submission, not of resignation, certainly, but a negative policy; now she is beginning a positive policy. Tomorrow it will be a policy of territorial demands with a formidable means of intimidation: her army . . . The instinctive reaction is to say that we will suppress not one man, not one gun.

He continued gloomily that if France reacted in that way, 'our country risks finding herself deprived of the support, so precarious in any case, that she can hope for.' Marshal Pétain asked a reasonable question: what guarantees would Britain and the USA give in return? Herriot produced an evasive reply. General Weygand complained of the prospect of the destruction of the French army and its defensive strength. Herriot replied, 'The defence of a country resides not only in its soldiers and guns, it resides in the excellence of its juridical position.' The French, unable to rely on their own force, could only anticipate with gloom the erosion of the artificial securities of Versailles and try to arrange that someone somehow would help her to meet the consequences when they came. Such was Herriot's argument.[329]

In November the French plan was revealed. It would have meant, if anyone had taken it seriously, a real approach to a world government exercised by a League equipped with the military means of enforcing its wishes. It implied equality for Germany, but the German government continued to insist that this equality be formally accepted before Germany would take part in the Disarmament Conference. M. Herriot disliked giving up in advance his major bargaining counter, but since he was committed to demonstrating that France was not obstructive, he was compelled to agree to a document which promised equality of rights for Germany. Security was promised, too, but this was a much more vague notion – indeed, many, especially in Britain and the USA, were prepared to argue that the granting of equality to Germany would itself bring security. In return Germany promised to resume its place at the Disarmament Conference. In December the conference adjourned until 31 January 1933. Its chairman, Henderson, declared that the period of waiting would then be over and the period of definite decisions would begin. By the time the conference re-assembled, Hitler had become German Chancellor.

As the international scene became threatening in Europe, dangers of change and conflict appeared in the Far East, with the appearance of an aggressive and militaristic Japan ready to use force to impose its wishes in China. The slump in the United States had an immediate effect on Japan. The population of Japan was increasing with great rapidity –

by nearly one million a year at the end of the 1920s. In order to maintain an increasing (but still very low) standard of living for the rising population a continued industrial growth was essential. This was threatened by the world slump. By 1929, forty-three per cent of total Japanese exports went to the United States. The most important export to the USA, raw silk, fell by nearly one-half between 1929 and 1931. The consequent fall in producers' incomes in Japan reduced demand for manufactures. In 1931 industrial production was nine per cent below the level of 1929 while Japanese exports fell by about forty per cent between 1929 and 1931. Meanwhile the government sought to hold prices down by deflationary policies involving curtailment of government expenditure including spending on armaments. Deflation was unpopular with producers and unpopular, too, with military men.

From 1931 onwards Japanese officers influenced or controlled or ignored the activities of civilian governments. These officers took the view, with more emphasis among junior officers than among many senior officers, that Japan's economic problems were capable of a political solution and that prosperity should be assured by force. In particular, threats offered to Japanese economic welfare by Chinese nationalists should be squashed. Such threats were immediately apparent in Manchuria. Originally the economic development of Manchuria had been undertaken by Russia and by 1904, when the Russo–Japanese war broke out, Russian railways had been constructed across Manchuria from west to east (the Chinese Eastern Railway) and northwards from Port Arthur towards Harbin (the South Manchurian Railway), and in 1898 Russia had secured a lease from China of the southern part of the Liaotung peninsula, including Port Arthur (the Kwantung leased territory). In 1905 Japan took over from Russia the rights Russia had acquired in Kwantung and over the South Manchurian Railway. The result was that Japan governed the leased territory and, through the South Manchurian Railway, administered the railway area, including several populous towns, and maintained an army in Kwantung and railway guards elsewhere. At the same time legal Chinese sovereignty remained. The result of the Japanese presence in Manchuria, which ensured relatively stable conditions compared with the bulk of the Chinese Empire, was that the economic development of the area proceeded rapidly. By 1930 Japanese investment there amounted to about 1,500 million yen (about 150 million pounds sterling or 600 million dollars or 3,000 million marks at 1930 exchange rates.) Japanese exports to Manchuria came to account for about twenty-three per cent of her exports to the whole of China and imports from Manchuria for about forty-six per cent. (Japanese trade with China was about one-fifth of her entire foreign trade.) Japan depended on Manchuria for soya beans and was seeking to secure there a supply of coal, iron, timber and oil.[330]

Chinese administration in Manchuria was exercised through military men who were always independent in practice of any central Chinese government that might exist at any time. Manchuria was ruled by Chang Tso-lin, the 'old marshal', from 1918 until 1928, when he was killed in a train explosion for which the Japanese were suspected to have been responsible. From 1928, his son, Chang Hsueh-liang, the 'young marshal', ruled Manchuria so far as effective Chinese rule existed. Both marshals showed signs of challenging Japanese predominance in southern Manchuria. The old marshal inaugurated attempts after 1924 to create independently owned and operated Chinese railway lines in south Manchuria to challenge the monopoly of the South Manchurian Railway. In 1928, the young marshal announced his allegiance to the Chinese central government. Thereafter organized propaganda against foreign interests was organized in Manchuria by the Kuomintang, the Chinese nationalist party. In April 1931 a conference was held in Mukden when the possibility of clearing the Japanese out of Manchuria was discussed and demands made for the recovery for the Chinese of the South Manchurian Railway. Japan objected to these developments and claimed that the Chinese government had promised, in 1905, not to construct any railways which might prejudice the interests of the South Manchurian. Negotiations were under way about railways in 1931 when officers of the Japanese army in Manchuria took matters into their own hands and set about imposing their policy on the Chinese (and on the Tokyo government) by force. This policy was to establish complete Japanese dominance over Manchuria, while avoiding too direct a challenge to Russian interests there. Operations began in December 1931 with the seizure of Mukden by Japanese troops after an explosion on the railway just to the north. The main Chinese forces withdrew from Manchuria at the end of 1931 and though the Japanese continued to meet sporadic resistance from scattered Chinese forces and from bandits their control of the three provinces of Manchuria was largely established in 1932. In that year the Japanese set up a new state, independent of China, which they named Manchukuo.[331]

These events strengthened widespread anti-Japanese feeling already existing in China. Already anti-Chinese riots in Korea (governed by Japan) following disturbances between Chinese and Korean farmers in Manchuria, had set off a boycott of Japanese goods in Shanghai, the major Chinese trading centre, and in other places inside China and outside China in areas where Chinese merchants were important. Japanese military operations in Manchuria caused the boycott to be intensified. Japanese exports to central China fell in the second half of 1931 by over sixty per cent compared with the second half of 1930.[332] A major Japanese trading outlet was thus threatened and the policy of the forcible seizure of secure export markets led to an attack by Japanese forces at Shanghai in the first months of 1932. Here Japanese forces had a foothold in the international settlement, part of which they occupied, while part was occupied by British, United States and Italian forces, with French forces in a separate French concession. At the end of January fighting broke out, and, with major reinforcements, the Japanese attempted to drive the Chinese away from the city boundary and to impose an end of anti-Japanese activity. Their operations met with stiff resistance and at the end of March fighting ceased. Japanese strength was reduced to normal in Shanghai and the status quo restored. Japanese officers had clearly miscalculated Chinese capacity for resistance and the attempt to establish a monopoly of the Chinese market by force was postponed. Early in 1933, the Japanese invaded the Mongolian province of Jehol and added it to their client state of Manchukuo. A truce followed between China and Japan and an uneasy peace descended on the Far East. In Manchuria, Japanese operations had been highly successful – and Japanese economic activity there was made secure; elsewhere in China Japan was less successful, and though the boycott movement died down in the latter half of 1933, Japan had not secured for herself either guarantees against renewed boycotts or a monopolistic control of trade with China. Operations to this end were begun in 1937. Meanwhile the Japanese made attempts, with fair success, to increase their share of competitive markets on the basis of low export prices, following a fall in the value of the yen, by 1933, to about one-third of its previous value.

It is quite clear that Japanese actions since September 1931 involved the use of force to settle issues and disputes in favour of Japan. This was not the sort of thing that was supposed to happen in the era of the League of Nations. There could be no doubt that Japan was breaking the covenant of the League of Nations, the nine-power pact of 1922, which laid down that the independence and integrity of China should be respected, and the Kellogg pact of 1928. However reasonable some parts of the Japanese case might be, it was absolutely certain that Japan had not exhausted the available means of peaceful settlement before resorting to force. What would be done about it? It was an issue that could not be avoided; the Chinese government, though not wholly successful in running China, was remarkably effective in arranging for the anti-Japanese case to be stated at Geneva and elsewhere. The answer emerged equally clearly: nothing was done to stop the Japanese use of force except varied and repeated verbal expressions of disapproval. The end of Japanese action at Shanghai was the result of Chinese resistance not of international intervention; in Manchuria Japan proceeded unchecked.

British policy was decisive. Britain had major interests in China and her power and influence in the Far East was clearly greater than that of any other member of the League of Nations (except Japan). Furthermore, Britain felt able to control and direct the activities of the League (there was no Afro-Asian group of the sort that has emerged in the United Nations). Sir John Simon, the British foreign secretary, told Stimson in February 1932, 'Everybody is prepared to follow our lead there [Geneva, i.e. the League]'.[333] In this crisis British policy seems to have been determined by the Foreign Office and the Foreign Secretary – much less interest was shown by the Prime Minister, Ramsay MacDonald, in these Far Eastern issues than was usually shown by him in European issues. The British foreign office regarded Japanese advance with fear and dislike.

If we stand aside and leave Japan to work her will unchecked upon China, British commercial interests may suffer severely from Japanese arrogance and Chinese xenophobia. A Far East where Japan was dominant and arrogant would not be a favourable sphere for the development of British trade and industry,

wrote Sir John Pratt in January 1932. Verbal protests and denunciations would do more harm than good: the chief official in the foreign office, Vansittart, telegraphed to Simon in February 1932,

I suggest that we should refrain from joining the United States government in a 'very strong indictment' of Japan at this juncture. Japan is not going to be deflected from her purposes in China by notes, however strongly worded, and in her present temper, as shown by our reports from Tokyo, a note of the kind advocated by Mr Stimson might well sting her into going further than she otherwise would.

Economic sanctions were agreed to be quite useless without the association of the United States.[334] The British ambassador in Washington, Sir R. Lindsey, declared in November 1931 on sanctions against Japan, 'I am sure they would be entirely abhorrent to United States government,' and confirmed this opinion after a talk with Stimson in which the latter was 'completely non-committal' on the subject. When Lindsey asked Stimson if he contemplated anything further than a note in reply to Japanese action in Shanghai, he replied that 'whatever his feelings might be, restraint was necessary'. In any case 'the application or perhaps even the serious threat of sanctions by the League or by America or by both combined would be immediately countered by an attack unheralded by any formal declaration of war', as Sir John Pratt put it. Although another foreign office official substituted 'might well' for 'would' the conclusion was accepted – that economic sanctions could only be undertaken if Britain were prepared to risk war with Japan.[335]

The British chiefs of staff viewed the notion of war with Japan with deep gloom. They announced that Singapore, Hong Kong and Trinco-mali (the British Naval base in Ceylon), 'could not, in their present condition, be expected to hold out in the event of hostilities suddenly occurring with Japan', that Japan might succeed in capturing or destroying bases and fuel supplies on which the British fleet would depend and that this 'would expose to depredation, for an inestimable period, British possessions and dependencies, trade and communications, including those of India, Australia and New Zealand'. Sir Robert Vansittart drew these gloomy conclusions:

If Japan continues unchecked . . our position and vast interests in the Far East will never recover . . . We are incapable of checking Japan in any way . . . therefore we must eventually be done for in the Far East unless the United States are eventually to use force . . . By ourselves we must eventually swallow any and every humiliation in the Far East.[336]

Thus it was recognized that Britain's position in Asia depended on the power of the United States. Until that power was brought to bear it seemed to most members of the foreign office that Japan should be treated with tact and caution. The Japanese militarists must not be provoked. Sir Victor Wellesley, deputy under secretary in the foreign office, put it thus in February 1932:

It is not impossible that, especially if exasperated by foreign pressure, we might see something like a fascist movement in Japan, or a government forced by popular excitement and militarist die-hards to embark upon a policy of adventure far exceeding anything which we have witnessed as yet . . . The success of our Far Eastern policy and the prosperity of our economic interests are largely dependent on Japanese good-will.

There were two serious embarrassments for the British government in seeking to maintain Japanese good-will: the League of Nations and Mr Stimson, the United States Secretary of State. Neither could be ignored. In Britain there was a substantial public opinion vaguely in favour of the League; this meant that Britain was expected to help to make the League work and in particular co-operate with it in doing something about Japan. Simon was fully aware of this feeling. In December 1931 he noted 'good relations with Japan . . . must be safeguarded: but we must, consistently with this, play our part as a member of the League'.[337] It was not easy to make the objects consistent. The difficulty was increased by Mr Stimson's desire to subject Japan to moral pressure; his public proclamations made it difficult in Britain to use the excuse of American reticence to tone down the League's pronouncements.

At first Stimson took much the same line as the British. He recognized that the civilian government of Japan was not able to control the army in Manchuria and sought to help it to reassert its influence by avoiding any direct challenge. With the change of government in Japan at the beginning of December and the further Japanese military advance at the end of 1931 in Manchuria, his attitude changed. In that month he considered carefully the possibility of applying economic sanctions against Japan. Stimson vacillated, but it became clear that President Hoover would not permit any such measures, however strong Stimson's own hostility to Japan became. Stimson fell back on the idea of asserting international order by refusing recognition to any ill-gotten gains. The British ambassador in Washington reported, in February 1932, that Stimson had said to him, 'that no such shock as events at Shanghai had been administered to the cause of international morality since August 1914'. He went on to state 'an important new principle' that would withhold 'from any aggressor, any legal title to whatever he might gain by his aggression'. This 'Stimson doctrine' he preached with vigour, and tried hard to persuade the British to join with him. He could not be kept quiet; he made it clear that he would promulgate his 'doctrine' whatever the British did. British governments were consistently anxious to maintain friendship with the United States. In particular, as we have seen, they depended, in the last resort, on America for rescue from the Japanese threat, and, at this time, were eager for American co-operation over reparations and war debts. Moves had to be made to support Stimson, with a reluctance engendered by the belief that indictments of Japan would only make matters worse. To do this the British used the League, which at last enabled them to make out to Japan that Britain was not a leader in hostility, while making out to Stimson that they were anxious to go along with him.[338]

Thus some clarity can be brought into the apparently cloudy picture of western reactions to Japanese activities. The Japanese challenge emerged after the League council resolution of October 1931 calling upon Japan to withdraw within a month from the territory it had occupied in Manchuria had been ignored by Japan. In December the council evaded the whole difficulty by setting up a commission of enquiry. In January 1932 Stimson made public a declaration that the United States would not recognize any situation brought about contrary to the Pact of Paris for the renunciation of war (the Kellogg pact). He urged other powers and especially Britain to join with him. Simon refused and merely sought assurances (which were given) that Japan would respect the Open Door in Manchuria. In February, Stimson tried to persuade Simon to join with him in an 'indictment of Japan' and in setting out the principle of non-recognition. Simon refused and presented as a substitute the League council's resolution of 16 February which made an appeal to Japan to respect the territorial integrity of China and pointed out that infringements of the territorial integrity of a member of the League could not be recognized by other members. Simon at once instructed the British ambassador in Tokyo, Lindley, to make it clear that this was an *appeal* not a threat and that Britain was not specially involved. Meanwhile Lindley had assured the Japanese that, 'there was no intention of applying economic sanctions'. (This was contrary to Stimson's attempts to bluff Japan into believing that sanctions might be applied.)[339] Stimson felt that Simon had let him down and produced his 'indictment' in the form of a published letter to Senator Borah. In it he accused the Japanese of breach of treaties and set out again the doctrine of non-recognition. On 11 March, on Simon's suggestion, no doubt to avoid resolutions which might put Britain into the position of defying a League call for sanctions, the assembly of the League declared that no member could recognize any changes brought about by means contrary to treaty. At last, Stimson's demand for a general moral statement was satisfied. The League then settled down to await the report of its commision of enquiry. The Lytton report was published in October. This made it clear that the Japanese régime in Manchuria and the means of its establishment could not be reconciled with the treaties which bound Japan, including the covenant of the League. In February 1933, the League assembly resolved that the report should be applied and Chinese sovereignty in Manchuria restored. In March Japan withdrew from the League and that was that. Until 1945 Japan remained in control of Manchuria.

Many criticisms have been made of the failure to stop Japan, and Sir John Simon has been particularly attacked. The assertion that

Simon rejected an offer from the USA of co-operation in firm action against Japan can be dismissed. The only difference between Stimson and himself was over the promptness and vigour of expressions of moral disapproval – there was no hope of anything more from America. It has been argued that a more vigorous condemnation of Japan by Britain, which would have encouraged other countries to follow suit, might have halted Japan. Thus Lord Cecil wrote in December 1931, 'I am not at all convinced that all the bluff we heard from Tokyo about the indifference of Japanese public opinion was really genuine. Sooner or later she would have had to give way if public opinion had been strong enough.' But, in fact, the moral condemnations came in the end and they made not the slightest difference. It is true that the League seemed shifty and evasive but it is not clear that an honest admission of weakness, such as Lord Cecil eventually called for, would have helped matters.[340]

Germany and Italy played little part in Far Eastern matters. Russia was concerned to avoid any clash with Japan and was ready to grant to Japan the use of the Chinese Eastern Railway to facilitate her operations, while Japan avoided any direct challenge to Russian interests in Manchuria. France was thought by the Japanese to be the most sympathetic of the great powers, but, as M. Massigli pointed out in July 1932, 'France must handle carefully other powers also. At the moment, when the question of war debts is posed, our relations with America are of supreme importance to us.' He explained, too, that France could not act contrary to the League. 'Under these reserves . . . the French government will continue to have the greatest care to maintain friendly relations with Japan and will lose no opportunity to show its friendship towards her.'[341]

It has been argued that the failure to check Japan made the Second World War inevitable, by encouraging Hitler to believe that aggression might be safe. However, the failure to resist Japan did not, in itself, make it clear that Britain, France and the United States could not or would not resist aggression in Europe, nor did it make it impossible to use the machinery of the League of Nations for such resistance. There is no convincing evidence that Hitler was encouraged by the outcome of the Far Eastern crisis of 1931-3. It is, of course, true that the Japanese threat could reduce the force Britain and the United States might bring to bear in Europe but it was Anglo-American resistance to Japan rather than surrender that would most effectively produce that weakening. What is quite certain is that the Far Eastern crisis put an end to hopes of a securely peaceful and orderly world.

13

The Coming of War

On 30 January 1933, Hitler became German Chancellor. What were Hitler's aims? By 1942 he had subjugated most of Europe. Did he intend to do this from the start? Or did he come to this through a series of reactions to outside events and circumstances? Did he seek only to follow policies similar to those of Seeckt and Stresemann, to destroy Versailles, to win back the German preponderance in Europe that had been lost in 1918, and then find himself driven forward into vaster projects?[342]

The major piece of evidence remains Hitler's own book, *Mein Kampf*. From its turgid pages there emerges the vague outline of a foreign policy: to conquer territory in eastern Europe, to be settled by Germans, 'the highest species of humanity on this earth'. Germany must be a world power, and to be a world power, a state requires a large territory. The German frontiers of 1914 were wholly inadequate; they did not even include all the members of the German nation. Land must be conquered and settled by Germans:

> The territory on which one day our German peasants will be able to bring forth and nourish their sturdy sons will justify the blood of the sons of the peasants that has to be shed today, and the statesmen who will have decreed their sacrifice may be persecuted by their contemporaries, but posterity will absolve them for all guilt for having demanded this offering from their people.

Colonial acquisitions overseas were useless, for the settlers must remain part of a political and geographical unit.

> We finally put a stop to the colonial and trade policy of pre-war times and pass over to the territorial policy of the future. But when we speak of new territory in Europe today we must principally think of Russia and the border states subject to her.

Mein Kampf was not disavowed or hidden after Hitler had come to power. Far from it; by the end of the war about ten million copies had been produced in Germany.

Immediately after Hitler had come to power, these ideas found new expression. On 3 February 1933, Hitler addressed senior officers of the *Reichswehr*. According to the notes of General Liebmann (confirmed by other evidence) he spoke as follows:

Rebuilding of the armed forces is the most important prerequisite for attaining the goal; reconquest of political power ... How is political power to be used after it has been won? Not yet possible to tell. Perhaps conquest of new export possibilities, perhaps – and indeed preferably – conquest of living space in the east and ruthless Germanization of the latter. It is certain that the present economic conditions can be changed only through political power and struggle. All that can be done now – land settlement – stopgaps ... The most dangerous period is that of the rebuilding of the armed forces. Then we shall see whether France has *statesmen*; if so, she will not leave us time but will fall upon us (presumably with eastern satellites).

At another occasion the year after, on 28 February 1934, the same theme recurred when Hitler spoke to a conference of senior SA, SS, and army officers (about thirty senior officers seem to have been present). According to General von Weichs, he said that unemployment might recur in about eight years' time. The only remedy was to create living space for the surplus population. (Hitler's grasp of economics seems always to have been very limited.) But the western powers might seek to prevent this so that short decisive blows to the west and then to the east could be necessary. The new army would have to be ready for defence after five years and for attack after eight years. In 1935, the same ideas reappeared. In the summer Hitler wrote a long memorandum, a thing, as he himself said, that he did only 'on very fundamental questions'. It dealt with the German economy. He wrote that it was pointless to continue saying that Germany lacked food and raw materials, something must be done about it.

It is essential to take those measures that for the future will bring a permanent solution ... The final solution lies in an expansion of living space, of the bases for raw materials and for the feeding of our people. It is the task of the political leadership to solve these questions in the future.

The memorandum concludes, 'The German army must be fit for operations in four years' time; the German economy must be ready for war in four years' time'.[343]

All this is certainly very vague. There is no evidence to show that Hitler had a plan, in the sense of any precise time-table of conquest, or even any clear notion as to how conquest could be brought about. It would require the threat, and probably the use, of armed force. The process would start sometime around 1940. Beyond that, circumstances would dictate the pattern of events. It is possible to agree with Mr A. J. P. Taylor's conclusions: 'Eastern expansion was the primary purpose of his policy if not the only one,' and 'Hitler intended to use his force or would at any rate threaten to use it'. The evidence does not confirm other statements made by Mr Taylor. 'In principle and doctrine, Hitler was no more wicked and unscrupulous than many other contemporary statesmen. In wicked acts he outdid them all . . . If western morality seemed superior, this was largely because it was the morality of the status quo.' But Hitler's 'wicked acts' (including his treatment of the Jews and his actions in Poland and Russia) *did* spring from his 'principle and doctrine'. The status quo *was* superior to the conditions that Hitler would predictably bring about if he could, and defence of the status quo, even of Stalin's Russia, *was* a morally superior cause. Mr Taylor has drawn, too, some conclusions about Hitler's intentions, or lack of them, from this history of German rearmament. 'The state of German rearmament in 1939 gives the decisive proof that Hitler was not contemplating general war, and probably not intending war at all.' 'Though he often talked of such a war [a great war against Russia], he did not plan it. German armaments were not designed for such a war.' It is, of course, true that Hitler did not expect, still less intend, the actual pattern of war that he got, especially after 1941. But it is important to point out that the evidence of German rearmament clearly suggests that Hitler was deliberately preparing to fight some kinds of wars or, at least, to be able to risk some. In the years 1933–8 Germany spent about three times as much for military purposes as either Britain or France; possibly nearly half as much again as the Soviet Union; more than Britain, France and the USA combined. (The United States, assuming that they would never be involved in conflict outside the Americas, maintained, except for the navy, defence forces of a minimal kind.) By 1938, Germany was using a higher proportion of her total resources for military purposes than any other major country (except Japan).[344]

These remarks have dealt with Hitler's aims. They were what mattered, since at least after the summer of 1934, Hitler controlled Germany. It is not to be understood, though, that these were personal notions of Hitler's or that Hitler burst on a startled Germany, equipped with new and revolutionary aims, of a kind that were so novel that no one could take them seriously until they began to be put into effect.

The notion that Germany should be a 'world power' and that this status must be secured by territorial expansion was, of course, thoroughly familiar. Innumerable schemes and plans from the years of the First World War (which Germany seemed likely, for most of its course, to win), including those of the imperial governments, embodied this theme. Some even contrived, in contrast to Hitler's greater moderation, to think in terms of aggrandizement in the west, in the east, and in Africa simultaneously. More specifically, plans for colonization in the east were rehearsed in these years. Among the papers of General von Seeckt is to be found a paper written in his own hand, in 1915, which sets out the following proposals: – 'All land forces should be directed against Russia after a separate peace with France and Belgium. Great areas should be conquered and the population expelled. Lands should be distributed to a million or more ex-soldiers, the amount of individual allotments to vary with rank. The war would probably cost Germany a million men. Against this what would it matter to expel twenty million men including a lot of riff-raff, Jews, Poles, Masurians, Lithuanians, Letts, Esthonians etc?' From 1915, comes, too, a memorandum to the Imperial chancellor, Bethmann Hollweg, from Friedrich von Schwerin (the Regierungspräsident of Frankfurt/Oder):

The German people, the greatest colonising people on earth, must again be called to a great colonising work; there must be given to it widened frontiers, in which it can lead a full life. The overseas regions suitable for settlement by Germans are shared out and are also not obtainable as the price of victory in this war so the attempt must be made to win new land for colonization linked to the present German region.

After the victory over Russia, notions of the permanent use of the economic resources of the Ukraine for the benefit of the German economy found ample expression and were given fleeting opportunities by the terms of the treaty of Brest-Litovsk. The idea of colonising the Crimea found some favour, especially from General Ludendorff.[345]

These arguments contained at least an implicit racial theory: that Germans were entitled to more advantages and privileges than the peoples of the east. In *Mein Kampf* Hitler explicitly stated racialist theories. Here again there was nothing new. The notion that there were divergent racial characteristics, that 'pure' races were capable of higher achievements than mixed races, that the 'Aryan' or 'Nordic' race was of special merit, that Germans were the best example of the 'Aryan' or 'Nordic' race in its pure form, but that this purity was threatened by lesser breeds, especially the rootless Jew, was a notion which had a considerable intellectual history, to which Hitler added nothing. Both

261

in Austria and in Germany, such ideas were widely disseminated before Hitler was heard of. In the form of a more or less energetic anti-Semitism and in the form of a diffuse belief in the superior virtue of a semi-mystical Germanic *Kultur*, such ideas were widely accepted. Hitler's originality lay in the vigour and success with which he put these ideas into practice: he could never have done so if the basic ideas had not been familiar before he set out to apply them.[346]

The first stage was to militarize Germany, materially and psychologically. This task, of course, was not executed by Hitler alone. Indeed, the preaching of the need for strength for the coming struggle, the heightening of Germanic self-consciousness, was much more the work of his national socialist associates and subordinates, since the international situation of the 1930's required Hitler himself to strike pacific attitudes to prevent interference with German rearmament. Thus Dr Goebbels told a mass-meeting in Berlin in June 1933 that his audience should be patient for eight years. During that time he promised that Germany would be converted into a 'furnace of patriotic national feeling such as the world had never experienced' and then the 'foreign political activity' of the Hitler régime would begin.[347] In this way, curiously, Hitler sometimes became thought of abroad as a 'moderate', a restraining influence on the 'wild men' of his party; this was a diplomatic card of high value. Still, it was clear enough to foreign observers that Hitler's rise to power in Germany involved something new, at least a more strident assertion of familiar claims, at most a clear prospect of a German bid for the mastery of Europe. The international history of Europe, from 1933 to 1945, is the history of the reactions of the other powers to this phenomenon.

There were many possible reactions; firstly, to set off a preventive war – to invade Germany, seize territorial pledges for German good behaviour and hope that the consequence would be a German rejection of Hitler, secondly, for threatened countries to join together in a defensive alliance to contain Germany by force, thirdly to conciliate Hitler in order to persuade him not to make Germany a European nuisance. Alternatively other countries might do nothing, and hope to be left alone, or might join with Germany in the hope of deriving profit for themselves from change in Europe.

In 1933 there was, in fact, talk of a preventive war. There were rumours that Marshal Pilsudski had invited France to join Poland in such a war and had received a refusal. It is impossible to be certain how much truth lay behind these reports. There is no satisfactory evidence that Poland made any such offer to France. It seems more likely that

Pilsudski knew well that France would not accept any such proposal and that the rumours were part of a scheme to frighten Hitler into accepting a bargain with Poland. It may be, though, that Pilsudski allowed unofficial soundings to be made in Paris in order to persuade his Polish associates that his policy was correct. In any case there was no need to ask Paris – a negative answer was shown to be certain by the conduct of French diplomacy in 1933. The most decisive evidence against the existence of any clear invitation from Poland lies in the unanimous denial of its existence by the responsible soldiers and politicians in France at the time (Weygand, Gamelin, Daladier, Paul-Boncour) and by the French ambassador in Poland.[348]

The nature of the major diplomatic activity of Britain and France in 1933 and early 1934 had a surprising and implausible object: an agreement on disarmament. The impulse for disarmament came from Britain. There, the view was generally held (even by many conservative supporters) that the mere existence of armies and weapons was a cause of war. The smaller armies became, the fewer their weapons, the less likely another war would be. It was politically unavoidable for the British government to seek some agreement to prevent a 'renewed arms race' and the revival of German nationalism seemed only to make this task more urgent. The foreign office favoured an agreement for other reasons. The essence of a disarmament agreement would be some limitation on German rearmament. If Hitler obeyed it, all would be well; if he broke it, at least it would be clear where the guilt for a renewed arms race lay. Sir Eric Phipps, the British ambassador to Germany, put the first point thus:

We cannot regard him [Hitler] solely as the author of *Mein Kampf*, for in such a case we should logically be bound to adopt the policy of a 'preventive' war . . . Nor can we afford to ignore him. Would it not, therefore, be advisable soon to bind that damnably dynamic man? To bind him, that is, by an agreement bearing his signature freely and proudly given? By some odd kink in his mental make-up he might even feel impelled to honour it . . . His signature moreover, would bind all Germany like no other German's in all her past. Years might then pass and even Hitler might grow old and reason might come to this side and fear leave that.

Sir Robert Vansittart, the chief permanent official in the foreign office, made the second point while urging the French not to take the lead in rejecting the latest British proposals:

It is important that the Germans should be allowed to reveal themselves unmistakeably in their true light so that our own public, which is in a state of confusion and bewilderment, should have a clear sight of where the true issues lie. It is the Germans who are the danger of the future and not the French. It would be a disaster if the wrong party should be seen by the public eye in the rôle of the obstructionist and disturber of the peace.[349]

For the French, 'disarmament' negotiations had certain obvious disadvantages. It was clear enough, both before and after Hitler's coming to power, that the Versailles level of armaments could no longer be imposed on Germany except by force, which France could not use without British and Italian support, which was not available. Germany was going to rearm and a disarmament agreement could mean, in fact, only the legalisation of German rearmament. This might make no difference in itself. The difficulty was that France was expected to pay a price in order to make an agreement possible. German demands were based on 'equality'; this would mean the disarmament of the so-called heavily armed powers which, in practice, meant France, or at least, the denial of any added strength to France, as well as the rearmament of Germany, the latter within paper limits which Germany would disregard when the time came. British anxiety to secure an agreement with a German signature meant that France was pressed to offer promises of future disarmament or even to disarm at once. This seemed unsuitable. Again, French participation in disarmament talks might create a fear of French weakness and readiness to yield to the exigencies of Germany among France's European allies, especially Poland, and they might therefore seek other ways to safety than co-operation with France. On the other hand, to refuse to discuss disarmament meant a danger of alienating Britain, while France might secure a firm committment from Britain to the European status quo in return for joining in disarmament schemes, (in fact, the British firmly refused any addition to the Locarno pledge of 1925). Thus negotiations dragged on even after Germany withdrew from the disarmament conference (and from the League of Nations) in October 1933. Indeed, the British became even more insistent on the need for French concessions. The whole process came to an end with the action of the French government under Doumergue when it firmly rejected the current British ideas, in April 1934, after the German announcement a month before of greatly increased spending on armaments. The World Disarmament Conference finally faded from the scene in June 1934.[350]

Hitler handled the situation with great skill and insight. He desired a 'disarmament' agreement (it would help to make Germany seem pacific). It must, of course, permit to the armed forces what Germany would be able to produce in the next few years; it must be a convention that would not need to be broken until Germany was strong enough to face the possible consequences of undisguised defiance. If, however, negotiations seemed likely to produce an agreement among the other powers that might be unacceptable to Germany, and thus produce the outlines of an anti-German coalition, then general negotiation must be torpedoed by a German withdrawal. Then it would be a matter of other powers disagreeing among each other about what to offer to persuade Germany to resume discussions. Germany could sit back and watch these conflicts with pleasure. There was no danger, Hitler asserted, of threatening steps against Germany (even so, the German war minister took the precaution of ordering preparations for resistance to attempts to occupy German territory). After the withdrawal of the Germans from the disarmament conference, Hitler encouraged Anglo-French discussions on how to bring him back by vague encouragements to the British ambassador in Berlin and to Anthony Eden, who, while visiting Berlin, was successfully persuaded of Hitler's 'sincerity' in seeking a disarmament agreement.[351]

To Mussolini, differences among Britain, France and Germany were welcome. He could not bring himself to be a conservative statesman; he was, in fact, a cautious adventurer. He was interested in 'greatness' for himself and Italy, concerned that he and Italy should be important, should be consulted, courted and, if possible, feared. His means to greatness were not fixed; he had none of Hitler's attachment to principles. He seems to have thought of establishing a preponderant influence in south-eastern Europe through association with Austria and with Hungary, of a Mediterranean hegemony, of expansion of the Italian empire in Africa. Unfortunately Italy had not the basic strength required for the status of greatness. In 1929, Italy's share of world manufacturing production was 3·3 per cent, against 6·6 per cent for France, 9·4 per cent for Britain and 11·1 per cent for Germany. In the same year, Italian steel production was about the same as Czechoslovakia's, less than the production of the Saar region, about half that of Belgium, less than one-quarter of France's or Britain's, about one-eighth of Germany's.[352] Mussolini could take no risks and never deliberately did so – his involvement in the Second World War was simply a disastrous mistake. Grandeur without strength, prestige without great war: these were the objects of Mussolini's activities. Obviously such aims were best sought when Europe was divided, when the other powers were quarrelling and ready to appeal to Italy for support. Thus the revival of German nationalism, the complete abandonment of the conciliatory manner of Stresemann, increased Mussolini's importance without requiring any effort. Understandably, Mussolini welcomed the German demand for 'equality of rights' in armaments and was delighted by the efforts of Britain and France to win his support for their respective views on this demand. In 1933, Mussolini sought to institutionalise and publicise this situation. In March, Ramsay MacDonald and Sir John Simon, the British prime minister and foreign secretary, went to Rome to secure Mussolini's support for their plan for disarmament. They were immediately presented with the draft of a Four Power Pact.

The Four Power Pact, as Mussolini set it out, was to establish effective collaboration between France, Germany, Britain and Italy, who would act together to induce other countries to adopt a 'policy of peace'. 'Disarmament' was to be worked out by the Four. The pact 'reaffirmed . . . the principle of the revision of the treaties of peace in circumstances capable of producing a conflict between nations'. This meant the setting up of a European directorate of the four powers which would preside over the solution of international disputes and arrange changes in the status quo by agreement. The great advanatage for Mussolini would be the acceptance of Italy as a great power and the opportunities such a mechanism would provide for profitable mediation between Germany and the others; Italy would be brought into everything. It is possible, too, that Mussolini was genuinely anxious to make a great European war less likely. In a great war Italy would either remain neutral, which would be humiliating to Mussolini, or find herself the subordinate ally of one of the two sides; threats of general war, not its reality, were what Mussolini liked. Mussolini may well, too, have been anxious to divert Hitler's attention away from Austria towards the Polish-German frontier by offering to Germany prospects of its smooth revision in the future. For the British, acceptance of the pact provided a chance of securing Italian help to moderate Hitler's demands over disarmament and of encouraging Italy to try to work to maintain Austrian independence; for Germany it offered exactly the reverse – a means of ensuring Italian support for the revival of German power.[353]

Thus the Four Power Pact, and the need to secure Italian favour, was pressed by Britain on France. For the French there were problems. The pact frightened France's allies, Poland and the Little Entente, beyond measure. Here was their protector considering acquiescence in a document which spoke of revision of the treaties on which their territorial possessions rested. The Little Entente (Czechoslovakia, Yugoslavia and Rumania) issued a public protest; the Poles were furious. The French government compromised by accepting the pact while watering it down with changes which made it clear that territorial revision would require League of Nations sanction and by assuring her allies that France would not permit this sanction to be given without their consent. The pact was signed in July 1933; it was never ratified. Poland was not mollified or reassured.[354]

The principal effect of the Four Power Pact was to create a rift between France and her eastern allies, especially Poland. Probably some time in 1933, Marshal Sosnkowski said,

We demand from France nothing else but that she be a true France as we conceive her, and that she defend her interests energetically and without compromises against Germany and against the others. Unfortunately what is happening in France cannot inspire us – above all, this constant fluctuation and a lack of determination.

With her ally wavering, Poland sought safety by other means than reliance on France. At an early stage there were signs that Poland was not wholly displeased by the advent of Hitler in Germany. Hitler could hardly be more anti-Polish than Papen or Schleicher and he promised to be a great deal more anti-Russian. Moltke, the German minister in Warsaw, reported early in March that the Poles were counting on a deterioration in Soviet-German relations. All the same, Hitler's government in its early months was faced with acts of Polish aggressiveness and rumours of worse to come. On 6 March, the Polish garrison on the Westerplatte in Danzig harbour was (illegally) more than doubled. There was, as we have seen, talk of Polish preparation for an attack on Germany, rumours which reached Berlin from many sources. In February, the Polish minister in Berlin actually spoke of Germany and Poland being on the eve of war. Significantly, however, Moltke reported from Warsaw that he did not believe that real preparation was being made for war. As early as 19 April, Moltke detected signs of an attempt by Colonel Beck, the Polish Foreign Minister, to improve relations with Germany. The turning point came on 2 May, when Hitler himself received the Polish minister in Berlin. Hitler spoke in a conciliatory way and disclaimed forceful designs on Polish territory. Thenceforward Poland and Germany moved through gestures of mutual conciliation towards an accommodation. In September, Beck told von Neurath, the German foreign minister, that 'the Polish government was tired of always letting itself be played off against Germany'. It looks as if the Polish demonstrations earlier in the year were designed to bully Hitler into an agreement with Poland. There was probably no need – Hitler was certainly ready to make treaties with individual neighbours of Germany in order to dislocate possible combinations against him. In January 1934, the negotiations culminated in a non-aggression pact, to last for at least ten years. The Poles firmly insisted on an explicit statement that existing international obligations were not affected by the pact; obviously, the Poles did not wish completely to discard the Franco-Polish alliance.[355]

It is impossible to be certain what Pilsudski and the Polish government thought they were doing. It may be, as the Poles subsequently claimed, that they were only making the best of the bad situation of French lack of resolve and that they were intending only to stave off threats from Germany until France should revive. There are signs, however, that the Poles took the pact seriously and imagined that they had made Poland secure. In September 1933, Beck wrote, 'Hitler is rather an Austrian, in any case not a Prussian' – that is, Hitler might not share the anti-Polish feelings characteristic of the Prussian upper class. In November, Pilsudski declared, 'I would like to see him [Hitler] stay in power as long as possible'.[356] It is easy enough to see what Hitler hoped to gain in the short-run – a weakening of the French system of alliances and a striking display of himself as the man of peace who should be left alone to pursue his harmless intentions. What Hitler's thoughts were for the long-term is more difficult to assess. Very probably he contemplated only the immediate benefits, possibly he thought of Poland as a future subordinate ally against Russia – certainly the German approaches in 1938–9 towards Poland hint at the latter. The treaty, whatever its formal purport, obviously brought the Franco-Polish alliance into question. In France, thoughts of other alliances, or of a new structure of security, were stimulated or, sometimes, thoughts of the need for increased attempts at Franco-German collaboration.

Hitler's emergence led to an even more important change in eastern Europe: the Soviet-German partnership of the years after 1922 was dissolved. The details of the dissolution are obscure: Russian policy is still almost impossible to document, while most German evidence is from the diplomatists and the German foreign office, who were certainly not thinking the same thoughts about Russia as Hitler. Indeed, there is still, in spite of Hitler's loquacity, little completely reliable evidence to show how Hitler's thinking evolved. He was not intimate with the foreign minister or his officials, not did he often descend to the day-to-day conduct of diplomacy. Still, it is fairly clear that the responsibility for the collapse of Soviet-German friendship was Hitler's. The Soviet government repeatedly showed anxiety to keep going the old relation of co-operation with Germany. It was the best guarantee against a threat from Europe to the Soviet Union, the threat that dominated Soviet policy.

The strictly defensive nature of Soviet policy was shown clearly in

1933, at a time when the threat from Japanese advance in the Far East to Soviet interests and possessions there had already become clear. The Russians showed extreme concern to avoid trouble in Europe; thus the Franco-Russian friendship that soon developed was a consequence of the German menace. As Molotov, one of Stalin's closest associates, put it, 'If German policy towards the Soviet Union remained unchanged, the latter would not change her policy towards Germany'. The pattern of events in the breakdown of Russo-German understanding was confused by the anxiety of the German foreign ministry and its representatives in Moscow to maintain it, on the assumption that German policy must necessarily be anti-Polish and therefore pro-Russian rather than the reverse. Thus the Berlin treaty of 1926, which had symbolized Stresemann's Russian policy, was renewed in May 1933, and it seems to have been only at the end of his period as German ambassador in Moscow, September 1933 to June 1934, that Nadolny at last grasped that higher authority in Berlin was no longer interested in efforts to improve relations with Russia – in May 1934 he even spoke of a future restoration of military co-operation. Underlying the diplomatic exchanges, however, lay, on the German side the belief expressed by Hitler in September 1933, 'In the relations with Russia the liabilities have always exceeded the profits'. The Russians showed a desire for some sort of proof that the new Germany was not hostile to the Soviet Union as a basis for a continued entente. Repeatedly the Russians pointed to *Mein Kampf*, and to the writings and utterances of Rosenberg, the Nazi propagandist, as evidence that Nazi Germany intended to attack Russia, and complained of Nazi manifestations praising war against Russia. As late as March 1934 Litvinov, the Soviet foreign minister, proposed a joint German-Russian declaration guaranteeing the independence of the Baltic states (Lithuania, Esthonia, Latvia and Finland). This proposal was intended as a test of the German attitude to Russia; in spite of Nadolny's pleading Berlin rejected it. By that time, the Soviet-German alliance was dead: military co-operation had come to an end by September 1933.[357]

The Soviet-German break was inevitable. Hitler, after all, was posing as the saviour of society from the Bolshevik peril. Thus he was obliged to be more anti-Bolshevik than previous German governments. Again, since Hitler intended to ignore the Versailles clauses on armaments, Russian co-operation lost its value. Russian policy was a reaction to Hitler's conduct and to the threat presented by Japan. Radek's remarks on 1 January 1934, those of the 'trusted agent of the central committee in foreign policy', seem sincere:

If, however, the Soviet Union were engaged in a hard struggle with Japan, there was a strong probability that Germany would use the opportunity to pounce on Poland and when she had conquered Poland would soothe Polish national pride by offering Poland compensation for the corridor in the Ukraine.

(The same effect could follow, of course, from a Polish-German alliance.) 'The Soviet Union had to take precautionary measures against that.' Hence the Russian attempt to secure a French counter-weight. It was a second best; obviously a friendly Germany was the most secure guarantee of Soviet safety. The end of military co-operation was attended by elaborate expressions of regret from the Russians – especially from Red Army officers, among whom was Voroshilov, whose relations with Stalin were close. 'Voroshilov and other key military persons . . intimated that they hoped that policy could permit the re-establishment of closer military relations again shortly.'[358] Even during the high period of Russo-French association, occasional friendly utterances towards Germany were made by the Soviet authorities.[359] The Russians were trying to maintain a free hand, so far as they could. If conditions changed, if Stalin felt confident of his control of the Soviet Union, if Germany were ready for a bargain, then the Soviet government might turn away from the west and rely on its own strength.

French links with Russia had come into existence before Hitler came to power. The revival of German nationalism in the early 1930s, particularly Papen's emergence in 1932, alarmed both countries. In France, Herriot watched German demands for arms with dismay, while the Russian government was frightened by what it had heard of an offer made by Papen of a Franco-German understanding, which it assumed to be directed against the Soviet Union. Thus a draft Franco-Russian pact of non-aggression, which had been initialed in 1931, was revived in the autumn of 1932 and signed at the end of November. Things moved forward in 1933. French and Soviet military attachés were exchanged, Herriot and the French air minister visited Russia and were received with emphatic warmth, and in the second half of 1933, Litvinov began to suggest a Russo-French alliance. This did not get very far at once. French policy in 1933 was still without a definite course; improved relations with Italy, solidarity with Britain, even, tentatively, attempts at direct Franco-German understanding, all these were being pursued. A Franco-Russian alliance would run counter to them all. Indeed, Daladier, French prime minister at the crucial time, seems, though he was certainly anxious to strengthen France, not to have accepted any inevitability in a Franco-German war, even with

Hitler in control.[360] The question began to be considered seriously when the Daladier government fell in October; the foreign minister, Paul-Boncour, re-opened the alliance issue soon after. Two conditions had to be met; that any pact should be limited to Europe and that it should come within the League of Nations, which Russia must join – without the latter condition any alliance would be incompatible with all France's existing security treaties. The negotiations were kept secret and not much is known even now about the details. In any case, they merged, after the February crisis in France, with discussions of wider schemes promoted by Louis Barthou, foreign minister in the Doumergue government.

The Doumergue cabinet inaugurated a more lucid and consistent French foreign policy. It assumed that Hitler was dangerous and rejected the idea that he could be persuaded not to be, and sought to make France safe against the future strength of Germany. The means was to be a grand alliance of threatened states who should combine to defend any member of the partnership who should be attacked. This was a defensive choice: preventive war was impossible to carry out, for French public opinion would never tolerate a government which set off a war of its own volition. Even if it could be launched, a preventive war would be futile. Germany would still have to be held down, however great the victory; and the 1920s had shown the difficulties. To contain Germany was the only possible course: by creating a defensive combination, to make the risks of aggression too great for Germany reasonably to accept. It was easier to see the need for such a combination than to get it.

The new course in French foreign policy was signalized by the rejection, on 17 April 1934, of disarmament discussions until the conditions of French security had been won. A clear rejection was imposed on Barthou by the French cabinet – he would have preferred to handle Britain more tactfully. It cleared the way, however, for Barthou's attempts to make France safe. There were two aspects: the first, to revive France's existing alliances, shaken by the Four Power Pact and the Polish-German non-aggression treaty; the second, to create a larger structure of mutual defence. In March, Barthou visited Belgium, in April, Poland and Czechoslovakia, in June, Rumania and Yugoslavia. He was now seventy-two, a veteran of French politics, learned, witty, honest and direct, the embodiment of the Third Republic at its best. His visits certainly brought comfort to his hosts but they were not entirely reassuring for himself. In Belgium, he found an anxiety to keep out of coming conflict; in Warsaw, a determination that Poland should stick to its independence of French tutelage; in Rumania, an undercurrent of hostility from the Fascist-minded right below flamboyant assertions of

271

pro-French feeling; in Yugoslavia, warm demonstrations of friendship which did not completely conceal an increasing economic dependence on Germany. Only in Czechoslovakia, did Barthou find complete and unconditional support. Still, these visits did display a genuine, if partial, revival of the French alliance system, and the Little Entente joined to approve Barthou's wider proposals.

These schemes were apparently evolved in discussions between Barthou and the Soviet foreign minister, Litvinov, in April and May. They worked out plans for a series of pacts of mutual guarantee; for eastern Europe, for the Mediterranean and even for the Pacific. (The third, which was no doubt Litvinov's suggestion, was never taken seriously.) The main plan was for a pact including Russia, Germany, Poland, Czechoslovakia, Lithuania, Latvia, Esthonia, and Finland; the Mediterranean security pact was to include Russia, Rumania, Bulgaria, Turkey, Greece, Yugoslavia, Italy, France and possibly Britain. Under the eastern European pact, each country would pledge itself to come to the assistance of any of the others attacked by one of the signatories. France would pledge herself to come to the help of Russia if she were attacked, and Russia to the help of France under the Locarno conditions of 1925. The whole was elaborately designed to harmonize with Locarno and with the covenant of the League. The Mediterranean pact Barthou thought of as a second step which he hoped would make for understanding between France and Italy and Italy and Yugoslavia.[361]

This Franco-Russian scheme naturally met with hostility in Berlin, and Neurath, the German foreign minister, soon began to repeat the conventional hostility to any 'bloc of powers'. The Germans were spared embarrassment by the hostile attitude of Poland towards the proposals. In an unpromising effort to arrange for the Poles to be pressed into sympathy, Barthou came to London to get British backing. There followed conversations of curious artificiality. Sir John Simon insisted that there should be no anti-German element in the proposed pacts and that they should somehow be linked with disarmament. He even demanded that Russia should guarantee Germany against French attack and that France should guarantee Germany against Russian attack. It is not clear how far Simon took all this seriously. Though his manner made him unpopular – he was a lawyer who never lost the habit of seeming to speak to a brief, and offended foreigners by treating them as hostile witnessess to be subjected to cross-examination – he was a man of high intelligence. Probably he was simply reflecting the predominant British notion that alliances and arms generated wars. Barthou accepted the British demands and a formula was worked out to demonstrate the complete reciprocity of his proposed pacts and to explain that they might make disarmament talks possible again. It is certain that Barthou regarded this formula as a virtuous façade to screen his real intentions – indeed, it is possible that the entire scheme for the eastern Locarno was simply a device for persuading the British to accept a French search for stronger and wider alliances. Barthou succeeded in his immediate aim and the British foreign office immediately gave strong support to his proposals in Rome, Berlin and Warsaw.[362]

At this stage violence broke out; Nazis attempted to seize power in Austria. Hitler's tactics in his early years in power required him to give an impression of peaceful inactivity outside Germany so that he could be left alone to rearm. Austria was an exception. There was no doubt about his ultimate aim for Austria – inclusion in the German *Reich*. To him this was a 'life's work to be carried through with every means'. He did not feel that Austria could be left alone until German strength was restored because there was a danger that too many Austrian Germans might come to feel themselves to be Austrians as distinct from Germans. 'There is a great danger that Germany might thereby definitively lose six million people, who are in the process of becoming something like the Swiss.' Hitler concluded that the Austrian Nazis must be enabled to secure a dominant position in Austria – then there would be no need for an immediate *Anschluss* at all, instead a process of *Gleichschaltung* would turn Austria into a Nazi state parallel to Germany, in which 'National' ideas would dominate i.e., German National ideas. This needed the weakening of the existing government in Austria under Dollfuss, who was certainly an upholder of Austrian independence – in May 1933, Hitler supposed that a collapse of Dollfuss' government would lead to elections, which would result in the *Gleichschaltung*. In order to overthrow Dollfuss, the Germans attempted to attack the Austrian tourist trade, by requiring a large fee for visas for Austria, and launched organized Nazi propaganda in Austria. Hitler was right to suppose that Dollfuss' political position was difficult but wrong in imagining that he could readily be tossed out of the way.[363]

Engelbert Dollfuss was a Christian-Social politician of peasant background. He was conservative enough to view the Nazis with deep dislike (in Austria the Nazis still showed the more radical face of opposition). He was a devout Catholic, a fact which probably provided the main basis for his belief in the 'Austrian idea'. On the right wing of Austrian politics his position was uncertain; the Nazis, of course, would support him only if he gave them effective power, his own party regarded him with suspicion, the powerful Austrian armed fascist group, the *Heimwehr*,

273

had its own ambitious leaders, Prince Starhemberg and still more, Major Fey. The natural support for a policy of independence of Germany would come from the Social Democrats, whose advocacy of the *Anschluss* had come to an end with the rise of the Nazis in Germany ; they, too, had armed forces, which might counterbalance the *Heimwehr*. Dollfuss' political course was settled for him, however, by the attitude of Mussolini. Italian objections to the *Anschluss* Dollfuss saw as the best guarantee of Austrian independence – and so they were, until, as Hitler anticipated, Italian consent to the union could be 'paid for with concessions in other areas'. Mussolini took the view (a view characteristic of his pseudo-statesmanship) that the Austrian Nazis derived their strength from their anti-Marxism and that Dollfuss, in order to weaken the Nazis, must be more anti-Marxist still. This meant that Dollfuss had to co-operate with the *Heimwehr*, with its rival leaders, Fey and Stahremberg, against the Socialists. It meant the suppression of parliament and of democracy and the destruction by armed force of the Socialist basis of power in Vienna. Dollfuss founded a new single party, the Fatherland Front, to rally Austrian sentiment.

In spite of terrorism and energetic propaganda from Munich and from inside Austria, the Nazis were held in check after the Nazi party itself had been prohibited in Austria in June 1933. From the Nazi point of view all was not lost: Dollfuss, Fey and Starhemberg all seemed ready to try and seek Nazi support against the others. As negotiations came and went inconclusively, Hitler and the Austrian Nazis began to diverge – Hitler seems to have been ready to wait for something to turn up, the Austrian Nazis wanted action. Hitler's attempts to persuade Mussolini to accept the nazification of Austria – Hitler met Mussolini in Venice in June 1934 – failed. Now Habicht, one of the leaders of Austrian Nazism, worked out a *putsch* in association with other Nazis. The Austrian President and the entire Austrian cabinet were to be taken prisoner, the radio station and the Vienna telephone exchange seized and a Nazi government formed under Rintelen, then Austrian minister in Rome. It is not certain how far Hitler controlled the details of Nazi activities in Austria but it seems that he gave his approval to the planned *Putsch*, if only because he was misled by the conspirators about the degree of support that could be expected from the Austrian army. On 25 July 1934, the plan was carried out. The Chancellery in Vienna was occupied by Nazis and the radio station taken over. However, the rebels failed to secure the whole cabinet – the President was not in Vienna and Dollfuss, having wind of the plot from Fey, had ordered the cabinet to disperse. Only Dollfuss and Fey were taken by the rebels. The President ordered the remaining ministers to squash the *Putsch*, which they did, using the army and police. Dollfuss was killed in the Chancellery while Fey appears to have wavered, waiting to see who would come out on top. In Germany, an announcement that the Austrian people had risen against its 'oppressors, gaolers and torturers' was hastily suppressed. Hitler quickly disavowed the *Putsch* and even despatched condolences on Dollfuss' death.[364]

The most striking reaction came from Mussolini. On the day after the *Putsch* he issued a statement: 'At first announcement of assassination of Chancellor Dollfuss . . . movements of land and air armed forces were ordered towards Brenner and Carinthia frontier districts.' These were, in fact, Italian troops training near the Austrian frontier and some of them were evidently moved to the frontier itself. This military operation created a great stir, even though it was almost certainly, for the most part, only a display of words. (The British embassy in Rome was told the same evening, 'that for political motives the most had been made in the communiqué of slight variations in troop movements primarily due to training'.) Mussolini seemed to be putting himself at the head of resistance to Hitler.[365]

The Austrian *Putsch* assisted Barthou's plans for the extension of French alliances. Eastern Locarno, however, soon ground to a halt. Obviously a German rejection was to be expected; it came on 8 September 1934 in a memorandum containing a remarkable amount of pious humbug. The Germans used the stale device of objecting to a security pact that did not advance disarmament and admit Germany's right to equality, they argued for bilateral non-aggression treaties, or at least, a general non-aggression treaty: 'The best guarantee for peace will ever be not to prepare for a war against war, but to extend and strengthen the means apt to prevent any possibility of an outbreak of war.' The Germans were already assured that Poland would reject the pact anyway. This was more serious; co-operation between Poland, Czechoslovakia and Russia could create a real barrier to Germany in a way the separate French treaties with those three countries could not. Poland objected to committing herself to the defence of Czechoslovakia, against whom there remained the grievance of Teschen and, above all, Pilsudski and Beck objected to any prospect of Russian forces entering Polish territory for any purpose whatever – even to defend Poland against Germany. Russian assistance seemed to them as dangerous as Russian hostility – if Russian troops entered Poland would they ever leave again? The Poles seem to have felt that the German danger was dealt with by the combination of the Franco-Polish alliance and the

German-Polish non-aggression treaty. The Soviet Union they assumed to have no aggressive intentions. Thus Poland could stand on her own feet and play enjoyably at being a great power.[366]

Barthou was left with attempts to bring about a direct Franco-Soviet alliance. The first stage was carried out on 18 September 1934, when the Soviet Union became a member of the League of Nations. Litvinov made the significance of the move plain: 'The exponents of the idea of war, the open promulgators of the re-fashioning of the map of Europe and Asia by the sword, are not to be intimidated by paper obstacles. We are now confronted with the task of averting war by more effective means.' At the same time, Barthou pressed forward with the task of creating a link with Italy. The prospects seemed good. Mussolini's concern to keep Austria independent had already led to demonstrations of solidarity with Britain and France. For instance, in February 1934, the three governments declared that 'they take a common view as to the necessity of maintaining Austria's independence and integrity in accordance with the relevant treaties'. The July *putsch* in Vienna strengthened this bond. One difficulty for Barthou was Yugoslavia. That country objected strongly to the encouragement Mussolini offered to those Yugoslavs (mostly Croats) who opposed Serbian dominance in Yugoslavia. The Yugoslav government suspected Mussolini of plotting with Hungary to bring about the disintegration of Yugoslavia. Mussolini's demonstrations at the time of the July *Putsch* made matters worse. The Yugoslav government made it clear that it would send troops into Austria if Italy did, in order to prevent a junction between Italy and Hungary. It was probably to persuade Yugoslavia to attempt an understanding with Italy that Barthou invited King Alexander of Yugoslavia to visit France.[367]

The King landed at Marsailles on 9 October 1934. Soon afterwards he was shot and killed by agents of the Croat terrorists, the *Ustači*. Barthou was in the same car and was also killed. This was a turning point; Barthou had a clear policy which he pursued with tenacity and vigour – he was succeeded as French foreign minister by someone very different, Pierre Laval. Laval was of peasant origin, shrewd and cunning, able and ambitious, without pretensions for himself and without belief in the pretensions of others. He started life as a left-wing socialist and evolved to the right in the years between the wars, while maintaining contacts with the left – including those that came from the mayoralty of Aubervilliers. He knew how to charm and when to threaten. He was a quick and responsive negotiator; in many ways he resembled Lloyd George, and, like Lloyd George, suffered because of the mistrust he eventually inspired. Laval's appointment to the French foreign ministry was welcomed by the Germans. Hoesch, who had served in Paris, regarded 'his appointment as an improvement on the previous Barthou régime', while a German who had talked to Laval before Barthou's death found, 'He was not in agreement with Barthou's foreign policy and considered a direct German-French understanding necessary'.[368] There seems little doubt that this was correct, though Laval was too calculating a politician to express this view, without restraint, in public. Indeed, interpretation of French foreign policy in the years before 1939 is made difficult by the existence of an official, respectable, public policy which could not be directly challenged by politicians anxious for power – the honouring of France's alliances, support for collective security and for the League of Nations, readiness to defend international legality and resist open aggression. Even Laval was compelled to make verbal obeisances to this orthodoxy and sometimes to act in accordance with it; his own inclinations were revealed more privately.

The projected Franco-Russian alliance that Laval inherited from Barthou became in his hands a political trap, a means of deceiving one section of the French right, which still believed in resistance to Germany. It was useful, too, on the left. As the German ambassador in Paris reported to Berlin, Laval's senatorial seat for the Seine department could only be secure if the Communists were restrained – by Moscow – from determined opposition. Again, after the Franco-Russian alliance had been made, the French ambassador in Berlin, François-Poncet, explained, according to Neurath, that Laval had signed it, 'in order to take the wind out of the sails of the powerful parliamentary group in France which consists of Communists, Marxists, Freemasons and Jews'. Indeed, Laval seems to have tried to evade the Russian alliance altogether. To do this he revived the idea of an eastern pact. Barthou's proposals had failed against German and Polish objections; Laval sought to negotiate a pact of a kind which Germany might accept, with the provision for mutual assistance against aggression removed. François-Poncet made it clear in Berlin that Laval hoped to 'tone down' the Franco-Russian rapprochement within a general pact and even after the Franco-Russian alliance was signed, he still argued that an eastern pact would make it invalid. The Franco-Russian alliance came about only because Hitler offered new provocation which made it impossible for Laval to resist the advocates of the alliance. At the end of 1934, Hitler congratulated himself on the understanding reached with Laval over the plebiscite to be held in the Saar – which decided its return to Germany in 1935. Hitler explained the conciliatory conduct of Laval as the result of Germany's resurgence as a great power and went on to say, 'the French had definitely missed the opportunity for a preventive war'. Rearmament could safely proceed on a larger scale. On 10 March 1935, Göring announced the existence of the German air force and, on 16 March, Hitler ordered the introduction of compulsory military service – both steps, of course, were flagrant breaches of the Treaty of Versailles. Laval came under strong pressure from the French cabinet, and from public opinion, and negotiations between France and Russia were accelerated. On 2 May 1935, the Franco-Soviet alliance was concluded. It provided, subject to the provisions of the covenant of the League of Nations, for mutual assistance against aggression. A few days later the Czechoslovak government concluded a similar treaty with the Soviet Union, but this treaty was only to come into effect if the Franco-Czech alliance had first done so. Laval went to Moscow, and on 15 May Stalin allowed to to be announced that he approved of French armed strength – a statement which turned the French communist party into advocates of French resistance to Germany, and made possible the French Popular Front: a left-wing success which soon brought doubts from the French right of the soundness of co-operation with Russia.[369]

Laval's heart was not in it. He prevented discussions between the general staffs on the military implications of the pact. In July, he reminded the German ambassador in Paris that the alliance was for five years only and declared that if Germany promised not to attack Russia, France would 'hand her paper back to Russia'. In November, he told a German journalist that he shared Hitler's feelings towards Russia. He boasted that 'both the Soviet Union and the French disciples of Franco-Soviet collaboration trusted him no further than they could see him', and he hinted that he expected Germany to attack Russia in the future – 'after all, you do mean to play the bolsheviks a trick or two one of these days'. He told the German ambassador in December, 'that French public opinion was increasingly coming to realize that the French army should only be used in defence of French soil, and in no circumstances beyond France's own frontiers'.[370] In fact, Laval took the view that Germany could be permitted to grow strong, to expand in the east, and that France could come to terms even with a powerful Germany. For Laval, at the best the Franco-Soviet alliance would provide a bargaining counter in negotiations for Franco-German understanding; at the worst, it would drag France into a war against Germany which he intended to avoid.

A better and safer bargaining counter would be an alliance with

Italy. Laval believed that this might make it easier to deal with Germany; it would lead to a revival of the Four Power Pact as a framework for Franco-German collaboration. Of course, even Laval wished to restrain Germany as far as could be done without risking a Franco-German war. He recognized that Franco-Italian friendship need not be a barrier to understanding with Germany in the way that a real Franco-Soviet accord certainly would be. Thus Laval pursued the second aspect of Barthou's policy – to win an Italian alliance – with vigour and enthusiasm. In January 1935, Laval went to Rome and received a very warm welcome from Mussolini. Agreements were quickly reached to settle Franco-Italian differences. Mussolini renounced all prospect of securing control of Tunisia from the French, a few unimportant African territories were to be ceded to Italy and some shares in the French railway from Djibouti to Addis Ababa, the capital of Ethiopia, were handed over. All this amounted to very little indeed in exchange for Mussolini's abandonment of Italian claims for compensations in accordance with the Treaty of London of 1915 and demands in Tunisia. The explanation will be set out below. In Europe, it was agreed that Italy and France should consult together on action to be taken in case of any threat to Austrian independence. Moreover, Mussolini at once inaugurated military conversations with the French general staff. The outcome was that France would dispatch one or two divisions to reinforce the Italian armies if they were faced with a German threat to Austria and that Italy would dispatch several squadrons of aircraft if the Rhineland were threatened with a German attempt at remilitarization and two divisions to Belfort in case of common action in defence of Austria. In July 1935, the chief of the French general staff, Gamelin, went to visit his Italian colleague, Badoglio, a visit returned in September.[371]

This Franco-Italian understanding was extended in April 1935, by the inclusion of the British at the conference which met, at Stresa, after the German announcement of the introduction of conscription and the creation of an air force. This meeting was arranged to counterbalance the curious action of the British government in allowing the foreign secretary to visit Berlin after the German declaration. At Stresa, the three powers declared that the maintenance of independence of Austria 'would continue to inspire their common policy', complained of 'the method of unilateral repudiation' adopted by Germany over armaments, while Italy and Britain reaffirmed that they would carry out their obligations under Locarno. A final declaration said that 'the three powers . . . find themselves in complete agreement in opposing, by all practicable means, any unilateral repudiation of treaties which may endanger the peace of Europe'. In a way, this courtship of Italy was a waste of time. Italy would never enter a war that she might lose, and was not likely to be strong enough to change a losing coalition against Germany into a victorious one. Mussolini would not miss a chance of joining a victorious Germany, whatever treaties and pacts he signed. Still, there is no doubt that most people in France and Britain thought it worthwhile to make treaties with Mussolini just as Hitler did later on.

Together with the Franco-Russian pact, the 'Stresa Front' seemed to have completed the isolation of Germany and to provide for effective resistance to Hitler. Now a network of anti-German treaties was spread over Europe: France, Russia and Czechoslovakia; France, Italy and Britain; in addition, the older alliances between France and Poland and between Czechoslovakia, Rumania and Yugoslavia. Essentially this structure, if it were ever to work, implied an alliance between France, Britain, Italy and Russia. Some reservations on the strength of the link between Russia and France have already been made. Mussolini was soon to strain the links with Italy. Britain had not abruptly been transformed into a sturdy and reliable advocate of collective security and of the curbing of German ambitions by force or the threat of force.

In 1935, British policy towards Germany was hesitant and variable. The government began to explain at home that German rearmament presented a threat, which must be met by increased British armaments, while it continued to call for a disarmament agreement with Germany. In February 1935, British and French ministers joined in suggesting a general settlement including an eastern pact, a general European pact, an armaments pact and an air pact. All this kept the diplomatists fully employed for the rest of the year without anything coming from their activities. Hitler was happy enough to join in a search for pacts which he might sign. The air pact had a special appeal – this was to be made by the Locarno powers alone and was to require signatories to use their air forces to assist any signatory attacked by air by any of the others. This had the desirable implication, from Germany's point of view, that eastern Europe was something of less importance to Britain, France and Italy than western. Laval, however, could not easily accept a public treaty with this implication and insisted that it should only be made together with the smoke screen of some sort of eastern pact, which, as we have seen would help him to emasculate the Franco-Russian alliance. Germany, however, had begun to realize that the Franco-Russian alliance provided a useful grievance and that it would be best not to give it up by joining with the Soviet Union in a general non-aggression pact. Discussions on an air pact revolved round these points for the rest of 1935. As late as 6 March 1936, Eden told the German ambassador in London that Britain wanted to get air pact negotiations moving. The most striking part of the discussions of 1935 was the visit of the British foreign secretary, accompanied by Eden, then a minister outside the cabinet, to Berlin to talk to Hitler. The visit followed a curious enquiry by the British government as to whether the Germans would welcome it, after the German announcement of conscription, and in spite of the British protests which followed – protests which this enquiry deprived of all plausibility. The visit made it clear that land disarmament was now hopeless, at least Hitler insisted firmly on a peacetime army strength of thirty-six divisions or over half a million men. Hitler, however, indicated that he might accept a limitation on German naval strength to thirty-five per cent of the British navy.[372]

Here was a piece of 'disarmament' the British were interested in. Soon after the British ministers returned from Stresa, an invitation was given to the Germans to begin naval talks. The Germans planned to stick firmly to thirty-five per cent, which was as much as they intended to build in any case. Negotiations began on 4 June 1935, with von Ribbentrop, the Nazi expert on foreign affairs, leading the German delegation. Ribbentrop assured the British that the negotiations, which in practice took the form of acceptance of German demands, were of 'world-historical significance', a phrase to which he and Hitler were much attached. On 18 June, an agreement was signed: the strength of the German navy was to be thirty-five per cent of the navies of the whole British commonwealth, while for submarines, the Germans were to be entitled to have a hundred per cent, though it was explained that only forty-five per cent would be built in the near future. This was a remarkable proceeding. The British action caused great resentment in France and Italy; objections from these countries to the British claim to dispense on their own with (admittedly moribund) parts of the Treaty of Versailles were disregarded. The Germans gave nothing whatever. In Berlin it was noted that any larger figures than those in the agreement could hardly be reached in the next decade.

As a result of the agreement, the most powerful of our former enemies and of the signatories of the Versailles treaty has formally invalidated an important part of this treaty and formally recognized Germany's equality of right. The danger of Germany's being isolated, which definitely threatened in March and April of this year, has been eliminated. A political understanding with

281

Great Britain has been initiated by the naval settlement. The Front recently formed against us by the Stresa powers has been considerably weakened.[373]

The Stresa Front was soon to be much more seriously weakened. On 5 December 1934, fighting broke out at Walwal. Here, Ethiopian and Italian forces disputed possession of an oasis claimed both by Ethiopia and by Italian Somaliland. The incident was not important in itself. What mattered was that it seems to have decided Mussolini to carry out a colonizing venture in Ethiopia which he had been meditating for some time. The real reason for this move lies in the nature of fascist rule. Mussolini claimed to be a great dictator. He claimed to be the creator and exponent of a revived Italian 'virility'. A new national vigour was the return the Italian masses were offered in exchange for the loss of liberty. In the 1920s the expression of national greatness could be verbal. With the appearance of a rival dictator, another man of force and action, something more solid was required. The Roman Empire must be reborn. The snag about this was that most of the former Roman Empire was in the hands of powers who were dangerously strong; a substitute empire must be found. Ethopia (with the exception of Liberia which, in effect, enjoyed the protection of the USA) was the only part of Africa that had not fallen under European control. It was an area where Italian colonial ambitions had suffered a serious set-back in the 1890s, when such ambitions were more fashionable than they had subsequently become. It would surely be unreasonable for the powers who still controlled the bulk of Africa to object to an Italian move in one isolated section outside their spheres of interest.

Prudently, Mussolini took steps to assure himself that the powers which might have objections, Britain and France, would let him carry out his design. Both were anxious that Italy should provide a counter-weight to Germany in Europe – would they pay the price of ignoring conquest in Africa? It appeared that they would. First, French assent was secured. The proceedings that took place during Laval's visit to Rome remain, in part, obscure and may always do so. Laval later denied that he had given Mussolini *carte blanche* and insisted that he had only conceded to Mussolini the right to secure economic concessions in Ethopia and to exploit them peacefully. This may possibly be what Laval had meant to convey to Mussolini in January 1935. Even if this is correct, he certainly gave Mussolini the impression that he was conceding much more. Mussolini assured Guariglia, an Italian diplomatist, that he was sure of the support of Laval in his east African adventure. When he met Eden in Rome in June 1935, part of the conversation was as follows, by Eden's account written at the time:

Signor Mussolini then went on to explain at some length that when M. Laval had been in Rome, it had in his view been clearly understood that Italy was to have a free hand in Abyssinia. I interjected 'economically'. Signor Mussolini replied that this might be so as far as written document was concerned, but since he had yielded to France the future of 100,000 Italians in Tunis and received half a dozen palm trees in one place and a strip of desert which did not even contain a sheep in another, it must be clear that he had understood that France had disinterested herself in Abyssinia ... I contested this, telling Signor Mussolini that M. Laval had ... emphasised to me that he had insisted that France had only given a free hand to Italy in economic matters ... At this Signor Mussolini flung himself back in his chair with a gesture of incredulous astonishment.

In December 1935, Laval wrote privately to Mussolini, claiming again that he had agreed only to peaceful economic penetration by Italy. In reply, Mussolini insisted that in conversation, if not in writing, there had been repeated references to the 'free hand' granted to him. In January, Laval wrote again to Mussolini claiming that, at least, he had never agreed to the Italian war on Ethiopia; Mussolini pointed out that he himself had not decided on war at the time of the conversations with Laval and asserted again that France had disinterested herself in Ethiopia.[374]

With Britain, the situation was less clear. In February 1935, Vansittart warned Grandi, the Italian ambassador in London, that any Italian attempt at conquest would be opposed by British public opinion and that it would therefore threaten Italo-British co-operation. On the other hand, and this must have been important to Mussolini, the British prime minister and foreign secretary said nothing about Ethiopia when they met Mussolini at Stresa (though Italian military preparations were openly going forward) and agreed, without demur, to the final statement which spoke of agreement to oppose 'any unilateral repudiation of treaties which may endanger the peace *of Europe*'.[375]

Thus Mussolini felt able to press forward military preparations for a campaign in East Africa. In February 1935, movements of fascist militia and army troops began from Italy to Eritrea and Somaliland. By October, when the war began, eight Italian divisions were available for the invasion; about 250,000 men, of whom 50,000 or so were local levies. This caused great embarrassment both to the British and French governments. Neither, if left to themselves, would have had the slightest objection to Mussolini doing anything he wished in Ethiopia – in June 1935, a British interdepartmental committee concluded that 'there are no vital British interests in Abyssinia or adjoining countries such as to necessitate British resistance to an Italian conquest of Abyssinia'. The difficulty was that if Mussolini engaged in aggression against Ethiopia,

e in breach of the covenant of the League of Nations. An
ion would be a much plainer defiance than Japanese action
had been – the situation in Manchuria had been confused
ce of legitimate Japanese rights within it. British public
opinion cared about the League. Ever since the war, it had been held
out as the great hope for a peaceful and orderly future. British ministers
had found it simpler to assert that they believed this too; it did no harm
to say it, even if it had led to some difficulty over Manchuria. A striking
display of British public opinion in 1935 resulted from a sort of
plebiscite, privately organized at the instigation of the League of
Nations Union – a British pressure group of League supporters. Over
eleven million people were persuaded to reply to six questions. Nearly
all of them wanted Britain to stay in the League, wanted international
disarmament, and the abolition of private armaments manufacture. All
but a few wanted to abolish military aircraft. Ten million against
600,000 came out in support of the application with other nations of
economic and non-military measures to stop one nation attacking
another; about 6,800,000 against 2,400,000 were prepared to join with
other nations to use force to do so. Here was an expression of public
opinion the government could not brush aside. Again, those in Britain
who were concerned about the threat from Germany must be interested
in strengthening the League; Vansittart explained to Grandi, in April
1935, that the League was the best means of persuading British public
opinion to accept commitments in Europe.[376] Unhappily, fear of
Germany could pull in a different direction; it made it important not to
offend Mussolini. Thus the British government could only seek
desperately to avoid conflict between Italy and the League, and, if it
came, try somehow to appear to back the League in public while
privately attempting to compromise with Mussolini. There were
differences of emphasis on the British side. Vansittart and the foreign
secretaries, first Simon and then Sir Samuel Hoare, tended to favour
the attempt to keep Mussolini's friendship. Eden, who was minister for
League of Nations affairs, was more anxious to make the League work,
and seems to have thought that Mussolini should be treated relatively
firmly to compel him to accept compromise.

In a rather different way, Mussolini's conduct embarrassed Laval in
France. His great triumph was the entente with Italy made at the
beginning of 1935. He intended to maintain it. As far as he was concerned, the covenant of the League might be useful as a bargaining
counter with Germany; if it stood in the way of friendship with
Mussolini, it should be ignored. The difficulty was to preserve the

British alliance. Laval was driven into a pretence of supporting Britain, and therefore the League, while keeping on good terms with Italy. He, too, had to worry about French opinion. Though it was less emphatic in support of the League than in Britain, the French left, including some of the Radicals, felt that the covenant should be upheld as a barrier against future German activities. Both France and Britain, wished, then, to patch things up while somehow working within League principles. They had one major advantage – between them, they could contrive to control the activities of the League. There was one great difficulty – Mussolini wished for a triumph; to have control over Ethiopia furtively smuggled to him was not enough. This set the pattern for negotiations – proposals from Britain and France for effective Italian dominance in Ethiopia turned down by Mussolini, because they did not fit in with his bombastic speeches. In May, the British ambassador in Rome, Sir Eric Drummond (later Earl of Perth), suggested the possibility of arranging for Italy something like the British position in Egypt (which was nominally independent). In June, Eden saw Mussolini in Rome, and suggested offering Ethiopia access to the sea by handing over British territory. This was meant to induce Haile Selassie, the Ethiopian emperor, to give Ogaden province to Italy. Mussolini turned this down insisting on more territory and a clear control of the whole of Ethiopia. On his way back through Paris, Eden heard Laval suggest an Italian protectorate over Ethiopia. In August, this suggestion was taken up in disguised form. Eden, Laval and Aloisi (for Italy) agreed on the idea that the League should arrange for 'assistance' to Ethiopia, by taking over the administration of the country, which would then be entrusted to advisers drawn from the three powers, among whom Italy would, no doubt, be allowed to take the lead. This plan would have given Italy every possible concrete aim in Ethiopia. But it would be a 'League solution' and it would leave the emperor in titular possession of his territories. By now, Mussolini had committed his prestige too far to accept this ingenious scheme. In September, a similar plan was evolved by a committee of the Council of the League and similarly turned down by Mussolini, perhaps partly because the reinforcement of the British Mediterranean fleet, which had just taken place, would make acceptance look like a surrender.[377]

At the beginning of October 1935, the Italian attack began. Since this display of martial vigour fulfilled one of Mussolini's objects, his terms began to moderate. In November, he suggested the cession of one province to Italy with an Italian mandate for the non-Amharic lands of Ethiopia, together with a collective mandate for the central part of

Ethiopia. These hints encouraged Laval and Hoare to work out, first through their experts, then in direct discussions, a similar scheme for buying Italy off. It was presented to Mussolini on 11 December. It suggested the cession of peripheral territories to Italy and the formation of a 'zone of economic expansion and settlement' reserved to Italy, in southern Ethiopia. It is possible that Mussolini might have been persuaded to negotiate on this basis. At this stage, there was profound gloom in Rome. It was thought probable that Ethiopia could not be conquered in the next few months (before the rainy season) and that war with Britain was possible (both views were quite wrong). Mussolini was spared the need to decide. In Britain Hoare and his plan were dropped. At first, the British cabinet approved the Hoare-Laval plan. But it got into the Paris press immediately after it was settled. The result was uproar in Britain. Here was the aggressor offered a reward for his evil deeds. The cabinet changed its mind and when Hoare refused to desert his own plan, he was compelled to resign.[378] This was the end of British attempts to settle the affair by private negotiation. British policy turned, with Eden replacing Hoare at the foreign office, to pretending to try to stop Mussolini.

This process had begun with an imprudent speech of Hoare's to the League of Nations in September. Of course, he had to announce British support for the League. In fact he sought to explain that this support was very limited. 'If risks for peace are to be run, they must be run by all. The security of the many cannot be ensured solely by the efforts of a few, however powerful they may be' – in other words, British action would be subject to a French veto. He did not emphasise the point sufficiently and wrapped it up in a string of what he regarded as harmless platitudes. The British government

will be second to none in its intention to fulfil, within the measure of its capacity, the obligations which the covenant lays upon it . . . The League stands, and my country stands with it, for the collective maintenance of the covenant in its entirety, and particularly for steady and collective resistance to all acts of unprovoked aggression.

To Hoare's surprise, this was treated as a resounding call for resistance to Italy. 'I myself was amazed at the universal acclamation . . . All this I had already said over and over again, and no one had become particularly excited.' Thereafter the British government had to live up to this speech. Privately, Hoare assured Mussolini that Britain would not consider either applying military sanctions, or closing the Suez Canal, and that economic sanctions would be decided on only with reluctance.[379]

On 7 October 1935, the Council of the League, however, declared Italy to have begun a war in defiance of the covenant. On 10 October a Committee of the League was set up to consider measures. This recommended a ban on the export of arms to Italy, the denial of all loans to Italy, prohibition on imports by member states from Italy, an embargo on exports to Italy of rubber and various metallic raw materials. These proposals were all put into effect by 18 November. There was a curious fact about these sanctions: the export of iron, steel and coal was not prohibited, and, above all, oil was left out. Of these, the decisive item would be oil. Without it, sanctions might inconvenience Italy, but would not prevent victory in Ethiopia, provided that the Italian armies could win quickly. The fact that the USA was not in the League would not have prevented an oil sanction having a decisive effect: the United States normally supplied only about six per cent of Italy's imports of oil and the administration was making serious attempts to restrict exports to the normal level – an attempt which relied on moral pressure, which could hardly succeed unless League of Nations powers themselves imposed an embargo.

A proposal to add oil was made on 2 November by the Canadian delegate to the League. On 6 November, the Committee of the League dealing with sanctions (Committee of Eighteen) adopted it in principle and began enquiries to governments. This proposal aroused the real fears of Mussolini. He told Laval that an embargo on oil would mean disaster to the Italian forces and would be equivalent to an act of war. According to Eden, Hoare believed that,

Mussolini would become more intransigent if we fixed a date for the oil sanction. Therefore, while approving the principle of an oil embargo, he was ready to delay its enforcement, hoping that the threat of it would influence Mussolini to serious negotiation.[380]

On 22 November, the chairman of the Committee of Eighteen summoned a meeting for the 29th with the oil sanction on the agenda. Laval promptly urged postponement, explaining that he was anxious to come himself and could not do so. He went on to suggest mid-December. The chairman found that the British agreed and the Committee was summoned for 12 December. On the 11th, the Hoare-Laval plan was sent out. Thus, on the 12th, consideration of the oil sanction was deferred until plans for a peaceful settlement had been explored. It was not until 22 January that the Committee of Eighteen met again. (A few days before, Aloisi, the Italian delegate to the League, received definite information that there was no danger of Britain and France accepting an oil sanction.) Then the classical delaying device was thrown in, of appointing an expert sub-committee to look into oil sanctions. This concluded its deliberations on 12 February. On 2 March, the Committee of Eighteen re-assembled. Flandin, now the French foreign minister, continuing Laval's policy, urged postponement during another attempt at mediation, and Eden (having telephoned to London) agreed. Attempts at mediation, spun out by the Italians, lasted until 17 April. This was enough, by then the Italian army had confounded the doubters and won the war – on 2 May the emperor fled and on 9th May, the King of Italy was proclaimed Emperor of Ethiopia.[381]

The sanctions that were applied were insufficient to stop Italy from winning a short war but they caused great economic stress. Indeed, if the war had not been brought to a surprisingly rapid end, it is probable that Mussolini would have been forced to accept a compromise – it is clear that Mussolini decided to annex the whole of Ethiopia only when the military victory was nearly complete. In January 1936, Italian exports fell off by nearly half and Italian imports by well over one-third as compared with January 1935. Figures for movements in British and French trade are as follows in thousands of gold dollars:[382]

	DECEMBER 1934	1935	JANUARY 1935	1936	FEBRUARY 1935	1936	MARCH 1935	1936	APRIL 1935	1936
Exports to Italy										
UK	2,796	313	2,935	158	2,742	226	2,645	267	2,060	82
France	2,330	1,038	1,331	735	1,968	603	1,702	386	1,473	422
Imports from Italy										
UK	1,903	930	2,004	79	1,842	82	2,142	9	2,083	23
France	1,942	501	1,395	159	1,660	83	1,343	158	1,431	150

Sanctions were continued for a time after the Italian conquest was complete. It took a few weeks for the League to grasp its total failure – only in July were sanctions formally ended.

Meanwhile Germany stood aside. Hitler seems to have been uncertain what to do. It was desirable to win Mussolini away from the Stresa Front, but, on the other hand the good relations with Britain embodied in the naval agreement were more important still. The simplest solution was to remain strictly neutral. As soon as the conflict began, the export of armaments to both contestants was forbidden. In November, it was announced that the government would prevent any increase in the export of raw materials or food which might threaten the German economy. In fact, German trade with Italy did not greatly increase during the months of League sanctions. The German attitude was highly successful. Without in any way upsetting British opinion, Germany was able to reap the benefit of Mussolini's resentment at the equivocal conduct of his Stresa partners. Evidently they were not prepared to pay the price for Italian co-operation against Germany. The year 1935 had seen the creation of a Franco-Italian alliance, concerned, above all, with the defence of Austrian independence. In 1936, the Rome-Berlin axis was born. On January 7 1936, the German ambassador in Rome reported that Mussolini had told him that it would now be possible to dispose of the only German-Italian dispute, Austria. 'The simplest method would be for Berlin and Vienna themselves to settle their relations on the basis of Austrian independence . . . If Austria, as a formally quite independent state, were thus in practice to become a German satellite, he would have no objection.' On 28 January Mussolini repeated his remarks. Meanwhile Mussolini assured the French that he intended to remain faithful to his Stresa policy. This seems to have been only a bribe to encourage the French to continue to sabotage sanctions.[383]

In February 1936, the French ambassadors in Berlin and Rome were perturbed to notice unusual activity on the part of the German ambassador in Rome, Hassell. They were unable to discover what it meant. In fact, Hassell was seeking Mussolini's permission for a German breach of the treaty of Locarno. On 14 February, Hassell conferred with Hitler in Munich. The *Führer* unfolded his thoughts. The French were, at last, about to ratify the Franco-Russian alliance. 'The question was whether Germany should take the Paris ratification . . . as grounds for denouncing Locarno and of once more stationing troops in the demilitarized zone.' (The provisions of Versailles, which had been given extra guarantees at Locarno, that Germany should have no troops or military material west of a line running fifty kilometres to the east of the Rhine, were still in force.) Hitler suggested that Hassell should persuade Mussolini to denounce Locarno first. Hassell then returned to Rome. On 18 February, he left again for Berlin. On 19 February, he saw Hitler twice. It was now made clear that Hitler had decided to move troops into the demilitarized zone. Hassell announced that he thought Italy would not co-operate with Britain and France in any action against German remilitarization of the Rhineland. Hitler told Hassell to sound Mussolini with great caution. On the 22nd, Hassell saw Mussolini in Rome. He led up to his point with skill and patience. Eventually, he put this hypothesis:

In the event of any German reaction whatever to ratification, she [Italy] would not co-operate with Britain in so far as the latter might declare that, as Locarno Powers, they were compelled to take action. This interpretation of mine Mussolini twice confirmed to be correct.

Mussolini was evidently not aware of what was coming. Hassell had to change the memorandum of his conversation with Mussolini which Suvich, the Italian undersecretary, had drawn up on the Duce's instructions, by securing the deletion of a phrase that German action would be confined within legitimate bounds. This was done without difficulty. Thus Mussolini gave a blank cheque.[384]

On 7 March, German troops moved into the demilitarized zone. The preliminaries provide a useful example of Hitler's processes of decision. The German foreign office had provided a pretext for ignoring Locarno – in 1935, German diplomatists spread the argument that the Franco-Russian pact was incompatible with Locarno; evidently they felt this might come in useful sometime. When Hitler was in Bavaria early in February 1936, he seems to have taken up the notion of using the excuse of the ratification (the Franco-Soviet pact came before the Chamber of Deputies on 12 February) as justification for remilitarising the Rhineland. On 12 February he made a rapid visit to Berlin and spoke to the army commander, Fritsch, about the Rhineland. Fritsch insisted that no risk of war should be run. Next day, General Blomberg, the war minister, was informed. The day after, Hitler explained his motives to Hassell, whom he told that he had so far discussed the question only with Neurath, Blomberg, Fritsch, Ribbentrop and Göring. At Hassell's next meeting with Hitler, he and the foreign minister, Neurath, advised delay. (Neurath feared that action might cause a hostile coalition to come into being, though he did not expect an immediate military reply.) Hitler argued that there was a danger of the demilitarized zone becoming an inviolable institution and that 'passivity was, in the long run, no policy. . . . Attack in this case, too, was the better strategy (lively assent from Ribbentrop.)' He would produce a smokescreen of offers of pacts to make it appear that he was not acting aggressively. On 28 and 29 February, senior officers conferred in Berlin. On 2 March, Blomberg issued the operation orders and on 5 March ordered their execution for the 7th. At this point Hitler enquired if the whole thing could still be called off, but did not do so. Here is a pattern of a general line of action, the execution and timing of which were dictated by external circumstances. Here, too, are to be found the last minute hesitations and fears that often seized Hitler's mind. Once the decision was irrevocable, however, it was pushed through. After a few days, Blomberg, frightened by possible French action, demanded a withdrawal of the small forces now stationed west of the Rhine. Hitler ignored him and thereafter claimed the success of the operation to be his own, imposed by him on his weaker subordinates.[385]

A challenge to Locarno and the demilitarized zone was expected, though not its timing. Repeated warnings had reached Paris of a coming remilitarization.[386] Though it was not expected to occur when it did, the French government had ample time to consider what it would do. The Ministry of Foreign Affairs consulted the service ministers. It emerged that the defence chiefs wished to preserve the demilitarized zone, but had no idea how to do it. General Maurin, minister of war, suggested taking precautions, in case remilitarization was followed by an immediate attack on France, but ruled out any individual action by French forces. On 19 February 1936, the Chiefs of Staff of the three services met. The Chief of Staff of the army set the tone. 'General Gamelin thinks there is no occasion to envisage that France alone could occupy the demilitarized zone.' He need not have worried. On 27 January, Flandin talked to Eden in London. He asked what the French should do if Germany took action in the Rhineland. Eden replied that this was, in the first instance, a matter for the French themselves. 'How much importance,' Eden says he asked, 'did they attach to the demilitarized zone? Did they wish to maintain it at all costs?' Or would they prefer to bargain? 'Flandin replied that these were just the subjects which he thought our governments should carefully consider and on which they should then consult.' 'This,' Eden goes on, 'was hardly the attitude or language of a man determined to fight for the Rhineland.'[387] On 27 February, the French Council of Ministers reached a conclusion, put thus by Flandin: 'The French government will not proceed to any isolated action. It will only act in agreement with the other signatories of Locarno ... While waiting for the views of the guarantor powers, the French government reserves the right to take all preparatory measures, including military measures, in view of the collective action which could be decided on by the Council of the League and by the guarantors of Locarno.'[388] This was clear enough; it meant that France would do nothing except hope that Britain would somehow negotiate the Germans out of the Rhineland. It was certain that nothing could be expected from Italy – with the Ethiopian war still going on, and with Italy still the object of sanctions, it was inconceivable that Mussolini would turn on Germany. As for Britain, there was ample evidence to show that no active steps could be expected.[389]

What is surprising is that the French government seems to have considered an immediate military counter-action to the German remilitarization when it happened. Even Flandin himself seems to have made some utterance in support of the use of force when the French cabinet met on 8 March. Presumably Flandin was aware that the minister of war would instantly object, causing these notions to fall to the ground at once. Certainly Flandin never presented to the British the question: what would they do if France acted alone? The French government would neither fight for the Rhineland nor give up the demilitarized zone. The result was the submission of the whole matter to the Locarno Powers and the League Council. In the various conferences which followed, the importance of Hitler's offer of new pacts became clear. The British were eager to renew the hunt for Hitler's signature. At the conference table, Flandin called for coercion of Germany to undo her unilateral repudiation of Locarno. In private, he was much readier to accept British policy. This was characteristic of the dualism between French public, official, policy – to maintain the demilitarized zone, as a means of making it easier to attack Germany to help any threatened ally of France – and the less openly avowed impulse to acquiesce in German designs. The outcome was certain, since France had accepted in advance a British veto on action. It was negotiation with Germany for some replacement of the security offered by the demilitarized zone. Since the suggestions put up by Britain and France were not backed by any threat of force, nothing whatever came of them. Discussions went on for the rest of 1936 without any weakening of Germany's hold on the Rhineland.[390]

The significance of French inaction was as a symptom of French lack of strength and lack of will to fulfill the rôle of policeman of Europe. Yet France's alliances with Poland, Czechoslovakia, Rumania, Yugoslavia, Russia and, indeed, with Italy (so far as that still counted) implied readiness to use force to defend the European status quo. The demilitarized zone mattered because it would make easier a French attack on Germany in carrying out these obligations. Its abandonment meant a further weakening of France's effectiveness as an ally. French passivity suggested that France did not take seriously her own official policy of honouring her eastern alliances. For many Frenchmen this was true; the whole structure was designed to prevent a new German war, not to bring one about. The eastern allies were there to help to frighten Germany into leaving France alone, or, if that failed, to weaken a German attack on France. The French army reflected this feeling much more clearly than French official policy. The latter, from the time of Millerand and Poincaré, had spoken as if France were the active guardian everywhere of the Versailles settlement, the active opponent of a German revival. Even at Locarno, Briand had repeated this. Barthou had vigorously reasserted it. Laval and Flandin were furtive, almost conspiratorial, in their questioning of this orthodoxy. The army ignored the orthodoxy altogether. It planned exclusively to defend France against a German invasion. 'Shall we be mad enough to advance in front of our fortified barrier to I don't know what adventure?' asked General Maurin in 1935. Gamelin showed no eagerness to resist a remilitarization of the Rhineland. When asked what the French army could do, he replied that there could be no entry into the Rhineland without general mobilization and that, even then, it could not be done without co-operation with Britain and Italy (that is, it could not be done at all). When pressed into suggesting possible operations for a seizure of some part of the zone, he repeated that nothing could be done without the League, or, at least, the Locarno Powers, and even then, all that could be done without general mobilization would be the occupation of the left bank of the Saar river, or, incredibly, the occupa-tion of Luxembourg. To justify these propositions, he produced figures for German strength in the Rhineland, swollen to 295,000 men by the inclusion of 235,000 for the SA, SS, NSKK (Nazi motorised volun-teers) and the Labour Service. Later, Gamelin expressed the hope that the foreign ministry should be 'well aware that the present organiza-tion of our army is such that without mobilization, we can occupy our defensive lines, stop an attack, but that all offensive action in enemy country is prevented.'[391] In 1939, Gamelin's inactivity provided the final proof that the French army thought only of meeting an attack, not of making one.

It was of critical importance that these hesitations lay below the surface. In public, France still insisted on her status as a great power and declined to abandon the rest of Europe to its fate. This meant that, when the excuse for resignation provided by British hesitation was removed, it became impossible for French governments not to live up to their own protestations.

The Rhineland crisis showed that French alliances were still in working order. On 7 March, the Czech Foreign Minister declared that Czechoslovakia would do exactly what France did. More surprisingly, Colonel Beck told the French ambassador in Warsaw, Nöel, that Poland would honour the Franco-Polish alliance. Nöel produced a plausible explanation. General Rydz Smigly, the Inspector General of the Polish army and one of the major personages in the Polish régime, had assumed that France would take military action against Germany and had imposed on Beck a declaration of support for France. Beck had assumed that France would do nothing. Thus Beck was able to argue that his policy of securing safety by friendship to Germany was justified. French failure to act caused dismay elsewhere. Yugoslavia and Rumania, already influenced by economic ties with Germany, were much alarmed, The French minister in Belgrade put their complaints in these words, 'You are leaving, in short, free play to the German tactic which seeks to cover itself in the west to secure a free hand in the east,' Even the Czechs, the most loyal of all the French allies, began to wonder if they should not make the best arrangements they could with Germany.[392]

Eden drew some 'conclusions' from the remilitarization.

> We must be prepared for him [Hitler] to repudiate any treaty even if freely negotiated (a) when it becomes inconvenient, and (b) when Germany is sufficiently strong and the circumstances are otherwise favourable for doing so. On the other hand, owing to Germany's growing material strength and power of mischief in Europe, it is in our interests to conclude as far reaching and enduring a settlement as possible whilst Herr Hitler is in the mood to do so.

The lack of logic in this statement resulted from its combining an expression of orthodox British policy, conciliation and concession, with doubts about the soundness of this policy. However, orthodoxy continued to dominate, indeed, grew in vigour as German strength grew. At the end of 1936, Eden used these words in a public speech: 'So far are we from wishing to encircle Germany that we seek for her co-operation with other nations in the economic and financial, as well as in the political sphere. We want neither blocs nor barriers in Europe.'[393]

In another way, Hitler derived benefit from Mussolini's resentments of 1936. Mussolini gave expression to his declining interest in the defence of Austria by ceasing to support Starhemberg and to pay for the fascist *Heimwehr*. The result was to make it possible for Dollfuss' successor, Schuschnigg, to seek to negotiate with Germany for a better understanding. It was not a matter of Schuschnigg's being compelled to take this course. He believed that, in the end, Austria's independence could only be secure with German acquiescence. Hence the so-called gentleman's agreement of July 1936. This permitted, in effect, more Nazi propaganda in Austria, while Schuschnigg promised to admit some members of the 'national opposition' to office and to permit the participation of the national opposition in political activity. This was a distinct step towards *Gleichschaltung*.[394]

All this soon retreated into the background when the Spanish civil war broke out. This was a conflict which aroused violent emotions. To many in Britain and France, and even in the United States, it seemed to be a clear cut fight between good and evil. To French and British left wing intellectuals, to most liberals, to some workers, it was a matter of a reactionary, fascist, clerical attack on a progressive democracy. To most Catholics, most of the French right and some British conservatives, it was the result of a virtuous crusade against godless, bolshevising terror. These themes were developed by two powerful propaganda machines: the Catholic Church (with some exceptions) and the Communist party (with none). What gave the incident international importance was foreign intervention. The hopes and fears of European governments must be considered.

Italian intervention on the side of Franco was the most substantial. There is no conclusive evidence to show that Mussolini planned or precipitated the revolt of 1936. Certainly, though, his decision to intervene was taken at once. There were some rational motives. If Spain could be turned into a satellite state, the French strategic position in the Mediterranean would be seriously weakened, especially if Italian bases could be set up on the Balearic Islands. The French communications with north Africa would be threatened, the British base at Gibraltar reduced in value. Mussolini told Ribbentrop, in November 1937, that the Italians

have established at Palma a naval and an air base . . . Franco must come to understand that, even after our eventual evacuation, Majorca must remain an Italian base in the event of war with France . . . Not one negro will be able to cross from Africa to France by the Mediterranean route.

In April 1936, Ciano told Göring, 'that there was a secret treaty with Franco, under which, in the event of a general conflict, Italy would be granted air bases not only in the Balearics but also in other parts of Spain.' Most of all, however, the Italians expected Franco to be a submissive satellite. In July 1939, Ciano noted complacently after a conversation with Franco,

Franco is completely dominated by the personality of Mussolini . . . He expects from the Duce – and he repeatedly said so in the conversations he had with me – instruction and directives. And he himself spoke to me of an even greater event, which I too, hold to be indispensable in order to complete the work carried out in Spain by our victorious legions – the Duce's journey to Madrid, whereby Spain would be definitely united to the destiny of the Roman Empire.

Franco was deluding Ciano and Mussolini.[395]

German intervention was decided on by Hitler personally, against the wishes of his foreign ministry. No one at that point imagined that the war would drag on for nearly three years. Probably Hitler calculated that the success of the rebels would weaken France, since they were much less likely to be friendly to France than the government they were seeking to overthrow. Other benefits revealed themselves and justified continued and expensive intervention in a long war. One was political, the other economic. Hassell, in Rome, put the political interest in these words:

> The rôle played by the Spanish conflict as regards Italy's relations with France and England could be similar to that of the Abyssinian conflict, bringing out clearly the actual opposing interests of the powers . . . All the more clearly will Italy recognize the advisability of confronting the western powers shoulder to shoulder with Germany.

Hitler, in November 1937, indeed, suggested that the Spanish war might lead to a war between Italy and France. To achieve these ends, Italy was to be encouraged to take the lead in helping Franco. In German economic policy, however, no priority was allowed to Italy. The Germans sought, with considerable success, somewhat limited by Franco's evasiveness, to secure control of Spanish mineral production – a vital factor in German armament manufacture. An extra benefit came for the German forces. The war provided excellent opportunities for tactical training with live ammunition; service personnel were rotated in order to spread the benefits of this experience.[396]

British policy was simply designed to prevent the war spreading to the major powers. It was clear enough that a victory for Franco would be harmful to Britain strategically but this threat was overridden by the main theme of British policy – to prevent a major war. In any case, British opinion on the war was sufficiently divided to have made British intervention difficult, even if the government had desired it. What is less certain is that British opinion would necessarily have prevented a more serious attempt to block the intervention of others, but to the government this involved dangers of war with Germany and Italy. The government sought to please all parties: Franco was not granted recognition until he had won the war and an elaborate pretence was maintained that Britain was working to prevent intervention, while diplomatic contacts were established with the rebels (which had some effect in hindering German economic ambitions).

The French government could be expected to help the Spanish government. By the time the civil war broke out, the Popular Front government, under Léon Blum, was in office. Its sympathies were naturally given to the analogous government in Spain. The Communist party, which was part of Blum's majority, was the most vociferous advocate of help to Spain. France would be most immediately affected by the strategic consequences of a hostile Spain. In fact the government responded to the appeal, which at once came to it from Spain, by dispatching arms. On 8 August, the government went into reverse, and direct deliveries of arms were brought to an end. Why was this? The attitude of Britain was not the decisive factor. When Blum and his foreign minister, Delbos, made a brief visit to London a few days after the Spanish conflict began, the subject, according to Eden, was not discussed at all, though it seems more likely that the British expressed reservations about French help to Spain. Even so, what really counted was the excitement Blum found when he returned to Paris. The secret of the government's help to the Spanish government had leaked out (through the treachery of Spanish diplomatists) and the *Echo de Paris* revealed it on 23 July. When Blum returned the next day, he received reports of a growing agitation against interference in Spain, and, in particular, Chautemps told him that most Radicals (who were a necessary part of the majority) could not support it. Here the Radicals were reflecting the dislike of adventure and risk felt by their supporters. Blum thought of resignation, but was pressed to remain by representations from the Spanish government – however little Blum could do for them, a purely Radical government would do even less.

Still graver fears inhibited Blum. The formation of the Popular Front in France, its electoral victory and the disturbances that accompanied Blum's coming to power, had generated paroxysms of fear and rage among the French right. Events in Spain seemed to confirm the worst fears of property owners and Catholics on the results of Popular Fronts. The last thing they wished to do was to strengthen the Spanish Popular Front government; on the contrary, its defeat might help to undermine Blum's French version. Blum expressed his fears later:

We would have had in France the pendant of Franco's coup. Before any foreign war France would have had civil war with small chances of victory for the Republic. That is to say that Spain could not have been delivered but that France would have gone fascist.

On 25 July, the Council of Ministers heard President Lebrun express fears of foreign and civil war. It was decided to allow deliveries and supplies to Spain only under the disguise of deliveries for Mexico, except for private transactions. On 2 August, a proposal was worked out for international agreement on non-intervention. On the 6th, Blum sent Admiral Darlan to London to try to persuade the British to intervene (which would have altered the position in France). They refused. Thus, on 8 August, deliveries were stopped. When it became clear that Germany and Italy were continuing to aid Franco, Blum accepted what he called 'non-intervention relachée' – the organization of 'virtually official smuggling'.[397]

The activities of the Soviet Union, which provided most of the aid received by the government in Spain, are shrouded in mystery. As usual in the 1930s, we know next to nothing about Stalin's methods and purposes. There exist innumerable assertions and hypotheses, none of which are supported by solid evidence. Two broad lines of interpretation hold the field. One is that Stalin was attempting to make the Popular Front policy work in practice: to encourage Britain and France to resist the advance of German and Italian fascism. The other is that Stalin was demonstrating to Hitler that the Soviet Union must be reckoned with, as a preliminary to arriving at some sort of bargain with him. One thing that is certain is that Stalin was preoccupied with internal affairs in Russia – in these years he was arranging for the murder of large numbers of his associates and subordinates. It is possible that the Communist International simply carried on its own policy – to strengthen foreign communist parties, a policy which had remarkable success, inside and outside Spain, as the communists came to seem the most reliable and active opponents of fascism. Meanwhile, perhaps, the foreign ministry was pursuing its own policy – to attempt to recruit Britain and France for an effective anti-German bloc. This would explain the contradictions that appeared in Soviet actions. We can be certain of nothing.[398]

The diplomacy of the civil war revolved round 'non-intervention'. On French initiative, all European countries declared that they would not assist either side in the Spanish war and a non-intervention committee was established in London to supervise the application of this principle. It went on throughout the war. Its success may be measured by contemplating a memorandum from the German foreign ministry of December 1938.

A victory for Franco requires that the volunteer units fighting for him in Nationalist Spain be retained, that their fighting power be preserved by means of regular reinforcements, and that Franco be supported with war material ... We ought not to permit the Non-Intervention Committee to dissolve ... We must rather attempt to retain the committee as an instrument for providing Franco with diplomatic support and tying down French and British policy in regard to Spain.

Every one wanted the Non-Intervention committee to continue even though it did not prevent intervention. France was the key. French governments needed the committee as an excuse for evading demands from inside France for full-scale intervention. The British wanted it because it kept the French, and therefore themselves, out of trouble. The Italians came to like it because it enabled the French not to intervene while leaving Italy itself, in practice if not in theory, free to do so without a major war. The Germans favoured it because they wanted Franco to win and because it made Italian intervention possible neither Hitler nor Mussolini was ready to risk a full-scale war for Franco's sake). Even the Russians accepted it, perhaps because they were afraid that their departure from the committee would hasten a revival of co-operation against them between the four western powers.[399] The committee was quite active. Sometimes it even reached agreement (especially at times when Franco seemed about to win anyway) on the end of 'volunteers' or even on their withdrawal – agreements which were then sabotaged in execution. Contemporaries called the whole process the 'farce of non-intervention'.

A consequence of the war, and of the existence of the Non-Intervention Committee, was that Germany and Italy came to work closely together on a day-to-day basis. Ciano visited Berlin in October 1936, and the next month, Mussolini announced the existence of an 'axis' linking Rome and Berlin. In the same month, Ribbentrop, still German ambassador in London, but with far larger ambitions, produced a personal achievement: the anti-Comintern pact. This was a treaty with Japan. Each signatory (secretly) promised the other that they would do nothing to make it easier for the USSR to attack the other. Each was clearly hoping that his partner would weaken Russia. The treaty was negotiated by Ribbentrop's private Nazi machinery; the German foreign ministry saw no reason for German interest in the Far East, except to maintain the privileged position Germany had secured in China since the war and it had no settled anti-Russian bias.

A year later, Italy joined the anti-Comintern pact. Ciano noted,

There nations are embarking together upon the path which may perhaps lead them to war. A war necessary in order to break through the crust which is stifling the energy and the aspirations of the young nations. After the signature we went to see the *Duce*. I have seldom seen him so happy. The situation of 1935 has been transformed. Italy has broken out of her isolation; she is in the centre of the most formidable political and military combination which has ever existed.

Meanwhile, the Japanese military had moved forward to another attempt to dominate China. The British had already concluded that they could not defend their Chinese interests unless the United States chose to use its strength; but the prospect was evident that a Japanese search for political and economic control of eastern Asia might reach to Malaya or beyond. In so far as Italy's signature of the tripartite pact had any meaning, it must be principally anti-British. 'Anti-communist in theory, but in fact unmistakably anti-British' wrote Ciano. Italy would distract Britain in the Mediterannean from resistance to Japan in the east. No doubt this was empty posturing on the part of Mussolini and Ciano – they had no coherent aims at all – but British eagerness to reach understandings with Hitler and Mussolini was sharpened. Without the absent United States, British interests could no longer be maintained by force of arms.[400]

Towards the end of 1937, the French Foreign Minister, Delbos, raised memories of Barthou by carrying out a tour of France's eastern allies. It seems that his purpose was to secure a mutual assistance pact joining France with Czechoslovakia, Yugoslavia and Rumania, and possibly Poland. This would, above all, strengthen Czechoslovakia against Germany – Poland had no commitment to Czechoslovakia, while the Little Entente was directed at Hungary. Nothing came of it. The Poles stuck to independence, though insisting that their alliance with France held good, the Rumanians and Yugoslavs were increasingly tied to Germany economically. Furthermore their unrepresentative governments were perhaps coming to feel that the axis powers might provide some sort of European barrier to social change. As usual, the Czechs alone showed complete sympathy for France.[401]

3

From this time, towards the end of 1937, the immediate origins of the Second World War can be dated. In the summer, Japan had begun a new attack on China which soon brought about a major conflict. There were signs that President Roosevelt was ready to begin to create a public opinion in the United States that would accept American intervention overseas. On 5 October, he spoke of the 'present reign of terror and international lawlessness' and went on, 'If these things come to pass in other parts of the world let no one imagine that America will escape'. There was a hint of action: 'When an epidemic of physical disease starts to spread, the community approves, and joins in, a quarantine of the patients in order to protect the health of the community against the spread of disease.' These remarks secured approval only from a minority in the USA and the President soon retreated, but his personal attitude was now clear.[402]

In Germany, Hitler began to talk of moving from preparation to action in the foreseeable future. On 5 November 1937, he spoke at length to Blomberg, the war minister, Fritsch, the commander-in-chief of the army, Raeder, the head of the navy, Göring, who, among other things, was commander of the air force, and Neurath, the foreign minister; Hitler's adjutant, Colonel Hossbach, recorded his speech. Hitler opened portentously. His remarks were the 'fruit of thorough deliberation'. They were to explain 'his basic ideas concerning the opportunities for the development of our position in the field of foreign affairs and its requirements'. If he died, this was to be 'his last will and testament'. The German racial community had the 'right to a greater living space than in the case of other peoples' and Germany's future was 'wholly conditional upon the solving of the need for space'. This would need strength: 'Germany's problem could only be solved by means of force and this was never without attendant risk.' After 1943–5 Germany's relative strength would begin to decline. 'If the *Führer* was still living, it was his unalterable decision to solve Germany's problem of space at the latest by 1943–5.' No suggestion about the nature of the 'solution' emerged. Hitler, however, went on to speak at length of the possibility of action before 1943. If France plunged into domestic crisis, so that the French army could not be used against Germany, 'then the time for action against the Czechs had come'. If France became involved in war with Italy then Germany must 'settle the Czech and Austrian questions', perhaps as early as 1938.

The annexation of Czechoslovakia and Austria . . . meant . . . a substantial advantage because it would mean shorter and better frontiers, the freeing of forces for other purposes, and the possibility of creating new units up to a level of about twelve divisions.[403]

Why did Hitler make these remarks? This conference was originally suggested by Blomberg to deal with a conflict between himself and Göring over priorities in armaments. Hitler turned it into a means of pushing Blomberg and Fritsch into accepting faster rearmament. This can explain his emphasis on the risks of war and the need to be ready for possible action in 1938. It does not mean that his statements are meaningless. They were not a plan for action, but they indicate Hitler's trend of thought. There is no reason to think it accidental that he used this particular argument – that aggressive war, firstly against Czechoslovakia, must be risked – rather than some quite different argument. Neurath, according to his own statement, urged on Hitler that his policy must lead to world war and that many of the things Hitler claimed to want could be secured by peaceful means – though slowly. Hitler replied that he could not wait. Blomberg, Fritsch, and Neurath all showed hesitation and fear. Early in 1938, they were all replaced.

Hitler became his own War Minister, Brauchitsch became army commander, and Ribbentrop foreign minister. Aggressive action was likely in the foreseeable future and would begin with Czechoslovakia.[404]

Towards the end of 1937, British foreign policy acquired a firmer tone and a clearer definition. Agreement and understanding with Germany had been a consistent British aim since the end of the war. Its pursuit had been restrained by dislike of Hitler's methods and by concern to fit in with French desires to maintain, at least on the surface, some remnants of the old policy of resistance to the expansion of German power. In May 1937, Neville Chamberlain became British Prime Minister. He presented many contrasts to his predecessor, Baldwin. He was active, forceful, clear and decisive. He disliked delays and evasions and prided himself on realism. As Prime Minister, he was authoritarian and confident. He was certainly not a weak man, nor did he advocate a weak foreign policy. He had been in favour of resistance to Mussolini over Ethiopia, though he demanded the speedy end of sanctions when their failure was clear. He wished to make a call for rearmament as part of the 1935 election campaign, for he believed that armed strength was an essential adjunct to British influence, though he wished to avoid straining the economy or interfering with normal commerce. He disliked fascism and Nazism; he described Hitler as 'a mad dictator'. Soon, Chamberlain began to devote attention to the foreign situation. Shortly after he became Prime Minister, he explained to the US government that Britain wanted to avoid simultaneous trouble in Europe and in the Far East and suggested that an attempt be made to reach an agreement with Japan. The United States reply embodied their standard policy: no agreement and no resistance – a line of policy curiously similar to that followed by French governments in Europe. Chamberlain could do nothing about Japan without American co-operation. In Europe he could act more freely. There, too, a choice was apparently approaching between compromise or war. He intended to look for compromise. In July 1937, he saw the Italian ambassador twice and wrote a friendly letter to Mussolini: 'I did not show my letter to the foreign secretary, for I had the feeling that he would object to it.' In the autumn Lord Halifax, a minister on good terms with Chamberlain, visited Göring and Hitler. Chamberlain wrote soon after,

The German visit was, from my point of view a great success because it achieved its object, that of creating an atmosphere in which it is possible to discuss with Germany the practical questions involved in a European settlement ... I don't see why we shouldn't say to Germany, 'Give us satisfactory assurances that you won't use force to deal with the Austrians and Czechoslovakians, and we will give you similar assurances that we won't use force to prevent the changes you want, if you can get them by peaceful means.

When Chamberlain, Eden and Halifax met the French ministers in November, he went further. Britain and France, he urged, should work actively for a peaceful settlement and press for concessions from the Czechs. Chamberlain was directing British foreign policy along a fateful path: towards interference in central European affairs.[405] From now on he came to dominate French policy, too; that was not because of relative French weakness but because he had one policy while the French had several.

Early in 1938, Chamberlain began to press for an attempt at an agreement with Italy. Eden, the foreign secretary, opposed it. He was impatient with Italian evasiveness over Spain and had come to believe that Mussolini should be treated firmly. Thus there should be no agreement unless Italy withdrew troops from Spain. The Prime Minister insisted on his own view, forced negotiations to go on and Eden resigned, to be replaced by Lord Halifax. Apart from the issue of policy involved, it is certain that Eden resented Chamberlain's high-handed interference and his obvious mistrust of foreign office advice. (These factors are more important than Chamberlain's rejection of a suggestion from Roosevelt for a general conference; Roosevelt had no desire to impede Chamberlain's efforts and was in no way offended, whatever some members of the US State Department might feel.) Chamberlain came to work most closely in foreign affairs with a civil servant from outside the foreign office, Sir Horace Wilson.

The first major event of 1938, however, did not test Chamberlain's skill as a conciliator. The union of Austria with Germany came in a way, and at a time, which no one had expected, and there was little opportunity to intervene by any means short of war. Schuschnigg, the Austrian Chancellor, recognized that Austrian independence could be made secure only with German permission, especially since Mussolini was unlikely to repeat his demonstration of 1934. At the end of 1937, Papen, who had been German ambassador in Vienna since 1934, suggested a meeting both to Hitler and Schuschnigg. Both agreed. As a preliminary, Schuschnigg engaged in negotiations with Seyss-Inquart, one of the 'respectable' Nazis, as distinct from the radical agitators of the local party organization. The meeting with Hitler was arranged for 12 February 1938. Its outcome was practically fixed in advance by the conclusions of Schuschnigg's negotiations with Seyss-Inquart, whose details were communicated to the Germans. Then, at the Berchtesgaden meeting, Hitler was able to impose terms which he knew in advance that Schuschnigg would accept. In addition, he used the meeting to insult and intimidate the Austrian Chancellor. It may be that he wished to make certain that Schuschnigg would tamely accept German wishes in the future, it may be that Hitler was driven to anger by the sight of an exponent of the 'Austrian idea', a concept which he regarded as simple treachery to the 'German idea'. The result was an agreement that Austrian foreign policy would support Germany's, that Seyss-Inquart would become Austrian Minister of the Interior, that the Austrian Nazis should have full opportunities for legal activity, without any discrimination against them, and that there should be an amnesty for Nazis already punished by the Austrian courts. Close relations between the Austrian and German armies, including exchanges of officers, were to be established.

Hitler was well contented with this. The *Gleichshaltung* of Austria should now be able to move forward. On 21 February, Hitler ordered that the radical group of Austrian Nazi leaders should leave Austria and, on the 26th, Hitler told these Austrian Nazis, 'the Austrian question could never be solved by revolution'. There were only two possibilities, force or evolutionary means.

He wanted the evolutionary course to be taken, whether or not the possibility of success could today be foreseen. The protocol signed by Schuschnigg was so far-reaching that if completely carried out, the Austrian problem would be automatically solved. He did not now desire a solution by violent means, if it could at all be avoided, since the danger for us in the field of foreign policy became less each year and our military power greater each year.[406]

This was important. Hitler evidently still took seriously the possibility of foreign intervention in Austria and did not think that German military strength had yet reached as strong a position relatively to others as it would come to do. It suggests that his remarks on 5 November represent his real views on timing: that military action in 1938 was possible only under special circumstances. His views were soon to be changed.

Schuschnigg was not content with the outcome of Berchtesgaden. The bullying to which he had been subjected became known, Nazis demonstrated in the streets, and his authority was called into question. In order to arrest the advance of Hitler's evolutionary process and the activities of Seyss-Inquart, and in order to make it more difficult for Hitler to have an excuse to use force, he determined on action to strengthen his position. The Austrian people were to be invited to declare their support for Austrian independence. On 9 March, Schuschnigg announced that a plebiscite would be held on 13 March in which voters would be asked whether or not they supported 'a free and German Austria, an independent and social Austria, a Christian and united Austria'. It was expected that Schuschnigg would secure a large majority. In the morning of 10 March, Hitler determined that the plebiscite must be stopped. Beck, the Chief of Staff of the army, was summoned and ordered to prepare for the invasion of Austria. By the end of the afternoon, preparatory orders were sent out to units. During the night the generals urged that the invasion should be abandoned, but Keitel, Hitler's new chief of the high command of the armed forces (OKW), failed to pass on their pleas to Hitler. Next morning, the 11th, Seyss-Inquart received instructions to demand postponement of the plebiscite from Schuschnigg, under threat of invasion if he did not agree by midday, a time limit extended by Seyss-Inquart to 2 p.m. At 2.45, Göring began the first of a series of telephone calls to Vienna. He learnt from Seyss-Inquart that Schuschnigg had called off the plebiscite. After a twenty minute conversation with Hitler, Göring put forward a new demand. Schuschnigg was to be replaced by Seyss-Inquart. The Austrian President, Miklas, refused. At 8.45 p.m. Hitler's order went out for the invasion of Austria next morning at dawn. It is significant that Hitler had earlier called off the invasion, at 6 p.m., when false information arrived that Seyss-Inquart had been appointed – he was still trying to cling to 'evolutionary' means, and had not decided to go through with the *Anschluss*. By the time Seyss-Inquart really was appointed, it was too late to stop the invasion. On 12 March, German troops entered Austria, received with enthusiasm by large sections of the population. No resistance was attempted.[407]

Meanwhile the diplomatic repercussions were unfolding. On the 11th, Lord Halifax informed Vienna that he could not advise Schuschnigg to take any action which might expose him to dangers against which Britain was 'unable to guarantee protection'. The French, irrelevantly, urged Schuschnigg to gain time and tried to get Mussolini to do something. Ciano replied that if the French wanted to talk about Austria, that was a subject on which the Italian government had no reason to concert with France or Britain. On the same day, Hitler dispatched Prince Philip of Hesse to explain away his use of force in Austria to Mussolini. In the evening, he reported by telephone that Mussolini had taken it well. Hitler broke into a startling outburst of relief and gratitude. It seems that he had not been completely confident that Mussolini really would do nothing, in spite of the evidence accumulated over a year or more. Again on the 11th, the British and French ambassadors delivered protests in Berlin. The British ambassador, Sir Nevile Henderson, also protested in the middle of the night to Göring, though he weakened his remarks by blaming Schuschnigg for 'precipitate folly'. Göring promised that German troops would be withdrawn from Austria as soon as the situation was stable; another sign that immediate *Anschluss* was not yet contemplated. The invasion was, in fact, carried out without fixed purpose. It was only after Hitler had crossed into Austria that he decided on immediate union. It was announced on the 13th, while Hitler gave a private commentary:

England has sent me a protest. I would have understood a declaration of war, to a protest I shall not even reply. France . . . cannot act alone . . . Italy is our friend and Mussolini a statesman of great stature who knows and comprehends that there can be no other development.[408]

This great success seems to have fortified Hitler's confidence. The caution and hesitation he had shown before the *Anschluss* became less evident. The timing laid down in the meeting of 5 November 1937, action against Czechoslovakia for 1943–5, was altered.

It was at once assumed that a crisis over Czechoslovakia would follow the *Anschluss*; that Hitler would soon seek some 'solution', at least of the problem posed by the three million or so Germans living inside the Czech frontiers. On 12 March, Lord Halifax and the French ambassador in London agreed that French and British ministers should meet to discuss what to do about Czechoslovakia. The British government quickly ruled out one possible reaction to future German demands on Czechoslovakia – the organization of collective resistance. On 17 March, the Soviet foreign minister declared readiness 'to participate in collective actions . . . which would aim at checking the further development of aggression' and announced readiness to consider 'practical measures' with other powers. Halifax made the British view plain in his reply a week later. Britain would welcome a conference of all European states (i.e. including Germany) designed to deal with and settle outstanding problems –

a conference only attended by some of the European Powers, and designed less to secure the settlement of outstanding problems than to organize concerted action against aggression, would not necessarily . . . have such a favourable effect upon the prospects of European peace.[409]

In other words, conciliation remained British policy, not coercion.

With Eden removed, the Chamberlain-Halifax partnership was free to pursue conciliation with energy. Newton, the British minister in Prague, pointed out the new emphasis in April 1938. The year before, Eden had advised Czechoslovakia to settle differences with the Sudeten Germans, but had insisted that Britain was 'not prepared to offer any advice, and still less to attempt any sort of mediation'. For Chamberlain in 1938, on the other hand, 'Now is the time when all the resources of diplomacy should be enlisted in the cause of peace'. This meant that the British government 'will at all times be ready to render any help in their power . . . towards the solution of questions likely to cause difficulty between the German and Czechoslovak governments'. The resulting policy was set out to the new French ministers, Daladier, the Prime Minister, and Bonnet, the Foreign Minister, when they came to London in April 1938. Halifax spoke thus: 'It should be made very clear to the Czechoslovak government and to Dr Beneš [the President of Czechoslovakia] that they must seize this opportunity . . . to make a supreme effort to reach a settlement.' On the other hand, 'The German government ought not to be encouraged to think that they could impose any settlement they would on Czechoslovakia by force or by threat of force'. This explains Chamberlain's carefully drafted pronouncement of 24 March. The Prime Minister refused to extend Britain's formal commitments under Locarno and the League. He would not promise that Britain would assist France if France attacked Germany after a German attack on Czechoslovakia.

But, while plainly stating this decision, I would add this: where peace and war are concerned, legal obligations are not alone involved and, if war broke out, it would be unlikely to be confined to those who have assumed such obligations. It would be quite impossible to say where it might end and what governments might become involved . . . This is especially true in the case of two countries like Great Britain and France, with long association of friendship, with interests closely interwoven, devoted to the same ideals of democratic liberty, and determined to uphold them.

This was intended to persuade Hitler that Britain might intervene while persuading Beneš that Britain might not. Both would be encouraged to be conciliatory and a conflict prevented.[410]

Why did the British government wish to avoid conflict with Germany? The obvious answer is the correct one: that such a war would be a great evil unless it was demonstrably unavoidable. If there was a chance of inducing Hitler's Germany to adopt peaceful ways, by giving satisfaction to its legitimate grievances, then that chance must be seized. It was not a question of surrender to Germany – at no time was Chamberlain ready to accept German mastery of Europe or to accept a state of affairs in which Britain would be dependent upon German goodwill for her independence and freedom. Quite different arguments were used in support of British policy, however, then and since. All of them were presented to the French ministers in April. Firstly, there were military arguments. British and French action could not, in any case, prevent Czechoslovakia from being overrun, and Britain and France were not strong enough to make ultimate victory certain. Secondly, the British Dominions – Canada, Australia, New Zealand and South Africa – would not join Britain in seeking to defend Czechoslovakia. Thirdly, British public opinion would not allow the government to risk war. These were supplementary agreements used to support a policy which would have been followed even if they had not existed. In the first place, Britain did, in fact, come near to war in September 1938 and did actually go to war in September 1939 without any great transformation in the strategic outlook – after all, in 1939, Poland could be defended no more effectively than Czechoslovakia in 1938. The British threat of war in September 1938 suggests, too, that the support of the Dominions would be dispensed with, if need be. Thirdly, while it is certain that the overwhelming mass of British opinion supported Chamberlain's efforts for peace in 1938, the British government made no attempt to change this opinion. Chamberlain's policy was based, in fact, upon the belief that Hitler's aims could be satisfied without surrendering Europe to Nazi domination. On the issue of 1938, 'He doubted very much whether Herr Hitler really desired to destroy the Czechoslovak state, or rather a Czechoslovak state' – that is, a Czechoslovakia modified to take account of the grievances of the Sudeten Germans.[411]

French policy followed the British line. This was obscured by the refusal of the French government to admit it openly. France was committed by treaty to the defence of Czechoslovakia. To fail to help Czechoslovakia against German demands was thus to accept that France was no longer a great power. The policy of Daladier and Bonnet, therefore, was to claim to be ready to honour France's obligations while arranging that this claim should not be tested. To avoid a situation in which France would be faced with a choice between open betrayal of Czechoslovakia or war, it was necessary to persuade Czechoslovakia to submit to German demands. The British were ready to take the lead in the persuasion. Daladier and Bonnet could indulge in verbal manifestations of French 'honour' and hope that Chamberlain would keep them out of trouble. The advantage of this situation was that it enabled Daladier to secure adequate political backing in France, whereas a definite choice for resistance or surrender would be likely to bring about the collapse of the government, either from disagreement within it, or from loss of support in the Chamber of Deputies. This policy was probably in harmony with the wishes of most Frenchmen. French policy had advocated resistance to the expansion of German power for so long that a clear reversal would be humiliating, while to uphold resistance would mean a war whose main burden would fall on France. To the British ministers, in the conference at the end of April, Daladier propounded the public line of French policy. He told them that he believed that the Germans were aiming at the destruction of Czechoslovakia and that, while Beneš should be urged to make reasonable concessions to the Sudeten Germans, he should be supported in resisting the dismemberment of his country. He urged that the frontier of Czechoslovakia was not alone at stake.

In his view, the ambitions of Napoleon were far inferior to the present aims of the German Reich . . . Today we were faced with the question of Czechoslovakia. Tomorrow we might be faced with that of Rumania . . . if and when Germany had secured the petrol and wheat resources of Rumania, she would then turn against the Western Powers, and it would be our own blindness which would have provided Germany with the very supplies she required for the long war which she admitted she was not then in a position to wage.

This call to resistance compares strangely with some remarks made by Daladier in private, remarks which were reported to the German embassy in London. To a British journalist he spoke thus:

Well, are you [i.e. the British] going to put pressure on Prague? Are you going to give the Czechs pressing councils of wisdom? . . . We are bound, bound in honour to Czechoslovakia by treaty . . . But you are free . . . The Germans themselves want the Czechoslovak question settled now – summer. And we must assume they mean it . . . Germany is in a dangerous mood. She is terribly strong . . . The peace of Europe probably depends at this moment on the Czechoslovak issue and on what your government and especially Mr Chamberlain will do.

On the same day, 30 April, this journalist spoke to the Comte de Brinon. The latter was one of the leading organizers of pro-German sentiment in France (he was shot, as a collaborator with the Nazis, after the war). He had known Daladier for some years, and had been used by Daladier and other French Prime Ministers for unofficial contacts with the rulers of Nazi Germany. Brinon reported that Daladier was hoping 'that Chamberlain and Halifax would themselves suggest that pressure should be put on Prague' so that Daladier could acquiesce without seeming to have taken the initiative . . . Bonnet was, if anything, even keener than Daladier on steering clear of France's obligations to fight for Czechoslovakia'. In May, Bonnet actually told the German ambassador in Paris that if the Czechs refused to fulfil 'well-founded demands' by the Sudeten Germans, the French would tell the Czechs that, 'they would be obliged to submit their obligations under the alliance to revision.' [412]

Only a small section of French opinion, from the political right, openly advocated the policy the government was following in practice, if not in theory. This fact had important effects. It meant that Daladier and Bonnet could carry out their own policy only if it seemed to be imposed on them by pressure of circumstances. It meant that they could not campaign openly for a change in the nominal foreign policy of France. Thus when circumstances changed, that is when the British ceased to impose restraint, they could not renounce their public policy of resistance to German expansion, without an impossible public volteface. Their refusal to appeal openly to French opinion meant that they could not find sufficient support for such a change of front when it became the only alternative to war. It should be added that these arguments are stronger for Bonnet than for Daladier. Bonnet had definite views which he worked for consistently, even if his love of office prevented their open expression; Daladier was more indecisive. He shared Bonnet's views to the extent of appointing Bonnet to the foreign ministry but found it less easy than Bonnet to put them into effect when they clashed with French pledges.

It seemed likely that British and French policy would ensure the isolation of Czechoslovakia, especially if the Czech government could be made to appear reluctant to grant the wishes of its German subjects. To this end Hitler devoted himself. Henlein, the leader of the Sudeten German party, received his instructions in Berlin on 28 March. Hitler told him that he intended to settle the Sudeten German problem in the not too distant future. He instructed him to make demands unacceptable to the Czech government. Henlein put it thus: 'We must always demand so much that we can never be satisfied. The *Führer* approved this view.'[413] Thus any attempt at reconciliation between Czechs and Germans was futile. However, Beneš had to make such attempts. His only hope of securing support from the west was to seem reasonable and conciliatory. He was restrained by fear of arousing equally unmanageable demands from other minority groups, and by reluctance to weaken the morale of the Czechs themselves, by calling the basis of the country into question.

The British government threw itself energetically into the hopeless task of securing agreement between the Czechs and the Sudeten Germans. In July, this process culminated in the dispatch of Lord Runciman as an 'investigator and mediator' – an idea which was presented to Beneš before the French were even told of it, though when they were, Daladier and Bonnet, of course, accepted it readily. The Runciman mission had no effect on the course of events, but it did collect some useful information on the situation of the Germans in Czechoslovakia. Germans who did not belong to Henlein's party pointed out to Runciman the unrestricted development of German culture permitted within Czechoslovakia. German Social Democrats showed that, until the world slump, most Germans had accepted the new state. However, the dependence of the Sudeten Germans on industry and the dependence of that industry on exports, meant that the depression had brought great trouble to the Germans in Czechoslovakia, on which anti-government and anti-Czech agitation could build. The Runciman mission ended in September, amidst the crumbling of the assumption on which it had been based – that agreement between Czechs and the Sudeten German party was possible. In that month, the Czech government's 'fourth plan' conceded virtually everything the Sudeten Germans had asked for within Czechoslovakia. The fraudulence of Henlein's demands at once became clear – in fact, no solution was acceptable to the Germans that left the Czechoslovak state intact. It was evident, at last, to everyone, that Hitler's wishes were what mattered, not those of Henlein, and that useful negotiations could only be carried on with Hitler. Runciman's only function, after he returned to Britain in the middle of September, was to persuade the British cabinet that no agreement on the basis of maintaining the existing Czechoslovakian frontiers was possible.[414]

Hitler's timing was fixed in May 1938. The army had been working on projects for an attack on Czechoslovakia (case green). On 20 May, the Chief of the High Command of the German armed forces (OKW), Keitel, submitted to Hitler a revised scheme to take account of the incorporation of Austria. The draft began, 'It is not my intention to smash Czechoslovakia by military action in the immediate future,' without a particularly favourable opportunity. On 30 May, Keitel passed to the three Commanders-in-Chief the new scheme as approved by Hitler. It began, 'It is my unalterable decision to smash Czechoslovakia by military action in the near future'. Keitel noted that the execution of the operation 'must be assured by 1 October 1938, at the latest'.[415] It is possible that this decision for violence was the result of the so-called May crisis of 1938. There were reports then of German troop movements preliminary to an attack on Czechoslovakia, the Czechs carried out a partial mobilization, and the British and French ambassadors in Berlin conveyed warnings to Hitler that any attack might lead to general war. It is clear that Hitler had not contemplated an attack at that time, but press comment took the line that he had been forced to 'climb down' by a firm allied stand. Hitler may have felt that a successful display of force was needed to restore his prestige. Probably he supposed that Britain and France would abandon Czechoslovakia to her fate, after a campaign of propaganda based on the alleged oppression suffered by the Sudeten Germans. Thus Czechoslovakia could be forced into submission by an attack or by the threat of an attack. The outcome was different.

As had been expected, the crisis of September 1938 was, so to speak, officially opened by Hitler in a speech at the Nuremberg party congress on 12 September. Amidst a series of threatening utterances, he demanded self-determination (i.e. union with Germany) for the Germans in Czechoslovakia. Bonnet and Daladier promptly collapsed. Bonnet told the British ambassador in Paris that 'peace must be maintained at any price' and expressed gratitude for a copy of a warning, first delivered in May, that Britain was not automatically obliged to take up arms if France helped Czechoslovakia. 'He indicated . . . that he had found this useful with certain bellicose French ministers.' Daladier explained 'with evident lack of enthusiasm, that if Germans used force, France would be obliged also', and proposed more talks on Czechoslovakia, or a conference between Britain, France and Germany. Chamberlain had written on 3 September, 'I keep racking my brains to try and devise some means of averting a catastrophe, if it should seem to be upon us. I thought of one so unconventional and daring that it rather took Halifax's breath away'. Now he put his scheme into effect. Without troubling to consult the French first, he told Hitler that he proposed to fly to Germany at once to try to find a peaceful solution.[416] Chamberlain and Hitler met at Berchtesgaden on 15 September.

Chamberlain was favourably impressed. He had once described Hitler as 'half-mad'. Now, he 'did not see any trace of insanity'. He told his sister, 'In spite of the hardness and ruthlessness I thought I saw in his face I got the impression that here was a man who could be relied upon when he had given his word'. Hitler spoke at length ('occasionally he became very excited'), with his usual historical reflections and with denunciation of non-existent atrocities committed by 'inferior' Czechs, and explained that this was the 'last major problem to be solved'. The substance was that Germany must bring the Sudeten Germans within the *Reich* and that he would risk war to do so. Chamberlain returned to London after promising to come back to Germany in a few days. Göring gave his view to the British ambassador in Berlin: there were only two alternatives, '(a) if British and French governments accept self-determination, for them to coerce Czechoslovak government into acquiescence, (b) if they failed to do this to allow Germany to do so.'[417]

On 18 September, Bonnet and Daladier came to London to hear Chamberlain's account of his meeting with Hitler and his views on what to do next. They accepted Chamberlain's proposal that Göring's first alternative should be adopted. Once again, Daladier challenged the assumption that Hitler could be satisfied, and peace secured, by accepting his demands, and ended by agreeing that they should be accepted. During the night, the details were sent to Prague. Areas in which more than half the population was German were to be transferred from Czechoslovakia to Germany. There was added an offer: Britain would 'join in an international guarantee of the new boundaries of the Czechoslovak state against unprovoked aggression'. This was added because Daladier and Bonnet had asked for it to make it easier for them to persuade the Czechs into accepting surrender of territory, and as compensation for the weakening of France's security system involved in the neutralization of Czechoslovakia. (Probably the French ministers thought it was needed to help to persuade the French cabinet to accept the new plan.) Chamberlain agreed, after discussing this request with Halifax, Simon and Hoare, but without consulting the cabinet, which was not told until the next day.[418] The guarantee did not come to much in the end, but its acceptance was a further and considerable move towards the involvement of Britain in eastern Europe—a result of Chamberlain's eagerness to get French and Czechoslovak acceptance of his plan for peace, so that he could take it to Germany before Hitler lost patience and attacked. Thus Chamberlain's eagerness to win peace pushed him into intervention in Europe and so, as it turned out, towards war.

The French council of ministers agreed, on the 19th, that the proposals should be presented to Prague. No decision was made on what to do if the Czechs refused them: Bonnet and Chautemps proposed that they should be warned that rejection would mean a French refusal to carry out her alliance obligations. This was not agreed to. At 2 p.m. on the same day the British and French ministers gave the proposals to Beneš. At 7.35 p.m. on the next day, the 20th, they received a reply from the Czechoslovak government rejecting the proposals. Next morning at 6.30 a.m., however, Newton, the British minister in Prague, received a telephone call from the Czech prime minister's secretary to say that the government had accepted.[419] There is controversy about what happened. One view was that Czechoslovakia was determined to keep out of war, even if France was in it, the other that Czechoslovakia was ready to fight, but only if she could count on France.

According to Bonnet, the Czech government knew well that any war, with or without France, would be disastrous for Czechoslovakia, but needed to carry its own public opinion by securing the pretext of a statement from France that France would not honour her alliance. 'The manoeuvre was skilful. We joined in it.' The Czech government claimed that the Anglo-French proposals were accepted only because Czechoslovakia would receive no assistance from the west if Germany attacked after a Czech rejection of the proposals. On the face of it, the message from the French minister in Prague, Lacroix, sent on the evening of the 20th, supports Bonnet. This declared that the Czechs would give way if Paris confirmed that France would not assist Czechoslovakia against a German attack, and that the Czech government required this statement to 'cover' it against its own public opinion.[420] During the same evening Newton was reporting that the government would give way if pressed sufficiently hard by Britain and France: 'A solution must . . . be imposed upon the government, as without such pressure, many of its members are too committed to be able to accept what they realize to be necessary.' At 2 a.m. on the 21st, the two ministers saw Beneš to tell him formally that Britain and France would stand aside if their proposals were rejected.[421] The Czech acceptance followed. But the exchanges of 20/21 September do not mean that the Czech government was simply seeking an excuse for surrender. It knew that the agreement between Britain and France, reached in London, meant that Czechoslovakia could expect no help. As soon as the agreement was known in Prague, it was recognized that the choice was between acceptance or risking a war against Germany without allies. From the first, acceptance was chosen since the desertion of France was assumed; the events of the 20-21st represented a protest and a demand from the Czechs that France should openly take the blame for surrender to Hitler's demands. These interchanges do not mean that Czechoslovakia would not fight under any circumstances, only that the government would not risk fighting alone. Bonnet, however, was able to use the message from Prague to suggest that the Czechs wished to avoid conflict, with or without allies. Thus the French government held together when it met on 21 September. Three ministers had intended to resign in protest against France's desertion of her ally: Bonnet could argue that the Czechs themselves wished it so.[422] The Czech acceptance of the Anglo-French proposals meant that the Czechoslovakian government had given up any idea of trying to force a general war by single-handed resistance. Thus Czechoslovakian policy became dependent on that of France; French policy remained dependent on British.

It is possible, however, that the Czech government was divided and that the call for surrender came from Hodza, the prime minister, and that he imposed it on Beneš, by working on the Czech general staff and by endeavouring to get clear statements from the two governments that Britain and France would not help Czechoslovakia. Indeed, the telegram from the Soviet minister in Prague, apparently sent in the night of 19/20 September, suggests that Beneš was then considering isolated resistance by the Czechs, even after a French and British refusal to help Czechoslovakia, a refusal he thought possible. Furthermore, Lacroix reports that his telegram to Paris resulted from a request from Hodza.[423]

On 22 September, a triumphant Chamberlain left for Godesberg to see Hitler again. 'European peace is what I am aiming at, and I hope that this journey may open the way to get it.' Hitler's response to the Anglo-French plan was not at all what he expected. Hitler insisted that a frontier line must be drawn at once, delimiting areas which Germany could occupy immediately – by 28 September, a date changed by Hitler to 1 October. At the same time Polish and Hungarian demands must be met. If the Czechs refused then Germany would attack and impose 'a military solution, which meant a military or strategic frontier'. This implied the absorption of the whole of Bohemia and Moravia. Probably this was what Hitler was trying to get. He would produce demands of a kind that the Czechs would be forced to reject, attack and destroy Czechoslovakia, and hope that Britain and France would stand aside. Hitler had told the Prime Minister and Foreign Minister of Hungary, on 20 September, that he

was determined to settle the Czech question even at the risk of a world war . . . He was convinced that neither England nor France would intervene . . . In his opinion, action by the army would provide the only satisfactory solution. There was, however, a danger of the Czechs submitting to every demand.

Hence the demands made by Hitler at Godesberg were designed to be rejected by the Czechs.[424] They were rejected. However, this time, Britain and France did not simply abandon Czechoslovakia to its fate.

In France, Daladier was suffering from his frequent worried desire to do something definite without knowing what it should be. He seems to have been coming to doubt the wisdom of accepting anything Hitler cared to demand. The preliminary stage before full mobilization began to be carried through by the French army, including the recall of reservists to man the *couverture renforcée*. Pressed by the French foreign ministry (though not by Bonnet), Lord Halifax agreed, on the 22nd, that the Czechs should no longer be told not to mobilize. On the 23rd, Halifax suggested to Chamberlain that the British cabinet might consider precautionary measures of mobilization. On the 25th, Daladier and Bonnet came to London again. Once again Daladier advocated resistence. This time, the British agreed. After a discourteous cross-examination of Daladier by Sir John Simon, apparently designed to show that France could not fight, Chamberlain told Daladier, on the 26th, that he intended to warn Hitler that if France stood by Czechoslovakia in a rejection of the Godesberg demands Britain would support France. Sir Horace Wilson was dispatched with this threat to reinforce attempts to talk Hitler out of an immediate invasion of Czechoslovakia. On the 26th Lord Halifax authorized a statement to the press. 'If . . . a German attack is made upon Czechoslovakia, its immediate result must be that France will be bound to come to her assistance and Great Britain and Russia will certainly stand by France.'[425] On the same day the British fleet was mobilized and reservists of coast defence units and anti-aircraft batteries ordered to report for duty. Here was something quite new: a British threat of war to enforce an orderly settlement 'of a quarrel in a far-away country between people of whom we know nothing', rather than one based on the naked use of force.

Hitler climbed down, abandoned his invasion and accepted an international conference – perhaps persuaded by pressure from Mussolini, who was anxious to avoid a general war, perhaps because of opposition from the German army command to running the risk of war with the western powers, perhaps because that risk had come to seem real. On 28 September, Hitler proposed a conference between Italy, France, Great Britain and Germany. Chamberlain, Daladier, Mussolini and Hitler met the next day at Munich. The Munich agreement provided for 'predominantly German' areas of Czechoslovakia to be ceded to Germany, their size to be determined by international commission. Specified areas were to be occupied by German forces between 1 and 7 October – Hitler got the entry into Czechoslovakia on 1 October which he had demanded – and the whole territory to be allotted to Germany was to be occupied by 10 October. 'The problems of the Polish and Hungarian minorities,' were to be settled by agreement or by a new conference. Britain and France repeated the offer of an international guarantee to the new Czech state. Germany and Italy promised to guarantee Czechoslovakia once Poland and Hungary were satisfied. The Czechs could do nothing unless they were prepared to risk war alone, which they had already decided not to do. After the proceedings, Chamberlain talked to Hitler, about disarmament, the Spanish civil war, and the world economy, and then invited Hitler to sign a document pledging them to use 'the method of consultation . . . to deal with any other questions that may concern our two countries'. With Hitler's signature, a triumphant

Chamberlain returned to London on 30 September. He spoke that evening: 'I believe it is peace for our time.'[426]

The Munich settlement aroused great controversy. Criticism came from those in Britain and France who believed that the expansion of Germany would have to be resisted some time. Most of them argued that Munich made future resistance more difficult. It neutralized Czechoslovakia, it alienated Russia, it made the small states of eastern Europe feel that an attempt to make the best bargain they could with Germany was their only course. On this line of argument, Munich even became a cause of war, since by weakening the forces of opposition to Hitler, it meant that war itself, and not the mere threat of it, would be required in future to curb him. This argument assumed that Hitler would have chosen to abandon even his demands for the Sudeten German territories if faced with a determined challenge from Britain and France. There is not enough evidence to support or to contradict this view. There was evidence available at the time, however, and some has emerged later, that Hitler might have been compelled to abandon those demands by some kind of internal coup d'état.

Hitler's plans for an attack on Czechoslovakia had been contemplated with dismay by the German army leadership. This was expressed most vigorously by the Chief of the General Staff, Ludwig Beck. Between May and July 1938, Beck sought to persuade the generals, and particularly von Brauchitsch, the Commander-in-Chief of the army, to take action to prevent Hitler from risking war with France, Russia and Britain. At the beginning of August, Beck secured a full conference of the high command of the army. He intended to arrange a joint ultimatum to Hitler: a demand for a halt to preparations for war, an end to the rule of party bosses, to attacks on the church, and a return to legal rule, and to 'Prussian cleanliness and simplicity'. Either for tactical purposes, or as a result of a grave misunderstanding, he argued in terms of saving Hitler from evil counsellors. If Hitler did not give way, then the generals were to resign in a body. Brauchitsch failed to convey Beck's appeal to the assembled generals and nothing came of the plan, except Beck's own resignation which was not even publicly known until after Munich. Beck's dissent, however, encouraged the formation of a more forceful plan. A scheme for a coup d'état was worked out, with the essential co-operation of officers who had troops under their command. The most important were General von Witzleben, commanding the Berlin military district, Count von Brockdorff-Ahlefeldt, in command of the Potsdam garrison, Count Helldorf, the police president of Berlin, and General Hoepner, the commander of an armoured division. Hitler was to be seized in Berlin, later to be put on trial or declared insane, and the army would take power. As soon as the final order for the attack on Czechoslovakia went out, Halder, who had replaced Beck, would inform the conspirators and the plan would go into effect. It was to be a last minute affair: it must be made obvious to German opinion that Hitler was deliberately launching a war against Czechoslovakia and taking the risk of war with the great powers. The conspirators assumed that this would happen and took steps to ensure that the Western Powers should make it plain that they would resist. Then Hitler would either call off his war or be overthrown: even if he abandoned aggression, his prestige would be so weakened that his régime might disappear. In August 1938, Ewald von Kleist, a distinguished conservative anti-Nazi, risked his life acting as emissary of the plotters to the British authorities. He insisted that his German associates needed the support that western firmness towards Hitler would provide. Information about the opposition inside Germany towards Hitler's policy came from other quarters, partly through hints dropped with the connivance of Weiszäcker, the state secretary in the foreign ministry. The proposed coup seems to have come near to reality after Godesberg; the outcome of Munich, a compromise between Hitler and the western powers, with Hitler securing the full satisfaction of his publicly stated demands, destroyed its basis. We cannot tell what the plotters might have done if Chamberlain had not gone to Munich or whether any action would have succeeded. Certainly, however, some of the conspirators were brave and sincere men.[427]

The Munich agreement, and the means by which it was reached, was certain to confirm any doubts about the possibility of co-operation with the Western Powers that the Soviet government may have felt. It was a return to the Four Power Pact, to the idea of remodelling Europe, without consulting Russia, under the aegis of an aggressive Germany and Italy, and a Britain and France evidently concerned to placate the dictators and divert them to the east. It would be interesting to know how far the directors of Russian policy, in 1938, were prepared to act as partners in resistance to Germany or how far they had already given up any such notion, if, indeed, they ever held it. Was the Soviet Union ready to assist Czechoslovakia? By treaty, since Russian obligations were only binding if France carried out hers first, the Soviet government had room to manoeuvre. It was able to proclaim its readiness to honour its engagements in full without these assertions being put to the test. So we cannot tell what Stalin had decided to do, or if he made any decision at all. Certainly, the Soviet foreign minister was distinctly vague about how Soviet forces might reach Czechoslovakia, when neither Poland nor Rumania would agree to allow their passage. Again, the German embassy in Moscow reported, in October, that the Soviet press had played down the crisis and that no preliminary measures of mobilization had been taken inside Russia. According to this report, 'The Soviets subsequently maintained that, in view of the policy of yielding followed by France and Britain towards the aggressors, they had never seriously believed in the outbreak of a war'. Probably this was correct. Since the fate of Czechoslovakia did not immediately concern Russia, its government was able to strike virtuously anti-Nazi attitudes without much practical content. The only concrete action taken during the crisis was to threaten Poland with a Russian reply if Poland attacked Czechoslovakia – a threat which had no influence on Polish policy.[428]

The period between September 1938 and March 1939 was the classical period of appeasement. In France, Bonnet sought to secure a parallel document to the agreement between Chamberlain and Hitler signed after Munich. To this end, Ribbentrop came to Paris in December 1938. A Franco-German declaration announced that the German-French frontier was recognized as final and that both governments were resolved, 'without prejudice to their special relations with third powers', to confer together on all questions affecting them in the future. There can be no doubt about what Ribbentrop wanted – a free hand in Eastern Europe. He thought he had got it. During a formal conversation with Bonnet, Ribbentrop denounced France's eastern alliances as

an atavistic remnant of the Versailles treaty and of the Versailles mentality . . . This kind of policy of encirclement must sooner or later be shaken off as an intolerable state of affairs, whether by means of negotiations or by some other means. If France would respect this German sphere of influence once and for all, then he, the *Reich* Foreign Minister, believed in the possibility of a fundamental and final agreement between Germany and France.

Bonnet replied vaguely that 'relations since Munich had fundamentally altered in this respect', and at once changed the subject to Italian demands on Tunis. In February 1939, when the German ambassador in Paris protested against Bonnet's talking in public of strengthening friendships in eastern Europe, Bonnet explained that

things were often said during a foreign affairs debate in the Chamber which were obviously designed for domestic consumption and had no significance beyond that. If a French Foreign Minister . . . drew his own conclusions privately from the changed situation in central Europe, he could not very well be expected to withdraw also all along the line when facing the Chamber. If he did, then the warmongers would only gain the upper hand.

In July 1939, Ribbentrop wrote to Bonnet to say that, in December 1938,

I expressly pointed out that eastern Europe constituted a sphere of German interests, and . . . you then stressed on your part, that, in France's attitude with regard to the problems of eastern Europe, a radical change had taken place since the Munich conference.[429]

Ribbentrop was struggling with the familiar discordance between French public policy and Bonnet's real policy; a discordance that continued to mean that Bonnet and his supporters might find themselves obliged to carry out a policy of resistance they disliked, since they refused to take the risk of creating a wider public opinion in their support.

In Britain, more confidently than in France, the Munich agreement was thought of as a settlement. If it was not enough to ensure peace, at least it showed how peace could be brought about. It is true that opposition to conciliation towards Hitler was growing in strength. About thirty Conservatives, notably Churchill, Eden and Duff-Cooper, the last of whom had resigned from the government after Munich in protest, expressed varying degrees of scepticism, while Liberal and Labour criticisms of the government's concessions to fascist dictators became more violent. German activities did not help to maintain the atmosphere of appeasement. The German government behaved with offensive arrogance in diplomatic exchanges, with savage brutality inside Germany, where organized attacks upon the Jews took place in November (which removed any remaining illusions in Britain, and presumably in Germany, on the nature of the Nazi régime) and with public discourtesy in speeches and newspapers. Even Chamberlain had his doubts: in October, he wrote, 'We are very little nearer to the time when we can put all thoughts of war out of our minds'. Rearmament continued, a fact bitterly complained of in Germany. But Chamberlain's policy did not change: 'The conciliatory part of the policy is just as important as the rearming.'[430]

Nor did it alter in March 1939, but the balance between conciliation and coercion was changed by the German destruction of Czechoslovakia. The settlement of September 1938 had been a concession on Hitler's part; the invasion and elimination of Czechoslovakia were postponed. They were not forgotten. On 21 October 1938, Hitler directed the armed forces that it must be possible at all times to liquidate the remainder of the Czech state, and on 17 December, a second directive made it clear that it must be done by the peacetime *Wehrmacht* without mobilization, since 'outwardly it must be quite clear that it is only a peaceful action and not a warlike undertaking'. There was no great hurry; the post-Munich Czechoslovak government was showing extreme subservience to German dictation. As with the Austrian *Anschluss* the year before, it was a question of an operation which Hitler intended to carry out at some future time, rather than part of any rigid plan of conquest. Although Hitler's dislike of a Czechoslovakia which possessed any remnant of independence was shown in his interview with the Czech Foreign Minister in January, and his interest in the Slovak independence movement in February, the decision for action seems to have come only after an internal crisis had arisen in Czechoslovakia. On 10 March 1939, the central government in Prague dismissed the Slovak prime minister, Tiso, on the grounds that he was working for Slovak independence. Here was an excuse for a claim that Czechoslovakia was breaking up. On 12 March, the *Wehrmacht* drafted military conditions for an ultimatum to the Prague government, requiring surrender to a German invasion, and instructions were issued to stir up anti-German demonstrations among the Czechs. On the 13th, the Hungarians were urged to invade Ruthenia at once, while Hitler directed Tiso to proclaim Slovak independence, with threats that if he failed to do so within hours, the Hungarians would be permitted to occupy Slovakia.[431]

To judge by Hitler's remarks in his meeting with Tiso, he intended then to use the 'intolerable conditions' created by the Czechs who had fallen under the influence of the 'Beneš spirit' as an excuse for an invasion to restore 'order', but a better device unexpectedly offered itself. The Czech government felt desperately anxious as it saw the signs of German impatience. Thus the President and foreign minister sought an interview with Hitler, hoping at least to secure some shadow of independence for Bohemia and Moravia. By the time they arrived at Berlin, German troops had already marched into Czech territory. Hacha, the Czechoslovak President, saw Hitler at 1.15 a.m. on 15 March. By 4 a.m., he had been bullied into signing a document in which he 'confidently placed the fate of the Czech people and country in the hands of the *Führer* of the German *Reich*'.[432] German troops entered Prague later in the morning. The next day, Hitler announced a Protectorate of Bohemia and Moravia, with a restricted autonomy left to a Czech government supervised and controlled by a *Reich* Protector. On 23 March, Slovakia placed itself under the protection of Germany;

German troops were given the right to establish themselves in parts of the country.

The basis of the next crisis were already being made. The friendship between Germany and Poland had worked well in September 1938. Still, sooner or later, any German government must seek some modification of the Versailles arrangements over Danzig and over the Polish Corridor to the sea. On 24 October 1938, Ribbentrop talked to the Polish ambassador, Lipski. It was a conversation 'in a very friendly tone'. Ribbentrop announced that the time had come for the elimination of all possible disagreements between Germany and Poland. This could be done without difficulty. Danzig should revert to Germany and Germany should have an extra-territorial road and rail link with East Prussia across the Corridor. Poland would be given a guaranteed outlet in Danzig and extra-territorial rights within it. The Polish-German frontier would be recognized as final. Poland would join the anti-Comintern pact. On 19 November, Ribbentrop saw Lipski once more. Lipski reported that Poland could not agree to the incorporation of Danzig in Germany, but said that the German link across the Polish Corridor might be considered. Ribbentrop urged that Colonel Beck should give more thought to his suggestions. On 5 January 1939, Beck met Hitler himself at Berchtesgaden. Hitler was conciliatory. He explained at length that Germany had no interests in pursuing a Ukrainian policy inimical to Poland (Poland's territories included areas inhabited by Ukrainians and Beck was concerned about German encouragement to Ukrainian separatism). He and Beck assured each other of their mutual friendship. Beck promised to think about the proposals made by Germany. Next day, Ribbentrop suggested to Beck that Poland and Germany might work together over Ukrainian matters, including the Soviet Ukraine, but 'of course, this pre-supposed a more anti-Russian attitude on the part of Poland'. Three weeks later, Ribbentrop went to Warsaw. Once again, he spoke 'about the policy to be pursued by Poland and Germany towards the Soviet Union and in this connection also spoke about the question of the greater Ukraine and again proposed German-Polish collaboration in this field'. Beck promised careful consideration. The Poles were not pleased at Germany's action against Czechoslovakia in March, about which they had not been consulted and, though pleased by the Hungarian absorption of Ruthenia [Carpatho-Ukraine], were upset by the German assumption of 'protection' over Slovakia. On 21 March, Ribbentrop saw Lipski. The tone had changed. To the now familiar proposals, there were added some threats. 'The *Führer* was becoming increasingly amazed at Poland's attitude . . . It was important,' Ribbentrop concluded, 'that he should not form the impression that Poland simply was not willing.'[433]

The Poles were not willing. Lipski went to Warsaw, to report to Beck, in a state of extreme gloom, and talked of the possibility of a German ultimatum to Poland. Beck expounded his policy. If Polish interests were threatened, 'we shall fight'. These interests included the defence of Polish territory and of the independence of Danzig. Danzig had a symbolic importance. Poland must not become one of those eastern states which allow themselves to be dictated to. Germany had lost all sense of moderation and there was only one way of restoring it – by firm resistance, something Hitler had not yet encountered. On 26 March, Lipski delivered the Polish reply to Ribbentrop. The German request for extra-territorial status for communications across the Corridor was rejected and the only offer was of a new status for Danzig based on a joint Polish-German guarantee. Ribbentrop declared that a violation of Danzig by Polish troops would mean war. Next day, Ribbentrop told Lipski that Poland had given 'an evasive answer to the generous proposal which Germany had made . . . Relations between the two countries was therefore deteriorating sharply'. On 29 March, Beck told the German ambassador in Warsaw that any German infringement of Danzig's sovereignty would mean war with Poland. Polish troops were concentrated near Danzig, partly as a reply to the German incorporation of Memel, the Lithuanian port, into east Prussia on 23 March. On 5 April, the German foreign ministry told its ambassador in Poland that the German offer to Poland 'will not be repeated' and that there should be no more discussions.[434]

Hitler's offers to Poland were certainly genuine. From the German point of view, they were truly generous; they represented terms for a final settlement with Poland far milder than any that Stresemann would ever have contemplated. Of course, as the Poles understood, the implication was the reduction of Poland to the status of a dependent satellite. That status the Poles would not accept – Beck could not do so, for Polish opinion would not tolerate it. Poland would be independent or nothing. Before Lipski came back to Berlin, Hitler had already begun to think of using force against Poland as a substitute for offers of friendship. On 25 March, he ordered that this 'should now be worked upon'. Still, this was very tentative: 'The *Führer* does not wish to solve the Danzig question by force, however. He does not wish to drive Poland into the arms of Britain by this . . . For the present the *Führer* does not intend to solve the Polish question'. Then Hitler went off to

Berchtesgaden to think about Poland. Early in April, after Beck's reply was known and the British guarantee to Poland had been announced, orders came from Hitler to prepare for an attack on Poland, to be carried out at any time after 1 September 1939. The Polish armed forces would be destroyed. The war was to be limited to Poland, 'if possible'. However, 'German relations with Poland continued to be based on the principle of avoiding any disturbances', unless Poland were to 'change her policy towards Germany'. Next month, there was something much more definite. On 23 May, Hitler addressed the highest officers of the armed forces. Poland was now assumed to be an enemy. 'We are left with the decision: to attack Poland at the first suitable opportunity.'[435]

Meanwhile great changes had taken place in London and Paris. The destruction of Czechoslovakia in March brought the policy of appeasement into disrepute. Evidently Munich had not satisfied Hitler. The notion that reasonable settlements of limited German grievances could be arrived at was brought into question. Those who had opposed this policy all along claimed to be justified; its authors began to doubt their own work. Most important of all was the evolution in the mind of Neville Chamberlain. On 15 March, he spoke as if his policy were unchanged. By the 17th, after he had heard the reactions of British public opinion and of the House of Commons, the tone was different: 'Is this the end of an old adventure or the beginning of a new? . . . Is this in fact, a step in the direction of an attempt to dominate the world by force?' On the 19th, he wrote, 'As soon as I had time to think, I saw that it was impossible to deal with Hitler after he had thrown all his own assurances to the winds . . . I have worked out a plan'. His object was still to secure peace, not to prepare for a certain war: 'I never accept the view that war is inevitable.' Now there was to be more coercion of Hitler and less conciliation, but the conciliation was not forgotten. On 30 July, Chamberlain wrote that Germany must be convinced 'that the chances of winning a war without getting thoroughly exhausted in the process are too remote to make it worth while. But the corollary to that must be that she has a chance of getting fair and reasonable consideration and treatment from us and others, if she would give up the idea that she can force it from us, and convince us that she has given it up'. French opinion was similarly affected. Flandin, who was still an advocate of Franco-German understanding, reported in May that 'public opinion in the provinces showed a visible readiness for war'. Daladier himself, ('one of those French politicians who sense the general atmosphere particularly well' according to Flandin) seems to have moved definitely to the side of resistance to Germany after March 1939. Bonnet remained 'the most conscious and steadfast pacifist in the cabinet', but he had never risked open advocacy of his own policies and was now even less likely to do so. His public acceptance of the policy of resistance made it more difficult for him to sabotage it in private – though, as events were to show, he did his best. However, with the change in British policy, he was to be deprived of his strongest argument.[436]

As in 1938, British diplomacy took the lead. Mr. Chamberlain's 'plan' was put into action on 20 March. At that time, as a result of statements made in London by the Rumanian ambassador, it was supposed that Rumania was under a threat of attack by Germany, in collaboration with Hungary. The British government proposed 'to proceed without delay to the organization of mutual support on the part of all those who realize the necessity of protecting international society from further violation of fundamental laws on which it rests'. 'As a first step,' a declaration was proposed, to be made by France, Poland and Russia, together with Britain, that those governments would concert together on joint resistance to 'any action which constitutes a threat to the political independence of any European state'. France and Russia agreed, the latter on condition that Poland agreed too. The scheme broke down because of Poland. Beck argued that a public association between Poland and Russia might provoke Hitler into an attack on Poland. He believed that an unprovocative Polish firmness might stop Hitler. Beck seems to have believed himself to possess special skill in dealing with Germany; still, he was anxious not to throw away the reinforcement that British support might bring. He suggested a confidential Anglo-Polish agreement in the terms of the proposed declaration. He got much more support than he expected. On 27 March, the proposal was sent out that Britain would promise to help Polish or Rumanian resistance to threats to their independence. Rumania was still principally in mind – the offer to Poland was to be conditional on a Polish pledge to help Rumania.[437]

Suddenly, this proposal was superseded. On 30 March, Halifax told the cabinet that he had information that Poland was going to be attacked, perhaps at once. The principal basis seems to have been information supplied by the Berlin correspondent of the *News Chronicle*, who had talked to Halifax and Chamberlain the day before. A message to Beck was drafted by Chamberlain asking his agreement to a British guarantee of Polish independence. At the same time, the agreement of the French was secured. Beck accepted at once. Chamberlain spoke in the House of Commons on 31 March. He repeated that his government had

constantly advocated the adjustment by way of free negotiations between the parties concerned, of any differences that may arise between them . . . In their opinion, there should be no question incapable of solution by peaceful means and they could see no justification for the substitution of force or threats of force for the method of negotiation.

He explained that consultations were going on. Until they were concluded,

in the event of any action which clearly threatened Polish independence, and which the Polish government accordingly considered it vital to resist with their national forces, His Majesty's Government would feel themselves bound at once to lend the Polish government all support in their power.

The British remained anxious to secure a Polish promise to help Rumania, and, indeed, Halifax at first made the future continuance of the British guarantee to Poland dependent on Polish acquiescence, which was never secured. Still, it is clear that the guarantee to Poland was not an indirect way of arranging help for Rumania; it was the result of fears for Poland herself. This conclusion is not affected by the curious fact that Beck told the British that Germany was not threatening Poland; probably Beck wished to avoid any British attempts at mediation between Germany and Poland after the 1938 pattern. In April, British and French guarantees followed to Rumania and Greece, the latter directed against Italy.[438]

These guarantees represented a startling change in British policy. The interference of 1938 in European affairs had developed into binding commitments. French policy, superficially, had not changed. France had never ceased to assert her interest in the rest of Europe, but British activities made it more likely that French action would correspond to French words. The British guarantees were not bluff; however much the British government hoped never to be called upon to execute them, it did not diverge from a reluctant readiness to do so, if the guarantees failed to deter aggression. Hitler had decided that he must destroy a Poland he could no longer trust, and, apart from some last-minute hesitations, he did not diverge from this decision. Thus by the early summer of 1939, the international situation pointed to a European war.

In retrospect, it seems that only one thing could have changed Hitler's decision: a firm and workable Soviet commitment to the defence of Poland. This was not obtained and may not have been obtainable. It is impossible to be certain about Soviet policy since we do not know what Stalin thought it should be. Since 1934, the Soviet government had called publicly for resistance to fascist aggressors. In Spain, the policy was put into effect, without arousing any response from the west. In 1938, the Soviet Union proclaimed its readiness to join in the defence of Czechoslovakia and was ignored by the western powers. It may be, and Stalin's speech of 10 March 1939 can be used to support this view, that Stalin had come to the conclusion, by the spring of 1939 at the latest, that the Western Powers could not be trusted to resist Hitler and that, in seeking Soviet co-operation in 1939, they were trying to involve Russia in a war with Germany from which they would stand aside. If this were so, then Stalin must attempt to frustrate them, by arranging that the western powers themselves should fight Germany or, at least, by making arrangements with Germany to prevent a German attack on Russia. If Stalin had adopted this view by March, then the negotiations with Britain and France in the spring and summer of 1939 were never seriously intended. On the other hand, it is possible that it was only during the negotiations themselves that Stalin decided that a bargain with Germany was the better course; if this is correct, then Poland and the west lost an ally they could have won. Zhdanov's article in *Pravda*, on 29 June 1939, supports the latter view, if the article is to be taken at face value.

It seems to me that the English and French do not want a real agreement . . . The only thing they really want is to talk about an agreement and, by making play with the obstinacy of the Soviet Union, to prepare their own public opinion for an eventual deal with the aggressors. The next few days must show whether this is the case or not.[439]

The course of the negotiations fits either hypothesis well enough. The Russians negotiated simultaneously with both sides – with Britain and France and with Germany. The negotiations with the west were carried on with considerable publicity and close attention to detail; the talks with Germany, until the end, were much more cautious and were conducted in secret (though rumours emerged from time to time). Nothing can be drawn from these discussions to show that either set of negiotations had higher priority for the Soviet Union. Both were protracted – the Russians showed no eagerness to conclude. They mistrusted both sides – if they accepted the offers of the west, then Britain and France might use this success to force an entente on Hitler; if Russia gave a free hand to Hitler against Poland too soon, then Hitler might frighten the west into giving him a free hand in the east of Europe. Soviet diplomacy sought to encourage both sides to persist in their chosen courses; the western powers to believe that Russian assistance might be available if they resisted Germany, Hitler that Russian neutrality might be available if he attacked. The Soviet side had no difficulty in spinning out the negotiations until the time of decision. The Germans feared that the Russians might use any eagerness they showed as a means of driving the west into alliance with themselves. As for the western powers, they found real obstacles in the way of a Russian alliance. Above all, through Molotov, who had replaced Litvinov, the Russians insisted that all their neighbours should be guaranteed by the Soviet Union against aggression whether they wanted to be or not. What is more, they were to be helped against aggressors whether they wanted help or not. Even if they actively objected to it, they were to have 'assistance' just the same. The Russians used the idea of 'indirect aggression', the notion that a country might fall under German influence without a direct attack (citing the precedent of Czechoslovakia in March 1939), to give them a pretext to interfere in any neighbouring country that seemed to them to be turning pro-German. The British government, which was genuinely concerned about the independence of small states, hesitated to accept this.

Again, and this was the point at which negotiations ended, the Russians insisted that Britain and France should secure the Polish government's consent to the passage of Russian troops across Polish territory if Russia were to 'help' Poland against Germany. This the Poles refused to give. The British would not coerce the Poles into giving it. They feared that if they tried to do so, Poland would go back to the German side and there would then be even less restraint on German aggression than if the Russian alliance were not secured.

The dénouement came in August. On 14 August, while the British and French military missions were in Moscow, the Germans began to show great eagerness to reach an immediate settlement with the USSR. Molotov was cautious and spoke of preparing the ground carefully. On the 18th, Ribbentrop instructed the German ambassador in Moscow to press for immediate discussions and expressed readiness to parcel out spheres of interest. On the 19th, Stalin agreed that Ribbentrop could come to Moscow, but only after a week's delay. On the 21st, Hitler himself urged Stalin to receive Ribbentrop on the 22nd or 23rd. Stalin agreed to the 23rd. The sudden burst of energy on the part of the Germans probably convinced Stalin that a German attack was imminent. By that time of year, it would be too late for an attack on Russia. Stalin could safely listen to German offers; Germany would attack Poland; then Britain and France might declare war, which would be good, or might not, in which case Stalin would have secured the most favourable position for the future. On the 21st, the Germans announced that a non-aggression pact would be signed with the Soviet Union. On 23 August, it was signed. A secret protocol set out agreed Russian spheres of interest in Finland, Esthonia, Latvia, much of Poland, and in Bessarabia, which had returned to Rumania after 1918. This was the bribe for Russian neutrality.[440]

Fortified by good news from Russia, Hitler expressed his intentions on various occasions in August. On 12 August, to Ciano, the Italian Foreign Minister, on 14 August, to the Chief of the army General Staff and other officers, and on 22 August, to the army and army group commanders, Hitler expounded broadly similar arguments. Poland had to be dealt with because it could not be trusted not to go against Germany in a future German war in the west. Arrangements could be made with Russia. Britain and France would almost certainly do nothing; if they did try to help Poland, it would probably be only a matter of a trade embargo, if they went to war, their intervention could not save Poland, which could quickly be destroyed without the western powers being able to launch serious attacks. If Britain and France went to war in earnest, it would only confirm that war with them was inevitable; the main German forces could be concentrated against them after a few weeks. It appears that Hitler was ready to risk war with Britain and France, even if he did not think it likely. After all, in such a war, Britain and France would appear to be the aggressors to German public opinion, which was firmly convinced of the reality of German grievances against Poland. On the 23rd, the date of the attack on Poland was fixed for August 26th.[441]

On the 25th, however, Hitler succumbed to indecision. The order for the attack was cancelled. The main reason seems to have been the attitude of Mussolini, whom Hitler always took seriously, and whose participation in a war would be highly desirable if Britain and France were to come in. On that day, Mussolini informed Hitler that he could not enter a general war without German supplies. On the same day, news came that Britain and Poland had just signed a formal treaty of mutual assistance; this made British and therefore French intervention seem more likely. Hitler now devoted himself to arranging Britain's neutrality and Italian readiness to come in. Both failed. Next day, requests for supplies, deliberately made to be impossible of fulfilment, arrived from Mussolini. On the other hand, hopes revived that Britain might stay out of war, although Hitler wrote to Mussolini on the 26th: 'As neither France nor Britain can achieve decisive successes in the west . . . I do not shrink from solving the eastern question even at the risk of complications in the west.' Hitler had not left himself much time. As he had told Ciano, the German general staff thought four to six weeks necessary for the elimination of Poland; after the middle of October, fog and mud might make military movements impossible. As late as the 30th, indecision continued. On that day, Hitler told the army command that the invasion would take place on 1 or 2 September or, after then, not at all. Next morning, things were different. Hitler had slept well, according to Halder's notes. Early in the morning, Halder was told that the invasion was to start on 1 September. Later he heard the time: 'Fixing of time of attack for 0445; intervention of west said to be unavoidable: in spite of this, *Führer* has decided to attack.' In fact, hopes of western neutrality remained, 'hopes that Mu[ssolini]s influence will contribute to the avoidance of big conflict', while Göring's impression was that 'England wants to keep out'. These were not certainties. Rather than postpone action against Poland, Hitler chose to risk war with Britain and France. Early on 1 September, the German attack began.[442]

Hitler's decision made war with Britain inevitable. This is a controversial assertion: it has often been argued that the British government and, above all, Chamberlain, having hastily guaranteed Poland at the end of March, were anxious thereafter to escape the consequences. If Hitler did not climb down, they would climb down instead. It is, of course, true that the British government thought of the Polish guarantee as a means of securing peace, not as a preliminary to war. Like all civilized governments, they went to war reluctantly. But the larger suggestion is made that British ministers were reverting, in the summer of 1939, to the policy of 1938, of accepting the idea of concessions to Hitler, even if those concessions involved the weakening or destruction of the independence of another country – Poland. This was certainly not the publicly proclaimed policy of Britain, which was to defend Polish independence if it were threatened. The evidence for the existence of a different, half-concealed policy is as follows: in British attitudes to Germany as exposed in various exchanges between British and German spokesmen in the three months before the war, in the British attitude to Poland after the guarantee was given and especially in the days immediately preceding the German invasion, and in the delay in the British declaration of war after the invasion. These pieces of evidence must be considered in turn.

There were several contacts between the British government and emissaries of Göring, who seemed to have taken upon himself the rôle of peacemaker with Britain, in June, July and August 1939. The principal persons involved were two Swedish businessmen, Wenner-Gren and Dahlerus, and Göring's subordinate, Wohlthat. The most important talks were those between Wohlthat and Sir Horace Wilson, Mr Chamberlain's closest collaborator. All of these discussions dealt with the same themes. On the German side, it was suggested that there was no reason for Britain to concern herself with eastern Europe since Germany would never present any threat to fundamental British interests. On the British side, it was constantly reiterated that German conduct had aroused mistrust, especially in destroying Czechoslovakia, and that, in future, force would be met by force. However, if only Germany would somehow demonstrate that she was to be trusted after all and if only Hitler would renounce force and threats of force, then all sorts of things would become possible. A 'general settlement' could be worked out, German claims in Danzig and Poland could be considered calmly, projects for disarmament could easily be revived. The only rational basis the British could see for Hitler's foreign policy was an economic one – therefore they promised economic co-operation in the future and an acceptance of the economic preponderance of Germany in eastern and south-eastern Europe.

The most striking evidence in favour of the view that Chamberlain was eager to escape from the post-March policy of 1939 is Wohlthat's report of his talks with Wilson in July. From this, it seems that Wilson was insistent that there should not be any aggression, but was ready to think that this might be guaranteed by a mere 'declaration'.

Here Sir Horace takes the view that such a declaration would make Britain's guarantees to Poland and Rumania superfluous, since, as a result of such a declaration, Germany would not attack these states, and they could not therefore feel that their national existence was threatened by Germany.

According to his own report, Wilson said that all the British commitments

were entirely defensive and if it was once made clear by the German government that there was henceforth to be no aggression on their part, the policy of guarantees to potential victims *ipso facto* became inoperative.

Probably Wilson supposed that he was simply stating the obvious – if Germany did not attack anyone and underwent a change of heart, the British guarantees would become irrelevant. Even in Wohlthat's July report, Wilson spoke with some firmness:

Certainly the British government would not like to create the impression that they desire to negotiate in all circumstances. If no other solution is possible, Britain and the Empire were today ready for, and determined upon, an armed conflict.

But it is understandable that Ribbentrop and Hitler should make the mistake of concluding that the British government was not in earnest, even though all these remarks are compatible with the policy set out in Lord Halifax's speech in June:

If we could once be satisfied . . . that we all really wanted peaceful solutions . . . we could discuss the problems that are today causing the world anxiety . . . but that is not the position that we face today. The threat of military force is holding the world to ransom, and our immediate task is to resist aggression.

Exactly the same impression as that presented in this speech was given by various leading 'appeasers' at Cliveden, and by Chamberlain himself, to Adam von Trott zu Solz, when he visited England early in June.[443]

A piece of evidence, which attracted Hitler's attention at the time, was the curious affair of the failure of negotiations for a British loan to Poland. It seems, however, that this was the result, not of any shift of foreign policy, but simply of the insistence of the British Treasury on what it regarded as economically acceptable terms.

With the crisis approaching, a letter from Mr Chamberlain was taken to Hitler by Henderson, the British ambassador in Berlin, on 23 August. This began the diplomacy of the last days of peace. The letter denied that the Nazi-Soviet pact would change British policy: 'It cannot alter Great Britain's obligation to Poland which His Majesty's Government have stated in public repeatedly and plainly and which they are determined to fulfil . . . If the case should arise, they are resolved, and prepared, to employ without delay all the forces at their command.' Any possibility of peace after Hitler had conquered Poland was ruled out. 'It would be a dangerous illusion to think that if war once starts, it will come to an early end, even if a success on any one of the several fronts . . . should have been secured.' More conciliatory utterances followed:

I cannot see that there is anything in the questions arising between Germany and Poland which could not and should not be resolved without the use of force, if only a situation of confidence could be restored.

Then there might be direct negotiations between Germany and Poland. Hitler's reply was uncompromising and threatening.

Two days later, on 25 August, Hitler changed his mind. He summoned the British ambassador, explained to him that he was 'a man of great decisions' and urged Henderson to fly to London with his 'last offer'. He expressed determination to 'solve' the Polish problem. However, if war was avoided, *i.e.*, if Britain abandoned Poland, he would guarantee the British Empire and place the power of Germany at its disposal, provided his demands for colonies were satisfied sometime in the future. Meanwhile, 'the *Führer* renewed his assurances that he is not interested in Western problems'. The British reply rejected this clumsy attempt to secure a free hand. The British 'could not, for any advantage offered to Great Britain, acquiesce in a settlement which put in jeopardy the independence of a state to whom they had given their guarantee.' It went on to suggest direct German-Polish negotiations, which the Poles had agreed to. Hitler was given this reply late on 28 August. At 7.15 p.m. on the 29th, Henderson was given the German answer. It demanded that a Polish plenipotentiary should appear in Berlin next day, the 30th. The way thoughts were moving in Berlin is shown by Halder's notes: he wrote on the 28th: 'We demand Danzig, Corridor through Corridor, and plebiscite . . . England will perhaps accept. Poland probably not. *Wedge between them*!' And on the 29th, he wrote: '30·8 Poles in Berlin. 31·8 Breakdown. 1·9 Use of force.'[444]

This attempt to divide Britain from Poland failed. Beck refused to send a plenipotentiary, and Halifax agreed that he should not. However, Halifax urged the Poles to enter into direct discussions with the German government 'provided method and general arrangement for discussions can be satisfactorily agreed'. The British ambassador in Warsaw was told to convey this message after midnight on 30/31 August. At that time, Henderson saw Ribbentrop who read out the German demands on Poland, demands which he now claimed to be irrelevant, since no Polish plenipotentiary had appeared. On the 31st, the Poles agreed to take steps to contact the German government, but ordered their ambassador not to receive any demands until methods of procedure had been worked out. At 12.50 a.m., on 1 September, Halifax sent a telegram to Warsaw urging the Poles to instruct their ambassador in Berlin to accept a document containing German demands. This was expressed only as an earnest hope and Halifax agreed that the Poles should insist on discussions about how negotiations were to be conducted before getting on with them.

A few hours later the German attack supervened. It is clearly going too far to say that 'Given another twenty-four hours and the breach [between Britain and Poland] would be wide open.' Nor is it acceptable to say that Hitler became involved in war through launching on 29 August, a diplomatic manoeuvre [i.e. the demand for a Polish plenipotentiary] which he ought to have launched on 28 August.[445] Hitler became involved in war with Poland because he chose to attack; war with Britain and France necessarily followed. There is no evidence to suggest that the British were preparing to desert Poland if the Poles refused to discuss Hitler's demands, or preparing to impose those demands on the Poles by a threat of withdrawal of their support. The Germans, who certainly still hoped for British and French neutrality, may have been misled by their knowledge of Henderson's views on the Poles; he no longer represented the views of his government. Even Chamberlain's remarks, of 23 and 30 August, to Joseph P. Kennedy, the American ambassador in London, did not go so far as some of Henderson's. Chamberlain was depressed by the prospect of war and recognised that the west could not save Poland. He hoped that the Poles would be ready to negotiate and feared that they might not. He hoped that Hitler might be tempted into a peaceful settlement. Still, he did not hint at any coercion of the Poles.[446]

We must now turn to the events between the German invasion and the British and French declarations of war. On 31 August, Ciano had telephoned a proposal from Mussolini for a conference to meet on 5 September to consider changes in the Treaty of Versailles, (*i.e.* to negotiate concessions for Hitler). The proposal opened a breach between Britain and France. Chamberlain's reaction was, 'that it was impossible to agree to a conference under the threat of mobilized armies', Daladier's, 'that he would rather resign than accept'. This was not Bonnet's view. Already, on 23 August, he had raised the question of whether France should honour her alliance with Poland. Now, he contrived to persuade the French cabinet to accept Mussolini's suggestion, though only on condition that Poland should be represented. On 1 September, Halifax instructed the British ambassador in Rome to reply that, 'it would seem . . . that the action of the German government has now rendered it impossible to proceed along those lines'. A quite different reply came from the French: 'a favourable reply.' Encouraged by this, and by a softening of Halifax's negative reply by the British ambassador in Rome, the Italians put their plan to Hitler, on the basis of an armistice leaving the armies where they were. (Bonnet, without consulting the British, urged the Poles to accept, receiving a contemptuous rebuff.)[447] The Germans seized the chance of gaining more time. 'The *Führer* . . . would draft an answer in a day or two.' Early in the afternoon of the 2nd, Ciano telephoned to Bonnet and Halifax to say that Hitler might accept a conference. Bonnet replied that the French would be in favour; Halifax, on the other hand, thought that the British government could not 'contemplate a conference with German troops on Polish soil.' Halifax confirmed this after a meeting of the cabinet later in the afternoon. That was the end of that.[448] Hitler had no intention of withdrawing from Poland and no interest in a Munich-type settlement. Even so, Bonnet made a last attempt, after the French cabinet had followed the British line on the evening of the 2nd. He suggested to Ciano that he might persuade the Germans to carry out a 'symbolic' withdrawal in order to get the British to withdraw their veto. Ciano did not bother to try. Thus Bonnet's attempts to escape were made hopeless by the British government.[449]

Last of all, there is the delay in declaring war. According to Bonnet, Halifax wished to deliver an ultimatum to Germany on 1 September, rather than the warning note which was delivered that day in Berlin. Bonnet insisted that the French constitution required parliamentary authorization before an ultimatum could be dispatched and added that the French parliament could only meet on the 2nd. This delayed British action. Kennedy reported, in the afternoon of the 1st,

They are anxious here closely to parallel French action, both in timing and form, and are desirous of avoiding giving the impression that Great Britain is dragging France into war. They wish rather to impress on the French public... that Great Britain is backing her ally France.

This point had been emphasized by the British ambassador in Paris. Then, on the 2nd, Bonnet urged an ultimatum with a forty-eight hours' time limit, which would have put off the outbreak of war to the 4th or 5th. His argument was that the French general staff wished mobilization to proceed unhindered, and big towns to be evacuated. This was too much for the British cabinet. On the afternoon of the 2nd, they agreed that war should begin at midnight.[450] Bonnet was unmoved. Halifax brought further pressure to bear, so that Chamberlain could produce a statement to the House of Commons, but was told that the French cabinet would be in session until 8 or 9 p.m. As a result, Chamberlain could only tell the House, at 8 p.m., that the British were in touch with the French about a time limit for a German acceptance of withdrawal of their forces from Poland. The result was a bitter outburst against Chamberlain in the House and among the cabinet. He was suspected of betrayal. It was clear that war must be declared before the House of Commons met at twelve the next day. Chamberlain telephoned to Daladier and found him insistent that France would not act before that time. Thus the British ultimatum was delivered at 9 a.m. and the French at 12 noon. Britain went to war with Germany at 11 a.m. on 3 September, France at 5 p.m. Clearly France caused the delay. However, even if Chamberlain had wished to evade the British pledge to Poland, he could not have done so, – British public opinion as expressed by the House of Commons would have compelled him to war.[451]

The short-term cause of the European war was Hitler's decision to attack Poland. The long-term reason was the growing conviction in British and French minds that Germany could not be allowed to become dominant in Europe. Hence a free hand for Germany in the east was refused. With Germany in command of the east of Europe, it was believed that the west could not be secure. The nature of Hitler's régime made this belief convincing. For Britain and France, the war was defensive. But modern wars require a moral basis, since they need mass-support. Thus the war immediately became a war for the destruction of Nazism. This was as good a war aim as any can be.

14

The Second World War

The war opened in September 1939 with Hitler's attack on Poland and the British and French declarations of war. Poland was conquered within a few weeks and the last pocket of organized resistance was destroyed on 6 October. The first phase of the war ended in June 1940 when France capitulated. From then until June 1941, Britain, almost alone, frustrated German attempts to compel or persuade her to make peace. In the summer of 1941, Germany attacked Russia. In December 1941, the war expanded into a world war when Japan attacked the United States, an attack immediately followed by a German declaration of war on the United States.

The European war, between September 1939 and December 1941, was dominated by the German strategy of *Blitzkrieg*. Hitler's intention was to limit conflicts between land forces to a series of short, decisive campaigns. It was war on the cheap, not total war. (As late as 1942, civilian consumption in Germany was almost as high as it had been in 1937.)[452] The military means were mobile armoured forces and motorized infantry, acting as spear-heads for slower moving infantry which was used to consolidate rapid advances by the mobile divisions, with aircraft, especially dive-bombers, used as highly flexible artillery. Airborne troops gave further tactical flexibility. Within this period, Hitler's methods enabled him to conquer Poland, Denmark, Norway, Holland, Belgium, France, Yugoslavia, Greece and much of European Russia and gave him dominance over Hungary, Rumania and Bulgaria. Of these conquests, Poland, Holland, Belgium, France and Russia were the result of German initiatives; the others were reactions to actual or anticipated moves by the enemy.

British and French strategy was defensive. German attacks on Britain and France were to be beaten off until the Allies had built up their strength to the point at which an offensive might be launched.

Meanwhile economic pressure – blockade and eventually bombing – would reduce enemy powers of resistance.[453] The British conceived of the application of economic pressure as their major contribution to the war – until March 1939, only two divisions were to go to France, with two more nearly a year later. However in that month, the commitments were doubled, and the government decided to expand the British army to an eventual thirty-two divisions. (In fact, there were thirteen British divisions in France on 10 May 1940, three of which were not fully trained or equipped.[454]) French determination to wait to be attacked rather than to attack themselves was shown most clearly in September 1939, when there were few German forces in the west.

The Norwegian campaign, however, came about as a result of a forward move by the allies. An essential source of iron-ore for Germany came from the mines in north Sweden: during the winter most of their production had to be exported through the ice-free port of Narvik in Norway. From Narvik, ships could sail to Germany within Norwegian territorial waters. To curtail the trade through Narvik would be useful, to seize the ore-fields themselves might be decisive. Thus when the Russians tried to impose their demands for bases in Finland by invasion, in December 1939 – March 1940, schemes were worked out by the allies for helping Finland. Norway and Sweden might be persuaded to allow passage of allied troops by rail from Narvik and Trondheim to Finland. On the way, they could move through the ore-fields. The railway line would then be guarded by a strong force. If the Germans countered by attacking Norway and Sweden, the allies would be there first and in a good position to resist. This ingenious scheme fell through when Finnish resistance ended. Another scheme was accepted early in April. Mines would be laid in Norwegian waters, and, if the Germans then attacked Norway, allied forces would land in the north, presumably with Norwegian consent. The Germans suspected that the allies had ideas of this kind. As early as December 1939, Hitler ordered plans to be made for a German occupation of Norway. On 9 April 1940, the allies found they had been anticipated: the Germans had seized Copenhagen, Oslo, Stavanger, Bergen, Trondheim and Narvik. British and French preparations had been made for unopposed landings: now they were faced with a quite different problem. Their replies were correspondingly disorganized. Narvik was taken only at the end of May and was evacuated again a week later. The campaign cost the German navy serious losses; on the other hand it demonstrated one of the dominating facts of the war – that it was dangerous for surface ships to operate, without air cover, in areas controlled by hostile aircraft.[455]

The western campaign of 1940 was the classical *Blitzkrieg* operation. Yet if most of the senior generals, German and French, had had their way, nothing would have happened at all. The French had no desire to attack; neither had the Germans. The senior officers of the German army command (OKH), including Brauchitsch, the Commander-in-Chief, and Halder, the Chief of the General Staff, hoped for peace, not for a European war, and doubted if it was possible to crush France and Britain. Hitler overruled them. In October 1939, he ordered that the attack should begin on 12 November. The date was postponed twenty-nine times as a result of bad weather and objections from the army commanders. It began on 10 May 1940, an altogether more suitable time for mobile operations than any previous date.[456] Hitler had no intention of allowing the war to settle down into a protracted affair in which economic strength would count as much as military, and rightly believed that it was necessary to secure Germany's position in Europe before the USA and the USSR were willing to intervene. He thought that the defeat of France would automatically cause Britain to leave the war (after all, he had no desire to weaken the British Empire) and he believed that, once the British were shown that they could not use continental allies against Germany, they would see reason and cease to oppose German domination of Europe. It was clear from the start that the attack would include the invasion of Holland, Belgium and Luxembourg, partly to avoid a frontal attack on the French fortifications on the frontier, partly to secure bases from which to threaten Britain.

The original German plan bore some resemblance to the pre-1914 Schlieffen plan: the weight of the German concentration would be on the right wing, north of Liège. The actual attack was based on quite different German dispositions, worked out by OKH, after repeated suggestions from General von Rundstedt's chief of staff, Manstein, had been taken up by Hitler. The new plan allotted the main weight of attack to the German army group under Rundstedt, with the bulk of the German armoured units. They were to secure crossings across the Meuse, between Namur and Sedan, and exploit westwards to the sea to cut off the allied troops which, as was known, would advance into Belgium to meet what now became the subsidiary German attack on Holland and Belgium. This concept brought about the defeat of France.

This defeat was a military defeat, in the sense that it was not rendered certain in advance by any disparity in the forces available to the contending commanders. This assertion runs counter to the line of argument which regards the outcome of military operations as necessarily predetermined by fundamental causes of a non-military kind, a line of argument which, as has been shown elsewhere, has had great appeal to those concerned to blame the French defeat on civilian mismanagement rather than military errors. To assert the contrary does not mean that all the causes of French defeat are to be found after 10 May, only that the pre-existing causes – errors of doctrine, training, organization and deployment – were matters within the command of the military authorities and that there was nothing in the nature of French society or education which necessarily created soldiers predisposed to make those errors.

Germany was inherently far stronger than France, and British power was not yet sufficiently mobilized to make up the difference. But this inherent disparity was not reflected in the balance of armed force in May 1940: that balance made it possible for France to be defended. On the German side, 114 divisions were available on the western front, a total which rose to a maximum of 142 by 23 June. These included ten Panzer (armoured) divisions, six motorized infantry divisions, one horsed cavalry division, three mountain divisions and forty-six infantry divisions of the first échelon. This meant sixty-six divisions of high quality. The French had the equivalent of ninety-one divisions on the north-eastern front, of which three were armoured, three were light mechanised divisions (DLM), and five of cavalry. Of the eighty infantry divisions, thirty-one had a preponderance of regular troops. The British had ten divisions of good quality. To these, provided the allies advanced into Belgium, could be added twenty Belgian divisions and eight Dutch. Including the British, but not the Dutch or Belgians, the allies had available fifty-two divisions of high quality. One further French armoured division, and one DLM, were in process of formation, while a British armoured division arrived late in May. Since the French DLM was, in fact, the equivalent of an armoured division, the disparity in major armoured units between the French and German armies was smaller than might appear. In total numbers of tanks, there was something like equality: the French had about 2,250 modern tanks, to which should be added about two hundred British tanks, the Germans about 2,500. French tanks were, on the whole, superior in armament and armour to the German tanks, though not in speed and radius of action. In the air, the allies were decidedly inferior. The Germans employed about 3,500 aircraft against about eight hundred French. There were over four hundred British aircraft in France at the beginning of the battle, which received some reinforcement during the battle, together with assistance from British-based aircraft. It seems that shortage of trained crews reduced the number of French aircraft available for operations to a figure well below what production had made possible.[457]

The allied plans for the battle might have provided an effective counter to the original German plan of attack. A strong left wing, including the British, was to advance into Belgium, link up with Belgian and Dutch forces, and form a front facing east. Between Namur and Antwerp, there were placed seventeen British and French infantry divisions, on a front of forty-two miles, with the Belgian army on their left completing the line. Another French army, of seven divisions, advanced to the mouth of the Scheldt. In the area where the heaviest German attack was to fall, twelve divisions, plus cavalry, held ninety miles between Longwy and Namur. Further south, thirty-six infantry divisions held the Maginot line sector. There were thirteen divisions in reserve, including the armoured divisions. Against the German attack, the Rhineland front was held in unnecessary strength, the left had a disproportionate share of the mobile units (about four-fifths) and the centre, or hinge, where the main German attack fell, was too weak. Mobile reserves were insufficient against a fast moving enemy. Even so, there were two occasions when the French armoured divisions might have interfered with the German victory. That victory rested on crossings of the Meuse in two places – near Dinant and near Sedan – on 13 May, and rapid advance by the Panzer divisions to the sea, which was reached on 20 May, thus cutting off the northern armies. French counter-attacks could have been launched against the Meuse bridge-heads immediately after they were established, or an attempt made to cut the German corridor to the sea, behind the advancing Panzer spear-heads and before the German flanks were consolidated. Thus, the 3rd armoured division could have attacked the Dinant bridge-head and the 1st towards Sedan with some prospects of success. Both attacks were mishandled, and delayed until too late, and those attacks made impossible the assembly by the French of a powerful spear-head for operations to cut the German corridor to the sea. (The acute German sensitivity to the latter possibility was shown, for example, by the near panic that a quite small British attack southwards from Arras created on 21 May.[458])

With the encirclement of the allied armies in the north, and the failure, amidst the consequent disorganization, of attempted counter-attacks on the German corridor to the sea, France was doomed. A new French line on the Somme-Aisne was hastily organized but the Germans were able to attack with greatly superior strength on 5 June. By the 12th, a breakthrough was made, and the French retreat turned into a rout. Reynaud, the Prime Minister, seems to have wished to continue the war from French North Africa, and there were many others who would have followed the government if it had done so. However, Reynaud's own appointments were damaging the cause of resistance – above all, that of Pétain, as deputy Prime Minister, and Weygand, as Commander-in-Chief. Weygand urged an armistice. The grounds were numerous – the war was lost, Britain could not survive alone, and further resistance could bring only a futile increase in suffering; there was fear of social revolution, if constituted authority broke down in France; there was a confused desire to keep some remnant of French sovereignty alive in France itself and a less confused desire to destroy republican democracy and inaugurate a 'new' France, under authoritarian direction, using Pétain as a figurehead. Reynaud's cabinet was divided, and Chautemps, out of parliamentary habit, produced a compromise – armistice terms would be asked, which would be so harsh that resistance would impose itself on all. This rallied a majority of Reynaud's cabinet. Reynaud tried to secure President Lebrun's support for the formation of a government of combat; the President preferred to follow the cabinet majority, and gave Pétain power to form a government of capitulation.[459] An armistice was signed with Germany, on 22 June, and with Italy, whose belated attack was wholly unsuccessful, on the 25th. Most Frenchmen accepted this surrender by the legal government; a few followed General de Gaulle, who appealed for continued war on 18 June. This opened a split in French political life which has not yet completely disappeared. At first, de Gaulle had little support outside French Equatorial Africa but as time went on, and his attitude of 1940 was more and more justified, he came to be the symbol of French independence, independence of the allies as well as of the Germans, against the conservative 'national revolution' of Pétain's government at Vichy. This split was not simply between right and left, but, on the whole, Vichy was supported by the conservative, prosperous, clerical, section of French life, while de Gaulle, though he and many of his leading associates were equally conservative, appealed most strongly to the radical, progressive, democratic, section of French society.

Mussolini had contemplated the war with uneasy embarrassment. He was torn between fear of Franco-British strength in the Mediterranean and dislike of the non-virile and unsuitable position of neutral dictator. The German victory in France removed the fears and, on 10 June, Italy declared war on Britain and France. Mussolini's object was to secure a place in the partitioning of the French Empire and, perhaps, the British as well; he involved Italy in an unwanted, unnecessary and destructive war.

For the war was not over. Hitler hoped that the British would now see reason; he asked for nothing beyond the return of former German colonies. The British obstinately declined to allow Hitler a free hand in Europe. On the contrary, they insisted that they were determined to defeat Germany. This conviction was expressed and fortified by the Prime Minister, Winston Churchill: 'We shall defend our Island home, and with the British Empire we shall fight on unconquerable until the curse of Hitler is lifted from the brows of mankind. We are sure that in the end all will come right.' The possibilities of defence were clear; if the Germans could be denied air supremacy, they would find it difficult to prevent crippling interference with an invasion of England by bombers and by superior British naval forces. The possibility of British victory in the war was much more obscure; blockade and bombing, together with revolts in German-occupied Europe, were relied on to make it possible for quite small land forces to deliver a final blow. This was highly optimistic. However, the assessment of the threat of invasion fitted that made by the Germans themselves. In July 1940, Hitler began to consider seriously the conquest of Russia; in that month he allotted the summer of 1941 for that crowning task. It would be convenient to end British resistance first. On 16 July, Hitler ordered preparations for the invasion of England. The navy insisted that air superiority must be secured and Hitler accepted this view. By 15 September, it was clear that this condition had not been met, and on the 17th, Hitler postponed the invasion indefinitely.[460] This was a serious defeat. It meant, above all, that if the USA were involved in the war, a first class base would exist from which to bring allied power to bear against Hitler's Europe.

Hitler's strategy was now dominated by the coming struggle with Russia. Against Britain there remained the economic war, principally from submarines and bombing, the former nearly successful, the latter ineffective. There was time before the war with Russia to attack British power more directly; final destruction could be left until Russia had been dealt with. Thus, in 1940, the Germans worked out an attack on Gibraltar and planned to encourage Mussolini's invasion of Egypt, if necessary with land forces. Britain would be excluded from the Mediterranean and her control of the Middle East, including the oil-producing areas, threatened. These operations failed – Franco ungratefully refused to bring Spain into the war while Mussolini found himself in danger of being driven out of North Africa rather than driving the British out of Egypt. Furthermore, Mussolini launched a war of his own – apparently largely to demonstrate his independence of Germany – by attacking Greece from Albania. The Italian attack failed.

A result was the appearance of British air forces in Crete and Greece, which did not amount to much, but suggested that British bombers might be able to reach the Rumanian oil-fields. Hitler intervened to reverse the consequences of Italian mismanagement. An invasion of Greece was ordered with Bulgarian and Yugoslavian co-operation. When Yugoslavia, after a coup d'état in Belgrade, rejected co-operation with the axis powers that country was itself marked down for destruction. On 6 April, German forces attacked Yugoslavia and Greece; both were conquered by the end of the month and, in May, Crete was taken – largely by airborne forces. These operations, extended by the defection of Yugoslavia, produced a delay of about four weeks in the great attack on Russia. To rescue Mussolini in Africa, German air forces were based in Sicily, and in February 1941, the German Africa Corps was dispatched to Libya under General Rommel.

On 22 June 1941, the great operation against Russia, 'Barbarossa', began. Russia was to be crushed in a rapid campaign and a barrier created against Asiatic Russia on the line Volga-Archangel. From that line, the German air force could destroy the last surviving industrial areas of Russia in the Urals. The newly conquered territories in the east were to be exploited economically. (One aspect of the *Blitzkrieg* strategy was shown by Hitler's directive, issued before the campaign had even begun, that armaments production for the army could be reduced and the main efforts of industry devoted to the navy and air force, for future operations against Britain.) By October, the Russian army seemed very near collapse. Concentrations of Panzer divisions repeatedly broke up Russian linear deployments and created encirclements which the infantry then cleared up. The German army had carried out the most successful offensive of the whole of history: probably about three million Russian soldiers had been killed or taken prisoner. The Germans had destroyed forces roughly equivalent to their own strength at the beginning of the campaign. In the same month, however, things began to go wrong, with rain and mud weakening already strained lines of communication and the fighting strength of mobile units. In December, the Russian winter descended on the unprepared German forces. The surviving Russian forces and their commanders were becoming more skilled and they were reinforced by levies in the rear, and by seasoned troops from the Far East. On 5 December, the Russians counter-attacked in front of Moscow. This was the end of Hitler's *Blitzkrieg*. Though great successes were secured in Russia, and in Africa, in 1942, and the end of German advance came only with Stalingrad and El Alamein at the end of the year, yet from

December 1941 the war had become the sort of war that Hitler had planned to avoid; a protracted struggle in which resources of man-power and munitions would determine the result. Germany was certain to be defeated for the United States were now ranged against her.

On 7 December 1941, Japanese aircraft, from carriers, successfully attacked the bulk of the US Pacific fleet (less aircraft carriers) at Pearl Harbor. The European war gave Japan the prospect of success in her long-term aim, the building up of an economically self-sufficient area in eastern Asia under Japanese control – the Greater East Asian co-prosperity sphere. It should include at least French Indo-China, British Malaya and the Dutch East Indies as well as Manchuria and the most important areas of China. The defeat of France, the German occupation of the Dutch homeland, the threats to Britain in Europe and Africa, together with the German attack on Russia, weakened or eliminated every potential opponent except one – the USA. The United States government, too, was preoccupied by the German threat. Ever since 1931 the USA had expressed disapproval of Japanese expansion through the use of force; after 1940, she tried to make Japan believe that America would join in resistance to Japanese attempts at conquest at the expense of the European friends of the USA, without actually pledging herself to do so. In 1940, exports to Japan of iron and steel scrap were stopped, and from August 1941, export of oil to Japan was forbidden. Since the Dutch applied a similar embargo, Japan faced a crisis. If these restrictions continued, the Japanese economy and war machine would be slowly strangled and Japan would be forced to with-draw from China, or Japan would be forced to accept America's terms for a settlement, but these equally meant withdrawal from China and renunciation of conquest. The further alternative was war, to break through the threatening economic encirclement and use force to seize the materials required to sustain that force. Growing United States pressure enabled the Japanese army to persuade the more cautious Emperor, and the heads of the Japanese navy, that the desperate gamble of war could not be avoided.[461]

Hitler had been eager for Japanese action, to distract the USA and thus weaken Britain. In April 1941, Hitler promised that Germany would declare war on the United States if Japan made war. On 29 November, this promise was repeated to the Japanese. Hitler kept his word. On 11 December, Germany declared war on the USA. President Roosevelt and his advisers certainly wished for (and expected) this event; it was extremely convenient for them not to have to persuade Congress to take the initiative. Hitler, on his side, may simply have

345

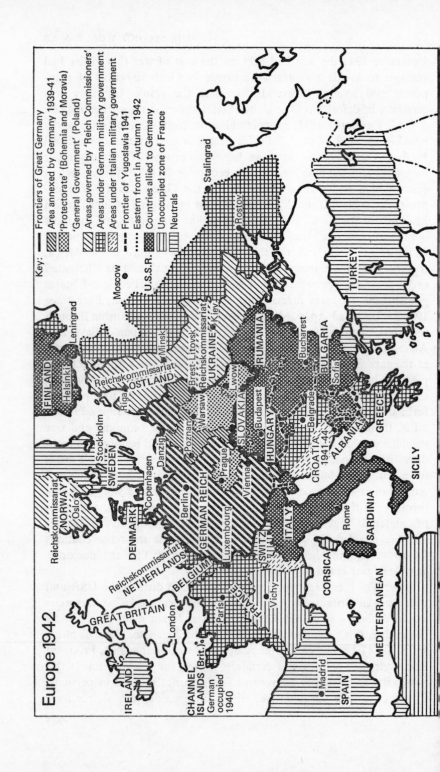

Europe 1942

Key:
Frontiers of Great Germany
Area annexed by Germany 1939-41
'Protectorate' (Bohemia and Moravia)
'General Government' (Poland)
Areas governed by 'Reich Commissioners'
Areas under German military government
Areas under Italian military government
Frontier of Yugoslavia 1941
Eastern front in Autumn 1942
Countries allied to Germany
Unoccupied zone of France
Neutrals

been anxious to honour his pledges. More probably he felt that it would make very little difference to have the United States formally in the war. United States' determination to prevent British defeat had already become clear. In March 1941, the Lend-Lease Act empowered the President to provide munitions of war to other countries without payment: this was applied to help both Britain and Russia on an increasing scale. From September 1941 American warships and aircraft began to protect trans-Atlantic convoys. Hitler still expected to defeat Russia in 1942 and then a consolidated continental European fortress could defy America.

United States entry into the war made certain that the struggle would become one of competing economic power; such a contest Hitler was bound to lose. The balance of forces is best shown in some figures.

VALUE OF WAR PRODUCTION IN 1943
(in thousand million dollars)[462]

Allied		Axis	
U.S.A.	37·5	Germany	13·8
Britain	11·1	Japan	4.5
U.S.S.R.	13·9		

TANK PRODUCTION 1940–44[463]

	Germany	U.K.	U.S.A.
1940	1,459	1,399	331
1941	3,256	4,841	4,052
1942	4,098	8,611	24,997
1943	6,083	7,476	29,497
1944	8,466	2,476	17,565
		(1st 6 months)	

AIRCRAFT PRODUCTION 1939–44[464]

	Japan	Germany	U.K.	U.S.A.
1939	4,467	8,295	7,940	2,141
1940	4,768	10,826	15,049	6,086
1941	5,088	11,776	20,094	19,443
1942	8,861	15,556	23,672	47,836
1943	16,693	25,527	26,263	85,898
1944	21,180	39,807	26,461	96,318

(Stalin claimed that Russia produced 40,000 aircraft in 1944)

It is surprising that the war lasted until 1945. One reason was that allied lines of communication were long, largely seaborne, and vulnerable to attack, while Germany had the excellent land communications of Europe at her disposal, which were shorter, quicker, and vulnerable only to bombing. Until allied communications were secure the full power of the USA could not be brought to bear on Germany. Until 1942, German attacks on shipping, especially from submarines, seriously threatened allied power and, at times, faced Britain with imminent defeat. In the years 1939–42, sixteen and a half million tons of allied shipping were sunk and just over seven million tons of new ships were constructed. However, from 1943–5 only four and a half million tons were lost while new building produced thirty-one million tons.[465] A second reason for the duration of German resistance was a doubling of German armament production between 1942 and 1944.

At last Germany had been forced into total war. First Todt, and then Speer, created a full war economy. Their success was partly the result of increased efficiency, partly the result of diverting resources from civilian production. However, the German civil population, because of the resistance of Nazi gauleiters to attacks on its standard of living, and because of the availability of labour and food from occupied countries, felt the economic strain of war less than the civilian population of Britain, which was more efficiently organized for war production. (Though, of course, the German civilians felt the military impact far more severely.)

CIVILIAN EXPENDITURE ON CONSUMPTION GOODS IN
GERMANY AND U.K. 1938–44[466]
(1938 = 100; constant prices)

	Germany	U.K.
1938	100	100
1939	108	100
1940	100	87
1941	97	81
1942	88	79
1943	87	76
1944	79	77

MOBILIZATION OF THE LABOUR FORCE (PERCENTAGES), MAY–JUNE 1944[467]

	U.K.	Germany	U.S.A.
Armed forces	22	24	18½
Civilian war employment	33	28	21½
Other employment	45	48	58
Unemployed	—	—	2

Another important symptom of the smaller intensity of German economic mobilization is in the position of women: in Britain, the number of women employed in industry doubled between 1939 and 1944, while in Germany, the numbers remained constant. This explains the remarkable fact that there were one and a quarter million German women in domestic service in September 1944, compared with one and a half millions before the war, while British domestic servants were probably about one-third of the pre-war number.[468]

Above all, however, the war was protracted by the German will to resist. This determination came not from any relative absence of material hardships felt by the German people, or from the fact that total war was inaugurated belatedly, but from the sufferings that were inflicted on Germany during the war and from the fear of the sufferings that might be inflicted after the defeat. The Germans expected little mercy from the Russians, especially the large numbers of Germans who were acquainted with the conduct of the German conquerers in Russia. The western allies fortified German will to resist in three ways. The first was the demand for 'unconditional surrender'. This was a demand caused by vivid memories of the use made by German nationalists of the alleged allied trick of 1918 by which an undefeated Germany had been induced to put herself at the mercy of the allies, and by anxiety to calm Soviet fears that the western allies might try to negotiate with a German régime, fears which might persuade Stalin to get in first himself. The second was the allied bombing of Germany which caused hatred of enemies equipped with an apparently indiscriminate remorse-lessness. The third was the news that came in September 1944 of the absurd Morgenthau plan, 'looking forward to converting Germany into a country primarily agricultural and pastoral in character'.

German resistance, however, could lengthen the war but could not win it unless the western allies or the Soviet Union could be induced to make a separate peace. There was never any serious prospect of this although the west and the Russians suspected each other's determination to fight to the finish. As it was, then, allied strategy was simply a matter of bringing their superior power to bear. Russian strategy was dictated by geography – it could only involve the defeat of the German land forces engaged against the Red Army – from the beginning of the Russian campaign to the end of the war this absorbed the major part of the German land forces. Anglo-American strategy was more flexible. The most important decision was taken before the USA had entered the war – that Germany should be defeated first and Japan contained until this had been done. Germany was recognized to be the more powerful enemy and it was believed that she could grow stronger still if time were permitted to her to organize her European conquests to support the German war effort. Apart from a few weeks in the summer of 1942, when the American chiefs of staff threatened to divert the main weight of American effort against Japan, (and were overruled by President Roosevelt), this strategy was adhered to without much dissension. Consequently Anglo-American discussions on strategy turned on the most effective way of defeating Germany. The major disagreement, largely, though not entirely, between the British on one side and the Americans on the other, was on the conditions needed before an invasion of France could be undertaken. The Americans were eager to concentrate all resources for this invasion and carry it out at the earliest possible moment; the British argued that it should be postponed until German capacity for resistance had been weakened by land operations elsewhere or by bombing. On the whole British strategy prevailed: until the spring of 1944 there were more ground forces from the British Empire in action against the enemy (Germany and Japan) than from the USA, and British views had corresponding weight. Again, Roosevelt was anxious to bring American ground forces into action against Germany quickly and since British arguments against an invasion of France in 1942 were clearly sound, this could only be done somewhere else. The result was the invasion of North Africa in November 1942. This led on to the invasion of Sicily in July 1943, and after this had brought about the fall of Mussolini, to the invasion of the Italian mainland in September. The Italian campaign, September 1943–May 1945, was the most controversial piece of Anglo-American strategy. Many Americans regarded it as a dangerous diversion from the main allied effort in France, some Americans and most British generals claimed that it diverted German strength from the main theatre. Who diverted whom? The most crucial moment was at the end of May and the beginning of June 1944. At that time the allies were engaging seventeen German divisions in Italy, of which six were Panzer or Panzer-Grenadier divisions, using twenty-seven allied divisions. This was a victory for the allies – what mattered was that the German forces available in France at the moment of the allied invasion, 6 June, and in the days immediately following, should be at a minimum, while the size of the first allied waves was determined by the availability of landing craft, not by the availability of troops.

The second highly controversial part of allied strategy was the strategic bombing offensive against Germany. There is no doubt that allied air power used tactically in direct support of ground forces or against lines of communication behind the fighting fronts, especially in France in 1944, was a major factor in allied military victory. What is questionable is whether the Anglo-American attempts to weaken the German capacity for war by bombing targets, mostly in Germany, without immediate tactical significance, produced returns commensurate with the effort expended. The controversy is made more acute by its moral implications: if the strategic bomber offensive was not an effective war weapon, then it is impossible to defend its concomitant destruction of lives and buildings which had no conceivable connection with the enemy war effort, even though, of course, the directors of allied bombing supposed that they were shortening the war, not murdering innocent people in the manner practised by the German government.

It is true that it was hoped that terror created by bombing would undermine the German will to fight. However, this hope, which seems to have been a delusion, did not cause the bombing of Germany to be undertaken. As with the equally indiscriminate German bombing of Britain in 1940–1, the underlying assumption, at the beginning, was that German capacity to fight, as distinct from will to fight, could be reduced or destroyed by attacks on war production or on transport. At first, it was supposed that limited targets such as railway yards, factories and oil refineries, could be identified and destroyed by bombers. These expectations were based on peace-time practice against undefended targets. It soon became clear that bombers could not operate in daylight at all without fighter escort and, more slowly, it emerged that night bombers frequently became completely lost and even if they did not, could not normally hit any defended target smaller than a large town. In August 1941, a British report on night-bombing operations in June and July 1941 concluded that of 6103 sorties sent out, only about 1200 had dropped their bombs within five miles [eight kilometres] of the targets. In the heavily defended Ruhr area only about seven per cent of bombers had reached even this degree of accuracy.[469] The result was that area bombing became accepted by the British as the normal method of bombing attack – what this meant was aiming at some point in a large town (usually near the centre) and trusting that the consequent devastation would somehow impede the German war effort, in addition to causing a great deal of useless damage and human suffering. In practice, it is now clear the damage done to the German war economy by area bombing was, except in rare instances, insufficient to justify the process either strategically or, therefore, morally. Even effective area bombing required improved training and navigational aids. Eventually these improvements, together with the defeat of the German fighter force as a result of the development of a long-range American fighter, went far enough to make possible a partial reversion to the precision bombing that had originally been attempted.

The United States bombing forces, which had never renounced the attempt at precision bombing, were able to strike with effect in daylight, once air superiority was secured. Even so, American 'precision' bombing was not accurate except under unusual conditions – absence of cloud and absence of effective defence. The consequences on the ground of American bombing were often indistinguishable from those of British bombing. In the last months of the war, however, area bombing against a weakened German defence became so devastating that it sometimes generated real economic effects. The start of this victory from bombing, though, coincided with rather than preceded the allied liberation of France and the Russian conquest of the Rumanian oilfields. Indeed, the allied occupation of France made a far larger contribution to the final success of strategic bombing than the strategic bombing of Germany had made to the allied campaign in France – by shortening the range of allied operations, pushing forward allied radar and pushing back the German air defences. It can be said, then, that British and American bombing showed no sign of being decisive until the war had obviously been won anyway and that area bombing, which the British particularly employed, largely because few of their bomber crews, until the summer of 1944, were capable of anything else (even in the last three months of 1944 British Bomber Command devoted just over half its efforts to area attacks on towns), was not justified by its results until near the end. The effort was substantial: nearly one-fifth of all men killed in the UK armed forces were in Bomber Command aircrews. Really serious results came only at the end of 1944 and in 1945, when German oil production was seriously curtailed and the rail transport system partially halted. In the process, the larger German towns faced total destruction. Given more time the Anglo-American bombing might have ended German resistance on its own, at enormous cost in human suffering; the invasion of Germany by the Red Army and by the allied armies from the west spared Germany most of such a climax of which a sample was provided at Dresden in February 1945. In May 1945, with Hitler dead, German forces surrendered.

The real climax of strategic bombing came in the war against Japan. The outline strategy of the Japanese war was fairly simple. The Japanese, having secured temporary supremacy over the waters of the Pacific by their surprise attack on Pearl Harbor, were able to seize territories making up an economically self-sufficient east Asian empire. By the summer of 1942, the Japanese were in control of Burma, Malaya, the Philippines, Hong Kong, nearly the whole of the Dutch East Indies and the islands of the central Pacific, as far as the international date line, in addition to their existing area of occupation in Manchuria, China, French Indo-China and Thailand. The Japanese assumed that the United States would negotiate rather than face the immense task of extruding Japan from her conquests. This assumption underestimated American power and determination. These were great enough to enable the United States, even though their main effort was directed against Germany, to reconquer maritime supremacy, well before the German war was over, through a combination of surface vessels with land-based and carrier-based aircraft. The mobility that command of the sea conferred enabled the Americans to by-pass Japanese island strongholds, rather than reconquering them one by one, and to concentrate on securing selected bases to make it possible to interrupt Japanese lines of communication, blockade Japan, and prepare a direct attack on Japanese home islands. The defeat of Japan was rendered imminent by the seizure of Iwo Jima (February–March 1945) and Okinawa (April–June 1945), against tenacious resistance. Plans were made for the invasion of Kyushu in November 1945 and of Honshu, the main Japanese island, in March 1946. It was confidently expected that the Japanese would meet these invasions with literally suicidal determination and at least half a million American casualties were expected. Meanwhile the American army air force had decided that it could defeat Japan on its own. The air-force had been depressed by failure to win the war against Germany and disappointed by the effect of precision attack with high explosive bombs. Like the British years before, the American air force in the east concluded that area bombing was the only answer and its commanders decided that fire-raising was the best weapon to maximise destruction. On 9 March 1945 Tokyo was set on fire: 261,000 buildings were destroyed and 83,793 men, women and children were killed. General Le May, commanding the heavy bomber force, calculated that, taking in thirty-three of the major cities of Japan, he would end the war in October. The army, which had heard this sort of prediction before, remained sceptical.

At this point the first atomic weapon was being prepared. It came at the precise moment when some device was being looked for to persuade the Japanese government that Japan had already lost the war. Discussion broke out among the small number of scientists and politicians who knew about the bomb, on how it could be used to do this. Some favoured a threat of its use, others a public demonstration on a desert island – both were ruled out on the grounds that this bomb might fail to go off and Japanese morale would be increased as a result. The most sensible suggestion of all, that the bomb should be dropped on uninhabited woodland in Japan, which it would dramatically devastate, escaped serious consideration. In spite of the argument put forward that the United States would lose all moral claim to demand international control over nuclear energy if it used the bomb, it was decided to drop the bomb on an intact Japanese town in order, if it worked, to demonstrate its power beyond question and, if it did not work, to avoid losing prestige. On 6 August an atom bomb was dropped on Hiroshima, on 9 August, a second on Nagasaki. The Japanese government had already been considering attempts at a negotiated peace which the military chiefs were resisting on the grounds that negotiations could best come after the American invasion had been launched, and, as they hoped, the American demand for unconditional surrender had been weakened by the losses the Japanese expected to inflict on the American invaders. The nuclear bomb reinforced the civilian politicians, and the Emperor, against the military, and, by a narrow majority, the Japanese government decided on surrender – even then, however, not an 'unconditional' surrender but one which stipulated the retention of the Japanese monarchy. The nuclear attacks killed over 70,000 at Hiroshima, about 35,000 at Nagasaki – the Nagasaki attack was probably unnecessary. By the grisly arithmetic of war the use of the bomb was justified – without it, Japan would probably not have surrendered until the United States air force had killed even more Japanese and, possibly, until the invasion had brought the killing of still larger numbers of American and Japanese troops.[470] The use of the atom bomb brought into view the prospect that humanity would soon be able to destroy itself – the contemporary world had begun.

During the Second World War probably about 35–45 million people were killed. The following figures, are, in many cases, no more than a rough approximation.[471]

	Military deaths	Civilian deaths
France	250,000	350,000
Germany	3,500,000	700,000
Italy	330,000	80,000
Japan	1,200,000	260,000
U.K.	326,000	62,000
U.S.A.	300,000	
U.S.S.R.	6,500,000	(?)10,000,000

Other major losses were suffered by Poland (pre-war boundaries) with probably over 5,000,000 killed and Yugoslavia with over 1,000,000 deaths: most of these were civilian deaths.

Another sort of human suffering was caused by deportation. This affected Germans most of all. Possibly 16,000,000 people, of whom perhaps 11,000,000 were Germans, were compelled to leave their homes in 1939–47. Some were moved during the war as a result of German schemes for creating a concentration of scattered German populations inside a greater Germany, most were refugees fleeing before the advance of the Russians in 1944–5 or were expelled by Poland and Czecho-slovakia after the war in reaction to German war-time policies.[472]

Apart from Japan, the war had its most devastating impact on the populations of Germany and countries to the east of Germany. (For Britain and France the war was far less severe than the war of 1914–18.) This fact was caused above all by the protracted Russo-German struggle. It was partly a matter of the immense size of the forces engaged, partly a matter of the ruthlessness of the conduct of the war. This ruthlessness came from the fact that German forces were usually operating in areas containing a hostile civilian population but much more from the nature of the doctrines that had brought about the war: that non-Germans and especially Slavs, had no right to exist except insofar as their existence served the ends of the German people. Thus about two and a half million Russian prisoners of war were killed or allowed to starve. This was the result of neglect and indifference but also of deliberate policy. It stands in contrast to the wholly correct treatment of western prisoners of war (with some exceptions attributable to the Waffen SS) maintained by the German authorities. Even western Jewish prisoners of war were safe. In Russia the army itself took part directly in the murder of prisoners of war of certain categories, political commissars etc., on orders from the OKW (the High Command of the Armed Forces), though some army formations disregarded the orders.[473]

A striking fact about the war years in Europe is that they produced more civilian than military deaths. The major reasons were as follows: aerial bombing, forced labour, resistance and partisan war in German-occupied countries, and murder, principally of Jews. Bombing is in a separate category; this was an act of war, however misguided and indiscriminate. Most casualties and most suffering from bombing were inflicted by the Anglo-American attack on Germany. The other categories are not completely separate from each other – many deaths cannot be ascribed with clarity to one line of German policy rather than another. The German war economy was consistently short of labour; the occupied territories of Europe contributed to the solution of this problem (never completely overcome for skilled workers) by providing labour in local workshops and factories, labour for German con-struction projects in occupied territories and labour for use in Germany itself, by September 1944 there were over seven million foreign workers in Germany or about one-fifth of the entire labour force.[474] In the east, first in Poland and then in the territories conquered in Russia, recruit-ment was both from volunteers and by compulsion; in the west, service was voluntary until 1942, when forced labour began. In the east, especially, measures were employed, as a German observer noted, which were typical of the worst eras of the slave-trade, for instance, the property of those who refused to work was confiscated, their houses burnt down and their relations arrested as hostages. They were frequently bundled off to Germany like ill-treated cattle, often without food for days. Conditions of employment in Germany varied widely. Workers from western countries were treated relatively decently – some valuable skilled workers, even generously. The workers from the east, especially the Russians, lived under conditions involving, at best, hardship and, at worst, starvation. As for those employed in concentration camps under the aegis of the SS, their employment was 'in the true meaning of the word, exhaustive', while many, not only Jews, were deliberately 'worked to death'.[475]

German occupation was met with resistance from the civilian populations of many of the conquered countries. In Poland, Russia and Yugoslavia, full-scale campaigns had to be waged against these partisans. In France and in Italy (after the Italian surrender to the allies and the German seizure of control) armed resistance was more difficult, but sabotage and even organized group resistance existed. German methods of suppression were brutal and blood-thirsty. This was deliberate policy. On 16 July 1941, Hitler explained, 'the Russians have now ordered partisan warfare behind our front. This partisan war has some advantage for us; it enables us to wipe out everyone who opposes us'. In September, Keitel, chief of the OKW, sent out an order:

It must be remembered that in the areas in question a man's life is not worth much, and that only the use of unwonted severity can make fear an effective deterrent. The death penalty for fifty to a hundred communists must be regarded in these cases as suitable atonement for the death of one German soldier.[476]

Collective reprisals – the shooting of previously imprisoned hostages or indiscriminate slaughter – became characteristic German reactions to measures of resistance. On 10 June 1944, for instance, an officer of the 2nd SS Panzer division was shot by a Frenchman near Oradour-sur-Glane. A battalion of the division burned the village and killed its entire population – 642 men, women and children. On 7 March 1945, four hundred Dutchmen were executed after an attempt on the life of the local head of the German police. In the west these were extreme examples, in the east such actions were common.[477] The result was to alienate the sympathies of most of the native populations in Russia – which were often available for the invading forces, and which were sometimes gained by the more enlightened army commanders and by a few civilian administrators. (Many of those Russians who helped the Germans eventually received ruthless punishment from the Soviet authorities, who could compete with the Germans in savagery.)

This volume has been in large part devoted to an examination of the revival of German power after 1918 and of the way in which Germany secured the mastery of Europe. The crowning achievement that German power made possible was the greatest crime in recorded history: a pure, unadulterated crime. Most of the horrors of the Second World War were the outcomes of struggling for military victory; the massacre of the European Jews was not, it was an end in itself.

The numbers killed are uncertain; it is safe to accept a minimum of four million and a maximum of about six million.[478] Some were killed by starvation, some by being worked to death, some in the suppression of the Warsaw ghetto rising, many more by shooting by mobile units in Poland and Russia or by mobile gassing apparatus, most of all in the death camps of Poland, usually by gas. Polish and Russian Jews could therefore be killed locally; Jews from the rest of German controlled Europe were deported. The process was controlled and organized by the German SS and security police. The murderers, however, were by no means exclusively German. Rumanian troops, indeed, indulged in haphazard killing operations of their own, which sometimes shocked the better organized German practitioners, Lithuanians and Latvians directly assisted in German-sponsored killings, Esthonians and Russians helped to round up Jews, while Ukranians provided eager auxiliaries for the German killers.[479] In countries under German occupation which had collaborationist governments, or in the territories of Germany's allies, co-operation was needed from the indigenous authorities for deportation to the killing centres. Sometimes this hindered the mechanism of destruction. Anti-Semitism had long been in evidence among the French right, and in 1940 the Vichy government produced autonomous anti-Jewish measures. The French authorities fed the German machine with immigrant and foreign Jews in France, rounded up by French police, but tried to protect the French-born and naturalized Jews, largely by evasion and delays – with considerable success. Many Jews living in France were protected by the Italian army in the extended zone of occupation it took over after November 1942. The Italians, though involved in the war by a frivolous dictator, retained their humanity. Mussolini, himself, though paying lip service to German policy, does not seem seriously to have tried to enforce it. As long as the Italian army controlled their region of France every Jew who could reach it was safe: the Italian army even used force to prevent French police from rounding up foreign Jews.[480] Unfortunately, after the Italian surrender to the allies, the Germans secured control of the areas of Italian occupation and much of Italy proper, where Mussolini had introduced anti-Semitic legislation, by way of imitation, but where no deportations had taken place. Then many Jews in south-eastern France and in Italy were caught.

The conduct of the Nazi rulers of Germany in wishing to destroy the Jews is explicable. They took their own theories seriously and believed that Europe would be a better place without Jews. It is surprising, though again explicable, that such men should have become rulers of a highly civilized, powerful, modern state. What remains difficult to understand, but essential for anyone who wishes to comprehend the behaviour of mankind in society, is how they were able to organize killing and carry it out on this scale without being stopped. The central problem is why the Germans, whose government was responsible for the murders, allowed them to take place. One crucial question is this: how many Germans knew what was being done? It is, unfortunately, impossible to find out. At the time, there were strong reasons, fear of punishment, fear of accepting responsibility, for avoiding enquiry into activities of the SS and the police. Since 1945, motives of self-exculpation necessarily induce professions of ignorance. Any answer to this question can only be tentative and hesitant. The German government did not proclaim what it was doing; on the contrary elaborate measures of deception were employed, including measures of self-deception on the part of many of those directly responsible: they wrote and spoke of Jewish 'emigration', 'resettlement in the east', the 'final solution of the Jewish question' and so on.

It is certain that everyone in Germany knew that Jews were being deported: in itself an inhuman measure. Probably many ordinary Germans believed that they really were being resettled. This belief could be strengthened by the fact that the original plan of the Nazis, until 1941, was to eliminate European Jews by compulsory emigration overseas – the favourite plan was to send them to Madagascar. Thereafter the talk of resettlement 'in the east' could satisfy many. The SS took the trouble to make up detailed reports of the life of 'resettled' Jews. Another practice was to encourage deportees to write postcards to friends and acquaintances – these were then stored and dispatched at intervals after the victims had been killed. Instructions were published on how to send mail to 'resettled' Jews.[481] The rumours of what was actually going on could be regarded as enemy propaganda.

The position of some of those working directly for the government was different. The administrative machine involved in the killings was complex and extensive; it was difficult not to suspect that something was wrong. Fear or indifference produced callous complicity or uneasy inaction. Here are two examples. Two visiting officials of IG Farben engaged in a revealing conversation at their synthetic rubber plant attached to Auschwitz killing centre. One commented on an inmate, 'This Jewish swine could work a little faster,' and the other replied, 'If they cannot work let them die in the gas chamber'. After the war, Werner von Tippelskirch, of the foreign ministry, explained that he had never protested against the killing of Jews in Russia because he had been 'powerless' and that his superiors, Erdmannsdorff, Wörmann and Weizsäcker, had equally been 'powerless'. They simply awaited for a 'change of régime'. Asked whether it was right to wait 'and in the meantime send thousands of people to their death', Tippelskirch replied, 'a difficult question'.[482]

Within the army, extensive knowledge of the mobile killing operations certainly existed, especially among the officers of the army rear areas and among the staffs of the front line formations. Some knowledge reached the troops themselves. (The combat SS or Waffen-SS units, though largely composed simply of fighting soldiers, contained some who had been directly involved in killings.) On 10 October 1941, Field Marshal von Reichenau (6th Army) issued an order: 'The soldiers must have full understanding of the necessity for harsh but just countermeasures against Jewish sub-humanity.' Army group South (Rundstedt) sent copies to the other army commands, 11th Army (Manstein) 17th Army (Stülpnagel) and 1st Panzer Army (Kleist). Reichenau explained that it was a matter of dealing with partisans and Manstein's order, based on Reichenau's text, added that the Jew was the liaison between the Red Army and the partisans.[483] Thus for the army, and, no doubt, for those at home who heard of the mobile killings in the east, these activities were part of the struggle against the feared and hated partisans. Thus the army could leave the SS and police to do their work and explain away their 'excesses', virtuously turn its back and go on trying to win the war.

Few Germans knew the full story. All knew of 'deportations', many of slaughter in the east. Both could be explained away – one was leading to resettlement and the other was part of the war, a branch of the struggle against partisans. Everyone was aware that the SS was harsh and ruthless and it was not admired or loved. (When conscription began in Germany for the Waffen SS in 1943, complaints poured in; even though this branch of the SS was not necessarily used for anything other than ordinary front-line combat, the reputation of the SS was such that respectable parents wished to keep their sons out of it.)[484] Even so, some contrived to believe that the misdeeds of the SS might be unofficial and unauthorised and not an inevitable aspect of the régime: the *Führer* would put a stop to them if he were not busy with the war. A startling instance is the story of the complaint made to Hitler himself by the wife of Baldur von Schirach, a prominent Nazi leader, of the disturbing nature of a round-up of Jews in Amsterdam – Hitler, of course, treated her remarks with irritable impatience.[485]

There was little direct resistance from Germans to the Nazi treatment of Jews. Opposition to the régime, however, certainly existed. Between 1933 and 1945, an estimated 32,000 executions of Germans for political reasons took place.[486] No doubt many of these suffered because of what they were, rather than because of active resistance, but the number is large. There were opposition groups, communist, socialist, christian and conservative, but their activities were largely restricted to discussion or to the secret diffusion of literature. There was lacking, with one exception, a strong organized centre of resistance, capable of facing the armed party organizations. That exception was the army. Many officers came to deplore the Nazi régime. The better-informed senior officers realised, in increasing numbers after 1942, that Hitler was dragging Germany to disaster by obstinate insistence on protracting a war that was already lost. At the same time many officers despised the party fanatics. Thus criticism and contempt for Hitler and the Nazis was freely expressed, in private, by army officers. For the most part, however, a curiously schizophrenic attitude prevailed and the army fought with skill and determination for Germany, in spite of the fact that this meant increasing and protracting the power of a régime it regarded as, at best, misguided, and, at worst, evil. Some, however, drew the conclusion that a coup must be launched to remove Hitler from power. In 1938, a group of senior officers had considered such action to prevent Hitler launching a war that they believed would lead to ruin. Such thoughts were weakened by the German triumphs of 1940-2. From then on, however, this motive for action, to save Germany from ruin by eliminating Hitler and making an honourable peace, perhaps on all fronts, perhaps with the west, perhaps with Russia, revived. From 1942, a group of officers, of whom the most active were Olbricht, von Stauffenberg and von Tresckow, began to evolve plans for a seizure of power after the elimination of Hitler. The ambivalent attitude of most leading generals is demonstrated by the extensive contacts and approaches these men made to them to secure their participation in the plot; none of them betrayed the plotters, few of them, as it turned out, were prepared to support the plot in action. After many false starts, Stauffenberg let off a bomb at Hitler's headquarters on July 1944 and the attempt to seize power was made. For the most part, the generals waited to see what would happen and, when it turned out that Hitler had not been killed, the plot was suppressed fairly easily. There can be no doubt that the plotters were principally inspired by the hope of saving Germany from disaster but there can be no doubt that some of them were concerned, too, to bring to an end the murderous brutality of the régime. After July 1944, amidst Hitler's violent revenge, the army went on to the end, fighting hard and permitting Hitler's men a few months more of bestiality.

It would be wrong to hold every German responsible for the wickedness of the Nazis and even if it were possible to do so, it would be wrong to regard Germans as the possessors of some special innate talent for evil. The historical significance of Nazi rule is quite different: it demonstrated the depths to which civilized human beings, collected in a highly organized society, can sink. Humanity's view of itself will never be the same again.

Notes

1 P. Mantoux, *Les Délibérations du Conseil des Quatre*. Paris 1955, Vol. II, p. 121.
2 *Ibid.*, II, pp. 267, 338, 355.
3 *Ibid.*, I, pp. 70, 73.
4 British State Papers. Accounts and Papers (14) S.P. 1924, XXVI. Cmd. 2169.
5 D. Lloyd George, *The Truth about the Peace Treaties*. London 1938, Vol. I, pp. 404–16.
6 P. Mantoux, op. cit. II, pp. 267–8, 392–4, 408–12.
7 A. Tardieu, *La Paix*. Paris 1921, pp. 188, 277.
8 D. Lloyd George, op. cit., I, p. 414.
9 P. Mantoux, op. cit., I, pp. 63–75, 89, 181–2, 209–10.
10 *Ibid.*, p. 47.
11 D. Lloyd George, op. cit., II, p. 988.
12 P. Mantoux, op. cit., II, p. 381–2.
13 D. Perman, *The Shaping of the Czechoslovak State*. Leiden 1962, p. 150 citing H. Nicolson, *Peacemaking 1919*.
14 D. Lloyd George, op. cit., I, p. 418.
15 P. S. Wandycz, *France and her Eastern Allies*. Minneapolis 1962, p. 36.
16 P. Mantoux, op. cit., II, p. 275–283.
17 H. W. V. Temperley (editor), *History of the Peace Conference of Paris*. London 1920–24, Vol. II, p. 285–6.
18 D. Perman, op. cit., p. 172; P. Mantoux, op. cit., I, p. 149.
19 D. Perman, op. cit., p. 178–80.
20 P. Mantoux, op. cit., I, p. 461–2; D. Lloyd George, op. cit., II, p. 957.
21 D. Lloyd George, op. cit., I, p. 589.
22 *Papers Relating to the Foreign Relations of the United States, 1919. The Paris Peace Conference*. Washington 1942–47. Vol. III, p. 718.
23 H. W. V. Temperley (editor), op. cit., II, p. 295–301.
24 *Ibid.*, III, p. 74–6.

25 *Ibid.*, III, p. 69–73.

26 V. S. Mamatey, *The United States and East Central Europe, 1914–18*, Minneapolis 1962. esp. pp. 235–6 and Temperley, op. cit., I, p. 453.

27 H. W. V. Temperley, *ibid.*, I, p. 452–3.

28 H. W. V. Temperley, *ibid.*, V, p. 384–91.

29 P. Mantoux, op. cit., I, p. 482.

30 R. Albrecht-Carrié, *Italy at the Paris Peace Conference*. New York 1938.

31 H. W. V. Temperley, op. cit., IV, p. 330 and V pp. 428–32.

32 *Documents on British Foreign Policy 1919–1939*, (ed. E. L. Woodward and R. Butler). London 1947— [Henceforward cited as D.B.F.P.] First Series, IV p. 7 footnote 4

33 See e.g. D.B.F.P. 1st Series, IV, pp. 83–86.

34 P. S. Wandycz, op. cit., p. 101. D.B.F.P. 1st Series, VI, pp. 159–60.

35 D.B.F.P. 1st Series, VIII, pp. 502–6, 524–30.

36 H. W. V. Temperley, op. cit., IV, pp. 271–3, 228, 211.

37 D.B.F.P. 1st Series, II, pp. 900–10 and A. Apponyi and others, *Justice for Hungary*, London 1928.

38 H. W. V. Temperley, op. cit., V, pp. 432–76.

39 *Ibid.*, V, p. 61.

40 D.B.F.P. 1st Series, I, pp. 547–9.

41 H. W. V. Temperley, op. cit., IV, pp. 453–59.

42 D.B.F.P. 1st Series, IV, pp. 444–9, pp. 241–51. Temperley, op. cit., VI p. 170. E. Kedourie, *England and the Middle East, the Vital Years 1914–1921*. London 1956, esp. pp. 56–7.

43 D.B.F.P. 1st series, IV, p. 1100.

44 S. H. Longrigg, *Oil in the Middle East*, 2nd edn. London 1961.

45 P. Mantoux, op. cit., II, pp. 137–43. D.B.F.P. 1st series, IV, pp. 256–7.

46 D.B.F.P. 1st series, IV, pp. 384–5, I pp. 700–1

47 D.B.F.P. 1st series, XIII, pp. 221–3 and 311–13.

48 D.B.F.P. 1st series, XIII, p. 37. E. Kedourie, op. cit., p. 189.

49 P. Mantoux, op. cit., I, p. 60, pp. 485–6.

50 *Ibid.*, I, p. 510, II, p. 49.

51 B. Lewis, *The Emergence of Modern Turkey*, London 1961, pp. 236–41; P. Mantoux, op. cit., II, p. 60.

52 P. Mantoux, op. cit., II, pp. 111, 133–5, 142, 517, 532.

53 D.B.F.P. 1st series, XIII, p. 20, p. 95, p. 100, p. 18.

54 D.B.F.P. 1st series, XIII, pp. 21–2, 184–5, 189, 193–4.

55 E. H. Carr, *The Bolshevik Revolution* III, London 1953, pp. 240, 294–7, 301–4.

56 H. Nicolson, *Curzon, The Last Phase*, London 1934. pp. 261–2, 266; E. H. Carr, op. cit., III, p. 475, footnote 1.

57 W. H. Chamberlin, *The Russian Revolution*. London 1935, Vol. II, pp. 165–7.

58 P. Mantoux, op. cit., I, pp. 20–23, 52–5.

59 D.B.F.P., 1st series, I, pp. 689–90, 696–8. Clause 12, Armistice of 11 Nov., 1918. D.B.F.P. 1st series, III, pp. 98–105.

60 P. Mantoux, op. cit., II, p. 401. D.B.F.P. 1st series, III, pp. 129, 134–5, 206, 221, 249–54.

61 E. H. Carr, op. cit., III, p. 277.

62 *Ibid.*, p. 154. J. Korbel. *Poland Between East and West.* Princeton 1963, pp. 23–40.

63 P. S. Wandycz, op. cit., p. 140. D.B.F.P. 1st series, VII, p. 216.

64 P. S. Wandycz, op. cit., pp. 177–8.

65 J. Erickson, *The Soviet High Command.* London 1962, pp. 84–110.

66 D.B.F.P. 1st series, II, VII, VIII.

67 *Ibid.*, II, pp. 867–75, 912. VII, p. 327. VIII, pp. 216, 323–8, 375–8.

68 P. S. Wandycz, op. cit., pp. 146, 177, 169. D.B.F.P. 1st series, XII, p. 733.

69 P. S. Wandycz, op. cit., p. 163. D.B.F.P. 1st series, VIII, pp. 709, 713–4, P. S. Wandycz, op. cit., p. 163. D.B.F.P. 1st series, VIII, pp. 709, 713–4, 734–5.

70 *Ibid*, XI, pp. 425, 455–6, 487–8, 514. VIII pp. 785–6. XI, pp. 421, 424, 429–34, 454, 466. P. S. Wandycz op. cit., pp. 165–74.

71 D.B.F.P. 1st series, XI, pp. 422, 438–9, 427–8, 484, 208–9.

72 *Ibid.*, XI, pp. 405–7, 409–11, 428, 442–3, 501–2, 510–3, 532. VIII, pp. 781–2.

73 E. H. Carr, op. cit., III, pp. 287–9, 344–6.

74 J. Korbel, op. cit., pp. 69–71.

75 D.B.F.P. 1st series, IX, pp. 256–60.

76 E. H. Carr, op. cit., III, 310–1, 315. D.B.F.P. 1st series, III, p. 511.

'77 E. H. Carr, op. cit., III, p. 315.

78 *Ibid.*, pp. 368–9.

79 G. Freund, *Unholy Alliance.* London 1957, pp. 92–3, 97–8.

80 E. H. Carr, op. cit., III, 368–9.

81 *Ibid.*, p. 359.

82 G. Freund, op. cit., pp. 124–5, 201–12.

83 F. Goguel, *La Politique des Partis sous la Troisième République.* Paris 1946, pp. 172–75.

84 P. S. Wandycz, op. cit., pp. 217–18, 300.

85 D.B.F.P. 1st series, IX, pp. 50–51, 170–71, 221–22, 317–18, 361–62, 379.

86 *Ibid.*, XI, pp. 1–197 esp. pp. 48–50, 54–55, 58–65, 141–151.

87 P. S. Wandycz, op. cit., pp. 231–37. Lord D'Abernon. *An Ambassador of Peace.* London 1929–30, I, p. 185. H. W. V. Temperley. op. cit., VI, pp. 261–65, 617–30.

88 Ministère des Affaires Etrangères. *Documents relatifs aux négociations concernant les garanties de sécurité contre une aggression de l'Allemagne.* Paris 1924. Numbers 18, 22. British State Papers. *Papers respecting Negotiations for an Anglo-French Pact.* Cmd. 2169 London 1924, Numbers 33, 40, 47.

89 D'Abernon, op. cit., I, pp. 27, 148, D.B.F.P. 1st series, VIII, pp. 522–23, 531. E. Weill-Raynal. *Les Réparations Allemandes et la France*. Paris 1938–47, I, pp. 564–69, 584–94. J. M. Keynes. *A Revision of the Treaty*. London 1922 pp. 17–21.

90 J. M. Keynes, op. cit., pp. 20–25. E. Weill-Raynal. op. cit., I, pp. 604–5.

91 C. Bresciani-Turroni. *The Economics of Inflation*, London 1937, pp. 45, 90–2, and Chapters 1 and 2.

92 E. Weill-Raynal. op. cit., II, pp. 78–84, 148–65, 191–92, 236–37, 260.

93 *Ibid.*, pp. 200–5.

94 For a different interpretation see L. Kochan, *The Struggle for Germany* Edinburgh 1963

95 *Papers respecting negotiations for an Anglo-French Pact*, Number 34. *Parliamentary Debates (Hansard)* House of Commons V Series. Vol. 152, columns 1894–95. R. N. W. Blake, *The Unknown Prime Minister*. London, 1955, p. 485. J. M. Keynes, *Economic Consequences of the Peace*. London, 1919, p. 14. *Hansard* V Series. Vol. 167, column 1816, Vol. 168, column 481, Vol. 160, column 509, Vol. 168, column 505.

96 E. Weill-Raynal, op. cit., II, pp. 328, 195–8.

97 Ministère des Affaires Etrangères. *Documents Diplomatiques. Demande de moratorium. Conférence de Londres. Conférence de Paris*. Paris 1923, pp. 54, 85. E. Weill-Raynal, op. cit., II, 327–60.

98 E. Di Nolfo, *Mussolini e la politica estera italiana 1919–1933*. Padua 1960, pp. 74–77.

99 E. Weill-Raynal op. cit., II, pp. 385–99. III 220–1.

100 *Ibid.*, II, pp. 418–48

101 *Ibid.*, II, pp. 509, 517–18, 522, 494–5, 493.

102 *Ibid.*, II, p. 600.

103 *Ibid.*, II, pp. 659–60

104 *Ibid.*, III, pp. 71–86, 119–20.

105 A. Thimme. *Gustav Stresemann. Eine politische Biographie zur Geschichte der Weimarer Republik*. Hannover and Frankfurt am Main 1957, pp. 65–69. G. Stresemann. *Vermächtnis*. (herausgegeben by H. Bernhard) Berlin 1932–33, II, p. 553.

106 H. W. Gatzke, *Stresemann and the Rearmament of Germany*. Baltimore 1954, pp. 28–29. A. Thimme op. cit., pp. 53–54.

107 A Thimme, op, cit., p. 85. G. Stresemann op. cit., II, pp. 553–5. Z. J. Gasiriowski *Stresemann and Poland before Locarno* in *Journal of Central European Affairs*. 18, Boulder 1958–59, p. 42.

108 G. Stresemann, op. cit., II, pp. 281, 554. A. Thimme, op. cit., p. 98.

109 Z. J. Gasiriowski, op. cit., p. 299. J. Korbel, op. cit., p. 198.

110 H. W. Gatzke, op. cit., pp. 70–5.

111 H. L. Bretton, *Stresemann and the Revision of Versailles*, Stanford 1953, pp. 96, 107.

112 E. Weill-Raynal, op. cit., III, pp. 403 391–2, 399, 868–79.

113   J. Korbel, op. cit., pp. 241–2.

114   Z. J. Gasiriowski, *The Russian overture to Germany of December 1924* in *Journal of Modern History*, 30, Chicago 1958. E. H. Carr. *A History of Soviet Russia. Socialism in one Country*. London 1964. Vol. III, pp. 275–9, 422–5, 432–3, 437–8, 1010–17.

115   G. Stresemann, op. cit., III, pp. 15–23. G. Suarez. *Briand*. Paris. 1938–52, VI, pp. 227, 241.

116   *Ibid.*, pp. 218–26. But compare A. J. P. Taylor. *Origins of the Second World War*. London, 1961, p. 57.

117   E. Di Nolfo, op. cit., Chapter 1.

118   *Ibid.*, pp. 79–98.

119   A. Cassels, *Mussolini and German Nationalism* in *Journal of Modern History* 35. Chicago 1963, pp. 143–4, 147–51.

120   E. Di Nolfo, op. cit., pp. 134–8.

121   *Ibid.*, pp. 153–8.

122   I. Svennilson, *Growth and Stagnation in the European Economy*. U.N.E.C.E. Geneva 1954, pp. 169–70.

123   A. Maizels, *Industrial Growth and World Trade*. Cambridge 1963. pp. 442, 424–5.

124   *Ibid.*, p. 220 (1913 figure excludes Netherlands).

125   I. Svennilson, op. cit., p. 190 (India includes Pakistan. Japanese figure is for 1914).

126   *Ibid.*, p. 152. A. Maizels, op. cit., p. 490.

127   I. Svennilson, op. cit., pp. 153–5.

128   *Ibid.*, p. 199.

129   A. Maizels, op. cit., pp. 477, 481.

130   I. Svennilson, op. cit., p. 87.

131   T. Wilson. *Fluctuations in Income and Employment*. London 1st. Edition. 1942, 2nd Edition 1948, pp. 117, 159. W. A. Lewis. *Economic Survey 1919–39*, London 1949, p. 61.

132   H. W. Arndt, *Economic Lessons of the Nineteen-Thirties*, London 1944, pp. 14–19, 36. W. A. Lewis, op. cit., pp. 51–57, T. Wilson, op. cit., pp. 143–72.

133   W. A. Lewis, op. cit., pp. 56–57.

134   E. W. Bennett, *Germany and the Diplomacy of the Financial Crisis, 1931*. Cambridge, Mass. 1962, pp. 100–1.

135   L. Robbins, *The Great Depression*, London 1934, pp. 91–7.

136   W. A. Lewis, op. cit., pp. 58–68.

137   H. C. Hillman, *Comparative Strength of the Powers* in A. Toynbee and F. T. Ashton-Gwatkin (eds). *The World in March 1939*, London 1952, p. 439. (The figures are approximate since they involve assumptions for the U.S.S.R.).

138   D. Kirk, *Europe's Population in the Interwar Years*, Geneva 1946, pp. 180, 255.

139 *Ibid.*, pp. 172, 263–77.

140 W. E. Moore, *Economic Demography of Eastern and Southern Europe.* Geneva 1945, p. 51.

141 D. Kirk, op. cit., pp. 54–60.

142 W. E. Moore, op. cit., p. 125.

143 *Ibid.*, p. 82.

144 International Labour Office, Studies and Reports G. 3. *Housing Policy in Europe. Cheap Home Building.* pp. 21–2.

145 *Ibid.*, p. 325. International Labour Office, Studies and Reports B. 30. *The Worker's Standard of Living.* Geneva 1938, p. 81. J. Strzelecki, *La Question de l'Habitation Urbaine en Pologne.* Geneva 1936, pp. 189, 206. H. Van der Kaa. *The Housing Policy in the Netherlands.* Geneva 1935, p. 44. Service Technique Central du Conseil supérieur du ministère des travaux publics d'Italie. *Rapport sur les habitations populaires et économiques en Italie.* Geneva 1936, pp. 55, 73.

146 International Labour Office. Studies and Reports B. 23. *Workers' Nutrition and Social Policy.* Geneva 1936, pp. 52, 46.

147 League of Nations. *The Problem of Nutrition. Vol. III, Nutrition in Various Countries.* Geneva 1936, p. 63.

148 United Nations. *Demographic Yearbook 1955.* New York 1955, pp. 464–9.

149 University of London, Institute of Education. *The Year Book of Education 1936.* London 1936, p. 115.

150 United Nations. *Demographic Yearbook 1963.* New York 1964, pp. 422–3. *Demographic Yearbook 1964.* New York 1965, pp. 734–7.

151 *Demographic Yearbook 1955*, pp. 464–69.

152 *Demographic Yearbook 1963*, pp. 398–99, 416–23. *Demographic Yearbook 1964*, pp. 730–37.

153 D. Kirk, op. cit., pp. 272–4.

154 International Labour Office. *Workers' Nutrition and Social Policy*, p. 208.

155 *Ibid.*, p. 197.

156 Service Technique Central etc., op. cit., pp. 51–2.

157 R. H. Tawney. *Equality.* London 1931, Edition of 1964, p. 137.

158 H. Van der Kaa, op. cit., p. 55.

159 A. M. Carr-Saunders and others. *A Survey of Social Conditions in England and Wales.* Oxford 1958, p. 222.

160 Political and Economic Planning. *Report on the British Social Services.* London 1937, p. 59.

161 International Labour Office. *Approaches to Social Security.* Geneva 1942, pp. iii, 97.

162 F. Edding, *Internationale Tendenzen in der Entwicklung der Ausgaben für Schulen und Hochschulen.* Kiel 1958, p. 36.

163 *Ibid.*, p. 30.

164 United Nations. *Demographic Yearbook 1955*, pp. 464–9.

165   J. Floud, *Educational Experience of the Adult Population of England and Wales as at July 1949* in D. V. Glass (ed.) *Social Mobility in Britain.* London 1954, pp. 120–1.

166   International Labour Office. Studies and Reports M. 13. *International Survey of Social Services 1933*, 2 vols. Geneva 1936.

167   J. F. Dewhurst and others, *Europe's Needs and Resources.* New York 1961, p. 400.

168   International Labour Office. *Housing Policy in Europe*, pp. 30–1, 45.

169   United Nations. *Demographic Yearbook 1953*, pp. 595–7.

170   Lord Beveridge, *Full Employment in a Free Society.* London, 2nd Edition, 1960, p. 47. The figures relate to those covered by unemployment insurance and exclude certain categories, notably agricultural workers, indoor domestic servants and certain public and railway workers. They exclude N. Ireland, where unemployment rates were higher.

171   S. Pollard, *The Development of the British Economy 1914–50.* London 1962, p. 4.

172   *Ibid.*, pp. 110–4.

173   I. Svennilson, op. cit., pp. 121, 123, 128, 272–3. Beveridge, op. cit., p. 318.

174   I. Svennilson, op. cit., p. 153. Beveridge op. cit., p. 318.

175   *Ibid.*, p. 318.

176   A. Maizels, op. cit., pp. 275, 280–1, 432–3, 490–3.

177   S. Pollard, op. cit., pp. 210–1. E. V. Morgan. *Studies in British Financial Policy, 1914–25.* London 1952. pp. 98, 152, 211, 377.

178   I. Svennilson, op. cit., pp. 304–5. *Key Statistics of the British Economy 1900–62.* London and Cambridge 1964, p. 13.

179   A. Maizels, op. cit., p. 432.

180   Beveridge, op. cit., 1st Edition. London 1944, pp. 63–4, 73.

181   W. Hannington, *Unemployed Struggles, 1919–1936.* London 1936. H. M. Pelling, *Modern Britain 1885–1955.* Edinburgh 1960, p. 130.

182   S. Pollard, op. cit., p. 267.

183   *Ibid.*, p. 290.

184   *Ibid.*, p. 275. J. Symons. *The General Strike.* London 1957, pp. 24–7.

185   W. H. Crook, *The General Strike.* Chapel Hill. North Carolina 1931, p. 384.

186   Lord Citrine, *Men and Work.* London 1964, pp. 162–72.

187   *Ibid.*, p. 189.

188   J. Symons, op. cit., pp. 138–43.

189   H. A. Clegg, A. Fox, A. F. Thompson, *History of British Trade Unions since 1889.* Vol. I, Oxford 1964, pp. 43–6, 314–5, 362–3, 393–5, H. M. Pelling, *History of British Trade Unionism.* London 1963, p. 127.

190   H. A. Clegg, A. Fox, A. F. Thompson, op. cit., pp. 471–5.

191   H. M. Pelling, *The British Communist Party.* London 1958, pp. 27, 62–3.

192   *Ibid.*, p. 192.

193   G. M. Young, *Stanley Baldwin.* London 1952.

194 R. Bassett, *Nineteen Thirty-One*. London 1958.

195 *Ibid.*, p. 333.

196 G. M. Young, op. cit., p. 202.

197 C. L. Mowat, *Britain between the Wars 1918–1940*. London 1955, pp. 506–12.

198 F. W. S. Craig, *British Parliamentary Election Statistics 1918–68*. Glasgow 1968, p. 6.

199 C. L. Mowat, op. cit., pp. 548–50, 581–2.

200 C. Cross, *The Fascists in Britain*. London 1961.

201 E. Di Nolfo, op. cit., Chapter 1.

202 A. Rossi, (Tasca). *The Rise of Italian Fascism*. London 1938, pp. 33–4.

203 R. De Felice, *Mussolini il rivoluzionario*, Turin 1965, p. 625.

204 K. R. Popper, *The Open Society and its Enemies*. London, 4th Edition 1962. Chapter 12.

205 Istituto Centrale di Statistica, *Sommario di Statistiche Storiche Italiana 1861–1955*. Rome 1958, p. 105.

206 S. B. Clough, *Economic History of Modern Italy*. New York and London 1964, pp 382–3 R De Felice, op cit , p 435 P Alatri, *Le Origini del Fascismo* 3rd Edition 1962, p 46. A. Rossi (Tasca), op. cit., pp. 75–81.

207 L. Einaudi, *La Condotta economica e gli effetti sociali della Guerra Italiana*. Bari, Laterza and Newhaven 1933, pp. 291–5. A. Rossi (Tasca), op. cit., 91–96. P. Alatri, op. cit., pp. 49–51.

208 Istituto Centrale di Statistica, op. cit., pp. 172, 204–5.

209 L. Salvatorelli and G. Mira, *Storia d'Italia nel periodo fascista*. Turin 1964, pp. 110–2.

210 *Ibid.*, pp. 148–9, 160–3.

211 *Ibid.*, pp. 151–6.

212 G. Perticone, *La Politica Italiana dal Primo al Secondo Dopoguerra*. Milan 1965, pp. 647–93.

213 P. Alatri, op. cit., pp. 72–80. R. De Felice, op. cit., pp. 607–8.

214 L. Salvatorelli and G. Mira, op. cit., pp. 195–6. P. Alatri, op. cit., p. 67.

215 L. Salvatorelli and G. Mira, op. cit., p. 179

216 R. De Felice, op. cit., pp. 603–4. L Salvatorelli and G. Mira, op. cit., pp. 201, 207, 230.

217 C. Sforza, *L'Italia dal 1914 al 1944 quale io la vidi*. Rome 2nd Edition 1945, pp. 117–8.

218 R. De Felice, op. cit., p. 607.

219 L. Salvatorelli and G. Mira, op. cit., pp. 221–30. P. Alatri, op., cit., pp. 129–31.

220 L. Salvatorelli and G. Mira, op. cit., p. 237.

221 P. Alatri, op. cit., pp. 85, 243.

222 A. Rossi (Tasca), op. cit., pp. 318–9.

223 P. Alatri, op. cit., pp. 88–9. L. Salvatorelli and G. Mira, op. cit., pp. 289–92.

224 C. F. Delzell, *Mussolini's Enemies*. Princeton 1961, p. 11.

225 P. Alatri, op. cit., pp. 90–91. L. Salvatorelli and G. Mira, op. cit., pp. 307–10.

226 *Ibid.*, p. 352. C. F. Delzell, op. cit., p. 16.

227 *Ibid.*, pp. 38–41.

228 F. Chabod. *A History of Italian Fascism*. London 1963, pp. 63–7. (translated from Italian, Milan 1961).

229 L. Salvatorelli and G. Mira, op. cit., pp. 465, 891–2.

230 S. W. Halperin, *Mussolini and Italian Fascism*, Princeton 1964, pp. 146–8.

231 W. G. Welk, *Fascist Economic Policy*. Cambridge, Mass., 1938, p. 76.

232 L. Salvatorelli and G. Mira, op. cit., pp. 541, 574.

233 I. Svennilson, op. cit., pp. 312–3.

234 W. G. Welk, op. cit., pp. 159–250.

235 I. Svennilson, op. cit., p. 251.

236 *Ibid.*, pp. 304–5.

237 P. Pétain, *Paroles aux français*. Lyon 1941, pp. 78, 80.

238 P. Tissier, *Le Procès de Riom*. London 1942, p. 5.

239 A. Sauvy, *Histoire économique de la France entre les deux guerres*. Vol. I, Paris 1965, pp. 339, 403, 501, 534.

240 *Ibid.*, pp. 282, 263, 350–3, 405–6, 355–6. J. Néré, *La Troisième République*. Paris 1965, p. 135.

241 C. P. Kindleberger, *Economic Growth in France and Britain 1851–1950*. Cambridge, Mass. 1964, p. 74. C. Bettelheim. *Bilan de l'Economie française 1919–46*. Paris 1947, p. 5. I. Svennilson, op. cit., pp. 70–1.

242 A Sauvy, op. cit., pp. 94–5. D. Ligou, *Histoire du socialisme en France 1871–1961*. Paris 1962, p. 366.

243 A Sauvy, op. cit., p. 118. G. Dupeux, *Le Front Populaire et les élections de 1936*. Paris 1959, p. 26. P. Reynaud, *Mémoirs I Venu de ma montagne*. Paris 1960, pp. 350–419.

244 J. Néré, op. cit., pp. 133. A. Sauvy, *La nature sociale*. Paris 1957, pp. 96–7. I. Svennilson, op. cit., p. 235.

245 G. Dupeux, op. cit., pp. 30–40.

246 A. Sauvy, *Le Pouvoir et l'opinion*. Paris 1949, pp. 100–10.

247 G. Lefranc, *Histoire du Front Populaire*. Paris 1965, pp. 310–21, 380–3. J. Néré, op. cit., p. 184.

248 G. Lefranc, op. cit., pp. 324–5, 386.

249 J. Néré, op. cit., p. 107. I Svennilson, op. cit., pp. 149, 262.

250 P. J. Larmour, *The French Radical Party in the 1930s*. Stanford 1964, p. 48. F. Goguel, *La politique des partis sous la Troisième République*. Paris 1946, p. 519. J. Plumyène and R. Lasierra, *Les Fascismes français 1923–63*, Paris 1963, pp. 28–30, 50.

251 D. Ligou, op. cit., p. 367. A. Sauvy, *Histoire économique* . . . p. 108.

252 F. Goguel, op. cit., pp. 206–14.

253   A. Kriegel, *Le Congrès de Tours*. Paris 1964, pp. xxix–xxx. J. Fauvet, *Histoire du Parti Communiste Français I 1917–1939*. Paris 1964, pp. 280–1. G. Lefranc, *Le mouvement socialiste sous la Troisième République*. Paris 1963, pp. 435–7. F. Goguel, op. cit., p. 260.

254   F. Goguel, op. cit., pp. 260–6, 327–8.

255   J. Plumyène and R. Lasierra, op. cit., pp. 56–63.

256   F. Goguel, op. cit., pp. 482–3.

257   J. Chastenet, *Déclin de la Troisième 1931–38*. Paris 1962, pp. 71–89. G. Lefranc, *Front Populaire*, p. 20. J. Plumyène and R. Lasierra, op. cit., pp. 72–4, 82. M. Beloff, *The Sixth of February*, in J. Joll (ed), *Decline of the Third Republic*, London 1959.

258   D. Ligou, op. cit., p. 399.

259   G. Lefranc, op. cit., p. 113. G. Dupeux, op. cit., pp. 65–95. J. Joll, *The Making of the Popular Front* in J. Joll (ed), *Decline of the Third Republic*.

260   P. J. Larmour, op. cit., pp. 172–6, 186–7.

261   L. Bodin and J. Touchard, *Front Populaire 1936*, 2nd Edition. Paris 1965, pp. 140–1. G. Lefranc, op. cit., p. 339.

262   G. Lefranc, op. cit., p. 465. L. Bodin and J. Touchard, op. cit., pp. 200–221.

263   R. Rémond, *La droite en France*. Paris 1963, pp. 222–6. E. Weber, *Action Française*. Stanford 1962, pp. 415–7. J. Plumyène and R. Lasierra, op. cit., pp. 122–41.

264   P. M. de La Gorce, *La République et son armée*. Paris 1963, pp. 309–21. E. Weber, op. cit., pp. 396–402.

265   D. Ligou, op. cit., pp. 447–9.

266   J. Fauvet, op. cit., pp. 255–7.

267   P. Pétain, op. cit., p. 235.

268   E. Bonnefous, *Histoire politique de la Troisième République*, Vol. VI. Paris 1965, p. 196.

269   C. Bettelheim, op. cit., p. 9.

270   L. Blum, *Oeuvre. Mémoires. La Prison et le Procès. A l'Échelle Humaine*. Paris 1955, pp. 323–4.

271   See e.g. B. H. Liddell Hart, foreword to Col. Goutard, *The Battle of France 1940*. London 1958, p. 10.

272   *Commission d'enquête parlementaire sur les événements survenus en France de 1933 à 1945. Dépositions etc.* Vol. I, Paris 1951, pp. 191–209, evidence of M. Jacomet.

273   *Ibid.*, Vol. I, pp. 266–83, evidence of M. Cot, Vol. II, pp. 259–359, evidence of M. La Chambre.

274   R. Carr, *Spain 1808–1939*. Oxford 1966, p. 472.

275   G. Brenan, *The Spanish Labyrinth*. Cambridge 1943, pp. 85–202.

276   *Ibid.*, pp. 59–62.

277   P. Broué and E. Témime, *La Révolution et la Guerre d'Espagne*. Paris 1961 pp. 25–30.

278 R. Carr, op. cit., pp. 509–19. G. Brenan, op. cit., pp. 65–77.
279 R. Carr, op. cit., pp. 564–91.
280 *Ibid.*, pp. 591–602.
281 G. Jackson, *The Spanish Republic and the Civil War 1931–39*. Princeton 1965, pp. 25–38.
282 *Ibid.*, pp. 43–102. R. Carr, op. cit., pp. 603–25. G. Brenan, op. cit., pp. 229–59. H. Thomas, *The Spanish Civil War*. London 1961, pp. 38–65.
283 For the view that Gil Robles was a pillar of democracy see S. De Madariaga, *Spain*, London 1942, pp. 325–43; for the opposite view see G. Brenan, op. cit., pp. 290–300. G. Jackson, op. cit., pp. 122–8, 172–5, 202–15 brings some evidence to support Madariaga; S. G. Payne, *Falange*, Stanford 1962, pp. 105–6 a fragment to support Brenan.
284 B. Bolloten, *The Grand Camouflage*. London 1961, p. 19.
285 G. Brenan, op. cit., pp. 265–89. H. Thomas, op. cit., pp. 74–85.
286 H. Thomas, op. cit., pp. 89–94.
287 G. Brenan, op. cit., pp. 302–12.
288 C. G. Bowers, *My Mission to Spain*, London 1954, pp. 226–38.
289 G. Brenan, op. cit., pp. 308–11. S. G. Payne, op. cit., 96–115.
290 P. Broué and E. Témime, op. cit., pp. 71–74. H. Thomas, op. cit., pp. 100–18.
291 G. Jackson, op. cit., p. 249.
292 *Ibid.*, p. 336.
293 H. Thomas, op. cit., pp. 637, 643.
294 G. Jackson, op. cit., pp. 356–8.
295 *Ibid.*, pp. 356–421.
296 B. Bolloten, op. cit., pp. 35–76.
297 G. Jackson, op. cit., pp. 526–40. H. Thomas, op. cit., pp. 631–3.
298 G. Jackson, op. cit., pp. 276–309.
299 C. Bresciani-Turroni, op. cit., pp. 286–333. G. Bry, *Wages in Germany 1871–1945*, Princeton 1960, p. 268.
300 F. L. Carsten, *Reichswehr und Politik*, Köln and Berlin, p. 185
301 *Ibid.*, p. 90. W. T. Angress. *Stillborn Revolution*. Princeton 1963, pp. 105–66.
302 *Ibid.*, pp. 426–59.
303 H. J. Gordon, *The Reichswehr and the German Republic*. Princeton 1957, pp. 233–4.
304 F. L. Carsten, op. cit., pp. 200–1.
305 *Ibid.*, pp. 205–18. E. Eyck, *A History of the Weimar Republic*. (Eng. trans.) Cambridge Mass. 1962–4. Vol. I, p. 294.
306 W. T. Angress, op. cit., pp. 240–1.
307 A. Milatz, *Wähler und Wahlen in der Weimarer Republik*. Bonn 1965, p. 151.
308 E. Eyck, op. cit., I, pp. 315–22, II, pp. 103–4. A. Dorpalen, *Hindenburg and the Weimar Republic*. Princeton 1964.

309   H. A. Turner, *Stresemann and the Politics of the Weimar Republic*. Princeton 1963.

310   F. Hiller Von Gaertringen, *Die Deutschnationale Volkspartei* in E. Matthias and R. Morsey, *Das Ende der Parteien*. Düsseldorf 1960, pp. 548-9. A. Bullock, *Hitler: A Study in Tyranny*. New Edition London 1965, pp. 147-51.

311   K. D. Bracher, *Die Auflösung der Weimarer Republik*. Villingen 4th Edition 1964, pp. 645-56.

312   R. Heberle, *From Democracy to Nazism*. Baton Rouge 1945.

313   W. S. Allen, *The Nazi Seizure of Power*. London 1966, p. 51.

314   A. Bullock, op. cit., p. 213.

315   D.B.F.P. 2nd series, III, pp. 140-3.

316   F. L. Carsten, op. cit., pp. 431-7.

317   D.G.F.P., series D., VII, p. 201 [No. 192].

318   D.B.F.P., 2nd series, Vol. I, pp. 312-24, 331.

319   *Ibid.*, p. 580.

320   *Ibid.*, Vol. II, p. 85. E. W. Bennett, *Germany and the Diplomacy of the Financial Crisis 1931*. Cambridge Mass. 1962, pp. 54, 150-2, 295-7, 300-1.

321   D.B.F.P., 2nd series, Vol. II, pp. 67-8, 96, 108.

322   *Ibid.*, pp. 435-514. Vol. III, pp. 52-4, 77, 178-9.

323   *Ibid.*, pp. 595-602. Ministère des Affaires Étrangères, *Documents Diplomatiques Français*. [Hereafter cited as D.D.F.] Iᵉʳᵉ série (1932-5). Paris 1964, Vol. I, pp. 1-2.

324   E. Weill-Raynal, op. cit., III, pp. 712-31, 890-1, 896-7.

325   A. J. P. Taylor, *English History 1914-45*. Oxford 1965, pp. 150-1.

326   D.B.F.P., 2nd series, I, p. 368.

327   D.D.F., Iᵉʳᵉ série, I, pp. 102-3.

328   *Ibid.*, pp. 423-4. D.B.F.P. 2nd series, IV, pp. 137, 182, 193.

329   D.D.F., Iᵉʳᵉ série, I, pp. 440, 476-91.

330   A. J. Toynbee and others, *Survey of International Affairs 1931*, p. 401. W. A. Lewis, op. cit., pp. 115-8. League of Nations, *Appeal by the Chinese Government. Report of the Commission of Enquiry*. [The Lytton Report]. Geneva 1932, pp. 37-8, 121-6. D.B.F.P., 2nd series, IX, pp. 374-83.

331   *Lytton Report*, Chapters IV, VI.

332   D.B.F.P., 2nd series, IX, p. 377.

333   *Ibid.*, pp. 487, 710.

334   *Ibid.*, pp. 266, 437-8, VIII, p. 798.

335   *Ibid.*, XIII, pp. 884, 923, IX, pp. 423, 567.

336   *Ibid.*, IX, pp. 677-8, 282-3.

337   *Ibid.*, pp. 289-90, 33.

338   For U.S. policy see A. Rappaport, *Henry L. Stimson and Japan 1931-33*. Chicago 1963. D.B.F.P., 2nd series, IX, p. 423. See also telephone

conversations between Simon and Stimson in D.B.F.P., ii, IX and in *Foreign Relations of the United States 1932*. Vol. III.

339 D B F P , ii, IX, p 515. A. Rappaport, op. cit., pp. 116–7.

340 D.B.F.P., ii, IX, pp. 61, 368 and see quotations in R. Bassett, *Democracy and Foreign Policy*. London 1951.

341 D.D.F., i, I, p. 9.

342 A. J. P. Taylor, *Origins* . . ., presents the argument that Hitler's actions were determined by circumstances and by the actions of others.

343 *Documents on German Foreign Policy*. London and Washington 1949. [Hereafter cited as D.G.F.P.]. Series C. Vol. I, p. 37. R. J. O'Neill, *The German Army and the Nazi Party*. London 1966, pp. 125–6, 39–41. W. Treue, *Hitlers Denkschrift zum Vierjahresplan* in *Vierteljahrshefte für Zeitgeschichte* 3. Stuttgart 1955, pp. 204–10. T. Vogelsang in *ibid.*, 2. 1954, pp. 434–5.

344 A. J. P. Taylor, op. cit., pp. 70–1, 218–9. H. C. Hillman, *Comparative Strength of the Great Powers* in A. Toynbee and F. T. Ashton-Gwatkin (eds.), *Survey of International Affairs 1939–46. The World in March 1939*. London 1952, pp. 452–4. T. W. Mason, *Some Origins of the Second World War* in *Past and Present*, No. 29. Oxford 1964.

345 G. Hilger and A. G. Meyer, *The Incompatible Allies*. New York 1953, p. 191 footnote 3. F. Fischer, *Griff nach der Weltmacht*. Düsseldorf 1st Edition 1961, 3rd Edition 1964, pp. 194, 714–38.

346 G. L. Mosse, *The Crisis of German Ideology*. London 1966. E. Nolte, *Three Faces of Fascism*. London 1964, esp., pp. 267–303.

347 D.B.F.P., 2nd series, V, p. 389.

348 *Ibid.*, pp. 28, 202. VI, pp. 80, 90. D.G.F.P., series C, I, pp. 328–33, 342–3, 364. Z. J. Gasiriowski, *Did Pilsudski attempt to initiate a preventive war in 1933?* in *Journal of Modern History*. Chicago June 1955, pp. 135–51. H. Roos, *Die Präventivkriegspläne Pilsudskis von 1933* in *Vierteljahrshefte für Zeitgeschichte* 3. 1955, pp. 344–63.

349 D.B.F.P., 2nd series, VI, pp. 90–1, 228, 378.

350 Franco-British negotiations in *ibid.*, IV, V, VI. See e.g., V, pp. 618–24, VI, pp. 68, 303, 631–3, 764–5.

351 D.G.F.P., series C, I, pp. 882, 887, 923. II, pp. 12, 39, 42, 173, 513–8, 520–3. D.B.F.P., 2nd series, VI, pp. 488, 490.

352 H. C. Hillman, op. cit., p. 439. I, Svennilson, op. cit., pp. 262–3.

353 D.G.F.P., series C, I, pp. 160–1, 181–2, 196–203. D.B.F.P., 2nd series, V, pp. 67, 87–8, 447–8, 492–3.

354 *Ibid.*, pp. 109, 114–5, 281.

355 Z. J. Gasiriowski, op. cit., p. 141. D.G.F.P., series C, I, pp. 127, 111, 325, 343, 364, 46, 332, 342, 307, 365-7, 840, II, pp. 365, 421–2.

356 Z. J. Gasiriowski, op. cit., pp. 149–50.

357 D.G.F.P., series C, I, p. 717. II, p. 863, I, pp. 851, 449–50, 819, II, pp. 297–8, 684–5, 731–4.

358 *Ibid.*, p. 297. I, p. 875.
359 E.g., *Ibid.*, II, p. 815 (May 1934) III, p. 521 (October 1934), IV, pp. 871, 898 (December 1935).
360 W. E. Scott, *Alliance against Hitler*. Durham, N. C. 1962, pp. 3–69, 125–9.
361 *Ibid.*, pp. 160–75. D.B.F.P., 2nd series, VI, pp. 752–3.
362 *Ibid.*, pp. 761, 803–22, 828–9.
363 D.G.F.P., series C. I, p. 488–9.
364 D.B.F.P., 2nd series, VI, p. 879. J. Gehl, *Austria, Germany and the Anschluss 1931–1938*. London 1963, pp. 46–100. G. Brook-Shepherd, *Dollfuss*. London 1961, pp. 191–284.
365 D.B.F.P., 2nd series, VI, pp. 871–2.
366 D.G.F.P., series C, III, pp. 396–402, 385–6. D.B.F.P., 2nd series, VI, pp. 858–61. W. E. Scott, op. cit., pp. 187–8.
367 *Ibid.*, pp. 201–2. D.B.F.P., 2nd series, VI, p. 426, 884–5.
368 D.G.F.P., series, C, III, pp. 494, 472.
369 *Ibid.*, p. 926. IV, p. 356. III, pp. 728, 956, 706. W. E. Scott, op. cit., pp. 231–53.
370 *Ibid.*, p. 266. D.G.F.P., series C, IV, pp. 495, 860, 926.
371 *Ibid.*, III, pp. 785–6. A. J. Toynbee, *Survey of International Affairs 1935*, Vol. I. London 1936, pp. 104–8. H. Lagardelle, *Mission à Rome. Mussolini*. Paris 1955, pp. 117–8. D.D.F. 2ᵉ série. II, p. 184.
372 *Survey of International Affairs 1935*. I, pp. 122–3. Earl of Avon (Anthony Eden), *Facing the Dictators*. London 1962, pp. 139–41. *Correspondence showing the course of certain Diplomatic Discussions directed towards securing an European Settlement.* (British State Papers 1935–6. Accounts and Papers 13. XXVII, Misc. No. 3. 1936).
373 D.G.F.P., series C, IV, pp. 87, 189, 588.
374 *Survey of International Affairs 1935*. I, pp. 109–10. L. Salvatorelli and G. Mira, op. cit., pp. 822–5. Lord Avon, op. cit., p. 244. H. Lagardelle, op. cit., pp. 112–6.
375 L. Salvatorelli and G. Mira, op. cit., pp. 824–5. *Survey of International Affairs 1935*. II, pp. 148–9.
376 *Documents on International Affairs 1935*. Vol. II. London p. 566. *Survey of International Affairs 1935*. II, p. 48. L. Salvatorelli and G. Mira, op. cit., p. 828.
377 *Ibid.*, pp. 829–34, 841–3. Lord Avon, op. cit., pp. 220–51.
378 D.G.F.P., series C, IV, pp. 903–4, 957–61. Viscount Templewood (Sir Samuel Hoare), *Nine Troubled Years*. London 1954, pp. 184–5.
379 *Ibid.*, pp. 169–70. D.G.F.P., series C, IV, pp. 674, 694.
380 Lord Avon, op. cit., pp. 293–5.
381 L. Salvatorelli and G. Mira, op. cit., p. 873. *Survey of International Affairs 1935*. II, pp. 271–359.
382 *Documents on International Affairs 1935*. II, pp. 244–8.

383 D.G.F.P., series C, IV, pp. 975, 1043. D.D.F. 2ᵉ série, I, pp. 336–7.
384 *Ibid.*, pp. 304, 309–10. D.G.F.P., series C, IV, pp. 1142–4, 1163–6, 1172–5, 1202–3, 1219.
385 R. J. O'Neill, op. cit., pp. 128–9. D.G.F.P., series C, IV, p. 1165.
386 E.g. D.D.F. 2ᵉ série, I, pp. 40, 52–4, 78–9, 91 etc.
387 *Ibid.*, pp. 260, 323–4, 158, 245–7, 301. Lord Avon, op. cit., 332–3.
388 D.D.F. 2ᵉ série, I, pp. 339.
389 See e.g. *ibid.*, pp. 162, 273–6, 303.
390 Lord Avon, op. cit., p. 359. R. A. C. Parker, *The First Capitulation. France and the Rhineland Crisis of 1936* in *World Politics*. Princeton 1956, pp. 355–73. *Survey of International Affairs 1936*, pp. 282–370.
391 D.D.F. 2ᵉ série, I, pp. 444–5, 504–6, II, p. 185.
392 *Ibid.*, I, pp. 419, 415, I, 120–1, 273, 277–9.
393 Lord Avon, op. cit., p. 345. *Survey of International Affairs 1936*, p. 370.
394 D.G.F.P., series D, I, pp. 278–81 (No. 152). J. Gehl, op. cit., 101–32.
395 G. Ciano, *Ciano's Diplomatic Papers*, (ed. M. Muggeridge, Eng. Trans. of *L'Europa verso la catastrofe*). London 1948, pp. 144–5, 295. D.G.F.P., series D, III, pp. 147–8 (No. 137). VI, p. 261 (No. 211).
396 *Ibid.*, pp. 1–2 (footnotes). 7 (No. 5), 10–11 (No. 10), p. 172 (No. 157). I, p. 37 (No. 19). K. W. Watkins, *Britain Divided*. London 1963, p. 7.
397 D.G.F.P., series D, IV, p. 4 (No. 3). Lord Avon, op. cit., p. 406. G. Lefranc, *Front Populaire*. pp. 186, 461, 465.
398 F. Borkenau, *European Communism*. London 1953. D. T. Cattell, *Soviet Diplomacy and the Spanish Civil War*. Berkeley and Los Angeles 1957. G. F. Kennan, *Russia and the West under Lenin and Stalin*. London 1961.
399 D.G.F.P., series D, III, p. 803 (No. 701). D. T. Cattell, op. cit., p. 106.
400 G. Ciano, *Ciano's Diary 1937–8*, (Eng. Trans. ed. A. Mayor). London 1952, pp. 27–9. E. Wiskemann, *Rome-Berlin Axis*. New Edn. London 1966. Chapter IV. E. L. Presseisen, *Germany and Japan. A study in Totalitarian Diplomacy 1933–41*. The Hague 1958. Chapters IV, VI.
401 D.G.F.P., series D, I, p. 88 (No. 49), *Survey of International Affairs 1937*. I, pp. 340–4.
402 *Ibid.*, pp. 273–6.
403 D.G.F.P., series D, I, pp. 29–39 (No. 19).
404 G. Meinck, *Hitler und die deutsche Aufrüstung*. Weisbaden 1959, pp. 174–87.
405 K. Feiling, *Life of Neville Chamberlain*. London 1946. Chapters XVIII–XXII. H. Feis, *The Road to Pearl Harbor*. Princeton 1950, pp. 8–9.
406 J. Gehl, op. cit., pp. 166–75. D.G.F.P. series D, I, pp. 515–7 (No. 295). 549 (No. 328).
407 *Ibid.*, p. 563 (No. 340). J. Gehl, op. cit., pp. 182–95. R. J. O'Neill, op. cit., p. 151.

408 D.B.F.P., 3rd series, I, pp. 13–14, 23–4. D.G.F.P., series D, I, pp. 578–9 (Nos. 335, 356). J. Gehl, op. cit., p. 194. (citing F. Langoth, *Kampf um Österreich*. Wels 1951, pp. 239–41).

409 D.B.F.P., 3rd series, I, pp. 35–6, 62–4, 101.

410 *Ibid.*, pp. 151, 214, 97.

411 *Ibid.*, pp. 212–26.

412 D.G.F.P., series D, II, p. 253 (No. 143), p. 257 (No. 147), p. 344 (No. 210). *Les Procès de collaboration: Fernand de Brinon, Joseph Darnand, Jean Luchaire*. Paris 1948. esp, pp. 12–13, 54, 179–206.

413 D.G.F.P., series D, II, p. 198 (No. 107).

414 D.B.F.P., 3rd series, I, pp. 563, 567, 600–2 *Survey of International Affairs 1938*, II, pp. 208–9, 215–7, 238–56, 334–7.

415 D.G.F.P., series D, II, pp. 299–303 (No. 175), 357–62 (No. 221).

416 D.B.F.P., 3rd series, II, pp. 310–4, 318, K. Feiling, op. cit., p. 357.

417 *Ibid.*, pp. 357, 367. D.B.F.P., 3rd series, II, pp. 338–54, 363.

418 *Ibid.*, pp. 373–99, 404–6. R. J. Minney, *Private Papers of Hore-Belisha*. London 1960, p. 142.

419 *Survey of International Affairs 1938*, II, p. 345. P. Reynaud, *Mémoires II, Envers et Contre Tous*. Paris 1963, p. 209. D.B.F.P., 3rd series, II, pp. 416, 438–9.

420 G. Bonnet, *Le Quai d'Orsay sous trois Républiques*. Paris 1961, pp. 212–3. D.B.F.P., 3rd series, II, pp. 447–8. D. Vidal, *Czechoslovakia and the Powers, September 1938* in *Journal of Contemporary History*, I, 4, London 1966, p. 54.

421 D.B.F.P., 3rd series, II, pp. 435, 438, 449–50.

422 *Survey of International Affairs 1938*, II, p. 363.

423 V. F. Klochko and others (eds.), *New Documents on the History of Munich*. Prague 1958, pp. 86–7. C. Serre, *Rapport fait au nom de la commission chargée d'enquêter sur les événements survenus en France de 1933 à 1945*. Paris 1951, II, p. 268.

424 *Survey of International Affairs 1938*, II, p. 376. D.B.F.P., 3rd series, II, pp. 463–73, 499–508. D.G.F.P., series D, II, pp. 863–4 (No. 554).

425 D.B.F.P., 3rd series, II, pp. 459–60, 483–4, 520–35, 536–7 (and footnote), 565–6, 550.

426 *Ibid.*, pp. 627–40. K. Feiling, op. cit., p. 381.

427 J. W. Wheeler-Bennett, *The Nemesis of Power*. London 1953, pp. 395–424. D.B.F.P., 3rd series, II, pp. 683–92.

428 *Ibid.*, p. 489. *Survey of International Affairs*, 1938. Vol. III, p. 55. D.G.F.P. series D, IV, p. 606 (No. 477).

429 *Ibid.*, p. 470 (No. 369), pp. 473–4 (No. 370), p. 497 (No. 387), *Survey of International Affairs 1938*, III, p. 189.

430 K. Feiling, op. cit., pp. 385–6.

431 D.G.F.P., series D, IV, p. 99 (No. 81), pp. 185–6 (No. 152). pp. 190–5

(No. 158), pp. 209–13 (No. 168) p. 235 (No. 188), pp. 240–1 (Nos. 197–9) pp. 243–4 (No. 202).

432 *Ibid.*, pp. 261–2 (No. 225), pp. 263–70 (Nos. 228–9).

433 *Ibid.*, V, pp. 104–7 (No. 81), pp. 127–9 (No. 101), pp. 152–6 (Nos. 119–20), pp. 167–8 (No. 126), VI, pp. 70–2 (No. 61).

434 J. Szembek, *Journal 1933–1939*. Paris 1952, pp. 433–5. D.G.F.P., series D, VI, pp. 121–4 (No. 102), p. 127 (No. 103), p. 136 (No. 108), pp. 147–8 (No. 118), p. 195 (No. 159).

435 *Ibid.*, p 117 (No. 99), pp 186–7, 223–7 (Nos 149, 185), pp 574–80 (No. 443). D.B.F.P., 3rd series, V, p. 46.

436 K. Feiling, op. cit., pp. 399–401, 409. D.G.F.P., series D, VI, pp. 569–71 (No. 430).

437 D.B.F.P., 3rd series, IV, pp. 400, 467, 500–3, 515–7. J. Szembek, op. cit., pp. 433–4.

438 I. Colvin, *Vansittart in Office*. London 1965, pp. 298–311. D.B.F.P., 3rd series, IV, pp. 545–6, 552–3. Compare M. Gilbert and R. Gott, *The Appeasers*. London 1963, pp. 230–6.

439 *Survey of International Affairs 1939–46. The Eve of War 1939*. pp. 426–9. D.B.F.P., 3rd series, VI, pp. 217–9.

440 For the negotiations with the U.S.S.R. see D.B.F.P., 3rd series, IV–VII, D.G.F.P., series D, VI–VII.

441 D.G.F.P., series D, VII, pp. 39–49 (No. 43), pp. 53–6 (No. 47), pp. 557–9 (Appendix I), pp. 200–6 (Nos. 192–3).

442 *Ibid.*, pp. 285–6 (No. 271), pp. 309–10 (No. 301), p. 314 (No. 307), p. 569 (Appendix I), *Documenti Diplomatici Italiani*. Ottava serie, XIII. Rome 1953, p. 39.

443 *Survey of International Affairs. The Eve of War 1939*, pp. 204–24. D.B.F.P., 3rd series, V, pp. 791–3, VI, pp. 389–91, 407–10, 579–82, 736–61. D.G.F.P., series D, VI, pp. 674–8 (No. 497), pp. 977–83 (No 716), pp. 1088–93 (No 783). Ministry of Foreign Affairs of the U.S.S.R., *Documents and Materials Relating to the Eve of the Second World War*. Moscow 1948. II, pp. 67–78 (Nos. 13–15), pp. 116–25 (No. 24).

444 D.B.F.P., 3rd series, VII, pp. 127–8, 177–9, 227–9, 330–2. D.G.F.P., series D, pp. 566–7 (Appendix I).

445 D.B.F.P., 3rd series, VII, pp. 391, 410–1, 427, 432–3, 447, 469–70. A. J. P. Taylor, *Origins . . .*, pp. 275, 278.

446 *Foreign Relations of the United States*, 1939 I. Washington 1956, pp. 355, 392.

447 D.B.F.P., 3rd series VII, pp. 442–3, 449, 477–9, 481, 498–9. D.G.F.P., series D, VII, pp. 509–10 (No. 535). M. Gamelin, op. cit., I, pp. 28–9.

448 D.G.F.P., series D, VII, p. 514 (No. 541), D.B.F.P., 3rd series, VII, pp. 505–8.

449 D.G.F.P., series D, pp. 538–9 (No. 565), *Documenti diplomatici italiani*. Ottava serie, XIII, pp. 375–6.

450 G. Bonnet, op. cit., pp. 296–7, *Foreign Relations of the United States 1939.* I, p. 405. D.B.F.P., 3rd series, VII, pp. 500, 504. R. J. Minney, op. cit., p. 226.

451 D.B.F.P., 3rd series, VII, pp. 513–4, 518, 524–5. R. J. Minney, op. cit., p. 226–8. M. Gilbert and R. Gott, op. cit., pp. 306–12.

452 A. S. Milward, *The German Economy at War.* London 1965, p. 29.

453 J. R. M. Butler, *Grand Strategy,* Vol II, London 1957, p. 10.

454 L. F. Ellis, *The War in France and Flanders, 1939–40.* London 1953, p. 5.

455 J. R. M. Butler, op. cit., pp. 91–150.

456 H. A. Jacobsen in H. A. Jacobsen and J. Rohwer (eds), *Decisive Battles of World War II,* Eng. Trans. London 1960, pp. 32–3.

457 Gen. de Cossé-Brissac, *L'Armée allemande dans la campagne de France de 1940* in *Revue d'Histoire de la Deuxième Guerre Mondiale,* Paris, Jan. 1964, pp. 4–5. Gen. Gamelin, op. cit., I, pp. 149–67. J. R. M. Butler, op. cit., pp. 177–9.

458 L. F. Ellis, op. cit., p. 36. Gamelin, op. cit., II, p. 311. Lt.-Col. Le Goyet, *La Percée de Sedan 10–15 mai 1940* in *Revue d'Histoire de la Deuxième Guerre Mondiale 1965,* pp. 25–52. Col. A. Goutard. *The Battle of France 1940.* (Eng. Trans.). London 1958, pp. 116–79.

459 P. Reynaud, op. cit., II, pp. 396–444.

460 R. R. A. Wheatley, *Operation Sea Lion.* Oxford 1958. J. R. M. Butler, op. cit., pp. 209–15, 284–93.

461 H. Feis, *The Road to Pearl Harbour.* Princeton 1950.

462 H. A. Jacobsen, *Der Zweite Weltkrieg. Grundzüge der Politik und Strategie in Dokumenten.* Frankfurt 1965, p. 168.

463 H. L. Thomson and L. Mayo, *The Ordinance Department: Procurement and Supply.* Washington 1960, p. 263.

464 W. F. Craven and J. L. Cate (eds), *Army Air Forces in World War II,* VI, Washington 1955, p. 350.

465 H. A. Jacobsen, op. cit., p. 169.

466 C. Webster and N. Frankland, *The Strategic Air Offensive Against Germany 1939–45.* London 1961, IV, p. 481.

467 *Ibid.,* pp. 472, 480. W. K. Hancock and M. M. Gowing, *British War Economy.* London 1949. p. 370.

468 A. S. Milward, op. cit., p. 47, Central Statistical Office, *Statistical Digest of the War.* London 1951, pp. 17–29. C. Webster and N. Frankland, op. cit., IV, pp. 473–4.

469 *Ibid.,* I, p. 227.

470 L. Giovanitty and F. Freed, *The Decision to Drop the Bomb.* London 1967. H. Feis, *Japan Subdued.* Princeton 1961.

471 G. Frumkin, *Population changes in Europe since 1939.* New York 1951.

472 X. Lannes, *Les Conséquences démographiques de la guerre en Europe* in *Revue d'Histoire de la Deuxième Guerre Mondiale.* Paris, July 1955, p. 7.

473 A. Dallin, *German Rule in Russia 1941–5.* London 1957, Chapter XIX.

H. A. Jacobsen. *Kommissarbefehl und Massenexecutionen sowjetischer Kriegsgefangener* in H. Buchheim and others *Anatomie des S.S.-Staates* II, Olten and Freiburg im Breisgau 1965.

474 A. Toynbee and V. M. Toynbee, *Survey of International Affairs 1939–46. Hitler's Europe.* London 1954, p. 234.

475 *Ibid.*, p. 245, 249, 253–4. A. Dallin, op. cit., pp. 435–6.

476 M. Carlyle (ed), *Documents on International Affairs 1939–46 Vol II Hitler's Europe.* London 1954, pp. 231, 188–9.

477 G. H. Stein, *The Waffen S.S.* Ithaca, N.Y. 1966, p. 276. A. Toynbee and V. M. Toynbee, op. cit., p. 506. A. Dallin, op. cit., p. 76, 210–2.

478 L. Poliakov, *Quel est le nombre de victimes?* in *Revue d'Histoire de la Deuxième Geurre Mondiale.* October, 1956, pp. 88–96. G. Reitlinger. *The Final Solution.* London 1953, pp. 489–501. R. Hilberg, *The Destruction of the European Jews.* Chicago and London 1961, p. 767. H. Krausnick. *Judenverfolgung* in H. Buchheim and others, op. cit.

479 R. Hilberg, op. cit., pp. 199–201, 203–5, 244–6.

480 *Ibid.*, pp. 389–421.

481 *Ibid.*, p. 470. W. Warmbrunn. *The Dutch under German Occupation 1940–45.* Stanford 1963, pp. 173–4.

482 R. Hilberg, op. cit., p. 596, 661–2.

483 *Ibid.*, pp. 211–2.

484 G. H. Stein, op. cit., pp. 204–5.

485 R. Hilberg, op. cit., pp. 651–2.

486 R. Collenot, *L'opposition Allemande contre Hitler*, in *Revue d'Histoire de la Deuxième Geurre Mondiale.* October, 1959, p. 24.

Select Bibliography

Sources

Documenti diplomatici italiani. Rome 1952–
Documents diplomatiques français 1932–1939. Paris 1963–
Documents on British Foreign Policy 1919–39. London 1947–
Foreign Relations of the United States: Diplomatic Papers. Washington 1861–
Mantoux, P. (ed.), *Les Délibérations du Conseil des Quatre*. Paris 1955.
Stresemann, G., *Vermächtnis* (herausg. by H. Bernhard). Berlin 1932–3.
International Military Tribunal, Nuremberg. Trial of the major war criminals. Nuremberg 1947–9.

International History

Albrecht-Carrié, R., *Italy at the Paris Peace Conference*. New York 1938.
Bretton, H., *Stresemann and the Revision of Versailles*. Stanford 1953.
Carr, E., *A History of Soviet Russia*. London 1950–
Freund, G., *Unholy Alliance*. London 1957.
Gatzke, H., *Stresemann and the Rearmament of Germany*. Baltimore 1954.
Gilbert, M., and Gott, R., *The Appeasers*. London 1963.
Keynes, J., *Economic Consequences of the Peace*. London 1919.
Lloyd George, D., *The Truth about the Peace Treaties*. London 1938.
di Nolfo, E., *Mussolini e la politica estera italiana 1919–33*. Padua 1960.
Scott, W. E., *Alliance against Hitler. The Origins of the Franco-Soviet Pact*. Durham, N. C. 1962.
Tardieu, A., *La Paix*. Paris 1921.
Taylor, A., *Origins of the Second World War*. London 1961.
Temperley, H., (ed.) *History of the Peace Conference of Paris*. London 1920–4.
Thimme, A., *Gustav Stresemann*. Hannover and Frankfurt a.M. 1957
Toynbee, A., and others (eds) *Survey of International Affairs 1920–1946* London 1927–58.

Wandycz, P., *France and her Eastern Allies*. Minneapolis 1962.
Weill-Raynal, E., *Les Réparations Allemandes et la France*. Paris 1938–47.

Economic

Arndt, H., *Economic Lessons of the Nineteen-Thirties*. London 1944.
Lewis, W., *Economic Survey 1919–39*. London 1949.
Maizels, A., *Industrial Growth and World Trade*. Cambridge 1963.
Svennilson, I., *Growth and Stagnation in the European Economy*. Geneva 1954.

Britain

Bassett, R., *Nineteen Thirty-One*. London 1958.
Mowat, C., *Britain Between the Wars*. 1918–40. London 1955.
Pollard, S., *Development of the British Economy 1914–50*. London 1962.
Taylor, A., *English History 1914–45*. Oxford 1965.

Italy

Alatri, P., *Le Origini del Fascismo*. 3rd edn. Rome 1962.
De Felice, R., *Mussolini il rivoluzionario*. Turin 1965.
Rossi, A., (Tasca). *The Rise of Italian Fascism*. London 1939.
Salvatorelli, L. and Mira, G., *Storia d'Italia nel periodo fascista*. Turin 1964.
Welk, W., *Fascist Economic Policy*. Cambridge, Mass. 1938.

France

Bonnefous, G., *Histoire politique de la Troisième République*. Paris 1956–67.
Chastenet, J., *Histoire de la Troisième République*. Paris 1952–63.
Goguel, F., *La Politique des Partis sous la Troisième République*. Paris 1946.
Lefranc, G., *Le mouvement socialiste sous la Troisième République*. Paris 1963.
Lefranc, G., *Histore du front populaire*. Paris 1965.
Ligou, D., *Histoire du socialisme en France 1871–1961*. Paris 1962.
Néré, J., *La Troisième République*. Paris 1965.
Sauvy, A., *Histoire économique de la France entre les deux guerres*. Paris 1965–

Spain

Bolloten, B., *The Grand Camouflage*. London 1961.
Brenan, G., *The Spanish Labyrinth*. Cambridge 1943.
Broue, P. and Temime, E., *La Révolution et la Guerre d'Espagne*. Paris 1961.
Carr, R., *Spain 1808–1939*. Oxford 1966.
Jackson, G., *The Spanish Republic and the Civil War 1931–39*. Princeton 1965.
Thomas, H., *The Spanish Civil War*. London 1961.

Germany

Allen, W., *The Nazi Seizure of Power*. London 1966.
Angress, W., *Stillborn Revolution*. Princeton 1963.

Bracher, K., *Die Auflösung der Weimarer Republik*. Villingen. 4th edn. 1964.

Bresciani-Turroni, C., *The Economics of Inflation*. London 1937.

Bullock, A., *Hitler, A Study in Tyranny*. 2nd edn. London 1965.

Carsten, F., *Reichswehr und Politik*. 2 Aufl. Köln and Berlin 1965.

Dorpalen, A., *Hindenburg and the Weimar Republic*. Princeton 1964.

Eyck, E., *A History of the Weimar Republic*. Cambridge, Mass. 1962-4.

Heberle, R., *From Democracy to Nazism*. Baton Rouge 1945.

Matthias, E., and Morsey, R., *Das Ende der Parteien*. Düsseldorf 1960.

Wheeler-Bennett, J., *The Nemesis of Power*. London 1953.

Second World War

The most important studies are the official histories published in London and in the U.S.A.

History of the Second World War. United Kingdom Civil Series. London 1949-

History of the Second World War. United Kingdom Military Series. London 1952-

The United States Army in World War II. Washington 1947-

Craven, W. and Cate, J. (eds.), *The Army Air Forces in World War II*. Chicago 1948-58.

Morison, S., *History of United States Naval Operations in World War II*. Boston 1947-62.

See also

Esposito, V. (ed.), *The West Point Atlas of American Wars*. New York 1959.

Hilberg, R., *The Destruction of the European Jews*. Chicago 1961.

Recent publications in English

(Some valuable works which appeared too late to be used in the preparation of this book.)

Barker, A. J., *The Civilising Mission: the Italo-Ethiopian War 1935-6*. London 1968.

Bradley, J., *Allied Intervention in Russia*. London 1968.

Carsten, F. L., *The Rise of Fascism*. London 1967.

Chapman, G., *Why France Collapsed*. London 1968.

Cienciala, A. M., *Poland and the Western Powers, 1938-1939*. London 1968.

Compton, J. V., *The Swastika and the Eagle: Hitler, the U.S. and the Origins of the Second World War*. London 1968.

Friedlander, S., *Prelude to Downfall: Hitler and the U.S. 1939-41*. London 1967.

Gilbert, M., *The Roots of Appeasement*. London 1966.

Mayer, A. J., *Politics and Diplomacy of Peacemaking*. London 1968.

Nicholls, A. J., *Weimar and the Rise of Hitler*. London 1968.

Northedge, F. S., *The Troubled Giant: Britain among the Great Powers, 1916-1939*. London 1966.

Richardson, H. W., *Economic Recovery in Britain 1932–9*. London 1967.
Robbins, K., *Munich 1938*. London 1968.
Roberts, J. M., *Europe 1880–1945*. London 1967.
Ryder, A. J., *The German Revolution of 1918*. Cambridge 1967.
Seton-Watson, C., *Italy from Liberalism to Fascism, 1870–1925*. London 1967.
Skidelsky, R., *Politicians and the Slump*. London 1967.
Thorne, C., *The Approach of War 1938–1939*. London 1967.
Ullman, R. H., *Britain and the Russian Civil War*. London 1968.
Warner, G., *Pierre Laval and the Eclipse of France*. London 1968.
Woolf, S. J. (ed.), *European Fascism*. London 1968.

Index

q denotes reference to a quotation

Abdulla, Emir of Transjordan, 36
Acerbo Law, 155–6
Action Française, 171, 174–5, 179
agriculture, 102–3, 200
Alcalá Zamora, Niceto, 196, 201
Alexander, King of Yugoslavia, 276
Alfonso XIII, King of Spain, 194–6
Allenby, Viscount, 33, 35
Allied Economic Commission, 30
Aloisi, Baron, 285, 287
Alsace-Lorraine, 8
Amendola, Giovanni, 155–6
anarchists, 191, 198
Anderson, Sir John, 124
Anglo-American Pledge, 1919, 59
Anglo-French Alliance, 39, 56, 59, 80
Anglo-Japanese Alliance, 246
Anglo-Polish Agreement, 325, 329
Anglo-Russian Trade Agreement, 1921, 50, 54
Anschluss, 16, 78, 242, 272, 305–6, 321
Anti-Semitism, 133, 180, 227, 238, 262, 320, 355–61
Aosta, Duke of, 153
appeasement, British policy of, applied by Lloyd George 5–16, 56–63, 66–8; by Bonar Law 68–70; by Curzon 72; by MacDonald 247–8; by Simon 254–7, 264, 272–273; by Hoare 280–1; by Eden

281, 292, 294; by N. Chamberlain 302–3, 306–8, 310–13, 315–17, 320, 324–6, 330–5
Atatürk, *see* Kemal, Mustafa
atomic bomb, 353–4
Auschwitz, 359
Austro-German Customs Union, 227, 240, 242
Avanguardisti, 157
Aventine Seccession, 156
Azaña, Manuel, 196, 198, 200, 202, 204, 208

Badoglio, General Pietro, 149, 279
balance of power, 32, 66–7, 100, 120
Balbo, Italo, 91, 152
Baldwin, Stanley, 68 *q.*, 125, 129–30
Balfour, Arthur J., 24, 30, 33
Baltic area, 43–4, 51
Banat, 28
Barthou, Louis, 73, 272, 275–7, 292
Bavarian Peoples Party, BVP, 219, 223, 228
Bayonne, 175
Beck, Colonel Joseph, 267–8, 275, 293, 322–6, 333
Beck, Ludwig, 305, 317
Beneš, Dr Edouard, 307, 309, 313–15
Berenguer, General, 195
Bergery, Gaston, 185
Berlin, Treaty of, 84, 269

Berthelot, Philippe, 82, 244
Bethmann-Hollweg, Theodor von, 261
birth rate, 102–3
Blitzkrieg, 337, 339, 344
Blomberg, General Werner von, 234, 236, 290, 301
Blum, Léon, 167, 171, 176, 179–84, 187–8
Bologna, 146–8
Bolshevism (*see* Communism)
bombing, 349–55
Bonar Law, Andrew, 69 *q.*, 74
Bonnet, Georges, 307–9, 312–14, 319, 325, 334–5
Bonomi, Ivanoe, 149, 151–2
boom, *see* slump
Borah, Senator, 256
Brauchitsch, Walther von, 317, 339
Brest-Litovsk, Peace of, 3, 261
Briand, Aristide, 59–60, 62–3, 81, 85–9, 171, 185, 239–40, 292
Briand-Kellogg pact, 89, 252, 256
Brinon, Comte de, 309
British Union of Fascists, 131, 133–4
Brockdorff-Ahlefeldt, Count von, 317
Brüning, Heinrich, 214, 227–32, 240–243, 247
Buchrucker, Major, 219
Buxton, Charles, 69 *q.*

Cagoule, 182
Calvo Sotelo, José, 203–4, 207
Camelots du Roi, 171, 175
Camere del Lavoro, 142
Cannes Conference, 54
capitalists, 41
Caporetto, 143
Carlism, 192, 198, 201, 204, 208
Catalonia, 192, 195, 200, 205
Cecil, Lord, 257
Centre Party, 223, 225, 228, 233–5
CGT, 172

CGTU, 172, 177
Chamberlain, Austen, 80
Chamberlain, Neville, 302, 306–7, 309, 312–13, 315–19, 324, 330–2, 334
Chanak, 39
Chang, Hsueh-liang, 251
Chang, Tso-lin, 251
Chautemps, Camille, 168, 174–5, 187, 297, 313, 342
Chicherin, 84
Churchill, Winston S., 320, 343
Ciano, Galeazzo, 295, 299–300, 305, 329, 334–5
Citrine, W. M., 125–6
Cittadini, General Arturo, 153
Clemenceau, Georges, 3, 4, 14, 16–17, 24, 34–7, 43–4, 47, 56, 172
Committee of Eighteen, 287
Committee of Union and Progress, 36
Commonwealth, 241
Communism, in Britain, 122–3, 127–128, 130; in France, 163, 172–3, 175–84; in Germany, 52, 67, 215–216, 222, 225–6, 229, 231, 233, 235; in Russia, 41–4, 46–8, 50–1; in Spain, 190–1, 200–2, 207, 209–10, 218–20
Communist International, 50, 183, 209, 218, 298–9, 322
concentration camps, 356
Confederación Española de Derechas Autónomas, CEDA, 198–201
Confederatión Nacional del Trabajo, CNT, 191–4, 197–8, 200, 202, 208
Constantine, King of Greece, 38
Cook, A. J., 128
cordon sanitaire, 43
Corfu incident, 89–90
Council of Action, 123
Council of Four, 6, 13, 35–7, 42
Council of Ten, 17
Creditanstalt, 101
croix de feu, 174–6, 178–9, 181

Cuno, Wilhelm, 77
currency, 68, 98, 101, 119, 124, 129, 161
Curtius, Julius, 241–2
Curzon, Lord, 49–50, 60, 72 *q.*
Curzon line, 46

d'Abernon, Lord, 49–50, 61
Dahlerus, 331
Daily Mail, 125, 134
Daladier, Edouard, 168, 174–6, 178, 181, 185–6, 188, 207–10, 271, 312–313, 315–16, 324, 334
d'Annunzio, Gabriele, 25–6, 143, 145
Danzig, 13, 49, 60, 78, 267, 322–3, 331, 333
Darlan, Admiral François, 297
Darwin, Charles, 139
Dawes, General Charles, 73
Dawes Plan, 72–5, 77, 79, 81, 86, 214, 222
death rate, 102–3, 109
deflation, in Britain, 119–21, 131; in France, 166–7, 170, 188; in Germany, 213–15, 241; in Italy, 160–2; in Japan, 250
De Gaulle, Charles, 164, 342
Delbos, Yvon, 297, 300
demilitarized zones, 39, 57, 59–60, 79, 85, 289–92
Denain, General, 188
Denikin, Anton, 42–3, 45
deportation, 354, 358–9
depression, 99, 166–7, 212, 214, 226–228, 236–7, 311
Deschanel, Paul, 56
devaluation, 100; in Britain, 101, 129, 166, 227; in France, 166, 168, 170–171, 180; in Germany, 214, 237; in Italy, 160–1; in Japan, 252; in U.S.A., 166
Diaz, General, 153
disarmament, 16–17, 57, 76, 78, 87–9, 93, 182, 242, 247–9, 263–4, 271–3, 275, 280, 316, 331

DNVP, *see* German Nationalist Peoples Party
Dollfuss, Engelbert, 273–5
Doumergue, Louis, 176–8, 264, 271
Drummond, Sir Eric, 285
Duesterberg, Theodor, 231
Duff-Cooper, Alfred, 320
DVP (*see* German Peoples Party)

Ebert, Friedrich, 216–18
Economic Party, 224
Eden, Anthony, 265, 281, 284, 291, 294, 303, 306
education, 106, 111–12, 193, 196–7
El Alamein, 344
Emergency Powers Act (UK, 1920), 124
emigration, 161
equality of the sexes, 107
Erzberger, Matthias, 18, 221
Ethiopia, 183, 282–7, 302

Facta, Luigi, 149, 151, 153
Faisceau, 171, 174
Falange, 203–4, 208
Far East, 246, 249, 252–4, 257, 299, 302
fascism, in Britain, 131–4; in France, 171, 174–7, 179, 181–2; in Germany (*see* Nazis); in Italy, 90, 137–41, 144, 146–62; in Spain, 203–4, 211
Faure, Paul, 184
fatherland front, 274
Federación Anarquista Iberica, FIA, 191, 200, 202
Federzoni, Luigi, 153
Feisal, Emir, 33–7
Fey, Major Emil, 274
FIOM, 141
Fiume, 24–6, 91, 143, 145
Flandin, Pierre Etienne, 166, 171, 178, 288, 291–3, 324
Foch, Marshal Ferdinand, 4–5, 8, 9, 17, 18, 42, 57
Fontainebleau Memorandum, 9, 12, 15

Four Power Pact, 266, 279, 318
Fourteen Points, 6, 13, 17, 21, 24, 29
Franco, General Francisco, 201, 204, 206, 208, 211, 295–6, 343, 299
François-Poncet, André, 277
Franco-Italian Alliance, 289
Franco-Czech Treaty 1924, 57
Franco-Polish Alliance, 82, 269, 275
Franco-Soviet Pact, 178, 183, 269, 270, 276, 280, 289–90
Franklin-Bouillon Treaty, 39
Franz Ferdinand, Archduke, 21
Free Corps, 51, 217, 219
free trade, 26, 29
Freikorps, see Free Corps
Fritsch, Werner von, 290, 301

Gamelin, General Maurice, 279, 290, 293
Garat, 175
Geddes, Sir Eric, 121
Genoa Conference (Economic), 54–55
German Army, *see Reichswehr*
German Democratic Party, DDP, 216
German Communist Party, KPD, 216, 218, 225–6, 229
German Nationalist Peoples Party, DNVP, 221–2, 224, 228, 230–1, 233, 239
German Peoples Party, DVP, 223, 228
Gessler, Otto, 220
Gilbert, Parker, 81
Gil Robles, José Maria, 199, 202
Giolitti, Giovanni, 144–5, 149–50, 152–5
Giral, José, 205
Goebbels, Joseph, 262
Goded, General, 201, 204
gold, 68
gold standard, 101, 120–1, 123–4, 131, 160, 162, 168
Goltz, General von der, 43, 50

Göring, Hermann, 278, 290, 295, 301, 305–6, 312, 330–1

Habicht, 274
Hacha, Emil, 321
Haile Selassie, 285
Halder, Franz, 318, 330, 333, 339
Halifax, Lord, 302–3, 305–7, 309, 312, 316, 325–6, 332–5
Hankey, Sir Maurice, 49
Habsburgs, 4, 20, 29–30
Habsburg Empire, 22, 29
Harding, President, 69
Hassell, Ulrich von, 289–90, 296
Hegel, Georg, 139
Heimwehr, 273, 294
Helfferich, Karl, 64
Helldorf, Count Wolf von, 317
Henderson, Nevile, 249, 306, 332–4
Henlein, Konrad, 311
Herriot, Edouard, 76, 173–4, 243–4, 247–9, 270
Hesnard, 87
Hindenburg, Marshal Paul von, 223, 229–34
Hindenburg, Oskar, 234
Hirohito, Emperor, 345
Hiroshima, 354
Hitler, Adolf, and Austria, 273–5, 294; becomes Chancellor, 232–5; and Czechoslovakia, 306–22; and disarmament, see 'and rearmament'; domestic policies of, 219, 225–7, 236–8, 262; foreign aims of, 47, 55, 227, 258–62, 273, 300–2, 306, 356; foreign views on, 183–5, 257, 262–3, 267–8, 308–9, 312, 323–325; and Munich putsch, 220–1; and Poland, 322–34, 336; and rearmament, 237–8, 262–5, 277–8, 280–2, 301; and Rhineland crisis, 290–1; and Soviet Union, 268–70; and Spain, 295–6, 299; strategy of, 337–9, 343–7; inherits Stresemann's work, 85; support for in Germany,

212, 224–8, 231, 238; other references, 177, 208, 216, 230, 240, 266, 271, 288–9, 352, 360–1
Hoare, Sir Samuel, 284, 313
Hoare-Laval plan, 286
Hodza, Milar, 315
Hoepner, General Erich, 317
Hoesch, Leopold von, 277
Hoover, President Herbert, 255
Hoover Moratorium, 227, 242, 248
Hossbach, Colonel Friedrich, 301
House, Colonel Edward, 15, 24
housing, 105, 108, 114
Hugenberg, Alfred, 224, 228–30
hunger marches, 123
Hussein, Sherif of Mecca, 33

Illiteracy, 102, 106, 111
immigration, 166
imperialism, 38
industrialization, 104
infantile mortality, 102, 107–9, 114–115
inflation, in Britain, 123; in France, 74, 86, 99, 164–6, 168–70; in Germany, 63–6, 71–2, 99, 212–15, 218, 237–8; in Italy, 140–3
International Labour Office (ILO), 110–11

Jeunesses Patriotes, 171, 176, 181
Jews (*see* anti-Semitism)
Jewish National Home, 34, 36
Jouhaux, Léon, 180
Jusserand, Jean, 10

Kahr, Gustav von, 220, 236
Kamenev, Lev, 48
Kapp, Wolfgang, 52
Kapp *Putsch*, 51, 58, 217, 219, 223
Keitel, Wilhelm, 305, 311, 356
Kellogg Pact, 89, 252, 256
Kemal, Mustafa, 37–40
Kennedy, Joseph P., 334–5

Keynes, John Maynard, 5, 7, 18, 62 q., 68
Kleist, Ewald von, 318
Kolchak, Aleksandr, 42, 45
Korfanty, Wojciech, 58–9
Kopp, 53
KPD, *see* German Communist Party
Kun, Bela, 28
Kuomintang, 251

Labour Charter, 208
Labour Party, 128, 135
La Chambre, Guy, 189
Lacroix, 314–15
Land reforms, 141, 200, 202, 208
Lansing, Robert, 6 q., 15
Largo Caballero, Francisco, 194, 196–7, 200, 208–10
Lateran Pacts, 157
Lausanne Conference, 1932, 227, 244
Lausanne, Treaty of, 1923, 20, 39–40
Laval, Pierre, 166, 178, 183, 188, 244, 276, 280, 282, 297
Lawrence, T. E., 33–5
League of Nations, 3, 8, 12, 14, 16, 18–19, 57, 59, 77–8, 83–8, 110, 182–4, 241, 247–9, 252, 254, 256–7, 264, 266, 211–12, 276–8, 285–8, 290–3, 307
Lebrun, President, 297, 342
Le May, General Curtis, 353
lend-lease, 347
Lenin, Vladimir Ilyich, 45, 53 q., 142
Le Rond, General, 58–9
Lerroux, Alejandro, 198, 200–1, 204
Leygues, Georges, 47
L'Humanité, 177
Liebmann, General Kurt, 259
life span, 102, 114
Lindley, Sir Francis, 256
Lindsey, Sir Ronald, 253
Lipski, Joseph, 322–3
Little Entente, 57, 92, 266, 272, 300
Litvinov, Maxim, 269–70, 272, 276, 328

Lloyd-George, David, 3, 4, 5–18, 24, 27, 34–9, 43–4, 47–8, 50, 54, 56, 58, 60, 62–3, 67–8, 86, 133, 246, 276
loans, international, 69, 73, 98, 100, 129
Locarno Treaties, 77, 79, 82–9, 91, 143, 222, 247–8, 272, 279–80, 289–293, 307
London Conference, 1921, 62
London County Council, 134
London, Treaty of, 1915, 22–4, 89, 92, 279
London, Treaty of, 1930, 246
Lossow, Otto von, 220–1
Loucheur, Louis, 7, 54
Lord, Professor R. H., 13
Ludendorff, Erich, 221, 261
Luther, Hans, 222
Lüttwitz, General Walther von, 52
Lytton Report, 256

MacDonald, Ramsay, 76, 129–30, 247 q., 253, 266
Maginot Line, 83, 188, 341
Manchuria, 183, 250–4, 256–7, 285
Manstein, Erich von, 339
march on Rome, 151, 153, 176
Martin, Germain, 171, 244
Martinez Barrio, Diego, 201, 205
Marx, Karl, 222
Masaryk, Thomas, 22
Massigli, René, 257
Matteotti, Giacomo, 156
Maurin, General, 291, 293
Max, Prince of Baden, 216
medicine, 109
Memel, 323
Mein Kampf, 258–9, 261, 263, 269
MICUM, 70
Miklas, President Wilhelm, 305
Millerand, Alexandre, 47–9, 58, 292
Modigliani, Emanuele, 142
Mola, General, 204, 207
Moltke, Helmuth von, 267

Molotov, Viacheslav Michailovitch, 269, 328
Mond, Sir Alfred, 126
Morgenthau Plan, 349
Mosley, Sir Oswald, 131, 133–4
Mosul, 91
Mukden, 251
Müller, Hermann, 228
Munich Agreement, 317–18, 320, 324
Mussolini, Benito, as fascist leader, 25, 137–40, 146, 151–60; foreign activities and ambitions of, 70–1, 73, 89–92, 133–4, 137–8, 178, 206, 246, 265–6, 274–6, 279–92, 294–5, 299–300, 302–3, 305–6, 316, 329–330, 334, 342; ideas of, 89, 137–9, 157–60; irresponsibility of, 89–91, 138, 246, 300, 342–4; fall of, 350

Nadolny, 269
Nagasaki, 354
Nationalism, 21, 30, 37–40, 89, 91, 138, 143, 219, 262, 265, 270
National Government, British, 129–131
Nazis, advance to power of, 231–6; in Bavaria, 219–20; murderous, 157, 227, 355–61; strength of, 221–222, 224–8, 239–40; other reference, 247
Nazi-Soviet Pact, 184
Negrin, Juan, 210
Neurath, Konstantin von, 236, 267, 272, 277, 290, 301
New Deal, 116
New Party, 133
Newton, Basil, 306, 313–14
Nicolson, Harold, 13
Nitti, Francesco Saverio, 38, 155
Norway, 338
Noske, Gustav, 18, 217
Nuremberg Party Congress, 312
nutrition, 105–6, 108, 112
NUWM, 123

Office du Blé, 169
Ogaden Province, 285
oil, 34–5
Okinawa, 353
Olbricht, Friedrich, 360
old age pensions, 112
Opera Nazionale Balilla, 157
Orlando, Vittorio, 6, 15, 23, 38, 152, 155
Ottoman Empire, *see* Turkish Empire
OVRA, 157

Papen, Franz von, 232–4, 236, 240, 244, 267, 270, 303
Paris, Peace of, 4, 20, 45
Parti Franciste, 174
Partito Popolare Italiano (PPI), 138, 144, 150–2, 154, 156
partisans, 356
Paul-Boncour, Joseph, 174, 271
Pearl Harbor, 345, 352
Perticone, G., 146
Pétain, Marshal Philippe, 163, 182, 185, 188, 249, 342
Philip, Prince of Hesse, 305
Phipps, Sir Eric, 263
Pilsudski, Josef, 44–6, 48–50, 82, 262–3, 268, 275
pleins pouvoirs, 186–7
Poincaré, Raymond, 4–5, 9, 18, 39, 54–5, 57, 60–1, 66, 70, 72–6, 81–2, 86, 166, 169, 171, 174, 221, 292
Polish German Non-aggression Treaty, 271, 276
political parties, statistics, 155–6, 222
population, 102–4, 249
Popular Front, French, 167, 173, 176, 178–80, 183, 187, 278, 296–7
Popular Front, Spanish, 201
POUM, 210
Pravda, 177, 327
Pratt, Sir John, 253–4
Prieto, Indalecio, 202–3
Primo de Rivera, General Miguel, 194

Primo de Rivera, José Antonio, 203, 207
proportional representation, 132–3
Pugliese, General Emanuele, 152

Quiroga, Casares, 202, 205, 208

racialism, 157, 261
Radek, Karl, 269
Raeder, Erich, 301
Rapallo, Treaty of (Italo-Yugoslavian), 25, 145
Rapallo, Treaty of (Russo-German), 54, 67, 83
Rathenau, Walther, 52, 55, 66, 221
Raynaldy, Eugène, 175
reparations, 7, 16, 18, 57, 61–6, 68, 70, 72–3, 74, 76, 78, 80, 85, 87, 101, 119, 242, 244–5
re-armament, 81, 85, 163, 185, 188, 230, 236, 247, 260, 264, 278, 280, 293, 301, 320
Red Army, 43, 45–6, 53, 83, 349, 352, 359
Red Peril, 44, 141–2
redistribution of income, 109–10
Reinhardt, General Walther, 52
Reichenau, Marshal Walther von, 359
Reichswehr, 51–3, 55, 71, 74, 81, 83, 91, 217, 219–21, 223, 227, 229–33, 247
reprisals, 356–7
revolution, 42, 44, 46, 116, 125, 139, 216
Reynaud, Paul, 166–70, 181, 341
Ribbentrop, Joachim von, 281, 290, 295, 299, 302, 319–20, 322–3, 328, 332–3
Riom Trial, 187
Rocque, Colonel de la, 174, 176, 181–2
Rohm, Ernst, 236
Rohm purge, 134
Rome-Berlin Axis, 289, 299

Roosevelt, President Franklin D., 303, 345, 349, 350
Rosenberg, 269
Rothermere, Viscount, 134
Rundstedt, General Gerd von, 339
Russo-German Non-aggression Pact, 329
Russo-Polish War. 45–7, 52, 124
Rydz-Smigly, General Edouard, 293

Saar, 11, 85, 87, 89, 277
S.A. (Sturmabteilung), 140, 227–8, 231, 235–6, 247, 259, 293
St Aulaire, Comte de, 59
St Germain, Treaty of, 20, 32
St Jean de Maurienne, Agreement of, 23, 89
Salandra, Antonio, 152–3, 155
Salengro, Roger, 180
Samuel, Sir Herbert, 126
sanctions, 62, 84, 253–5, 287, 302, 329, 345
Sanjurjo, General José, 195, 198, 204, 207
Sarraut, Albert, 174, 178, 186
Sarzana, 148, 151
Sauvy, Alfred, 167
Schlageter, Leo, 71
Schleicher, General Kurt von, 229–234, 236, 247, 267
Schleswig-Holstein, 12
Scheidemann, Philipp, 81, 216
Schlieffen Plan, 339
Schober, Dr Johann, 242
Schuschnigg, Kurt, 294, 303–6
Schwerin, Friedrich von, 261
Schwerin Krosigk, Lutz, 236
Seeckt, General von, 44, 52–3, 55, 217, 219, 221, 223, 258, 261
Seisser, Colonel von, 220
Seldte, Franz, 234
self-determination, 10, 12, 14, 27
Serrano Suñer, Ramón, 203
Sèvres, Treaty of, 20, 38
Seyss-Inquart, Arthur, 303, 305

SFIC (French Communist Party), 172
SFIO, 171, 173, 179
Sforza, Count Carlo, 149
Silesia, 13
Simon, Sir John, 253, 255–7, 266, 272, 284, 313, 316
Simons, Walter, 53, 62
Slovakia, 321–2
slump, 68, 99, 120–1, 123, 160, 164, 214, 249
Smoot-Hawley Tariff, 100
Smuts, General Jan Christiaan, 18
Smyrna, 37–39, 91
Snowden, Philip, 69 q., 130
Social Democratic Party, SPD, 216, 218, 224–30, 232, 274, 311
Socialism, maximalist, 141–8, 200–2, 208–9, 216
Socialism, reformist, 110; in Britain, 123–32; in France, 163, 171–3, 176–181, 184, 187; in Germany, 216–9, 224–35; in Italy, 142, 151–2, 156; in Spain, 190–2, 194, 196–7, 199–202, 209
Socialist League, 134
Solidarité Française, 174–5
Sonnino, Sidney, 23
Sosnkowski, Marshal Kasimir, 267 q.
Soviet-German Alliance, 53, 268, 329
Spa Conference, 26, 61–2
Spanish Civil War, 180–3, 205, 294–298, 316
Speer, Albert, 348
SS (Schutzstaffel), 236, 293, 356–7, 359
Stahlhelm, 229, 231, 234–5
Stahremberg, Prince Ernst von, 274, 294
Stalin, Joseph, 92, 178, 218, 269, 298, 318, 327–8
Stalingrad, 344
standards of living, 107, 127, 141
state regulation of trade, 102
Stauffenberg, Claus von, 360

Stavisky, Sacha, 174–5
Stimson, Henry L., 248, 253–5, 257
Stinnes, Hugo, 61
Stresa Conference, 279–82, 288–9
Stresemann, Gustav, 76–88, 92, 222, 239, 258, 269, 323
Strike, General, 121, 124–6
strikes, 141, 198, 202, 213
Sturzo, Don Luigi, 144, 151–2, 154
Sudetenland, 26, 306, 309, 312
Suez Canal, 35
Suvich, Fulvio, 290
Sykes-Picot Agreement, 33–5

Taittinger, Pierre, 171
tanks, 340
Tardieu, André, 10 q., 171, 244, 248
tariffs, 29–30, 80, 96, 98, 100, 117, 122, 186, 214
Taylor, A. J. P., 260
Tellini, General, 89
Teschen, Duchy of, 26, 275
Thälmann, Ernst, 231
Thaon di Revel, Admiral, 153
Third International, 172, 190
Thoiry, 87–9
Thomas, J. H., 125, 133
Thorez, Maurice, 177, 184
Tippelskirch, Werner von, 359
Tiso, Josef, 321
Todt, Fritz, 348
total war, 349
Tours, Congress of, 172
Tower, Sir Reginald, 50
trade, 47–8, 68, 84, 94, 97, 101, 119–120, 122
trade cycles, 99
Trades Union Congress, 123, 125–6
trade unions, 123, 127, 135, 141, 159, 166, 232, 237
Tresckow, Hans Henning von, 360
Treves, Claudio, 142, 152
Trianon, Treaty of, 20, 27, 32
Trott zu Solz, Adam von, 332

Turati, Filippo, 142, 152
Turkish Empire, 4, 6, 33, 36

unconditional surrender, 349, 354
unemployment, 69, 96, 116, 118, 121–122, 129–30, 133, 160, 165–9, 212, 214, 226, 259
unemployment insurance, 113
Union des Intérèts Economiques, 171
Union General de Trabajadores, UGT, 190–2, 194, 196
Upper-Silesian Plebiscite, 54, 57–60, 62, 78
Ustači, 276

Vansittart, Sir Robert, 253–4, 263, 282–3
Veniselos, Sophocles Eleuthios, 37–8
Versailles, Treaty of, 2, 4, 18, 20, 23, 32, 43, 47, 52, 54–8, 60–2, 72, 76–9, 85, 93, 184, 215, 217, 242, 245–7, 244, 258, 264, 269, 278, 281, 289, 292, 319, 322, 334
Vichy, 185, 187, 342, 357
Victor Emmanuel III, 148, 153, 156
Voroshilov, Klementi, 270
Vuillemin, General Joseph, 189

wages, 123
Washington Treaty, 245–6
war debts, 69, 81, 101, 245, 257
Weichs, Maximilian von, 259
Weill-Raynal, 245
Weimar Republic, 215, 218
Weiszäcker, Ernst von, 318
welfare, 102, 109–13, 122, 160
Wellesley, Sir Victor, 254
Wenner-Gren, 331
Westarp, Count Kuno, 224
Weygand, General Maxime, 49, 342
Wilhelm, Crown Prince, 78–80
Wilson, Woodrow, 2, 3 q., 5–13, 15, 16, 19, 21–6, 29, 36–7, 42, 44, 143
Wilson, Sir Horace, 303, 331

Witzleben, General Erwin von, 317
Wohlthat, Helmuth, 331
workers, 41
workers' defence groups, 127
World Disarmament Conference, 264
World War I, defensive struggle, 1
Wrangel, Peter, 43–4, 46, 48

Young, Owen D., 73, 82
Young Plan, 81, 87–9, 93, 224, 227, 239, 243
youth movements, 157–8

Zhdanov, 327
Zogu, Ahmed, 91